Peter Thompson and **Anthony Delano** were Senior Executives of Mirror Group Newspapers when Robert Maxwell took over. They were appointed to the board and stayed with the company another two years. Thompson became editor of the *Sunday Mirror* in 1985. Delano became director of Maxwell's electronic media operation. He is the author of several books, including *Slip Up*, the celebrated account of a classic Fleet Street caper.

A note from the publisher

This book was first published in a hardcover edition by Bantam Press in February 1988 but withdrawn from sale after legal objections from Robert Maxwell. It was amended to take account of Mr Maxwell's objections and published in a Corgi paperback edition in April 1988, but that too was withdrawn following a further objection by Mr Maxwell to the cover. Following his death in November 1991, it was decided to release the book with the 1988 paperback edition text intact.

'What's he really like?' – Prince Charles

'I am a jungle man' – Robert Maxwell

'He is a business brigand. He almost physically loves
the feel of power' – Rupert Murdoch

'ou only meet a man like Bob once' – Elisabeth Maxwe

'My family will not inherit one penny of the wealth
I have created' – Robert Maxwell

'He is the nearest thing we have in this country
to a genius' – Lord Kearton

'I am not on an ego trip' – Robert Maxwell

'He is a mysterious personage' – Lord Rothermere

'My aim is to make this world a little better than
if I had never lived' – Robert Maxwell

'He should be sent packing to Liechtenstein'
– William Jovanovich

MAXWELL
A PORTRAIT
OF POWER

**Peter Thompson and
Anthony Delano**

CORGI BOOKS

MAXWELL: A PORTRAIT OF POWER

A CORGI BOOK 0 552 99353 0

Originally published in Great Britain by Bantam Press,
a division of Transworld Publishers Limited

Bantam Press edition published 1988
Corgi edition published 1988
Corgi edition reissued 1991

Corgi Books are published by Transworld Publishers Ltd.,
61–63 Uxbridge Road, Ealing, London W5 5SA, in Australia
by Transworld Publishers (Australia) Pty. Ltd., 15–23 Helles
Avenue, Moorebank, NSW 2170, and in New Zealand by
Transworld Publishers (N.Z.) Ltd., Cnr. Moselle and
Waipareira Avenues, Henderson, Auckland.

Printed and bound in Great Britain by
Cox & Wyman Ltd., Reading, Berks.

MAXWELL

A Portrait of Power

ONE

I am a salesman.

<small>ROBERT MAXWELL</small>

He is a business brigand.

<small>RUPERT MURDOCH</small>

MAXWELL

IN A BEGUILING FLASH of self-deprecation, Robert Maxwell once likened a set of documents that brought him lingering infamy to a Victorian novel because of the headings scattered through them: 'A Succinct Reply', 'A False Statement', 'An Unhappy Meeting', 'Exaggerated Claims', 'Another False Statement'. An account of the evening of Friday, 7 June 1985 has to be entitled 'A Family Gathering'.

But it was clear long beforehand that it was also going to be 'A Hell of a Party'. Mr and Mrs Robert Maxwell had requested the company of an astonishing array of people at Headington Hill Hall, Oxford, for – as the elegant italic hand-lettered invitations advised – 'a Gala Dinner and Dance on the occasion of their 40th Wedding Anniversary'. They would also be celebrating, it had been let drop, Bob's sixty-second birthday.

Like Trooping the Colour and turning out rascally newspapers, a summer bash in the garden is one of the things the English like to think they do well: a vast marquee tethered alongside a great country house, women in long gowns, men in black ties, the muted brassiness of a 1940s-style band, champagne in magnums. Rain.

There was a widespread impression that Prince Charles would be among those showing up at Headington, which might have justified the small army of security men in yellow slickers whispering into radios on the sodden lawn and the intense scrutiny at the red and white barrier that barred the main gate. His Royal Highness was known to be greatly intrigued by the antics of the extraordinary man who was soon to be acclaimed as one of the two wealthiest commoners in the realm. (Charles had once asked one of Maxwell's editors in a plaintive whisper: 'What's he really like?') But the guards, it was soon realized, were there to protect Maxwell. Now that he had realized the ambition of a lifetime and become as recognizable as he was rich he was beginning to have misgivings about his personal safety. Charles, anyway, would not have been a bigger draw than Maxwell himself: a socialist multimillionaire with obscure beginnings and an opaque past who, virtually at retirement age, had suddenly conjured up a rumbustious present in which he glowed far more visibly than any mere prince.

The phenomenon was all the more arresting because less than a year earlier Bob Maxwell had seemed to be a spent force in British public life. Not that he was a failure – anything but. He was a millionaire several times over, the largest printer in Europe. Great magazine empires, some of them deadly rivals, depended on the mighty rotogravure presses of his resoundingly named British Printing and Communication Corporation. Maxwell printed *Radio Times*, the BBC programme guide that sold 3 million copies a week, and he printed just as many copies of *TV Times*, the Independent Television competitor. Maxwell printed *Vogue* and he printed bibles. Maxwell plants stamped household names on to cans, bottles and plastic packaging; embossed rare and expensive paper for banks and brokers; churned out chocolate-bar wrappers by the hundreds of millions.

Even more important, there was Pergamon Press, the enigmatic foundation-stone of Maxwell's fortune – and the rock upon which he had once all but foundered. Even though they might never have laid eyes on a book bearing the Pergamon imprint (relatively few people had), connoisseurs of financial scandal among the guests were well acquainted with the rise, fall and rise again of this idiosyncratic publishing house whose offices sprawled around the grounds of Headington like some joyless Bible Belt seminary transplanted to the wrong side of Checkpoint Charlie.

Even those too young to recall the succeeding waves of investigations and court battles that had swirled around Maxwell and Pergamon in the early 1970s were familiar with the devastating verdict that had nearly become Maxwell's business epitaph. 'We regret having to conclude', two distinguished Department of Trade inquisitors had written, 'that, notwithstanding Mr Maxwell's acknowledged abilities and energy, he is not in our opinion a person who can be relied upon to exercise proper stewardship of a publicly quoted company.' And that was not all they wrote.

But most people of reading age in the country would also have some idea, however vague, that despite this uncompromising indictment Maxwell had somehow pulled off a comeback for Pergamon and for himself that had won the admiration of the financial community – if not yet its universal confidence – although at the price of being branded, like a beer-can, with the condescending sobriquet of 'The Bouncing Czech'.

Even more obscured by the passing of time was Maxwell's political career. If a week (as Harold Wilson, his erstwhile patron who was one of the guests, had been the first to observe) was a long time in politics, then the fifteen years that had passed since Maxwell was voted out of Parliament should ensure oblivion.

One thing that might, since then, have endeared him to a nation obsessed with football was his purchase a few years earlier of Oxford United, the local team. But United had only just been promoted to the First Division, and their fate was of concern to few apart from their most faithful fans.

Most effacing of all, fifteen months earlier Maxwell had been humiliatingly defeated yet one more time in his repeated, and at times desperate, efforts to become the proprietor of a national newspaper – something he had always regarded as the ultimate token of acceptance and influence in Britain. Another interloper, richer and in some ways as mysterious as himself, 'Tiny' Rowland, had teased him with the prospect of letting him buy the *Observer*, a venerable Sunday newspaper of liberal views and enormous prestige. Rowland had got the *Observer* himself by snatching it from under Maxwell's questing nose in 1981. But no sooner had Maxwell shown interest the second time than Rowland changed his mind and put the prize back in his pocket.

Such a public trouncing on top of similar ones he had suffered at the hands of an even more formidable adversary (and interloper), Rupert Murdoch, might have convinced a less dedicated aspirant that the time had come to stop trying; to withdraw to Headington and enjoy the seemingly endless and effortless Pergamon profits. But once again Maxwell had bounced back. His bruises from Rowland's calculated rebuff not yet faded, he had spotted one last chance to realize the ambition of a battling lifetime. Bold as a bank robber, he had mounted a raid on another prestigious stronghold of public print. Pulling millions of pounds from seemingly nowhere, wielding them like a sock stuffed full of sand, he had torn from the protesting hands of its custodians a very different newspaper that was even more of a Great British Institution than the *Observer*: the *Daily Mirror*.

And everything that went with it, which in Maxwell's case meant, foremost, the attention of the nation and as far beyond as he could throw his voice with the new resources at his command. From the moment he strode into the *Mirror* office in the early hours of the morning and announced that the place was his, Maxwell's face, Maxwell's views and Maxwell's interests – even Maxwell's wife and Maxwell's children – had dominated the pages of the paper as though it were a family album. So spectacular was this coup, and so flamboyant Maxwell's behaviour in proclaiming that he was on top again, that rival newspapers were compelled to give him almost as much space as his own and television, bowing to a virtuoso performer, was his for the demanding.

In no time at all the latest Maxwell revival was playing in different versions to fascinated audiences not only in Fleet Street but also on the other stages from which the protagonist had in the past been driven by boos and hisses: drama and suspense at the Stock Exchange and the City of London banks; low comedy in the arena of politics. War might be, as Clausewitz said, simply the continuation of politics by other means. So is running a famous newspaper. Maxwell, forced – against his every verbose instinct – to define himself in a single word, would answer: Politician.

If Prince Charles's question about Maxwell also had to be answered in one word, it might be: Lucky. For, although the drama and tragedy visited upon Maxwell throughout his life were nothing less than operatic, he is, even in relatively trivial ways, remarkably lucky. Just recently he had been driven to a local fête in his Rolls-Royce (personalized number-plate, 'PP 1923', the year of his birth and the initials of Pergamon Press), bought tickets in a raffle and won a Bentley. His lucky number was thirteen.

•

As the barrier rose and fell at the gates of Headington that night the arriving guests were ushered into the circular hall of the house which was dominated by a spectacular stained-glass window of Maxwell as Samson at the gates of Gaza. Their names were announced by a costumed retainer, which was just as well, since many of them were meeting their host and hostess for the first time. They had been given a rendezvous at this milestone in a marriage that was as exceptional as everything else with the Maxwell name on it not because they were intimate acquaintances but in the hope that they would be useful in business or, at least, 'friendly'.

There were people among the arrivals scuttling up to the porch in the downpour who had known the Maxwells for many years. But few, even of those, would have described themselves as close friends. In the rather dated English that Maxwell uses to refer to himself as 'having a couple of bob', he once also said offhandedly: 'I'm not a man for chums.'

The host and hostess were chummy enough in their greetings, though: Betty Maxwell in a blue Murray Arbeid dress which was greatly admired, Bob in a dinner-jacket as broad as an opera cloak and with eyebrows that looked as though they had been put on in the dark. They distributed handshakes and kisses in distinctly un-English profusion. Bob's pride in being British, proclaimed even more fervently than ever now that he could write his own headlines, did not extend to his party manners. Or any other manners. Betty, it was apparent as much from her well-corseted chic as from her charming accent, could not be anything but French.

The reception line led through a huge salon where Jeannette Cordrey, the celebrated harpist, strummed sweetly away, swamped by the excited chatter. A number of guests sidled over to the bookshelves to confirm what they had heard – that many of the impressive volumes on the famous publisher's shelves were simply spines pasted to backings.

That was not the only suspicion in the scented air. There were men and women of great eminence at Headington that night who regarded Maxwell as a benefactor and valued collaborator, a figure of towering importance in the cloistered world of scientific publishing. To others he personified everything that, six years into Margaret Thatcher's go-get-it Britain, could go right; living proof that a man of humble alien origin and no recognizable education could, by his own efforts, transcend his background, make fortune upon fortune and still persist in the romantic contradiction of calling himself a socialist while behaving like a ruthlessly efficient capitalist.

Others, however, perhaps the majority, were far from convinced that any of Maxwell's accomplishments was admirable. To them he was nothing more than a charlatan, an opportunist, a poseur, a buffoon. The quintessential Englishness of the superbly mounted event in the setting of stately Headington – which, to add injury to insult, they knew to be rented from the local council for an enviably low sum – only emphasized the fact that Maxwell was still trying to make himself into something he was not: an Englishman like themselves. And a damn sight richer one at that. One thing Maxwell had found out the hard way in his mission to make himself one of them was how little the British admire success.

For a man topping three score who had only one lung, weighed twice as much as he ought to, slept only half as much as everyone wished him to, smoked a dozen huge cigars a day, gambled until dawn with £1,000 chips and could outdrink anyone in the room Maxwell was setting a spanking pace and most of them were glad to be there, guzzling his vintage Moët et Chandon and watching the latest Maxwell of so many they had seen down the years do his stuff.

Protected from the rain by a covered walk, the guests were guided beneath the enormous canopy spread over and around a circular swimming-pool in the grounds. Only then could they take in the scale of the event: tables for at least 500 had been set beneath sparkling chandeliers hung from the canvas ceiling, sheaves of summer flowers stood everywhere, the Salon Orchestra of the Royal Air Force in powder-blue dress uniform tootled soothingly. No desert monarch could have made a tent more sumptuous.

The guests began to take stock of each other. A neatly printed guest-list and table-plan lay at every place together with gifts: scent for the ladies, leather sponge-bags for the gentlemen. It was an impressive crowd. Whether they knew Maxwell or not, many of them knew each other: hardy troupers of politics past and present, tycoons, bankers, media celebrities, trade union grandees, academics, a rich crust of lords and ladies. Except for the royal family, for whom his adoration is boundless – he is so fond of the Queen that he once breached royal protocol to the extent of giving her a pat on the back, while she named one of her dogs, a cocker spaniel, Maxwell because it was noisy and energetic – Maxwell proclaims a hearty socialist contempt for titles. He fought a very loud lawsuit over the suggestion that he had tried to buy one. 'I despise the aristocracy,' he has said.

Not that life peers and knights are aristocrats. Their titles are the British equivalent of the honours Maxwell is only too happy to flaunt: the Royal Swedish Order of the Polar Star (First Class), the Bulgarian People's Republic Order of Stara Planina (First Class), his honorary doctorate from Moscow University. He always has plenty of nobles and knights of the realm on the payroll. His closest assistant, Peter Jay, described as his 'chief of staff' – inappropriately, since in Maxwell's tribe everyone else is an Indian – is a former British ambassador to Washington. The gardener at Headington is the Marquis of Kildare.

There were guests who would rather have stayed at home. Sir Monty Finniston at table K2, for one. Now chairman of Clyde Cablevision, an embryonic network in Scotland that was part of the Mirror Group when Maxwell bought it, he had seen his business life jarred six years earlier by contact with Maxwell and was – justifiably – apprehensive that the same thing might happen again. Others would soon regret having put in an appearance. At table H2 was Sir Clive Sinclair, inventor of the pocket calculator and the flat television screen among other wonders. Maxwell was about to take over his promising but ill-run business and put it to rights. After he had made the announcement Maxwell had to abandon the rescue mission after looking at the figures. At table E3 was Jo Foley, newly appointed as managing editor of the *Mirror* and given to understand by Maxwell that she could expect to be the first woman to edit a national British newspaper. Within months she was threatening to sue him for constructive dismissal. Not until – as in so many things – Murdoch had appointed the first woman editor did he follow suit. George Gale at table J3, a conservative columnist and one of Maxwell's oldest friends among the journalists, had no idea that he, too, would soon be suing. Maxwell was to hire him with a confidential brief to write, in contradiction of the *Mirror*'s avowed policy, in support of Prime Minister Margaret Thatcher.

Usually it is Maxwell who does the suing. Not only does he deal out writs almost as a matter of routine whenever he is thwarted in business, but he also frequently resorts to the stifling British laws of libel and slander – a reaction difficult to reconcile with his pride in publishing newspapers to which intrusion is a way of life or with his stance as a champion of the right to information. But, then, one thing Maxwell is not is a champion of consistency. In 1987 he was even to issue a writ against the *Independent*, a newspaper in which he owned a 4.9 per cent stake; suing himself, in part.

At table A4, Baroness Birk's solicitor husband Ellis bore no title of his own. But in the overlapping worlds of Labour Party politics and national newspapers, of which, until recently, Maxwell had been confined to the fringe, he was a discreet but major power. Moreover, Birk was just as influential in the Jewish community. The *Jewish Chronicle* reported in 1964 that Maxwell had notified them that he had joined the Church of England. While never intruding on his religious convictions, Birk had gently kept Maxwell in touch with the community and its works. The Church of England missed its chance. Maxwell now describes himself as an agnostic, although his latest pronouncement to the *Chronicle* was: 'I was born a Jew and I shall die a Jew.'

Maxwell has a talent, too, among his formidable array of abilities, of inducing inconsistency in others. At table B3 sat Joe Haines, looking, as a financial reporter had once described him, 'like a 1950s Hollywood villain'. Maxwell is far too headstrong, impetuous, unpredictable to support an *éminence grise* in the sense of a power behind his throne. But in Haines he had found a political guru who personified the axiom that politics is the art of the possible.

Haines was the *Daily Mirror*'s leader-writer, its editorial spokesman, keeper of the paper's conscience. Right up until the eve of Maxwell's arrival he vowed repeatedly before his colleagues that he would never work for such a monster. He was now speedily accumulating titles (and the salaries that went with them): Assistant Editor of the *Mirror*, Group Political Editor, Director of Mirror Group Newspapers, Chief Leader-Writer, official biographer and general amanuensis. 'Only two people in this organization can write a letter,' Maxwell had become fond of saying.

'Joe Haines and myself.' It was a rare compliment. Maxwell's most frequently uttered pronouncements begin: 'I am the only man who can . . .' Haines's influence was demonstrated at the next election when he manoeuvred Gale's column out of the *Mirror* despite the contract Maxwell had given him.

There were some who had come along in the spirit of reconciliation, like Donald Trelford, editor of the *Observer*. One of the reasons 'Tiny' Rowland had considered selling was a public row he had had with Trelford over the principle of editorial independence. At the time, Maxwell had snorted away such a puerile concept. If he had owned the paper, he left no doubt, Trelford would have done what he was told or been fired. The breach was soon to be reopened. When an investigation began the following year into allegations of improper dealings over Guinness shares Maxwell complained that the *Observer* linked his name too closely with that of financier Sir Jack Lyons (table E1) and Lord Spens of Henry Ansbacher, the merchant bank (table H2). Trelford refused to apologize. Maxwell took his objection to the Press Council – whose chairman, Sir Zelman Cowan, was at table E9 – which, to the surprise of many journalists, upheld it.

There were also those present who would soon be touched by the random generosity with which Maxwell frequently disarms the leery. Penny Stott, for instance, at table E7, the pretty blonde wife of one of his editors. Maxwell suddenly made her a present of a car. Not a company car, as he might bestow on a favoured employee with a wave of the hand, but a personal gift. At table C1, Michael Molloy, the editor of the *Mirror*, was well on the way to winning a bet Maxwell had offered him: £5,000 that he could not stop smoking cigarettes for a year. Molloy turned to cigars in emulation of his publisher and at the end of the year pocketed his tax-free cheque.

There was a diplomatic contingent, too, from territories where Maxwell did go out of his way to be chummy. At the E-shaped table dominated by Maxwell himself the place of honour had been given to the Russian ambassador, His Excellency Victor Popov. Madame Natalia Popova was shown to the equivalent place on the adjoining E over which Betty presided. The affectionate respect Popov always showed his host reflected the regard in which Maxwell was held in Moscow. Popov and Maxwell popped in on each other regularly, Maxwell invariably delighting the Russian by addressing him as 'Dear VIP'. When Mikhail Gorbachev visited London in 1984 the only non-official guest he received was Maxwell – as ever, heedlessly late for the appointment.

At table J3 the Romanian ambassador, M. Vasile Gliga, sat with Lord Grade. The Polish plenipotentiary, M. Stefan Staniszewski, had to settle for Jimmy Reid, a former Scottish communist union organizer now a Maxwell columnist, at table A2. At Maxwell's sixtieth birthday party, a rather less impressive occasion, the Bulgarian ambassador had made a speech which veterans among the guests recalled with a shudder. He had spoken in his own language at a length which was no doubt intended to convey high regard. The only people in the room who understood were his wife, the interpreter and Maxwell.

At least it was generally accepted that Maxwell had understood. Perhaps the most frequently referred to of his attainments was that he spoke nine languages. These certainly included, in addition to his singular style of English, Yiddish, German, Russian, Hungarian, Czech and French. But if one of the other two was Bulgarian no one really knew. This time the Bulgarian envoy, M. Kiril Shterev, was left to practise his English on television interviewer Russell Harty at table E3.

At table G3, strategically placed within eyeshot of Maxwell and, in any case, hard to miss in the vivid colours she had chosen for her matching taffeta skirt and turban, was the most indefatigable and powerful person in the Maxwell organization apart from himself. Jean Baddeley, who bore the sonorous title of Director of the Chairman's Office, had served the Maxwells devotedly for nearly a quarter of a century. While he was awake, she was rarely out of reach. She saw far more of him than anyone else, including his wife. Baddeley, it was, who had mounted the drive to seed the guest-list with 'friendlies' – not without some disagreements with Betty, whose priorities were slightly more sentimental.

With Baddeley sat Laszlo Straka, chief executive of the Pergamon operation in America. Like the predecessor from whom he had taken over, he was originally Hungarian. He had worked for the company for thirty years. 'Mr Maxwell expected his executives to carry out his instructions to the letter and nothing more,' another reproachful paragraph of the Department of Trade and Industry report on Maxwell's activities in the 1960s had read. 'And not to doubt or question the wisdom of their instructions. It is difficult to envisage how any worthwhile executive could operate for long under such conditions.' Baddeley and Straka went back to that time, and it was precisely those qualities in them and a very few others that had made them so enduringly worthwhile to Maxwell. Together with something even more important. Despite his irrepressible weakness for the limelight, Maxwell operates, most of the time, on a level of obscurity and duplicity that few national security networks could match. Silence is what Maxwell wants most from those who do his bidding. Under her gaudy turban Baddeley kept more secrets than the CIA.

The entire glittering scene made a particular impression on a smallish bespectacled man sitting at table H2 with Spens and the unfortunate Sinclair. Henry Poole, a partner in Alexanders Laing & Cruickshank, one of the most active and prestigious brokerage houses in the City, had been pondering the problem of renovating Maxwell's image to give Pergamon and BPCC more appeal to investors. Quite a lot of City folk believed – as Maxwell certainly did himself – that he had been less than fairly treated by the Department of Trade report, scraps of which were all that the public at large knew of his financial history. Maxwell's efforts over the last decade or so, thought Poole, surely showed that the inspectors had not been entirely justified in their appraisal.

The famous names, the frothy clothes, the expectant tension of the vast crowd put Poole in mind of a scene from the masterpiece of a favourite author, Anthony Trollope: the banquet for the Emperor of China in *The*

Way We Live Now. Trollope's host, the financier Augustus Melmotte, had invited five ambassadors, fifteen City merchants, ten peers, three wise men, two poets, Cabinet ministers and politicians, three editors (and three bores 'endowed with a power of making themselves absolutely unendurable if not admitted'). It occurred to Poole that Melmotte, too, had been a misunderstood man, abused as much as he was praised, and whose honesty was questioned. Perhaps there was an idea there. . . .

Something else lay at every place-setting alongside the gifts and the table-plan. A menu, its cover a sepia photograph of Bob and Betty as bride and groom, he in his Second World War subaltern's uniform with the single ribbon of the Military Cross on his left breast, she with her veil stunningly thrown off, stunningly pretty.

Inside the folder the dishes of the evening had been named for milestones in the whirlwind courtship four decades earlier of the dashing young infantryman and the *jeune fille de bonne famille* who had found him irresistible. From this enchanting picture it was easy to see why. Until quite recently women had confessed to weakness at the sight of Maxwell's tall figure. A lady journalist had gushed that he looked like a combination of Victor Mature and Frankie Vaughan – comparisons that presumably appealed to her.

The little souvenir was a heart-winning touch. But on the back was a caption to the romantic picture: Bob and Betty on their wedding day, Paris, 15 March 1945. Not only was 7 June 1985 anything but a sentimental family occasion. It was not even the wedding anniversary.

Nor was it Bob's birthday, Betty blandly confessed when the excellent meal had been eaten and she stood to address the expectant crowd. That was in three days' time. The reason this party was being held on this night was that the hugely expensive marquee was also to be used on the following day for the reception given every year by Pergamon Press. It was an explanation to delight those waiting to see if Maxwell's latest bound back into the public eye had left some of his ways unchanged. It had. As always in the Maxwell scale of values function rated higher than fact. The most sentimental of dates was just a number on a calendar when compared to the figure on a cheque.

No matter how much they might have come to respect, admire, fear or even feel deep affection for Maxwell, few people – including his own children – can ever have found him lovable. Betty worships not only what he is but also everything he has ever been. The first year they were married she collected the few scraps of paper about his life up until then and pasted them into a scrapbook. She has done the same every year since, the file waxing and waning with Maxwell's public fortunes. There were now forty volumes bound in hand-tooled leather and embossed with the Maxwell name. 'I can live my husband's life peacefully at night by gluing in the cuttings,' she had once confided – something apt to give a misleading impression to anyone not aware of her steely intellectual achievements and the fact that she liked it to be acknowledged that she, more than anyone, was now involved in the day-to-day affairs of Pergamon Press. That year's clippings would weigh in at 60 lb.

But it was as the wife and partner of forty tempestuous years rather than as the family historian that Betty now set out to take her audience on a tour of the menu through which they had just eaten their way with enjoyment. *Terrine de Homard Normandie*, she explained, was to commemorate her beloved husband's part in the Normandy invasion. *Selle d'Agneau Cancellier, Panaché de Légumes Versaillais* were named for the places in which they had met and courted, *Le Plateau de Fromages Parlo* after the town in which he had won his Military Cross, and *Bombe Glacée Queen's Royal* after the regiment whose uniform he wore in the photograph. *Gâteau du 40e Anniversaire.* . . . Well, she had already explained how they came to be eating that a few weeks late.

At first the well-fed tentful gave Betty no more than its polite attention. The shadow of the Bulgarian ambassador lingered over the liqueurs. But the nervous determination with which she set out to tell them what she, at any rate, was marking on this occasion, whatever the date, soon found the wavelength of her audience. Even those who had come just to mock and mop up the Moët found themselves entranced as, the echo of darker days in her engaging accent, Betty spoke to them of the wartime Paris of 1944 in which she had been a skinny hungry young woman, of her first memories of the outlandish suitor who had won her heart, of their uncertain summer of courtship. Haltingly, she recalled the misery of seeing her Bob off to the front again after they had fallen in love; her rapture at his safe return. She giggled at the recollection of the parachute silk he had 'liberated' for her wedding dress. A rapt silence gradually settled on the great hall of canvas. The worldly gathering had not expected this. When at last she described the dread she had felt for the great battle that both she and her new bridegroom had known was still to come after they married and the parting that took him back to the war once again, there was many a moist eye beneath the preposterous chandeliers.

Then her son the doctor stood up. Unlike most of his brothers and sisters, who were readily capable of addressing the United Nations without a tremor of misgiving, Philip Maxwell was nervous before such a large audience. He had, he said, been elected to speak on behalf of the children. What was more, he added, making an uneasy joke of the egocentric zeal with which Maxwell controlled his empire and his family, what he had to say had not been submitted for official clearance.

It was apparent that this came as a surprise to Maxwell himself, and not a particularly welcome one. But Philip, too, was determined to pay his own tribute to the early years; a eulogy as unexpected as Betty's, to his elder brother Michael, the Maxwells' firstborn, who in the full bloom of adolescence had suffered a miserable fate. He spoke of the dead boy and their distant childhood over which his father had loomed as a demanding but indulgent tyrant, of the excitement stirred up by the streams of distinguished visitors to Headington with whom the children were expected and encouraged to deal on equal terms, of the tribal bond that united the seven surviving young Maxwells.

Philip even gave the invincibly suspicious a new morsel to toy with. He recalled how he and Michael would play with their father's old uniforms. How, he remembered wondering, could it be that the clothes he had worn when he had gone to war were so much smaller than the ones he had come back in? Ah ha! breathed the mesmerized audience. Was the man who went the same one who returned?

Quite an array of preconceptions had been demolished by the time Philip sat down. But there was no time to reflect on the baffling contrast between Maxwell's place in the midst of this puzzling and complex clan, of which they had been given such a tantalizing glimpse, and his legendary rapacity and abrasiveness in the market-place. With the same commanding charm with which he had welcomed them their host rose to respond.

When he was a financial writer on the *Observer* in the 1960s, Anthony Sampson offered an inspired description of Maxwell. 'With his broad boxer's frame and relentless talk, he seems, as he is, defiantly insulated from other men's susceptibilities, like something from outer space.' And there is something about Maxwell of the man from Mars, who provides such a useful device to describe the reactions of someone unfamiliar with the usual way of doing things, although it is more in his manner than in his looks. Many of the methods Maxwell applies in his operations have the rigidity of something adapted from a self-help manual: one of the few people he admires is Edward de Bono, whose book *Lateral Thinking* gave a memorable buzz to business executives of the 1960s but who now writes mail-order texts on how to run the office. Many of Maxwell's gambits with people or in business dealings have the feeling of a trick learned by painstaking imitation and adapted over and over again to new circumstances. Few of the ideas and innovations he has promoted so boisterously down the years have been his own to begin with. Their effectiveness comes from the vigour and persistence with which he hammers them home.

Maxwell's enthralment with newspapers and newspapermen had always, of course, been amply reciprocated. From his earliest beginnings in business – from his first spectacular disaster, to be precise – he cultivated reporters and editors; above all, financial writers. Some were ready to take him at his own highly coloured evaluation. Others dismissed him as a man who always added a couple of noughts to everything he said. Others still suspected that there must be even more to the intriguing phenomenon than was apparent. The first to scrutinize him and his activities with the care they deserved was the *Sunday Times* in 1963.

The paper was encouraging a new reporter, Margaret Laing, who was beginning to make a reputation for herself in financial subjects – an unexpected speciality for a woman at that time. Laing went to Headington not long after the Maxwells had moved there and, with a deft grasp of financial details, pieced together a profile that became the model for many to follow, an intriguing impressionistic portrait of a man who was only just preparing to unleash himself on unsuspecting British institutions. But she came no closer to discovering if there was more to Maxwell and his money than any journalist before or since. She was outclassed. 'I am a jungle man,' Maxwell told Laing – she used it for her introduction – and she melted. 'He charmed me senseless,' she recalled twenty years later. 'I didn't stand a chance.'

That commanding charm was not the only means by which Maxwell was ready to ensure that he was presented in the light that served him best. In his early days in politics he asked a columnist how much he would take to mention him every week. Such steadfastly un-English clownishness – he also embarrassed BBC executives he wanted to thank for the *Radio Times* business by pressing autographed fifty-pound notes on them – kept Maxwell insulated for a time from the place in British life he believed he deserved; he was regarded as a sort of *idiot savant* of commerce and Parliament. When he first displayed signs of becoming a newspaper proprietor it was another *Sunday Times* writer, the late Nicholas Tomalin, who rather mischievously tempted him to acknowledge similarities between himself and Lord Beaverbrook, the impish Canadian who made the *Daily Express* into a legend of the 1930s.

In 1968, when Maxwell tried to buy the *News of the World* – as much a British institution in its way as the *Mirror* – Tomalin wrote in a profile of Maxwell that can hardly be bettered today:

> *Both were poor foreigners who sprang to notice with an arduous financial coup which has inspired mysterious, malicious rumours ever since. Both came to Britain and conquered the most jealously guarded anti-foreigner, gentleman's citadel of our national life. Both suffered calumnies from disgruntled natives swept aside by this process and caused controversy as to just how wicked they were which will last forever. Both sought political power and courted party leaders to gain it. Both were baulked because their pushiness and lack of scruple united the conventionally minded against them. Both turned back in their disappointment to publishing and propaganda. Both tried to be influential but were lamentable failures. Both were quick to hire talent and to fire it. Both were brilliant at making enemies. Both as they grew older and mellower came to be grudgingly accepted, even admired, by the more raffish and realistic sections of the same society that had denounced them as caddish outsiders for so long.*

Tomalin found that Maxwell warmed to this suggestion. 'Superficially, I suppose there is a real comparison between us,' Maxwell mused. 'Beaverbrook was a man who was ultimately forgiven all his, er . . . his activities. I may be also. But he was a man of property and I am not. I'm not interested in money except as a means to power. And I only want power in order to do things. I'm just a chap who's interested in making communications and the printing industry more efficient. Just a chap who wants to stop Britain sliding.' It is very much what Maxwell might say today except that the 'communications' have become an absorbing global ambition.

But when, in 1969, it had become apparent that the Pergamon–Leasco scandal, the most explosive financial story of its day, was taking shape and Maxwell was about to go down for the third time, taking a lot of shareholders with him, it was once again the *Sunday Times*, in the shape of its formidable investigative department, 'Insight', which pulled out its magnifying glass. The first reporters assigned to ask questions soon discovered that they had strayed into baffling territory. Few people who knew Maxwell were ready to talk about him (something that is just as true nearly twenty years later). Many of those approached were quick to let Maxwell know that questions were being asked.

The investigation that Insight launched into Maxwell and his affairs was epic, involving dozens of reporters in Britain, on the Continent and in the United States. Maxwell fought them for every inch of ground, counter-attacking tirelessly. He issued writs for slander based on questions they asked of his associates. He hired private detectives to investigate the investigators. When some of the Insight team went to interview Maxwell he had their dossiers on his desk.

Like Laing and Tomalin – and Sampson later – the Insight journalists might not have discovered everything there was to know, even then, about Robert Maxwell. But they drew some penetrating and durable conclusions. Laing concluded that it was the savage suddenness with which Maxwell seemed to strike that baffled Maxwell's critics. 'The elemental attack leaves them unsure whether he is naïve or sophisticated. He has a primitive grasp that undercuts convention, energy to pursue an opportunity while others are still digesting their kill and an instinctive aim at weak spots.'

The Insight writers decided that the most remarkable thing about Maxwell was not that he had collided with 'The Establishment' but

> *That a man so expert in the arts of capitalism should be so easily accepted as a socialist; that an entrepreneur and a salesman without any scientific qualifications should be so easily accepted as the apostle of technology; that after all the deals and all the spiels he should have become a hero of our times; that is the true wonder of Robert Maxwell.*

Tomalin took it from the horse's mouth. 'The thing about me', Maxwell had told him, 'is that I move fast. It's both efficient and politic. When there's an object in my way I smash it down or race around it. And I move so fast that when people put bombs on my road I'm a hundred yards beyond before they explode.'

With his sixty-second birthday in sight, the athletic frame that caught Anthony Sampson's imagination had long since run to fat. On a bad day Maxwell weighs over 250 lb. The self-conscious young subaltern of the sepia photograph had taken on the look of a lugubrious all-in wrestler; his face not so much lived-in as taken over by squatters.

Under the spotlight that picked out the microphone his hair was a flagrant jet black, dyed each month by a visiting barber; and since he had not recently caught the sun – he tans easily – he had the florid complexion of a relentless bon viveur. Contact lenses hide the colour of his eyes: they are black. Maxwell is well over six feet, and everything about him is big: his jowls, his belly, his hands. But he moves as fast as a bear, not shambling but striding, covering the space between himself and an objective with disconcerting speed, using his bulk to overawe and menace. He is a consummate bully with a disarming smile.

In the booming well-rounded cadences with which he welcomed his audience there was not a flicker of anywhere more distant than Dover; there would not be unless he was forced to pronounce one of the few words that still give him trouble – 'wilderness', for example. Nor was there the slightest hint of the readiness with which his unctuous tones can turn to a carping bellow, the practised politician's patter to a torrent of violent banal curses. Maxwell's voice is deep and oratorial, like a stage Churchill – the kind of Englishman they simply do not make any more (or, as the guests who were determined not to be impressed might insist, that they never did make).

His command of a language he had never even heard until he was seventeen is truly impressive. And to emphasize that it was no isolated accomplishment Maxwell could not resist throwing a couple of phrases to the diplomats in their own difficult tongues before he faced up to responding to Betty and Philip.

It is rare for a sentimental word to pass Maxwell's lips in any language. That night, however, he was unable to keep the pride from his voice as he introduced his remaining six sons and daughters, the subjects of a lot of neck-craning since it had been realized that they were making a rare appearance together. Maxwell had missed no opportunity down the years to let it be known that none of his offspring would inherit a penny of whatever wealth he accumulated. They would have to make their own way in the world, he insisted, aided perhaps by the superior education he had bestowed upon them – to say nothing of being given, each and every one of them from time to time, a job in one or another of the family firms. High achievers for the most part, the young Maxwells had massively outweighed the lack of formal education on which their father based so much of his image by earning an Oxford degree each. Betty took one, too, at the age of fifty-three.

As he called the names, beginning with Anne – at thirty-eight the eldest, a striking soft-faced woman who also had careers as an actress and a kindergarten teacher – the children stood where they had been scattered strategically throughout the tent. After Anne came Ian, twenty-nine. Like her he was not married and, since he also had a healthy capacity for enjoying himself, was as close as the family could offer to a playboy. It was well known that Maxwell had once fired him for being too involved with a young woman to meet his father at the airport.

Slighter, but no less attractive than their elder sister, came Isabel and Christine, twins aged thirty-five, the first a film producer, the second an executive of a Maxwell company in California. Then Kevin, a gaunt workaholic of twenty-six, already marked as the one most likely to inherit responsibility, if not reward. When Kevin's wife Pandora had complained to her mother-in-law about how little she saw of her husband, Betty replied with lofty lack of sympathy: 'If you marry a man like my son, what can you expect?'

When he came to the last name Maxwell's voice softened noticeably. The Benjamin of the family he called this one fondly, the raven-haired, lovely – and undoubtedly his best-beloved – Ghislaine, twenty-four. Of all the young Maxwells she was the only one their father truly indulged. Hers was the only photograph in his vast office where, whatever his mood, she was always welcome, to hug him, to slide behind his desk, slip into his lap and cajole for favours: a trip to St Moritz, a new BMW – a new business. He made her a director of Oxford United, which bemused the players even more than it did her but made some good pictures for the *Mirror*.

Once Ghislaine had taken her bow, however, the true business of the evening could begin. Boasting. No Maxwell occasion is complete without a robust bout of it.

Much of what Maxwell had to tell his listeners had heard before. Getting his hands on the *Mirror* and its sister papers was not an end but a beginning. In no time at all he would have settled the hash of their opposition, the market-leading titles owned by Rupert Murdoch. Newspapers, though, were to be but one element of the worldwide communications empire Maxwell had now set out to build. There was television, cable, satellite broadcasting, films, books, data transmission – any medium that conveyed information. By 1990, a scant five years hence, BPCC, which was to be his – Pergamon's – vehicle in this great crusade, would be among the top ten of communication megacorps, right up there with RCA, the American networks, the BBC. And, of course, Murdoch's News Corporation. There would be a long way to go. The only television interest Maxwell had was an investment in Central Television, one of the larger British networks, and some creaky cable television systems of limited potential. The only data retrieval system was Pergamon Infoline, an experimental system picked up for next to nothing in 1980 from his old Nemesis the Department of Trade. It seemed a useful beginning but hardly a match for Dow-Jones or Reuter.

Maxwell then called upon Lord Wilson of Rievaulx to say a few words. This plainly came as something of a surprise to the former prime minister, under whose leadership of the Labour Party Maxwell had held his seat in the House of Commons. But, seasoned old word-spinner that Harold Wilson was, he got up from his Moët after only the briefest of bemused hesitations and launched into a speech of wondrous circuitousness. It was several minutes before it became clear to his listeners that, skilled though his improvised soliloquy was, he simply could not bring to mind the name of his host. But when he did he assured all there that, had

Bob Maxwell stayed in politics, he, too, would have become prime minister.

One of the reasons Maxwell became – and has remained – so security-conscious is that he gave it as his opinion in front of television cameras that IRA bombers ought to be tried by court martial and, if found guilty, promptly shot. Maxwell had displayed a taste for summary justice during the war. Four years after the Headington party, some of his letters to Betty were included in the authorized biography serialized in Mirror newspapers. One that attracted particular comment told of how he had shot a German mayor in reprisal for an attack by soldiers who were supposed to have surrendered.

The RAF band gave way to the sedately stirring strains of the Joe Loss Ambassadors. Some of the diners danced; some went in search of the one comfort in rather short supply for those unwilling to tramp out in the rain to the portable toilets erected in the grounds. Gentleman standing in line for a guest washroom that one of them had discovered on the ground floor of the house passed the time by browsing through the contents of the cupboards lining the passageway. One was stacked with jars of salad cream, presumably awaiting the Pergamon lunchers of the following day. They worked up an ungrateful joke to bring back to the tables. 'We've found what he puts on his hair.'

Most of Maxwell's listeners had been neither interested nor impressed by the braggadocio they had sat through. Those who had known or heard of him for only a short time had already learned to take into consideration the gap between what Maxwell said and what he meant. Some who had known him longer wondered if it was a fundamental design fault – the Martian blueprint perhaps – the inability to distinguish between what might be so and what could never be.

Maxwell pledged, publicly and repeatedly, that if the printing of the *Daily Mirror* was impeded by the print unions for any reason whatever he would never allow it to be printed in Fleet Street again. The unions called his bluff. They did stop the paper. But the *Mirror* was still being printed in Fleet Street long after most other titles had moved out. No less solemnly he had sworn that he would sell the *Sporting Life*, the group's unique racing-sheet. Years later it was still flourishing under his ownership. Rather less rhetorically he had pledged that his circulation-boosting bingo games would create at least two winners of a £1 million prize. One was enough. There was never a second. 'He will say whatever he thinks will impress people,' said a despairing admirer. 'And once it is out of his mouth he regards it as fact.'

Nothing caused more confusion to the many people who attempted to help Maxwell succeed in his soaring ambition than this seemingly innate inability to understand that he was actually expected to do what he said he was going to do. Among those who did not wish him well nothing generated greater scorn. 'That is a Murdoch promise, not a Maxwell one,' jibed a News International director, spelling out one of their rigidly enforced ultimatums. Seasoned observers only realized that Maxwell's ill-fated *London Daily News* was about to be shut down when he assured them he would keep it going for another two or three years.

Even the most loyal of Maxwell employees had learned not to try too hard to spare him the consequences of his grosser blunders. As another paragraph in the Department of Trade report had read, 'He is a man of great energy, drive and imagination, but unfortunately an apparent fixation as to his own abilities causes him to ignore the views of others if these are not compatible'.

More than one man beneath the rain-soaked canvas could vouch for that personally. They had seen colleagues reduced to tearful trembling fools by Maxwell's thunderous disapproval. 'The one way to stop influencing Bob Maxwell', an outsider was breezily assured, 'is to work for him.'

It was something that had been apparent ever since Maxwell's earliest days in what he refers to as 'the Knowledge Market'. To John Halsall, who managed a division of Pergamon producing school books, 'It always seemed that Maxwell regarded any able employee as a competitor to be driven out rather than an ally to be encouraged'.

Driven out they were, in a steady stream. 'Gone,' Maxwell would bellow in the wake of another departure. 'Gone into the Outer Darkness!' But the stream flowed in as well as out. Maxwell would snap up talented people, pay them large salaries, give them titles that implied serious responsibilities and then insist on doing their work for them. There was only one way – Maxwell's way. 'I am the only man who. . . .' Maxwell was the only man who could agree contracts, authorize work of any importance, approve any but the most routine expenditure. Executives had to have his approval for their every move. Given the extent to which Maxwell's time and attention were stretched as his patchwork empire spread, the delays and frustrations were boundless. A manager who had spent weeks laying the groundwork for a deal could have the galling experience, when it finally won Maxwell's attention, of watching the Only Man Who pick up a phone and in five minutes settle for something rather less advantageous than he was being offered.

Employing people, Maxwell practised a certain bracing equality. Doorman or director, it made little difference. No matter what the accomplishments or achievements of anyone who worked for him, their status was defined by taking his wages. As far as he was concerned they were, with rare exceptions, mere minions. One of the exceptions sat at table B5: Marje Proops, the *Mirror*'s regal agony aunt, to whom Maxwell had become devoted. 'You know how much I think of you, Marje,' he had told her. 'You're not like these other schmucks who work for me.'

It is not hard to understand Maxwell's attitude. Most of his battles – and especially the one to re-establish his financial credibility – had been fought singlehanded. What was really being celebrated at Headington was a monumental victory over the money Establishment that in the past had despised and rejected him.

Memory of Maxwell may have faded in most sectors of the nation's life by the time his astonishing resurgence began just over a year before, but he was never far from the minds of the worried men at the Piccadilly headquarters of Reed International, a prosperous conglomerate with large holdings in the United States as well as in Britain. Originally a manufacturer of newsprint and other paper products, Reed had diversified into a vast range of paint and decorating products and into publishing – including now *Variety*.

Reed's wholly owned subsidiary, IPC (for International Publishing Corporation) Magazines, was by far the largest magazine publisher in the country. Maxwell printed many of its titles in plants that Reed had been glad to sell to him at bargain rates so that he, rather than they, could deal with the intransigent print unions.

It had been for much the same reason that the Reed board (which Maxwell was soon to describe as 'a committee of wallpaper manufacturers') wanted to get rid of their newspaper group, also the largest of its kind in Britain until Murdoch had assembled his.

The *Daily Mirror* was the problem. As recently as 1967 when it had been the only tabloid newspaper of consequence in Britain, it sold 5 million copies a day, the largest circulation in the Western world. It was the only popular national daily on which the Labour Party could rely for support. Although the Conservative Party held a hundred-seat majority in the House of Commons, the *Mirror* had many friends inside Parliament and out. It was unthinkable that Reed would be allowed to dispose of it however they wished.

The wallpaper manufacturers decided to skirt controversy by 'floating' Mirror Group Newspapers as a separate company on the Stock Exchange. At a time when the Government was encouraging Britain to turn itself into a nation of shareholders by privatizing State-owned enterprises they hoped that the majority of shares might be bought by the papers' own readers. An elaborate prospectus was drafted, according to which only a certain number of shares would be sold to any individual. This, said Reed, would keep the group, which included, in addition to the *Daily Mirror* and the *Sporting Life*, the *Sunday Mirror* and the *People*, another Sunday, and two important Scottish papers, the *Daily Record* and the *Sunday Mail*, out of the hands of a predator who might wish to turn its influence to his own ends.

It was a proposal of blinding fatuousness. From the moment that Maxwell was sighted circling the derelict ship it was plain that if he could once get a line aboard the prize would be his. In the event, Reed handed him the rope themselves and he used it to hang them. Like a movie Godfather he made them an offer they could not possibly refuse. It was a brilliant exercise in brute force, swift, unexpected, no quarter given or asked. For all the tomfoolery in the papers that followed, if Maxwell, a name to scoff at in the City for as long as most bankers could remember, could pull off something like that on one of the most eminent outfits in the game, then

Henry Poole was quite likely right. The time had come to take Maxwell seriously.

'Carriages at midnight,' the invitations had said. Before that unusually early hour the following day's *Mirror* was delivered from London – great piles of it, warm from the presses, the ultimate publisher's conceit. Then the ultimate publisher was off to bed. He would be up again at six the next morning, and a thousand people were coming for lunch.

Peter Marsh at table E7, one of the more colourful advertising entrepreneurs in London, was summoned to a presentation for the *London Daily News* as its launch was being planned. Maxwell asked all the advertising men present what they thought the editorial content of the paper ought to be. 'I thought it rather strange to be asking us, rather than telling us, particularly at that stage.'

Marsh fell into conversation with Ian Maxwell. 'Your father takes a lot on his shoulders. And he's not in very good physical shape, is he? Tell me, does he ever think about . . . er, his mortality?'

'Yes, he does. It makes him very angry.'

Three weeks short of two years after the gala at Headington a huge white yacht, 145 feet and five storeys – they could hardly be called decks – of gleaming marine plastic and curved glass, lay with its shapely stern tethered to the sea-wall in Cannes. High on each side her new name stood out in huge letters. *Lady Ghislaine*. Her previous owner, Adnan Khashoggi's brother Essam, had called her *Lady Ida* for his own daughter. It was a perfect Riviera spring evening, not a wisp of smog to mar the view of the Croisette shoreward, nor enough movement on the sea beyond the breakwater to test the vessel's stabilizers – the least of the space-age innovations which raised her value to $16 million.

A mere ten kilometres away at the tip of Cap d'Antibes stood the most sumptuous retreat on the French Riviera, the Hôtel du Cap, and in its grounds by the rock-pool the Eden Roc restaurant, a David Hockneyish dream in green and blue looking out over the Mediterranean from Monte Carlo to the deep red-purple Maures Mountains. There the Maxwells were expected for dinner. 'We'll take the boat,' decreed the proud new owner. And in no time at all the crew of thirty or so had *Lady Ghislaine* under way.

For all its readiness to please those who pay its astronomical charges, the Hôtel du Cap makes it difficult for anyone who arrives by yacht. The only landing-place is by the pool, impossibly cramped for a vessel the size of *Lady Ghislaine*. The order was passed to lower Number One Tender, largest of the boats carried on board.

Even then, so crammed together are the huge villas of the rich that line the shore of the Cap, and so closely do their well-heeled owners protect their access to the water, that the only place the Maxwells could find to come ashore was inconveniently distant from the hotel. Betty, scrambling out of the launch in her dainty Charles Jourdan shoes, demonstrated a command of her native language that took the salty crewmen by surprise.

Nothing else went wrong, however, with *Lady Ghislaine*'s flag-showing visit. Maxwell had come to love the boat since Betty had talked him into getting it a few months earlier. Twin-domed satellite communications kept him in touch with London or wherever else he wanted to speak to. The vessel was based in Majorca. She could easily cross the Atlantic if he wanted her in the Americas. Now he had brought her to Cannes for his first appearance at the MIP-TV Festival, an annual international television market-place, the more dramatically to unveil his latest boasts.

In the tomb-like Palais des Festivals, Maxwell told a press conference he planned to share a 12 per cent interest in the operation of TF-1, a newly privatized French television channel, and also to launch a pan-European television news network that would be the equal of the great American systems like CBS, NBC and ABC: the European Coalition Broadcasting Corporation.

Maxwell had an attentive audience. The journalists knew that only the month before he had taken *Lady Ghislaine* to the Spanish mainland and bearded King Juan Carlos in his own capital to petition for a 25 per cent stake in a Spanish television channel that was also due to be privatized. He had come away, he said, convinced that he would be successful, having also discussed such matters of moment as the future of Gibraltar and a forthcoming holiday by Prince Charles and Princess Diana. 'Hundreds of millions of people speak Spanish,' Maxwell reminded them, 'and are influenced by its culture.'

Then, remembering that he was in France, he added: 'As it is my ambition to create the first worldwide communication company, it is clear that we cannot do without France and its language – the third most-spoken language in the world of creativity.'

The French, at least, among Maxwell's listeners were well aware that a year earlier he had tried to participate in the setting-up of a French DBS (Direct Broadcast by Satellite) television operation. But a new French government had revoked the agreement. Now he was asked once more if he was still interested, and indeed he was, he assured them, for the music channel that his British cable interests had developed.

He had also bought a small organization called the Agence Centrale Presse, which for years had operated in the shadow of the main French news agency Agence-France Presse, and invested in the picture agency Sygma. Now he announced that he planned to launch a national popular daily newspaper in France which would sell 2 million copies a day. 'I want to implement the same system I created in England,' he said, puzzling reporters who knew that Maxwell had frequently discussed the possibility of printing the same centrally edited paper in different parts of Britain but had not done anything more about it. What impressed the French reporters most was his claim that he planned to buy *La Provençal*, the Marseilles newspaper which had been the power base of the late Gaston Deferre, another legendary socialist millionaire who had been the godfatherly mayor of that turbulent old town.

Maxwell, who was billed in France as President of the Pergamon Media Trust – one of the dependencies of the Liechtenstein foundations which had, by then, become newsworthy – was taking up his stake in TF-1 in partnership with Francis Bouygues, a French cement baron who also wished to be a Great Communicator. The pair of them were photographed handing a cheque for 3 billion francs to Edouard Balladur, the Minister of Communications. The yellow cheque with its nine zeros, drawn on the Banque Indo-Suez and certified by the Banque de France, was photographed assiduously, too.

Not nearly as much notice was taken of the contract permitting the use of the channel for ten years which required 40 per cent of the financing to be provided by public investment. For in Cannes, where the visitors to MIP-TV were sharing the town with delegates to the Fortune Tellers and Astrologers convention, it was party-time once more. From *Lady Ghislaine's* afterdeck the blue and white Pergamon house flag fluttered alongside the Red Ensign and the tricolour. As every arrival stepped on board he or she was requested by the white-uniformed gangway watch to remove their shoes, which were placed in a plastic bag and lined up to await their departure. Not only did Betty not want to have her silky teak decks marked; she would not even allow anyone to enter the salons where the carpets were thick enough for smaller vessels to run aground on.

Mystifyingly, the background tape played 'Jerusalem' over and over. Stewards and stewardesses passed the champagne – Mumms this time. Jean Baddeley in flowing silk and a carefree new hairdo rarely left the side of Mike Maloney, the tall *Mirror* photographer with whom she had become close friends and who was now the yacht's official cameraman. Ian and Kevin helped their father, suitably nautical in a vast blue T-shirt, entertain a stream of guests most of whom, once again, he was meeting for the first time.

The man in the Maxwell contingent who did know who the guests were was Bryan Cowgill, a former managing director of Thames Television whom Maxwell had telephoned as soon as he saw that he had resigned after a row. The recruiting style was typical of the way in which Maxwell will swoop upon a man whose expertise can be useful to him but whom he has no intention of allowing to share credit for the result. Cowgill had structured most of the plans Maxwell had been flaunting at MIP-TV. But he spent most of the party relegated to the jetty to check off the names of the arrivals before they were allowed to take their shoes off. A few weeks later he had hauled down his flag as a deputy managing director of BPCC and survived on the manifest only as a 'consultant'.

A group of papparazzi climbed up on to the sea-wall and yelled to Maxwell to pose for them. He pulled Betty and the deal-signers alongside him. The photographers were jabbing their thumbs in the air, a gesture that might easily be misunderstood in Britain but which in France means 'one'. Maxwell got it. TF-1. He and the others stuck their thumbs up for the cameras, all of them in a row.

'The amazing thing about Maxwell', Lord Spens has said, 'is the way that he can keep fifty deals in the air at once and keep control.' The acquisitions and activities Maxwell was talking about in Cannes were no more than a glimpse of the ventures he was feverishly launching. Three years after his triumphal re-emergence, he had collected a bewildering, seemingly patternless array of businesses and investments across the world. Acquiring the helicopter division of British Airways made him the biggest helicopter operator in Europe. He picked up struggling engineering companies at bargain rates. He bought up an undervalued investment trust and realized its assets. He nurtured stakes in magazine groups, film production companies, radio stations and picture agencies that could be judged strategic; others in stationers, property, furniture manufacturers, banks and brewers that looked as though he simply could not resist a bargain. But he seemed to be making serious money. For year three the profit forecast for the main Maxwell businesses in Britain was £150 million on a turnover of £1 billion. And he had formulated a target. By 1990, Pergamon/BPCC was to have a turnover of £3–5 billion – which was going to take some doing.

No one knew better than Maxwell himself that he could not earn that kind of money in Europe alone. A series of timely buy-ups in the United States had already made him the third-largest printer there in addition to his publishing and growing database service. But printing was neither glamorous nor high-powered enough to let him make it big. Only something like a major newspaper, a film studio, a television network or a top publishing house could do that. This was Maxwell's second really bad decision of 1987. The first had been to launch a newspaper of his very own.

'Never start a business,' Maxwell would always cry, whenever an idea was put to him. 'Always buy a going concern.' Nevertheless he had succumbed to the temptation that far more seasoned Fleet Street proprietors had found easy to resist and decided that London could use a second evening paper. After a year of the turbulence, melodrama, contradiction and confusion that accompany every Maxwell venture the *London Daily News*, put together independently of Mirror Group Newspapers, had first hit the streets at the end of February 1987.

For a while in the next few weeks it looked as though Maxwell might, as he said himself, have been in danger of realizing his ambitions, even though they remained easier to proclaim than to define. The crucial American plunge he had decided on had as its target the mammoth Florida-based publishing conglomerate of Harcourt Brace Jovanovich Inc. To finance it he had to overcome the resistance of City investors to what had been defined by a *Financial Times* writer as the Maxwell Factor.

Henry Poole, the literary stockbroker, won the crucial institutional investors over. Turning the notorious assessment of the Department of

Trade investigation around, he made the spirited assertion that 'in three or four or five years all those people who say they will not back BPCC will have to explain to their trustees or shareholders whether they are fit and proper persons to run a public company'.

Poole did not even have to show them the forty-eight-page analysis of BPCC's prospects he was preparing for general sharebuyers entitled *Unravelling the Melmotte Skein.* In that he gave four reasons for BPCC stock being worth less than it deserved to be, the last of which was:

> *A feeling of unease, even hostility, towards the Group's chairman which is captured in the following quotation from Chapter 10 of* The Way We Live Now *by Anthony Trollope, 'But still there was a feeling of doubt and a consciousness that Melmotte, though a tower of strength, was thought by many to have been built upon the sands.'*

Cheerily, Poole continued:

> *It appears Robert Maxwell has suffered every accusation, apart from being drunk in the House of Commons, that was borne by Mr Melmotte and others besides. Our review is entitled* Unravelling the Melmotte Skein, *because it is clear that in contrast to Mr Melmotte Robert Maxwell has built on secure foundations.*

It seems unlikely that Maxwell would ever have read this lengthy Victorian epic (though one of his companies printed the standard paperback edition). Poole, of course, made the comparison only to dismiss it, but it is not one that his client might relish. Augustus Melmotte, described in the blurb as a 'horrid big, rich scoundrel . . . a bloated swindler . . . a vile city ruffian', was a large man with bushy eyebrows who came from a mysterious background to make a fortune in the City, had dealings with Russia and China, claimed to have risen above the profit motive despite his great wealth, made a speech in the House of Commons when he was not supposed to and was brought down by a financial scandal.

'The City hasn't changed all that much,' explained a Poole assistant. 'Possibly we're a little more subtle now. They were rather more openly crooked then.' The professional investors and underwriters decided that Maxwell was once more an acceptable risk. They stuffed the credibility gap with money, gobbling up a huge issue of BPCC shares which matched Maxwell's own investment and which raised a total of £630 million for the American war-chest.

But Maxwell had underestimated the opposition. William ('Billy Jo') Jovanovich was as tenacious a defender as he was a fierce attacker. He had no intention of being colonized by another empire-builder. He fought back with deft legal manoeuvres and a superb intelligence service. Indeed, he raised the question of Liechtenstein: Was it a hideaway?

Black Friday came on 24 July 1987 with a United States federal court ruling that barred the portals of Harcourt Brace Jovanovich to Maxwell.

That month had started badly. Maxwell's old enemy Rupert Murdoch had outwitted him once again by plucking another paper, the pioneering full-colour *Today*, out of his grasp. Worse, Murdoch's *Sun*, the detested rival Maxwell had vowed to beat with the *Mirror*, was claiming that under his guidance the *Mirror* had actually fallen behind it by another quarter of a million in circulation. His old financial crony Lord Stevens had not fulfilled the expectations he had aroused of letting Maxwell have the valuable printing contracts for the *Daily Express* and the *Sunday Express* – an important consideration for the BPCC investors. Nor was the news from France much help to his global aspirations. When the TF-1 shares had been placed on the Paris Bourse their opening price had not risen above 165 francs, about half the cost of Maxwell's own. The family Deferre of Marseilles had sold *La Provençale* to Robert Hersant, who, because he owned so much of the French press – and television – already, was sometimes known as France's Robert Maxwell.

But by far the worst realization was that the *London Daily News*, the paper Maxwell regarded as his very own, had turned out to be a disaster. At lunchtime on Black Friday, without a moment's warning, he ordered it shut down. It was the most spectacular collapse of its kind in memory.

As he is fond of saying at times like that, 'You've got to learn to take a kick in the goolies'. Maxwell fights back by reflex, although what he decided upon then sounded suicidal. He immediately gave orders to plan the launch of up to three new papers in Britain.

The idea of starting more papers seemed to become a preoccupation. When he made a bid for the large Dutch publisher Elsevier, probably the only serious rival Pergamon has in scientific publishing, newspapermen were puzzled to hear him talk of founding a Sunday newspaper in Holland, where Sunday newspapers are not legal.

Elsevier gave him a cool reception (they had already been talking to the wallpaper manufacturers at Reed). Maxwell has never succeeded in a hostile takeover bid, unless his two-stage acquisition of BPC (he added the C for Communication) counts. And there, he now relates with pleasure, 'I was about as welcome as swallowing a frozen dead rat'.

For the moment, though, Maxwell took to cruising the world's stock markets, a kind of financial Flying Dutchman unable to find a port, a home for the huge sum that was burning a hole in his coffers. The Grumman Gulfstream II jet – registration BO-VIP – he now used for air travel spent as much time in the air as on the ground. In Tokyo, where he arrived in the same week as Murdoch, he told Japanese publishers he wanted one of them to partner him in an English-language daily newspaper published simultaneously in London and Tokyo. He already prints such a paper for the Chinese. In Moscow he made a similar proposition to the Russians. In Portugal, where Murdoch, also with an eye on the huge Brazilian market, had made his own pitch, he got a multi-media deal and the scent of yet another to be had in Macao, the Portuguese colony adjoining Hong Kong. The Gulfstream headed in that direction, and Maxwell announced he would be bidding for the Macao television franchise, which could beam a Chinese-language service into Hong Kong and Canton province.

Nor was this frenzied activity confined to business. Ever since his financial rebirth no good cause had been safe from Maxwell. In 1984 he had set out to end the famine in Ethiopia. In 1986 he had flung himself into rescuing the Commonwealth Games in Edinburgh from collapse after quarrels over race threatened to decimate the competitors. In 1987 it was AIDS. He became chief fund-raiser for a Government-backed charity, promising an equivalent £500,000 from his own charitable funds. In fact, when the scheme was announced, the *Mirror* said the Maxwell half-million had already been handed over. Seven months later Maxwell and the Government were still arguing about who was supposed to put their money up first. During that time, however, Maxwell had faced the epidemic like a global Canute, travelling to Canada to warn against the 'plague mentality' and to Edinburgh to tell the Royal College of Surgeons he would set up a worldwide information service on the scourge. He pressed on with plans for a huge teach-in on the Holocaust to be held in the Albert Hall in the summer of 1988.

He still found time to play the stock market. While the BPCC investors watching this hyperactive performance were beginning to wonder what was going to be done with the £630 million intended for a major expansion, the only real news to come their way was that the company was no longer to reflect Maxwell's oft-proclaimed pride in his adopted land. Too many people in other countries thought BPCC must be something like British Rail. It was to become the Maxwell Communication Corporation. 'It's not an ego trip,' said Maxwell before anyone could suggest such a thing. 'I was forced into it by my colleagues.' The pace began to tell. In Paris, speaking at the Anglo-American Press Club (to announce the launch of an English-language paper there in 1989), Maxwell keeled over backwards and continued his speech lying prostrate – a feat his audience acknowledged with a spontaneous round of applause.

Maxwell was back in Cannes once more, this time for MIP-COM, the second big electronics market of the year, to do some bragging about Portugal when, four months after Black Friday, on 19 October, Black Monday dawned. Within a week of the Great Crash of 1987 the shares in all Maxwell enterprises and investments had suffered as badly as anyone else's. But so had the important American and British conglomerates both he and Murdoch could use to expand their domains been drastically marked down. And whereas Murdoch had, on paper, lost an almighty $1 billion, half his personal fortune, Maxwell's luck had been at work. Maxwell boasted that his losses had barely dented the unspent £630 million. As he had said when the flabbergasted staff of the *London Daily News* – on which £50 million had been squandered – enquired about compensation for the abrupt ending of their employment: 'The one thing I'm not short of is money.'

TWO

There is no topic on which more haziness prevails than the identity of Czechoslovakia.

MR JUSTICE ROWLETT, 1933

I was never young. I never had that privilege.

ROBERT MAXWELL

MAXWELL

AFTER HE HAD PLAYED HIS PART in saving Ethiopia from famine Maxwell became fond of saying that he had been born in the African part of Czechoslovakia. Few people who heard this little joke – which like much of his repertoire had been fed to him by someone else – would be likely to remember that it was the Nazi intimidation of that small country in 1938 that led to the Second World War.

Following the shambles of the Great War of 1914–18 the principal victors, France, Britain, Italy and the United States, set out to redraw the map of Europe. One of the new countries they planned was to be assembled around the ancient kingdom of Bohemia, a province of the disintegrated Austro-Hungarian Empire.

Since the days of the Holy Roman Empire the Czechs of Bohemia had been Western civilization's 'acceptable' Slavs, a buffer state holding off the barbarous Slav lands to the east. In the seventeenth century the Austro-Hungarians added the sibling provinces of Moravia and Silesia. Soon the enlarged territory began to exhibit signs of modern nationhood. By the nineteenth century the energetic and innovative Czechs were recognized as an important economic asset to their languid Habsburg rulers in Vienna. Skoda engineering, Bata shoes, Pilsen beer – and the fine glass from which it was drunk – were famed. Prague became the second city of the Empire.

The Czechs had long urged the Austrians to grant them nationhood. Invited to plead their cause at the Paris Peace Conference, their leaders decided to enlarge their territory by aligning themselves with their similar-sized but more pastoral eastern neighbour, Slovakia, another Habsburg orphan. The two countries petitioned for joint independence. The victorious powers not only agreed to the establishment of the Czecho-Slovak Republic – the hyphen seemed crucial at the time – they threw in Sub-Carpathian Ruthenia, also known as the Carpatho-Ukraine or 'Little Russia', another former Hungarian province on Slovakia's eastern border.

The nation-builders knew little about Ruthenia, as it was most frequently called, but they were happy to have all the territory they could get and this addition would provide an eastward corridor through the Ukraine to Russia, the Slav mother-nation. To the Czechs and Slovaks the original German purpose in the First World War had been a land-grabbing drive to the east. Torn though she might be at the time by the

Bolshevik adventure and its aftermath, Russia was still the best insurance against the same thing happening again.

The new country's founders might well have named it Czecho-Slovakia-Ruthenia. One reason they did not was that many Ruthenians had emigrated to the United States. Their nationalist spirit aroused, they lobbied President Woodrow Wilson, most influential of the Paris map-makers, to make their native province autonomous.

Treaties that supplemented the Treaty of Versailles in 1919 duly pro-vided for the establishment, within Czechoslovakia, of the Autonomous Republic of Podkarpatska Rus. Its administrators, its police, its civil servants were all to be Ruthenian. Its first governor would be one of the nationalists, imported from America.

The Czech and Slovak delegates hurried back to Prague and forgot all about Podkarpatska Rus. Their priority was a model modern state on the sturdy foundations of Czech heavy industry and Slovakian agriculture. A compelling idealism convinced them that this was possible despite seri-ous obstacles the planners had ignored.

Setting up a parliamentary system to accommodate some fourteen political parties was among the least of the problems. The redrawn fron-tiers encompassed a bewildering array of 'minority' populations: Poles, Hungarians, Romanians, Ukrainians, Yiddish- and Hebrew-speaking Jews. The Czech and Slovak delegates had pledged in Paris that the ethnic identities of all these citizens of the new republic would be respected, and the efforts to do so were impressive.

But since 7 million Czech-speakers far outnumbered all the others put together Czech inevitably became the official language of national administration, parliament, the courts, the army, universities. People born to other tongues soon realized that if they wanted to make the most of their citizenship they would need to learn it. Nevertheless, grudgingly, this was accepted as the price of admission to what one of Czechoslo-vakia's early admirers called 'a unique and luminous experiment in multi-national democracy' by all except the largest and most cohesive minority, the Germans.

There were 3½ million Sudeten Germans in Czechoslovakia. Most of them lived in the northern and western region that bordered on Germany, overshadowed by the mountain range for which they and their largest piece of territory were named. The rest were scattered, like bits of fruit in a dumpling, in enclaves throughout all three provinces.

The committee at Versailles to which had fallen the task of making practical recommendations about the various 400 million or so Europeans whose lives were being redirected had no doubt what this meant. 'It is clear that the prosperity and perhaps almost the existence of the new state will depend upon the success with which it incorporates the Germans as willing citizens,' it reported doubtfully.

The Sudeten Germans had no intention of becoming 'willing citizens' if it meant giving up being German. Their right to stay where they were and be themselves, they wanted the world to know, was at least as good as that of most Czechs. It might even have been better. Czech history was tendentious and obscure. No one could really say if there had been, as the romantic nationalist view had it, some sort of a Czech republic as early as the seventh century. Germans were known to have been there in the twelfth century, and it was from them that the Sudetens claimed descent. In the days of Austro-Hungarian rule the German language alone had guaranteed cultural and economic superiority.

The Czechs, on the other hand, asserted that the 'historic' Germans of Bohemia had all been driven out long ago and that the present-day occupants of Sudetenland and the other areas were mere colonial settlers like the 'ethnic' Germans finding *Lebensraum* in Russia, Poland, the Ukraine and the Balkans.

In the 1930s the bitter resistance of the Sudeten Germans to the loss of their historic 'apartness' from the Slavs among whom they lived would come to dominate European politics. But in the early 1920s the Sudeten Germans were lying low, numbed by the financial disasters they had suffered through supporting Kaiser Wilhelm in the Great War and glad to be insulated from the revolutionary turmoil which had gripped Germany and Austria.

Some Germans could see that their new homeland had a lot going for it. It had inherited more than two-thirds of Austro-Hungarian industrial capacity with only a quarter of the old empire's population to feed. But since they could not agree with their Slav partners about the future any more than about the past, and since they scorned the newly erected democratic institutions, some of their morbid prophecies of second-class citizenship became self-fulfilling.

At first the Germans were divided amongst themselves about what they did want: an independent Sudetenland or one incorporated into Germany proper. Fanatical leaders had not yet drilled them into intransigence. But Adolf Hitler made up their minds for them. His most rousing slogan, 'Ein Volk, ein Reich, ein Führer', was nowhere repeated more stridently and ominously than in Sudetenland. Right up until 1938 a lot of Czechs clung to the hope that their Utopian political institutions might outweigh the ominous geopolitical jigsaw. But a lot of the pieces of the puzzle were simply swept off the table right at the start – among them Ruthenia.

Grigory Zatkovic, the first governor-designate of Podkarpatska Rus, arrived in Chust, the provincial capital, in 1921, two years after Wilson and his colleagues had done exactly as he asked. But he saw almost immediately that the promise of autonomy was unlikely to be fulfilled and returned, disillusioned, to Pennsylvania.

Eduard Beneš, one of the delegates to Paris, who was by then the country's president, felt sorry for him. Admitting that Ruthenia had already deteriorated into a neglected ramshackle colony, he said gloomily: 'Czechs have taken the rights of domination but have failed to carry out corresponding duties.'

Apart from Prague's impatience at Ruthenian national ambitions it was not difficult to see why. Janet Flanner of the *New Yorker*, one of a new breed of journalists, found her way there in 1938 and offered it to her readers as an example of why central Europe was likely to remain a mystery to them. She told them something of what they would find.

> *That in any big country house the owner is an aristocratic Hungarian, usually broke; that the house servants are Slovaks; that the tradesmen they buy from are Czechs; that the estate farmers are Jews; that the stablemen are Magyars; and that the gamekeepers are Germans, originally imported by Queen Maria Theresa, mother of Marie Antoinette.*

The place was simply too far away. Paris was closer to Prague than Chust was. This splinter of the Carpathian Mountains shaped like a Neolithic arrowhead, buried deep in the heart of the continent, was the most remote and backward corner of Europe. Of its 600,000 inhabitants, two out of three were illiterate landless peasants indifferent to who their rulers might be. One in five lived on the verge of starvation.

Much of the province was inaccessible wilderness, the few roads choked with frozen snow in the winter and in summer made all but impassable by the hard-baked ruts ploughed out by ox-carts and gypsy-caravans. For centuries the only really effective power across its thickly forested slopes and sinister valleys, packed with bear and deer, had been wielded by the *voivodes*, the omnipotent estate-managers of the Hungarian landowners. Well into the twentieth century these tyrannical figures, fur-hatted and high-booted, were ready to enforce their *droit de seigneur* on a village bride or brutalize the latter-day serfs.

Their places and those of the few Hungarian colonial functionaries who had been stationed there were taken not by Ruthenians, as poor old Zatkovic had been promised, but by transplanted Czechs, strangers to the local languages – rustic dialects of Ukrainian and Hungarian. In the larger villages and towns the triangular-patterned tricolour of the new state was stuck up over a few log-cabin prefectures, the uniforms of the gendarmes and the Customs collectors changed, but not much else. The ways of feudal Hungary lingered on, although there were always the *Karpathendeutsch*, as Queen Maria Theresa's Germans had become known, to see that the Sudeten question was not forgotten.

Slatina-Selo (*selo* means 'village' in Czech) was, until the Second World War, a huddle of wooden shanties, abject even by Ruthenian standards, around a water-point on the railway to Bucharest and a solitary salt mine. Among its miserable inhabitants were Mechel and Anna Hoch and their six children. It was on 10 June 1923 that Anna gave birth to Jan Lodvik, the boy who, several names later, became Robert Maxwell. Maxwell has always described his parents as farm labourers of the kind that Janet Flanner unearthed. But the friends of his earliest days of exile believe that Mechel was also the Orthodox Jewish community's *shochet*, the ritual slaughterer who enjoys an important religious standing.

Not much else of note happened in Slatina that year or for several years to come, except that life became steadily harder and the *Karpathendeutsch* gradually more truculent. When people spoke of the capital they still meant Budapest, a mere 120 miles away, rather than Prague. The River Tisa on the outskirts of the little town formed the frontier with Transylvania, the province of Romania renowned for Vlad the Impaler and Count Dracula. Occasionally the border guards took a pot shot at a smuggler sneaking something across. But in the main the people of Podkarpatska Rus, Gentile and Jew alike, lapsed back into the obscurity out of which great but distant events had briefly heaved them, the hillbillies of Mitteleuropa.

There was little work for Mechel most of the time. The family had virtually no money at all. Understandably, Maxwell and the two of his sisters who were also to survive the new war which, even in that remote place, would all too soon be upon them have never forgotten the misery of the one-room hovel in which eight of them lived. In winter, with snow thick on the ground and wolves howling on the frozen slopes, the children had to huddle for warmth around the old black stove on which Anna cooked. There were barely enough hand-me-down clothes to go around and no shoes for the younger ones. They wrapped their feet in rags against the cold or went barefoot. There was never enough to eat. Most of the year their diet was potatoes and *kasha*, the buckwheat groats that are an Eastern European staple, cabbage and pickled cucumbers. On the sabbath there would be *matzoh*, unleavened bread.

The children grabbed at every scrap. The appalling table manners familiar to anyone who has ever shared a table with Maxwell were bred in his bones. Even now he eats every meal as though it might be his last. No matter what the chef has sent in when he is eating at home or in his office, where the kitchen is always staffed; no matter what fine vintage he may have had brought up from his cellar – no meal is complete for Maxwell without some of the coarse delicacies of that hungry childhood: three or four large dark-green sour pickles or a basket of *matzoh*.

To the family the boy was known as 'Lajbi'. Despite the sparse diet he grew tall and heavy-boned. He was the family favourite. 'Mother spoilt him a great deal. We were all jealous,' one of the sisters, now Sylvia Rosen, remembers. But of course the girls knew there was no arguing with the pride of place due to a male child in a Jewish family. They, too, took a proprietary interest in their brother, embroidering little yamulkas for him, and seeing that they stayed on his wiry dark hair.

Among themselves the Hochs spoke Yiddish, the lingua franca of European Jews. But Mechel taught Lajbi the ancient Hebrew prayers. According to Maxwell, his mother was a decisive influence. Anna, he relates, had been properly educated and spoke good Hungarian. More important still, perhaps, he believes she was a member of a political party, the Social Democrats, from whose meetings she would bring home ideas which even at such an early age had an influence on him. 'I asked my mother why my father was hanging around in doorways. She told me it was because of the conservative politicians who made it impossible for him to get work.'

Not until the age of eight did Lajbi get his first pair of shoes and was able to go to the primitive local school. Lessons were given in Czech, and Russian was a compulsory subject. Some of the other children were *Karpathendeutsch*, who spoke German outside school. Lajbi picked up all those languages as well, although with more speed than accuracy – the first sign of the major talent he was to display throughout life. The boy had what is popularly known as a photographic memory. Whatever he read – or, even more particularly, heard – he soaked up instantly. So fast and readily in fact that his ability to absorb far outstripped his capacity to record what he had learned. Maxwell will unhesitatingly dictate a document twenty pages long (and then change his mind and dictate it over again and again); but only rarely does he attempt to write anything by hand, and when he does it is a hesitant process, the result barely legible. 'He couldn't even write "three pounds" on a cheque,' said one of the old soldiers who used to play poker with him in the murky postwar London days when Captain Robert Maxwell, MC, was setting out to fulfil his improbable destiny.

Nobody in Slatina – except possibly Anna – could have realized that young Lajbi was already displaying the extraordinary capacity for absorbing information which powered his progress in later years. But he was acknowledged to be a clever child, and one of the hopes that the Hochs had; assuming the money could ever be found, was to have him train as a rabbi. However, when he turned eleven and Anna tried to enrol him in a higher grade of school the teachers looked over his ragged clothing and turned him away.

Maxwell had been a member of the British Labour Party for some time before he was ready to pinpoint this childhood rebuff as the wellspring of his socialism. In his earliest campaigns to get into Parliament he avoided dwelling on his origins. He was already in Parliament before he began to invoke the memory of people like his father to whom money had a meaning only because they had none. 'A lucky man would aspire to a bicycle . . .' he would recall. 'I am a socialist because until the age of eight I had no shoes; because as a child I have never forgotten the pang of cold and hunger; because I was turned away from school because I was too poorly clothed and only received three years' education; and because my father spent most of his life unemployed. Just because I've made a couple of bob on the way I'm not about to renounce my working-class origins.'

It was, to be sure, a wretched childhood – and worse was yet to come – but not unrelentingly so. It was not always winter in the Carpathians, and in summer there were trees heavy with plums, there were pike to be caught in the Tisa and trout in the mountain torrents, if the gamekeepers could be evaded. Outside the inns old men sat drinking tea from tall glasses, arguing with Talmudic deviousness and rhetoric, bartering and bargaining mercilessly over a horse or a calf or a crop. Or a bicycle. Little Lajbi listened and learned the immortal truths of hustling; an argument is not lost simply because it is ended, a bargain made can always be remade, people buy what you say not what you deliver, the less you have to sell the louder you have to shout. An advertising director of Mirror Group Newspapers once complained to Maxwell about the space-buying methods of a chain of electrical-goods shops. 'They're tough going,' he said. 'Real street-traders.' Maxwell chuckled mightily. 'So am I,' he said. 'So am I.'

Many of Maxwell's consultations with the directors of his companies and others he employs are no more than brief midnight telephone calls, hurried exchanges in corridors, cars or lifts – even in adjoining *pissoirs*. He never chats; any niceties are for a purpose. He despises smalltalk. But to watch him at work, especially at Headington, on someone with whom he wants to do serious business conjures up at once his long-gone past in that distant drowsy place, and rituals more oriental than European. There will be a table to sit at – none of the restless pacing and bellying-up to people of the long, long office hours. There will be a stack of small plates. Soon a servant will appear with a tray. There will be drink within reach, but food, small delicacies, is more important. Maxwell will seat himself, settling his paunch between his thighs. Leaning across he will take a plate from the pile and push it in front of his guest. Eat, eat. It is the carpet bazaar, rather than the leafy fringe of Oxford; the horse market, the far side of the Bosporus.

Lajbi went to school in Slatina until he was eleven. The year was 1934. Czechoslovakia had based its economic hopes on Germany and Austria, the traditional markets for its manufactured goods and other exports. But the worldwide depression on top of the astronomical inflation those countries suffered – the miserable conditions that helped breed the Nazi movement – held back their recovery.

Nevertheless the Czechs beavered away in mines, fields and factories. Czechoslovakia was unquestionably the biggest little country in Europe. Tourists came to wonder at the dramatic Tatra Mountains, the forests and peaceful villages, the stirring contrast of magnificently preserved medieval cities with the functional modern buildings in which the local architects excelled. A remarkable national movement of gymnasts and dancers known as the Sokol became world-famous. In Germany the Nazis copied it as Strength Through Joy.

Sensitive by now to the menace of Germans both inside and outside the country, the Czechs took care to safeguard what they had built. As early as 1926 they had signed a mutual defence treaty with France. Keen to see Germany ringed by states friendly to them, the French had always tried to cultivate a special relationship with the Czechs. The Czechs, in turn, took a great deal of intellectual inspiration from France but for political guidance they looked to Britain with whom they had no treaty but whose ways were so admired that traffic in Czechoslovakia drove on the left. In 1935 the long-envisioned alliance with Russia was sealed.

Rather more pragmatically, the Czechs built themselves mighty frontier fortifications, raised a strong army and equipped it well. The locomotives and trucks produced in the great Skoda works were among the best in

Europe. So were the tanks. And the guns. Artillery was a national speciality. The Czechs had invented the howitzer, classic siege weapon of modern armies, and a lot of other weaponry besides.

But even in the developed provinces there was still not enough work for all. Which meant that in far-off Ruthenia things could only get worse. The Hochs decided to send Lajbi away to relatives in Slovakia. He might get a better education there, and in any case a growing boy could not go on sharing one room with all those sisters in varying stages of womanhood.

Maxwell is not the only Czech of his generation who still thinks well of Britain. It is hard to understand why. The Munich agreement of 1938, which bought a year or so of grace for the governments of Neville Chamberlain and Edouard Daladier, was the most futile and cowardly diplomatic act of the epoch. It brought the 'luminous experiment' to an abrupt end after a mere twenty years, inflicting on a bold and ingenious people the humiliation of a defeat without any of the glory of a war.

Hitler always had it in for the Czechs. They were too cocky, too accomplished for Slavs, and their condescension to the Sudetens was intolerable. As an Austrian, he held their nationalistic aspirations partly to blame for the weakening of the old empire. He spoke with loathing of the ambitious Czechs he had seen in his youth arriving in Vienna 'penniless, dragging their worn-out shoes over the streets of the city' where, all too soon for his baneful liking, they would 'instal themselves in key positions'. As early as 1932 he had confided to cronies that he planned to make Bohemia completely German. 'The Czechs we will transplant to Siberia. . . .'

He meant it. In 1935, two years after he had been elected Chancellor, Hitler informed his military chiefs that he intended to annex first Austria and then Czechoslovakia. Two million Czechs would be driven out to make *Lebensraum* for more Germans. A whiff of this brutal ambition was enough to clear what doubt might remain on the part of any Sudeten Germans. The principal democracies, Britain and France, it turned into dithering cowards.

In 1938, while Lajbi, like Hitler's penniless Czechs of Vienna, was dragging his worn-out shoes across Slovakia, the occupants of the Sudetenland, backed by Germany, demanded outright that it be made an autonomous region. It was the question upon which, most Czechs immediately understood, the future of their country depended. Even though Lajbi was only fifteen, to him as to the rest of the Hoch family and to the rest of Czechoslovakia's Jews it meant something more. Even in Slatina the Jews had heard whispers, at least, of what was going on in Germany.

Throughout that fateful year of 1938 a sorry lethal farce unfolded. Hitler gave the Sudeten Germany Party its instructions. 'We must always demand so much that we can never be satisfied.' Although the Allies were not to know it, nothing short of their direct intervention could have stopped Hitler.

Czechoslovakia turned to her treaty partners. Would France fulfil her obligations? Would the Russians? Yes, but only if France would. Daladier consulted Chamberlain. The best that could be offered by the two great nations that had sponsored Czechoslovakia's creation was a polite expression of concern.

Neither Britain nor France was ready to face the prospect of disturbing Europe's fragile peace. Dictators were springing up all around – Mussolini in Italy, Franco in Spain, Horthy in Hungary, Salazar in Portugal. In both London and Paris bare-knuckled shirt-colour politics already threatened the fragile authority of Parliament and the National Assembly. The sacrifices of 1914–18 were far too close in memory to risk repeating.

Nazi propaganda and conspiracy had some success in making it appear as though it was Germany which stood in danger of imminent attack by the Czechs. The Sudetens marching through the streets under their swastika banners were presented to the world as victims with a legitimate grievance. In desperation President Beneš summoned their leaders and pushed a piece of blank paper at them. 'Write out your demands,' he said. 'I pledge in advance to grant whatever you want.' Cornered, the negotiators could only present their ultimate demand: secession. Very well, said Beneš, it is yours. But the Germans would not even accept capitulation. They wanted a fight. There was rioting and upheaval throughout Sudetenland. Beneš could only place it under martial law.

Three times altogether Chamberlain, a man whose smile reminded a colleague of the silver handles on a coffin, flew to try to curb Hitler. After the first visit he and Daladier made a proposal: all Czech territory in which more than half the inhabitants were German would be handed over to Germany. Britain and France would guarantee the frontiers of the shrunken remainder. Beneš saw what he was up against. 'We have no choice,' he told his cabinet. 'We have been betrayed.'

On his second visit Chamberlain discovered that Hitler was no longer satisfied with the timetable for the transfer he had previously accepted. Germany must occupy all of the Sudetenland within a week. Matters were sliding out of Chamberlain's control. In a sickeningly spineless broadcast he lamented: 'How horrible . . . it is that we should be digging trenches and laying in gas masks here because of a quarrel in a faraway country between peoples of whom we know nothing.'

The third time Chamberlain came back from Munich he clutched the celebrated 'piece of paper' that guaranteed, he told the newsreel cameras, 'Peace with honour . . . peace for our time'. The Sudetenland would become part of Germany. In return Hitler had promised Chamberlain that Germany would not fight Britain again. But the piece of paper said nothing about fighting anyone else. In Prague the Sudetens in their leather shorts and knitted white stockings were already beating up their Czech fellow-citizens in the street, forcing them to salute the swastika.

On the whole the Czechs accepted their humiliation stoically. The Army, which the Germans later estimated could have defended the Sudetenland for two or three weeks, laid down its arms in October 1938 without protest. Neither the National Assembly nor the generals opposed Beneš' orders. Fighting Germany alone, Beneš explained to his secretary Jaromir Smutny, before he left to take refuge in Britain a few months later, would mean the sacrifice of countless lives, not to mention 'the odium that peace has been broken because of our apparent desire to hold a territory inhabited by Germans'. He believed – correctly, if pessimistically – that Germany was bound to bring about a European war out of which Czechoslovakia would be rebuilt.

The next month Kristallnacht, the night of broken shop-windows, descended upon Germany. In an unmistakable sign that the brutalization of Jews was the Nazi government's deliberate policy, a wave of inspired thuggery swept Germany. Thirty-five Jews were killed, thousands were injured and arrested, millions of marks' worth of damage was done to their homes and businesses.

'There are two things in life I hate,' Maxwell became fond of saying years later. 'Taxes and Germans.' Putting down the phone after a fulsome exchange of compliments with one of his German contacts, he will say: 'Fucking kraut.' Ian and Kevin have picked up the habit, too.

In 1938, Lajbi did not yet have to worry about taxes. But he became possessed by the conviction that he, personally, should start doing something about the Germans.

Like thousands of other restless and resentful adolescents he roamed from group to group beneath the leafy summer trees of Slovakia arguing, boasting and threatening. The undependable adhesive of democracy that had kept the state together was losing its grip. Divisions between Slovak and Czech, ethnic Pole and Ukrainian, Christian and Jew were in danger of becoming as consuming as their common hatred of the Germans. Quick-witted and with his remarkable memory, Lajbi absorbed and recycled all the arguments he heard in his search for a role. At one stage he swung nearly full circle from his maternal Social Democrat politics and joined a right-wing youth movement.

Not only was patriotism a confusing matter. Germans upon whom to vent the head of patriotic ire that was being stoked up were quite difficult to find. Germans, to Lajbi, did not mean the Sudetens, provocative though he might find them now that they had emerged to take over most official functions throughout the country. The target he had in mind, the full-fledged, jack-booted, goose-stepping stormtrooper, was not yet a familiar sight. In fact in Ruthenia another predator appeared.

It had taken Hitler five more months to realize his plans for Czechoslovakia to the full, but in March 1939 he bullied Beneš' successor into signing over Bohemia as a German *Protektorat*. Chamberlain's placatory manoeuvres had robbed him of the triumphal entry into Prague that a military victory would have brought. But now he arrived as the nation's 'deliverer', rolling in his massive Mercedes-Benz across the ancient cobblestones of Wenceslas Square, through crowds of delirious Sudetens to spend a symbolic night in Hradčany Castle, seat of the old Bohemian kings. 'Czechoslovakia', he proclaimed, 'has ceased to exist.'

It was true. Once the Beneš government collapsed it was more difficult than ever to administer Slovakia and Ruthenia from Prague. The distracted National Assembly shrugged both provinces off, told them to elect parliaments and govern themselves. In Ruthenia the clock was pushed back twenty years overnight. Democracy was forgotten. The dominant Ukrainian population seized power led by an archbishop of the Orthodox Church who believed he enjoyed Hitler's backing.

He did not. Hitler was cultivating Hungary's 'man on horseback', Admiral Miklos Horthy, leader of the Arrow Cross fascists, as a likely partner in crime. Long before he had any conceivable authority he had begun the dismemberment of Czechoslovakia by 'restoring' to Hungary the Felvidek, a wide strip of southern Slovakia and Ruthenia. Now he invited Horthy to help himself to the whole of Ruthenia. 'He who wants to eat at the table', said the Führer magnanimously, 'must help in the kitchen.'

Janet Flanner, who had been impressed by the concrete anti-tank dragons' teeth of the Czech defences, was soon to be followed by Sefton Delmer of the *Daily Express*, a master prospector of news who gave a vivid account of German and Slovak thugs dragging Czech Jews off the train he took from Prague to Chust. He watched the archbishop's Ukrainians, with only a few rifles between them, prepare to fight off the advancing Hungarian army, to which the concrete tank-traps presented no obstacle.

> *They suddenly arrived on bicycles, dark little men in khaki uniforms, pedalling away, bent low over their handlebars, as though they were a group from the Tour de France. . . .*
> *'Follow those bicycles,' I commanded our taxi-man.*

Not a line the modern foreign correspondent is likely to find himself uttering. Soon Delmer was witnessing the casual savagery that usually marks civil war. The local Hungarian population appointed themselves to authority over the Ukrainians and others.

> *I saw one fellow in a towering frenzy of histrionic Hungarian patriotism club down the wife of a Ukrainian leader with the butt of his shotgun. Then he shot her in the face as she lay on the ground. A gang of prisoners were marched down the main street carrying a heavy log on their shoulders, their hands manacled to it above their heads. They looked typical Slav peasants with their round, flat faces and blue slit-like eyes. Seconds later I saw them shot, all six one after the other. They went down in a shrieking, sobbing, kicking tangle, still chained to the log.*

Events were moving with a speed that all Europe found bewildering, let alone young backwoods patriots like Lajbi. In August 1939, Hitler and Stalin baffled the democracies by signing a non-aggression pact. 'This unnatural act', as Winston Churchill labelled it, contained a secret agreement to partition Poland, Czechoslovakia's northern neighbour, between Nazi Germany and the Soviet Union.

The German invasion of Poland, which both Britain and France were bound by treaty to defend, on 1 September was the actual beginning of the Second World War. To the motley underground band to which Lajbi had at last been allowed to attach himself – although hulking and aggressive, he had only just turned sixteen – it was the signal to move. Germans to kill, the Czech rebels calculated, would be easier to find in the direction of Poland. That was the direction in which Lajbi's group wandered, nervous but determined. They found not Germans but the Red Army, which had walked across the eastern part of Poland virtually unopposed and were now poking around the Slovakian frontier.

'We got into trouble with the Russians,' Maxwell remembers. But they got out of it. The Russians had no quarrel with Czechs. Just as in Ruthenia not too many Czechs of other origins kept up their quarrel with the Hungarians once they had settled in. The Hungarians were a familiar presence after all and, it was soon seen, far preferable to the Germans. For in Bohemia and Slovakia the Germans lost no time in getting down to the sinister undertaking that was soon to spread through most of Europe: Adolf Hitler's extermination plans.

All over Czechoslovakia there were raids, torture, imprisonment, extortion, murder. The Gestapo – enthusiastically aided, as it so often was in all Nazi-occupied territories, by local police – cast a wide net. Into it were swept intellectuals, clerics, trade unionists, socialists and communists, right-wing nationalists, gypsies; but, above all, Jews.

By comparison with her neighbours Czechoslovakia had few Jewish citizens – some 365,000 or about 2.4 per cent of the population (Poland had nearly 3 million). But the Germans wanted every one of them and, although the killing-ovens still lay in the future, the ghastly bureaucracy of deportation to concentration-camps and forced labour was soon established.

Hungary, too, had a national anti-Semitic policy, partly devised to ingratiate itself with Hitler. But in those early days it was hesitant to act too forcefully against its Jews for the bluntly practical reason that they represented a very large part of its workaday middle-class population – half the lawyers and doctors, a third of the merchants and industrialists, a similar proportion of academics and other intellectuals. Even many of its legislators. Without all these the country would simply not function properly. Eventually the very worst was to befall the Jews of Hungary in the hyena shape of Adolf Eichmann. But in 1939 they were merely being 'classified'. Where there was judged to be too many Jews in an industry or profession, their property would be confiscated and their job given to an 'Aryan'.

But there was not as yet anything like the perils that haunted Germany, Austria and now the *Protektorat* and Slovakia. Hungary struck many Czech Jews – Maxwell among them – as by far the lesser of two evil places. Once there he became a 'conductor' of trains taking little groups of refugees further on. He bought food and tickets for the escape, and watched out for guards.

·

Flying into Budapest in 1984 as an honoured guest of the Hungarian government, Maxwell finished his British Airways lunch, carelessly tossing the last of it – a pear that was not to his liking – on to the floor of the first-class cabin, and told his travelling companion, Sir Tom McCaffrey, then his Director of Public Affairs: 'It's forty-five years to the day, almost, since they sentenced me to death here.' He then took out one of his mighty havanas and, indifferent to the rules, filled the aircraft with fragrant smoke.

Maxwell has always treated airlines in a splendidly cavalier fashion. Before he had the Gulfstream he usually got one of the children or a director of one of his companies to go on trips with him. It would be their job to take care of the baggage. If he ever found himself returning home alone, he simply abandoned his bags, prominently labelled with his name, on the carousel. Usually the airline was sufficiently impressed to see that the luggage got to his office before Maxwell did.

He took a notable pleasure in telling the story of his extraordinary youthful adventure to his Hungarian hosts. And for anyone who knows Maxwell it is easy to envisage young Lajbi, reckless, headstrong, determined, shepherding his charges through to their destination. 'It was dangerous,' he said, relating the story forty-eight years later. 'But very exciting – until I got caught.'

For the moment, at least, the rest of the Hoch family seemed relatively safe back in Slatina. Soon it might be necessary for them, too, to go to Hungary. But what would they live on there? The question was never answered. The Hungarians were arresting Czechs by the hundred. Something about young Lajbi did not look quite right, and it was not long before a hand descended upon one of his broad shoulders.

'I was tortured and beaten up, sentenced to death as a spy,' Maxwell relates. But the Hungarians were still abiding by their own laws. And Hungary was not yet at war with Britain and France, both of which showed some vestigial responsibility for the citizens of their abandoned protégé state. The French embassy intervened to point out that many of the Czechs were under eighteen and ought to have been tried by a juvenile court. 'Instead of having two guards I was sent off with only one and he had lost an arm in the First World War.'

It was a perfect set-up for the impulsive violent offensive which was to become the favourite Maxwell tactic. 'I hit him on the head with a stick and escaped. It was fairly easy.'

Clearly, young Lajbi could not go back to Slatina. 'We often talked about what would have happened,' Betty says. 'He would have been killed.' There was only one way to go – onwards. There was only one place to turn: the terminal of the underground pipeline to which he had recently delivered his charges. Lajbi joined the trudge into exile, along the escape route which had now been extended through Yugoslavia, Greece and Bulgaria to Turkey and on to Syria, then a French protectorate.

He never saw his parents, or three of his sisters, again. But he did go back to Slatina more than forty years later. Ruthenia was annexed by the

Soviet Union in 1945 and made part of the Ukraine. He could find no one who remembered him, no mementoes of Anna and Mechel or the girls.

After Lajbi's departure the family must have lived in heartbreaking suspense. In 1941, although still prevaricating over their own Jewish population, the Hungarians rounded up most of the Jews of Ruthenia. Trying to avoid further responsibility, they drove some 7,000 of them across the border into the Ukraine where the Germans had set up mobile extermination units. At first the Germans tried to oblige. Later they complained that their killing resources were overstrained and sent the sorry survivors back to the Hungarians.

Surprisingly, a new Hungarian government showed more scruples. Jewish property was plundered, Jewish rations cut to starvation level, the civil rights of Jews were expunged and their humiliation completed by branding them with yellow stars. They were trundled here and there across the country, herded into ghettoes and concentration-camps. But they stayed alive.

Hitler held his notorious Final Solution conference in Berlin in early 1942. Horthy and his prime minister, however, kept the bloodthirsty Nazis at bay until 1944 when Hitler, fearful that Hungary would not be able to withstand the advancing Russians and determined to have his way with the Jews before they got there, imposed his own shadow government and with it the unspeakable Adolf Eichmann and his Sondereinsatzkommando.

In May and June 1944, while Maxwell, by then a British soldier and out for German blood, was preparing for D-Day, Eichmann and his SS cohorts put into operation a plan that in some ways was just as complex as the Normandy landings. The Jews had been marshalled into five zones scattered around central Hungary and its newly acquired provinces. Zone 1 included the Carpathians. Even though it meant straining the country's war-battered railways and other facilities to the limit, 437,402 Jews were assembled, registered, loaded on to trains and sent to the industrialized slaughterhouses of Auschwitz, near Cracow in Poland.

Jan Lodvik Hoch had only been in Britain a few hours before he was locked up again. Nobody called him Lajbi any more. The time for baby names was long past. By now his childhood was over beyond doubt. He had not yet killed a German – not even laid eyes on one – but, although still only seventeen, he had become a soldier, of sorts, in the army of the Czechoslovak Republic. Maxwell has always been fond of pointing out to people tempted to describe him as a refugee that he landed in Britain with a rifle in his hand. The image, with its echoes of Dunkirk, invokes a certain sentimentality.

Sometimes, in this frequently recycled account, he steps ashore from a British destroyer, which had picked him up after he escaped from occupied France in a small boat. In the abbreviated biography he now issues he describes himself as having been wounded and captured in the battle for France.

The famous rifle young Lodvik was carrying when he and his comrades shambled on to the Liverpool dockside in late July 1940, to be immediately surrounded by stony-faced British military police wearing red caps and large revolvers, would soon have been taken from him. During the two weeks it had taken the grimy old troopship to bring him and a couple of thousand other bedraggled fugitives to Britain from Sète in unoccupied southern France all the weapons on board had been confiscated. The beleaguered British government was understandably wary of fifth columnists of the kind thought to be largely responsible for the fall of France. The last thing it wanted was a bunch of armed enemy aliens – as, technically speaking, the Czechs seemed to have become by their homeland's surrender – swarming ashore. Their officers had been given orders to disarm them.

After the disintegration of the Czech Republic it soon became apparent that aggrieved patriots who still wanted to fight the Germans had better find their way to France, where anti-Nazi refugees of all kinds – even Germans – had been gathering ever since Hitler came to power. Many of military age had avoided deportation by enlisting in the Foreign Legion. Others had been detained in camps or were hiding out, one step ahead of the police.

Czechs, however, were welcome in France. In the First World War a Légion Tchèque of renegade Czech Nationalists had fought alongside the French army. (A similar legion in Russia had sided with the Whites against the Bolsheviks and found its way home again only after a legendary trek by armoured train across the Continent to the Pacific.) Now the two old allies were able to come to each other's aid again. In May 1939, only two months after Hitler had arrived in Prague, the Czech Military Bureau under General S. Ingr opened its doors in Paris. In the autumn a Czech National Committee led by Beneš signed an agreement under which the French would arm and equip a Czech force that would be at the disposal of the French high command. But it would go into battle under its own flag and be led by its own officers.

The trickle of bellicose refugees that found its way to the new Légion Tchèque was never to become a flood, which was just as well. It was one thing for gallant gestures to be exchanged; quite another for the over-whelmed French military bureaucracy to turn them to useful purpose. France's own reserves had been mobilized indiscriminately, and every camp and barracks in the land was overflowing with confused recruits.

There were never more than about 2,500 Free Czech soldiers, but not until the autumn was somewhere found for them to train. It was about as far from Paris as it was possible to go and still be in France: the town of Agde on the south-west Mediterranean coast near the Spanish frontier, in a tumbledown collection of huts surrounded by barbed wire thrown up to house refugees from the Spanish Civil War. The National Committee made contact with the escapees who had got to Syria, and they were brought to France by a returning supply-ship. Thus, in early 1940, was Lodvik Hoch, still only sixteen, delivered to the Czech army – which was far from pleased to see him.

The Czechs were an ill-matched assembly of professional soldiers led
by Lieutenant-General Rudolph Vierst, communist veterans of the
Spanish Civil War and released Foreign Legionnaires who had learned
their rudimentary military wisdom in that hard and alien school. But the
few with any experience were far outnumbered by eager volunteers like
Lodvik who came from every part of the defunct republic, spoke between
them every one of its languages and were anything by background
except soldiers. Many of them were too old to take orders readily; their
average age was close to forty and one man, at least, was thought to be
seventy. Many, like Lodvik, were too young to be given them. Even in
exile regular army rules applied, and the age for enlistment was
eighteen. But scores of boys as young as fourteen had found their way to
Agde and could hardly be turned away. They became a sort of unruly
auxiliary to the First Czech Division, as the new legion was to be called,
unpaid, clothed in oddments of uniform, running errands for the real
soldiers, constantly brawling among themselves.

Lodvik's arrival at Agde is still vivid in the memory of men who were
already there. Lou Rosenbluth, for one, whose own first name then was
Lodvik, a glamorous young man of twenty who was goalkeeper for the
Slovak national soccer team and had been in Brussels when the Germans
took Prague. Freddie Strasser, for another, who with his brother Arthur
had got from Prague to Agde via Milan and Nice. The cosmopolitans had
never come across anything like this gangling yokel, illiterate in several
languages, 'big and dark . . . clumsy like a young bull from the mountains', as yet another veteran recalled Lodvik.

'He spoke a little Yiddish,' remembers Freddie, 'a little Hungarian, a
little Czech. But he couldn't speak any of them properly. And he could
read but he couldn't write very well. Even after the war he couldn't write
well. He's a linguist. But language isn't the same as writing.' Strasser was
responsible for the African joke Maxwell was later to adapt. 'You're so
backward,' Freddie would tell Lodvik, 'you must have come from Africa.'

Rosenbluth, a Jew himself, felt obliged to defend young Lodvik from
the other boys when they discovered his father's trade and teased him
about it. 'A lot of bullying went on. They would call him "shochet". He
was just a child. We would protect him. I'd give him a few centimes to
clean my boots. He was glad to have it.'

The older men soon discovered that Lodvik was painfully determined to
improve himself. His respect for anyone educated was profound. An
astonishing proportion of the Czechs were professionals: doctors, lawyers, teachers. In one of the three regiments into which the division was
split up as it expanded into other camps in the nearby towns of Béziers,
Pézenas and La Nouvelle, one man in eight was a lawyer – which may be
how Maxwell acquired his unslakeable thirst for litigation.

An old soldier Margaret Laing found, called Klopstock, had noticed
Lodvik's early ability to charm. 'He always had a smile and he was very
polite to people who had a university education. He had no friends of his
own age – he was far too clever for them – and most of the people he liked
looked down on him.' Insight found a veteran who recalled Lodvik's

persistence in learning by imitation – another Maxwell characteristic in evidence many years later. 'He used to drive everyone wild because he would follow you like a dog – trying to do anything one had just done and do it slightly better. If you jumped over a ditch he would, too.' A penetrating observation, this, particularly followed up by the same man's analysis made nearly thirty years later: 'He has this talent for taking what someone else has conceived and improving it slightly. It's a basic trait.'

Since overrunning Poland the Germans had made no more hostile moves. It was the period Britain knew as the Phoney War. The French, peeping out from the delusory fortifications of the Maginot Line, called it the *drôle de guerre* – the 'joke war'. It was no joke to the Czechs as they marched up and down rocky parade-grounds in baggy French breeches and flanged steel helmets, long old-fashioned Lebel rifles on their shoulders. They had little money and few comforts. The French government was making an emergency payment of 50 centimes a day (on top of rations and the standard litre of rough red wine per man per day) until the National Committee straightened out its finances. But they did not go short of friends. Some of them had wives and girlfriends who had also escaped from Czechoslovakia and who could stay locally if their documents were in order. Some walked out with the local girls. Some availed themselves of the bordellos which, in hallowed French military tradition, soon established themselves nearby. Strange soldiers they might have been, but they were the only soldiers that Agde had, and as the spring gales from the Golfe de Lyon died away and mosquitoes infiltrated the draughty barracks the little town came to take a peculiar pride in its legion.

Young Lodvik had not yet discovered his appeal to women, nor could he afford the whorehouse. And he did not drink wine. He stuck close to his elder brothers-in-arms, listened to their arguments – there were as many political factions in the division as the Czech Republic – and learned. Among other things, they taught him to play cards – poker and a game like gin rummy called *kaluki.* What money he got for selling his wine ration and cleaning boots he usually lost. He also learned to play chess – to win.

In the spring of 1940, Hitler struck again, first at Denmark then at Norway. In May the Panzers rolled into Holland, Belgium and, on the 14th, France. Blithely bypassing the Maginot Line, the Panzers hammered their way right across the top of the country like a knife decapitating an egg, routing a French army twice as big and pushing the British Expeditionary Force into the Channel at Dunkirk. Blitzkrieg.

For a short while it looked as though the Germans might be contained in the north. Where the structure of command and supply stayed intact and officers did not desert their men the French often fought hard before being overwhelmed. But by 6 June, when the impatient Czechs still in Agde finally got marching orders, the main armies were once more falling back. The First and Second Regiments were sent north. The third, still inadequately trained, stayed at Agde. And young Lodvik stayed with it, frustrated and furious. 'He was too young,' said Rosenbluth, who went with the 10th Company of the First Regiment. 'Only the older boys were sent to the front.' Age did not stand in Maxwell's way. His official biographer Joe Haines records:

> He was a private in a motorized brigade dispatched to assist his fellow countrymen in the battle for Orleans. He was slightly wounded in the knee by shrapnel, but not badly enough to keep him out of the line. For a few hours in the thick of the fighting he was captured by the Germans but in the confusion of battle he easily made his escape.

The French Seventh Army had collapsed under the brunt of the initial Panzer onslaught. Now it had been pulled together again under a new commander and deployed to the north-west of Paris. Both Czech regiments were attached to its 239th Division, commanded by General Dunoyer, which had been ordered to make a stand on the River Marne about sixty miles from the capital between Chalons-sur-Marne and La Ferte-sur-Jouarre. 'The rest of the French were coming back,' says Rosenbluth. 'We were going forward.'

It was the most critical moment of the war so far. The world hung on the question of whether the French would risk the destruction of Paris by defending it. On 9 June the French commander-in-chief, General Maxime Weygand, in a famously ominous proclamation, had urged his soldiers to hold on to their ground. 'Nous sommes au dernier quart d'heure.' He did not tell them he was about to declare Paris an open city and that the government was preparing to flee.

Even if they had known that their stand was to be in vain, the Czechs would still have had plenty to give them hope. Chamberlain, the man who sold out their country, had been driven from office and Winston Churchill was now the British Prime Minister. British troops taken off the beach at Dunkirk would soon be back, they believed, to fight alongside the three British divisions which had never left France, and a Canadian division was expected to land at any moment. The First Czech Division might not be the best-trained or most battle-ready unit in the French line but there could be none more highly motivated or more ready to stand its ground.

Two days later the Germans fell upon the Czechs, not in an all-out Blitzkrieg (unknown to the Allied commanders the Panzer columns had overreached themselves and their lines of supply were stretched perilously thin) but in a First World War style infantry offensive, infantry brought up by railways and forced marches, artillery pulled by horses. But the Stuka dive-bombers were there from the first, and the attack was heralded by the harrowing shrieks of their approach.

Through two long hot days of full-scale battle the 239th held the riverbank, dug in against howitzer shells and the screaming 500 lb bombs. They had to fit their fire to the ammunition-supply. No dead or wounded man was let go to the rear with a bullet left in his pouches. But eventually the German *Pioneeren* in their rubber boats got across the Marne and gained a foothold on the French-held side from which they could not be dislodged. These assault engineers, already a legend for their feats earlier in the campaign, were the spearhead of every German advance, blowing up fortifications, wielding flamethrowers, throwing bridges across rivers and fighting to defend them until the Panzers could cross. They were the harbingers of doom.

General Dunoyer was ordered to fall back. The French retreat was gathering momentum. It would have been even more cataclysmic had Weygand let it be known that Churchill (accompanied by his friend and Cabinet minister Lord Beaverbrook) had flown to Tours, where the French government was cowering, to give a reluctant nod to its intention to seek a separate peace.

A fighting withdrawal is the most hazardous of tactics, nerve-racking for a commander, demoralizing for soldiers. But Dunoyer kept his division together as the Germans battering through the refugee-choked roads pressed it south to another of the great rivers that France had always considered impregnable obstacles to an invader. In the rearguard, the Czechs, covered in dust from the torn-up roads, sweating in their heavy serge, scavenged for food and ammunition, turned and skirmished with the advancing *Pioneeren* and cursed their inability to stop them. Then came the final indignity. 'We recognized our own tanks coming at us,' says Rosenbluth. One in three of the tanks the Germans were using had come from Skoda.

Near Gien on the Loire the 239th heard that it was all over. The French had asked for an armistice. On 25 June, the day the armistice became effective, General Dunoyer issued an order of the day praising their valour and discipline. He distributed thirty-two Croix de Guerre. Envoys from the National Committee somehow got through to the Czechs. Churchill, they were told, had insisted that everything be done to allow them to escape.

All around the Czechs the French soldiers of the division, some numbed with relief, some forlorn with shame, were simply throwing down their arms and making for home as best they might get there. The only place in France the Czechs could call home was Agde, 500 kilometres away, and that was where most of them decided to go. 'We wanted to report to our headquarters or we would be deserters,' recalls Rosenbluth. 'We were without food for eight days. Drink we had plenty – champagne. But no food.'

The stragglers walked as far as Toulouse. At the railway station some French soldiers offered Rosenbluth's party a truck and they drove the rest of the way. They got a warm enough welcome in Agde. Under the terms of the armistice the southern third of France was to remain unoccupied. There were still many foreigners on the coast. Only a couple of days earlier the Duke and Duchess of Windsor had motored through the town on their way to safety in Spain.

Awaiting the return of the combat-weary soldiers was Lodvik, spared from battle and unwounded. 'I was so pleased to see him,' Rosenbluth remembers. 'We didn't know what had happened to him.'

Once back in the camp the full misery of their plight descended upon the Czechs. Where could they go? There were rumours that the French might try to continue the war from their North African colonies. Should they go there? How? Surely Britain, too, would soon fall. Once again the Germans had defeated them. The fragile unity that had kept them together in battle began to show signs of strain, the old factionalism breaking out again. Not all the soldiers were satisfied with the performance of their officers, either in battle or out. And vice versa. But once again the tireless National Committee decided their fate. 'They took us straight from Agde to the ship at Sète,' says Rosenbluth. The ship was *Mers El Kebir*, and Lodvik, Rosenbluth and the two Strassers were packed on board, together with most of the division and a few French soldiers who wanted to fight on.

As he became known in academic circles Maxwell began to mention that, rather than deciding to go to Britain at this moment, he could have accepted a scholarship to the University of Southern California offered to him by the American consul in Marseilles. In Marseilles, 120 miles from Agde, every neutral consulate was besieged by refugees desperate for a visa to anywhere.

Many of the Czechs had relatives in America and no doubt some of them found their way into Marseilles and joined the long lines that formed each day at the consulate in the Place Félix Baret. It would be understandable for young Lodvik, now seventeen and with the need to assert himself in the world becoming urgent, but with no papers apart from his First Czech Division identity-card, to indulge in some wishful thinking.

But something else that, Maxwell has since claimed, decided him to choose Britain is a matter of record. Literally. As a guest on the uniquely British radio programme 'Desert Island Discs', he named as one of his favourite recordings to be played Winston Churchill's great speech promising that Britain would fight on alone. Although he had not understood a word of it at the time, it had decided him 'to come to Britain to help Britain fight Germany.'

Lou Rosenbluth and his other friends did not believe that they had a choice. The broadcasts which affected most of the Czechs were one on 29 June by Beneš, who by that time had reached London, and another on 14 July by Anthony Eden, the British Foreign Secretary. Eden, an elegant moustached Conservative, epitomized British decency to many Europeans of that era. 'All this about Maxwell being a Labour man is boloney,' says Lou Rosenbluth. 'He was an Eden man. He tried to model himself on Eden.'

The isolation and strain of the days at sea in the filthy overcrowded *Mers El Kebir*, an old colonial transport, were too much for the fragile unity of the division. There was open confrontation between rightists and leftists, Czech-speakers and others, those who questioned whether it was worth trying to continue the war and those – of whom Lodvik was certainly one – who insisted that it was. Above all, the men had no faith in their officers and there was little hope that any orders given would be obeyed. The polyglot mob that filed down on to the dock looked like a lot of trouble to the local military commander. Soon a few more improbable signposts were added to the exiles' progress: Cholmondeley Park, Lord Cholmondeley's requisitioned estate near Chester, then an internment camp at Sutton Coldfield, near Birmingham. There, on the BBC, they heard Anthony Eden once again. He was welcoming these Free Czech warriors to Britain.

Their new home had a lot in common with Agde. Mosquitoes for one thing. Another – for they were soon allowed into town – was that the natives were friendly, if rather more difficult to understand than the French. The Potteries accent back in those days was as sing-song as Cantonese. Even professors of English among the overeducated Czech contingent had difficulty understanding what was said to them.

However, before they could leave the camp there were tedious days of arguing with Czech diplomats who came up from London and replying to the questions of ponderous English coppers. The Czechs might have been an army to the French but to the British they were, first of all, aliens and therefore a matter not for the military authorities but for the police.

Considering the turmoil that prevailed in Britain, now Germany's only remaining enemy and preparing, stoically, to be invaded in her turn, the Czechs did not have too hard a time. The most vociferous left-wingers were weeded out and shipped to another camp at York. A few rightists were interned on the Isle of Man. The Czech government-in-exile was encouraged, like the Poles, Norwegians, Dutch and French, to set up a 'free' force, the Czech National Army, which many of the First Czech Division internees, particularly the professional soldiers, joined.

Plenty of the men from *Mers El Kebir*, however, were resolved not to serve under Czech officers again. About five hundred of them were told they would be welcome in the British army. In the Pioneer Corps. The *Pioneeren*? Everyone who had been to the front in France had been impressed by the professional derring-do of the élite German units: Lodvik had heard endless stories about them during the voyage. A pioneer would surely get to kill a lot of Germans.

'It was a trick,' Maxwell recalled, still rueful, many years later. And it probably was. The new Pioneer Corps the British army was raising bore no relation whatever to the fearless shocktroops of the Wehrmacht. It was to provide, as it had in the First World War, the Army's navvies, its hewers of wood and carriers of water, pourers of concrete, diggers of ditches. Worst of all so far as the aliens were concerned, who were to form such a large part of it, they were not to be allowed to bear arms at all.

Lodvik was still to discover any of this when, in October 1940, he signed on as 13051410 Private Hoch, L. I. Jan had become Ian. He was still only seventeen, but he certainly looked older, and nobody questioned that or anything else about him. If they had, he would have been able to give a good account of himself – and in English. He had discovered women – or at least one woman – and the English language simultaneously. As soon as he had been allowed into Sutton Coldfield he had made the acquaintance of a girl who worked in a tobacconist's shop in the town. Speedy learner as he had always been, in six weeks of conversation he had a firm grounding in English – even if he spoke it, as she did, with a Welsh accent – with overtones of Birmingham.

Long after Maxwell had become fluent in the plummy tones picked up from Eden and similar models that he thought were suited to his place in British life, Terry Coleman, the brilliant interviewer of the *Guardian*, asked him about the lady who had provided him with the greatest single advantage in his life up until then. Had he learned the language in what was recognized as the best possible way – from a mistress? 'I was too young to have a mistress. I was very innocent in that respect. No: we talked a lot and walked and read.'

Had he ever seen her after that time? Maxwell seemed surprised at the question. 'No.'

Loathe it though Lodvik undoubtedly did, the Pioneer Corps of that time was a remarkable body of men. Many of them were, to be sure, too thick-witted, short-sighted or otherwise inadequate for the infantry. But there were a number of companies whose average IQ was boosted by refugee intellectuals and professionals to even higher than that of the First Czech Division. These 'alien' companies were organized, as far as possible, according to languages, which meant that most of them were German/Austrian. (But there were two Spanish companies.) In the autumn the Czechs were divided, after some preliminary backing and filling, between 226th and 227th Companies. Lodvik, Rosenbluth and the Strassers were assigned to the 227th and sent to Ilfracombe to be fitted out in uniforms even less flattering than their French ones.

The officers and all but one NCO in the company were British, and only the British were permitted, outside training, to handle the few rifles and revolvers the unit was allowed. This may have been a wise precaution with exiles of uncertain future and un-British temperament. When 13803821 Private J. K. Kliske did manage to get his hands on a rifle within days of joining 226th Company he used it to kill himself.

So far as the Czechs were concerned there was not much difference, in terms of humiliation, between the Pioneers and internment. Throughout the winter of 1940 – and for nearly two years after that – they built aircraft runways and tank standings, laid cables, worked on railways and erected barracks huts all over East Anglia. They ate stodgy English rations but managed to get coffee in place of the murky army tea they were first offered. Only the occasional training they received on weapons that they might eventually be entrusted with reminded them that they were soldiers. Sometimes the instructors were preaching to the converted. The two final letters of the name of the British army's most important automatic weapon, the Bren-gun, stood for Enfield, where it was manufactured under licence; the first two came from Brno in Czechoslovakia where it had been invented.

They were also given English lessons and lectures on British wartime life. One of the more interesting of these to men whose horizons were not limited to their meagre army pay was on the subject of National Savings. It was delivered by an elderly First World War lieutenant-colonel named Maxwell. It was being suggested to the aliens that they take *noms de guerre* to protect their families back home from reprisals should they become known to have enlisted in the British cause. Maxwell has told – or allowed to go uncorrected – various fanciful accounts of how he adopted his name (the most romantic being that it was bestowed upon him by a Scottish officer called Maxwell who was briefing him for a perilous secret mission to Berlin). But this would seem to be the first time he could have encountered it.

By that time 227th Company was quartered in Lord Derby's stables at Newmarket. And Lodvik, who by now spoke impressive English and read it so well that he soon exhausted the limited resources of the army's circulating libraries, had formed some conclusions about Britain. It may have been the imagery evoked by Eden and Churchill or it may have been the impression of the huge estates he was seeing in such unusual circumstances. But, not yet twenty, he confided to Lou Rosenbluth: 'One day I will be in the British Parliament.'

First, however, he had to get out of the Pioneers. Lodvik's determination to get into a fighting unit fell only just short of an obsession. For months he had been pestering the Pioneer unit commander, Major A. J. Wilcock, to recommend him for a non-commissioned officer's course as one possible way. Opportunity struck when he was stricken with appendicitis and went to hospital in Bury St Edmunds.

Freddie Strasser, whose brother Arthur regularly lent Lodvik half a crown whenever he lost at poker, was there already, suffering from asthma, and pleased to have his company.

From hospital, Lodvik was sent to a convalescent home in Ely where he met the first of a series of young women who helped him, each a little further, along the pathway on which he had been set by the lady tobacconist of Sutton Coldfield. The last of these ladies, a widow Maxwell will name only as 'Sylvia', introduced him to Brigadier M. A. Carthew-Yourston, commanding officer of 176th Brigade. She took to the tall dark-haired young foreigner, muscular from his months of labouring and with unexpectedly suave ways. 'He was a bit like Gregory Peck then,' Dr Klopstock had told Margaret Laing. 'All the girls were after him.'

The brigadier's daughter took the recuperated Lodvik home. Displaying the talent for persuading people of influence to give him a hand up, which from then on became one of the keynotes of his life, the obscure alien Pioneer made his pitch. 'Gary' Carthew-Yourston was impressed. There would soon be a keen demand for young men who were determined to kill Germans. He sent him to Lieutenant-Colonel Wilkins, commanding one of the brigade's battalions.

Thus, in October 1943 the 6th Battalion of the North Staffordshire Regiment, a unit whose battle honours went back to the Indian Mutiny and which was about to start training for the counter-invasion of the Continent, gained its most improbable recruit. It did not particularly want one with a Germanic name like Hoch, and the War Office stricture meant that Lodvik could call himself whatever hé liked. Perhaps because he liked the French ring of it, perhaps with the lady tobacconist of Sutton Coldfield in mind, he chose the name of a superior brand of cigarette, Du Maurier. If his English had not been so good, it might have been Woodbine.

Most of the men in the battalion were from Derbyshire, the Potteries, Stoke-on-Trent, stocky, beer-drinking and light-hearted. The large and sombre stranger stood out; something of a mystery. But they soon got to like him. 'Very brave, very go-ahead, a very pleasant person,' recalled Major A. W. Mitchell, then a young lieutenant.

Significant developments in Maxwell's life often seemed to occur around his birthday. When his twenty-first arrived in 1944 the invasion had begun four days earlier. He was now a corporal, acting sergeant. Because of his languages, particularly German, he had been kept in the battalion's intelligence section, but he had no intention of staying there. He had also been trained as a sniper; he carried a rifle fitted with a telescopic sight, the better to zero in on the Germans he wanted so badly to kill. He was beside himself with impatience to get about the business for which he had trained for a year and a half.

But the 6th North Staffs were still languishing under canvas at Margate. There is no telling what Corporal Du Maurier might have done if he had known that at the same time as the huge hordes of men and machines of which he was part were being moved towards the British coast the wretched Hungarian and Ruthenian Jews from Zone 1 were being trundled towards the final horror of Auschwitz.

On 7 July, thirty-one days after D-Day, the 176th Brigade, part of the 59th Division, marched ten miles inland from M Beach where they had landed. At 0400 the next morning they were to join in a new offensive against Caen, from which the commander of the British and American ground forces, General Bernard Montgomery, had expected to drive the Germans within a few hours of the Allies first landing in France.

The battle had plainly not gone well. The Allies' lost momentum had given Hitler time to bring battle-hardened units to the front from as far away as Russia. Worst of all, despite murderous Allied air attacks, the Germans had been able to transfer an immense array of Panzer strength to Normandy, especially their dreaded Tiger and Panther tanks. The 6th North Staffs had been left in no doubt that heavy fighting lay ahead of them. But they were far too cocky for their own good. One of them, a Lieutenant Brown, recalled for Normandy historian Alexander McKee some twenty years later: 'We had spent the whole war in the UK. We were pretty fit and hard trained but the majority had no battle experience. It was with, perhaps, a little over-confidence that we approached our task in Normandy.'

On the eve of their baptism the 6th North Staffs watched in awe as a vast air armada plastered Caen with high explosive. Five thousand French civilians were killed, but only a handful of the enemy. The Germans had moved out of the city into a ring of outlying villages which had long been fortified and linked together in an almost impenetrable system of tunnels and trenches backed with dug-in Tigers. On La Bijude, the village which the North Staffs had been given as their objective, not one bomb fell. At 0420 Du Maurier's unit crossed their start-line, a perfectly calibrated artillery barrage marching ahead of them. It was a classical infantry manoeuvre they had exercised time and again in training.

The German resistance was fierce but brief, hand-to-hand fighting, grenades hurled to and fro, a lot of men hit. Both commanders of the leading companies were killed almost immediately, plunging the advance into confusion. The North Staffs had had the misfortune to come up against the 12th SS Panzergrenadier 'Hitlerjugend' Division. The 'Baby' Division, as it was deceptively called, was led by a swaggering thirty-three-year-old fanatic, General Kurt Meyer, nicknamed 'Panzer', whose exploits on the Eastern Front had won him a ferocious reputation. It was made up of volunteers from the Hitler Youth Movement, Aryan archetypes in health and appearance, dedicated unquestioning Nazis. These dreadful 'babies' had never been in action before D-Day, either, and hardly any of them was as old as Du Maurier; most were only fifteen or sixteen. But they were one of the most formidable German elements in Normandy.

As officers fell or became separated Corporal Du Maurier swapped his rifle for a more wieldy Sten-gun and moved about giving orders. The battalion rallied, and by 0730 it thought it had captured La Bijude. But, as they invariably did after giving way, the Germans counter-attacked viciously. Another battalion had to take La Bijude for a second time. The 6th North Staffs fell to clearing another trench system to the west of it, dangerous work, going on the second day to capture a flyspot on the map named Malon. There they had to stop. In the brigade's first forty-eight hours of action 124 men had been killed and 259 wounded. Half these casualties had been suffered by the 6th North Staffs.

Both the Allied commanders and the men they were sending into battle soon had second thoughts. It was sickeningly apparent that despite the huge industrial effort behind the British and American armies many of their weapons were inferior to those of the Germans, especially the ones that mattered most: tanks and anti-tank weapons. The same was true of the soldiery. The British in particular were sluggish in attack. After the first setbacks, veteran units that had excelled in Italy and the North African desert seemed to feel they had done their bit. The greater mass of novices, conditioned by four years of wartime deprivation, were short on aggression and initiative. Since victory, they had been assured, was a foregone conclusion, they were understandably inclined to leave as much as possible to the impregnable air forces and the safely distant artillery. 'Let metal fight metal,' was one of their axioms, 'and keep flesh in one piece.'

The generals soon came to accept that, man for man, the Allied troops were often no match for Germans – and not just the youthful desperadoes of the 12th SS – who believed there was still a chance of bottling up the Allies in Normandy and preventing them from reaching the Fatherland. It was not simply that the Germans were brave. Many of them had been fighting for years and were masters of their craft. The German national reputation for rigid conformity was anything but justified in battle. German soldiers, particularly the totally Nazified SS, rarely hesitated to seize the initiative and carry the fight forward; whereas when British officers were cut down, as at La Bijude, it usually brought chaos. Looking down at a ditchful of corn-haired young corpses, their Nordic jaws set aggressively even in death, one North Staffs officer doubted that his stubby dogged Midlanders would ever defeat such a foe. Du Maurier, whose sniping had accounted for a share of them, would spit and growl, 'Fucking krauts'. There were all too few Du Mauriers in the British ranks.

All through the end of July and into August the battalion pushed patrols into enemy territory, bracing themselves against instant reprisals from huge mortars and field-guns. They captured 160 prisoners at Les Nouillons and 290 more at Haut de Forges but lost thirty-two of their own men. The Germans had learned the value of picking off officers. More and more Du Maurier found himself in command, and able to do what he wanted. On one expedition into a village he came back laden with bottles of calvados, which would have cheered up his comrades. On another occasion, when accepting the surrender of a hundred German prisoners, he relieved them of all their banknotes. Any small change he gave to a companion.

What the 6th North Staffs were being saved for, though, was the crossing of the River Orne, a vital point on the painfully slow Allied advance. It was a slaughter. In the early evening of 7 August the rifle companies crossed the river in rubber dinghies – Pioneeren at last. Lieutenant Brown had to wait for a bridge to be built during the night to get his anti-tank guns over. 'When I reached the far bank I discovered that the two forward companies no longer existed as such. The Germans had brought up Tigers by the dozen, and the British Churchills, an inferior tank, could do little about them.'

But the British planners decided that the advance must not be halted. The order from the brigade commander was 'No pulling out'. Not even the wounded – and there were more by the hour – could be got out under the unrelenting German fire. Huddled in the rubble thrown up by their own artillery barrages, Du Maurier and his company commander, one of the few surviving officers, watched a Tiger grind its way towards them. 'Its gun looked as big as Nelson's Column,' he related years later, laughing as easily at the recollection as when he told the story of the stolen francs.

Maxwell had a PIAT, a kind of bazooka, far inferior to either the American or the German version, but all that was available to the British. 'I was shaking. I just couldn't hold it. I was so afraid I was going to die.' The CO had a bottle of gin. 'I took a swig. It was the first alcohol I'd ever drunk. And I knocked that tank out.'

The North Staffs held out against the powerful German counter-attacks. Ahead of them rocket-firing Typhoon fighters battered at the

Panzers. Behind them artillerymen doused the barrels of the guns with water to stop them melting. 'The British line bent,' said a BBC broadcast, of this heroic effort, 'but never broke.'

The 6th North Staffs were broken, though. By 9 August three of its four companies of a hundred men each had been reduced to six, seven and fifteen men respectively. At least 202 were dead, wounded or missing. There were no replacements. Montgomery's staff decided that the entire badly mauled division ought to be disbanded. Evil luck still dogged the battalion. On 17 August, Lieutenant-Colonel Wilkins and his intelligence officer, Captain Terry, were killed when a truckload of mines beside which they had stopped to confer was hit by a German shell. But the colonel had already put his signature to a recommendation which would provide Du Maurier with another vital rung in his upward climb. It was usual for soldiers to be given a Military Medal for getting a Tiger. Du Maurier was not put up for an award, but for something far better.

Even if the battle for Normandy was not quite over, its outcome was settled. The German army was retreating, although the chance to destroy it had been lost. Slovenly Allied generalship and cautious soldiering were allowing enough of it to escape – including 'Panzer' Meyer and the remnants of his murderous brood – to ensure that there would have to be a winter campaign to take Germany itself. Behind the advancing Allies all the Channel ports except Dieppe would remain in German hands for months. Despite all that, for the moment the main objective of every right-thinking battle-weary soldier was newly liberated Paris. Acting Sergeant Du Maurier, his pockets full of liberated francs, headed that way, knowing he had been recommended for a battlefield commission.

Many young Parisiennes went hungry during the German occupation. But unlike the girls in Britain, who seemed to have become resigned to a dutiful dowdiness, most managed to keep up their legendary chic. In the shoulder-length brunette bob and carefully arched eyebrows of twenty-two-year-old Elisabeth Meynard there was already, in September 1944, much of the elegance she would, in the fullness of time, display as châtelaine of Headington Hill Hall.

Elisabeth had only just arrived in Paris when the Germans first marched in. She had been brought up near Lyons in a family that had made its living from that city's historic trade in silk. They were Protestants – Huguenots. Before the war they had been well-off but, in the way of the provincial bourgeoisie, unassuming. The Elisabeth of Headington could recall having to go to bed by candlelight and solemn gatherings of the local Girl Guides. 'A puritanical Protestant upbringing taught me to be thrifty.' She also had an unusual father. When Elisabeth's older sister wanted to go to Paris to study medicine and she herself had decided to study international law he retired from business and, at the age of sixty-four, enrolled at the Sorbonne with them.

For a long time many of the foundation-stones of French existence remained unmoved by the Occupation. Bureaucrats registered births, deaths and marriages, policeman tracked down stolen bicycles, the dread baccalaureate examination still hung over the weary head of every child who wanted to do well. But after the Normandy landings there was too much disruption to study. The sisters spent most of their time looking for food. When the city suddenly became heady with freedom and the streets filled with light-hearted and open-handed foreign liberators, Elisabeth, like thousands of other young women withered by boredom, went forth to greet them.

Speaking some English, Elisabeth signed on with a group called the Allied Welcoming Committee. Its worthy aim was to place lonely but respectable soldiers with Parisian families willing to offer them hospitality. When she got her first look at Du Maurier, fresh from the battlefield, she was by no means certain he was a suitable case. The word Elisabeth used later about her impression of him was 'raw'.

Du Maurier was not on leave while he was awaiting his promotion, although he was able to get plenty of liberty. While the fate of the North Staffs survivors was being decided he had been posted to Versailles, twenty kilometres outside Paris. SHAEF (Supreme Headquarters Allied Expeditionary Force) had now been established there and it had an urgent need for anyone who spoke German, or even French – to say nothing of the more exotic languages of which he had some mastery.

Paris was awash with stragglers and deserters from both sides. Some of the Germans and their conscript cohorts – Ukrainians, Czechs, Russians – had been hiding out for months. Every day the Free French, who had swiftly taken over the running of the city, made arrests and pinpointed suspects. Du Maurier joined a motley group of Allied soldiers, both male and female, who were sent to interrogate and eavesdrop on these fugitives. Working clandestinely, the investigators would wear civilian clothes or conceal their true background with a strange uniform. Thus, one day he might dress in the blue smock of a Parisian labourer and the next as an American air force officer. It was his first real contact with the world of deception and conspiracy. He also developed, for no good reason, except that the conspiratorial nature of intelligence work seemed to demand it, a couple of new names. One was Jones. The other was – wherever he got it from – Maxwell.

He happened to be Jones at the time the officer in charge of his makeshift outfit gave him the obligatory written recommendation to the Welcoming Committee, so that was how he introduced himself to Elisabeth. 'I never thought of him as anything but English,' she remembers.

The rest of the multilingual investigators seemed to have no difficulty finding congenial company, but Sergeant Du Maurier appeared a little shy. Elisabeth, two years older and far more confident, put that down to English reticence. She sent him to a family she thought would be kind to him. Then he came back again, and she sent him to another. And another.

Soldier visitors were very welcome to these Parisians. They brought food. Paris had been shorter of food than ever since the Normandy breakthrough. Vast amounts of supplies were being brought in from the makeshift invasion-harbours, but civil and military racketeers were diverting much of it to the black market. For the Meynards, life was becoming desperately difficult.

SHAEF, by contrast, was packed to the doorjambs with the best that two powerful nations could offer their fighting men. One day, his interest in Elisabeth still undeclared, her raw admirer noticed she was not at her best. There's nothing wrong with that girl, he remembers thinking. She's hungry. Elisabeth could not resist his invitation to an army hotel. 'It was my first square meal since the Occupation,' she recalls. 'And that is something you don't easily forget.'

By wartime standards it was hardly a whirlwind courtship, although it must sometimes have seemed so to Elisabeth during that Paris autumn as the plane trees shed their leaves, the evenings grew chillier and the battles that would soon part them came nearer. Their frequent visits to Versailles were commemorated on the anniversary menu of forty years later. The more she saw of her unexpected suitor, the more she saw how different he was from any man she had ever known or imagined. He was interested in everything but never for long; far too impatient to learn things that did not come to him easily or immediately. She could see that he really enjoyed being mysterious. She found his generosity, his restlessness and his indefatigable self-assertion irresistible. 'You only meet a man like Bob once in your life,' she said many years afterwards – a view that not many people would argue with.

As it became evident that Maxwell's intentions were not only honourable but, like everything else to which he addressed himself in life, pressing, there was Meynard *père* to be consulted. 'It was not the way we did things in our family,' says Elisabeth. 'Usually one family would know the other one.' The French, particularly French like the Meynards, did not take alliances lightly; and this was not, on the face of it, a promising one: the object of the cherished daughter's affections was not only a rootless soldier and a foreigner but also a Jew. That seemed to matter less to the Meynards than it might have to French Catholics. On more than one occasion the monolithic Catholic French had driven earlier Meynards from the country, and the present generation had sometimes wondered whether the anti-Semitism of the Vichy regime might not easily spread into wider intolerance. Many Protestants, particularly around Lyons, had been helpful in smuggling French Jews out to Switzerland.

At least her fiancé was not entirely penniless. Quite early in his army service an officer had helped him open an account at Grindlay's Bank in London. Even before he had discovered how to 'liberate' money, he had found some way to make it. The letter to the bank, which Betty preserved in the first volume of her archives, is a splendid example of the mixture of bafflement and concern the young soldier was capable of evoking. 'I am unable to give you a forecast of subsequent credits,' his kindly patron had written for enclosure with the first deposit. 'His regular source of income is of course his army pay, which is negligible and does not warrant a banking account. His other sources of income seem to be incidental to war and of a non-predictable nature.' Feeling some further explanation was required, he added: 'I discovered that he was carrying some £30 about with him and considered that at his age, and with his possible future, it was high time he opened a banking account.'

By now, though, all the Meynards had good reason to be grateful to Du Maurier – and to SHAEF. If the old man had doubts, his prospective son-in-law managed, as he had before and would do countless times again, to siphon up a sufficient volume of charm and conviction to float him over them. Elisabeth's family became an important support in future Maxwell enterprises.

The War Office had been nonplussed by the recommendation that Du Maurier be given a commission. Particularly since he now seemed to have settled on Maxwell for a name. The provisional Czech government in London was asked what it knew about this outlandish candidate for the King's Commission. The Czechs, just as baffled, could only reply that it seemed unlikely that he had been convicted of any offence by a Czech court. But, pondered the War Office, was this fellow actually a Czech? The Hungarian takeover of Ruthenia might well have been legally sound. Was he, therefore, a Hungarian? In that case he would be not only an alien but also an enemy alien. Making an officer and a gentleman out of the former Jan Lodvik Hoch of Slatina-Selo was only slightly less complicated than getting together the voluminous documentation required for a French marriage. He did not even have a birth certificate – which, given the variety of names, was probably just as well.

To the chagrin of the newly affianced couple it was the Army that got its dossier together first. Before the Normandy campaign it would have been a rare event for a soldier to be commissioned in the field; by the end of 1944 it had become a necessity. Infantry subalterns were by far the highest category of casualty. If the British armies were to regain their aggression, then suitable gun-fodder had to be found to lead them into battle.

Montgomery, newly promoted to field-marshal, was under intense pressure. Allied strategy now called for the defeat of the German army before it could retreat across the Rhine and organize a final vast battle to defend the Fatherland. But a good deal more immediate was the need to capture the German missile-launching sites in Northern Europe. Even before D-Day the first-generation V1 'buzz-bomb' had destroyed or damaged nearly three-quarters of a million houses in London alone. Now the V2 – forerunner of the intercontinental ballistic missiles of today – was being launched in ever-increasing numbers. Great areas of Britain could be laid waste by this monstrous weapon.

Montgomery complained to the Secretary of State for War, Sir James Grigg, that he was short of nearly two thousand subalterns and demanded such 'ruthless methods' to replace them as combing the Royal Air Force for non-flying officers. The prospect of gaining a genuinely battle-hungry young leader of men – as Maxwell had been portrayed in his recommenda- tion – far outweighed any legal niceties. Monty was delighted to endorse the recommendation. On 7 January 1945 the *London Gazette* duly recorded the promotion of Corporal Ian Robert Maxwell to second lieu- tenant. The War Office was still not ready to assign him a new number so that he could be paid, but that did not stop Monty's headquarters from giving him his marching orders.

As she said *au revoir* to her new young officer, Elisabeth was filled with foreboding. A pall had been cast over Christmas 1944 by a shattering and unexpected German counter-offensive in the Ardennes forest of Belgium which drove a deep bulge in the Allied line. Only a spirited stand in bitter winter weather by the American 101st Airborne at Bastogne prevented two huge Panzer armies from driving through to Antwerp on the coast, shutting off the Allied supply-line. Versailles had been gripped by panic when it was reported that an SS suicide force dressed as American paratroopers was in the area bent on assassinating the commander-in-chief, General Dwight D. Eisenhower.

Then on New Year's Day the Luftwaffe launched a raid of which it had not been thought capable. Nearly 200 Allied aircraft were destroyed on the ground. The war which had come to seem far away from Paris was, it suddenly became plain, far from over. The Battle of the Bulge cost the Americans 70,000 casualties and set the Allied war effort back so much that in London and Washington it was seriously being questioned that a drive across the Rhine could be mounted. It was an immense relief at SHAEF when, in mid-January, the Russians at last began to advance and occupied Warsaw.

When the British army does commission a man in the field it is customary to ease the process by transferring him to a new unit. In any case Maxwell's old one was no more. He was posted to the Queen's Royal Regiment, a rather smarter outfit than the North Staffs, although hugely expanded by the war, and told to report to the 5th Battalion. It was up on the Dutch–Belgian border. Maxwell made the journey by himself, driving the last part in a jeep through a snowstorm, the sky overhead regularly raked by roaring buzz-bombs, and caught up with them on 28 January.

The 5th Queen's belonged to the 131st Brigade of Lorried Infantry – the best the British could come up with to match the Panzergrenadiers – part of the Seventh Armoured Division, the celebrated 'Desert Rats'. For some days past they had seen all too little of their lorries. Or, indeed, the tanks alongside which they were supposed to operate. The division was in the middle of Operation Blackcock, a gruelling push to clear a German-held pocket between the River Roer and the River Meuse or, as it is known to the Flemish-speaking Belgians, the Maas. Although it was still miserably cold, the great frost had broken and the thaw had begun. The Meuse rose six feet in a night.

Maxwell was welcomed by the battalion's commanding officer, Major Hubert Nangle, and sent to A Company under Major D. J. Watson. Watson put him in command of 7 Platoon and briefed him on the attack they were to make the next day. Supported by tanks, including flame-throwing versions of the Churchill called Crocodiles, they were to advance to the bank of the swollen Roer and take the village also immortalized on the fortieth-anniversary menu: Paarlo.

Even with its many replacements 5th Queen's was a battle-wise and tight-knit unit. 'Jock' Nangle, a regular Gurkha officer, had won a Distinguished Service Order in Normandy (and was about to win another). Since the start of Blackcock the battalion had paid dearly for every foot of canal bank and village street they gained. The brigade had lost 101 killed and 650 wounded since the beginning of the operation, and the Queen's had taken more than their share. Casualties would have been worse still except that it was so cold that blood froze on wounds, sealing them.

Many of the enemy units they faced were hardened veterans of the Russian campaign, ghostly in white winter camouflage-suits. The Germans had thought up a nasty trick of bricking Tiger tanks into cottages out of which they would burst at an unexpected moment, spraying machine-gun fire and grenades. But Maxwell was warmed by the business-like preparations he noted going on around him. He had missed killing Germans, and this was the kind of outfit in which a man might get to slaughter as many as Hitler could send. On 29 January when 5th Queen's started to advance the Germans nearly got Maxwell first.

Winning the Military Cross is probably the most significant event in Maxwell's life, certainly the achievement of which he is most proud – and deservedly. Only officers are decorated with 'crosses'. With the exception of the Victoria Cross, other ranks get medals. The Military Cross and its ranker equivalent the Military Medal are the Army's 'basic' grade of award for bravery in the face of an enemy. But that is not to say that they are handed out lightly. Why Maxwell prefers to circulate a version of how he won it which to most people seems far less favourable than the facts available can only be put down to the vagaries of his ego. His own biographical notes say:

> 'Ignoring an order to retreat and under heavy enemy fire at a battle on the Dutch–German border, for heroism in the face of enemy action', he is decorated with the immediate award of the Military Cross by Field Marshal Montgomery.

The quotation is unattributed. Perhaps it was the bit about disobeying an order that appealed to him. The citation that accompanied the Military Cross begins:

> Lt. Maxwell was leading his platoon when a heavy artillery barrage fell on and near the platoon killing and wounding several men. The attack was in danger of losing momentum but this officer showing powers of leadership of the highest order controlled his men with great skill and kept up the advance.

Eventually the Germans withdrew across the river and, having satisfied themselves the banks were clear, the battalion fell back a little to shelter for the night, leaving A Company and a troop of tanks in possession of Paarlo. Maxwell and the men of 7 Platoon established themselves in the fortified tenement buildings the Germans had only just abandoned. It was completely dark, and for a long time the only sound on the freezing night was the distant throb of Churchill engines as supporting tanks found their way forward across the pontoons that had replaced the bridges blown up by the Germans. But, as the tense British soldiers feared it would, the reprisal came without warning:

> *During the night another platoon of this company was counter attacked and partially overrun.*

Pioneeren-style the Germans came back across the river in rubber boats and hurled themselves into the Paarlo tenements, fighting fiercely from room to room, rolling grenades along corridors, Schmeissers blazing in the blackness. Number 8 Platoon bore the brunt of the onslaught. Its men, scattered through several houses, found themselves in danger of being cut off from their commander, Lieutenant M. L. Baker. The sole defender of one building was Lance-Corporal R. Dennis armed only with a Sten. A German machine-gunner had the approach to the house covered, and the rest of the platoon could not reach their comrade. Firing short bursts to spin out his ammunition, Dennis boldly held off the attackers and prayed that the tanks would get there soon. This was the moment the man who had been with the regiment only for a matter of hours chose to emblazon his name on its roll of honour.

> *An attempt to restore the position with another platoon failed but Lt. Maxwell repeatedly asked to be allowed to lead another attempt which request was eventually granted. This officer then led two of his sections across bullet swept ground with great dash and determination and succeeded in contacting the platoon who had been holding out in some buildings.*

The Queen's official history also records the relief of Lieutenant Baker's hard-pressed soldiers by 7 Platoon 'splendidly led' by Second-Lieutenant R. Maxwell. Sten-gun in hand, Maxwell himself headed the charge on the German machine-gunner. The citation goes into more detail.

> *Showing no regard for his own safety he led his sections in the difficult job of clearing the enemy out of the buildings, inflicting many casualties on them and causing the remainder to withdraw. By his magnificent example and offensive spirit this officer was responsible for the relief of the platoon and the restoration of the situation.*

The Crocodiles arrived breathing fire, and it was all over. The Germans had lost their company commander, but only ten of them surrendered. The cost to the British was seven killed and wounded. The 5th Queen's got the largest share of decorations earned in Blackcock, but it was not a lengthy list. A Corporal Dolly who destroyed a Tiger with a PIAT did get a Military Medal. For holding out singlehanded Corporal Dennis was awarded a Distinguished Conduct Medal. Lieutenant Baker and Major C. V. Lilley also got the Military Cross, and Jock Nangle got a bar to his Distinguished Service Order.

On 21 February the division was pulled out of the line to prepare for the final offensive against Germany, and in March Montgomery himself

visited it to make the awards in person. The 5th Queen's had the privilege
of providing the guard of honour. Their band, brought out from England
for the occasion, played the regimental march, 'Braganza', and in a
requisitioned schoolhouse the victor of Alamein – and shortly of the Rhine
– stretched up to pin the white-blue-white scrap of ribbon on Maxwell's
battledress blouse.

For a long time after he left the Army it seemed that Maxwell regarded
his decoration as the key that would admit him to the kind of life he was
just beginning to see might be possible. When the might of the commercial Establishment descended upon him a few years later, in the shape of
the Department of Trade inspectors, he refused at first to answer their
questions. As though he had been taken prisoner on the battlefield he
would tell them only his name and that he held the Military Cross.
Unfortunately for him, it was not enough.

But it was enough for the battalion. That night in the makeshift though
comfortable mess the table glittered with ceremonial silver, the port went
round rather more than a couple of times, and Maxwell was formally
'dined in' to the Queen's Royal Regiment. He could have drunk a toast to
the important lesson he had learned at Paarlo had he known how well it
was to serve him in later life: the value of surprise; the power of the frontal
attack.

Back in Paris the other *rite de pas-
sage* in the making of Robert Maxwell was proceeding apace. The wedding was arranged for 15 March, and Bob got a week's leave. Having a
bridal gown made and assembling a trousseau were no easier for the
daughter of a silk merchant than for anyone else at a time when every
scrap of decent fabric seemed to have been plundered by one or other
belligerent. But once more the resources of SHAEF came to the rescue.
Betty's 'something borrowed' was the sheet of parachute silk that Bob
liberated for her bridal gown.

The photograph on the fortieth-anniversary menu froze the moment:
the bride in the simple white dress trimmed with lace and a veil of finest
chiffon, white sandals, a huge bouquet of lilies in one hand. Beside and a
little behind her the groom smiles, proudly but a little uncertainly. Either
his new brother officers or his old accomplices at Versailles had come
through with enough bits and pieces to turn him out respectably; he is the
very model of a gallant subaltern, single pips on the shoulders of a tunic
that he could not possibly have had time to get made for himself, MC
ribbon on his left breast, and a gleaming Sam Browne belt. Somehow the
lack of a birth certificate had been overcome, but to avoid complications
nobody mentioned to the *mairie* that the groom was no longer known by
the name in which the licence had been applied for. Among the guests
was Maxwell's patron, Brigadier Carthew-Yourston.

There was no time for a honeymoon.
There were still Germans to be killed. Much of the German army had by

now been forced back into home territory where it was preparing its last stand. Given a second chance to end the war the Allied generals were again divided over strategy. The Americans argued for a vigorous dash across the Rhine. Montgomery insisted on steady progress along a wide front to buy time for an enormous build-up. Operation Plunder, the vast crossing he launched on 22 March, was eventually to involve a million men.

Before their second parting the newlyweds decided that the course of the war was still so uncertain that Elisabeth would be better off in Britain. Despite the difficulties of civilian travel, arrangements were somehow made for her to be sent there where some friends that Maxwell had made would look after her. He went back to his battalion, which had been training hard for the final push. The officers who were to make the Rhine crossing had their photograph taken together. Maxwell stands in the rearmost of three ranks, his smile distinctly more confident than in the wedding picture.

By April the Allied advance was unstoppable. Ahead of the armies huge air armadas drenched German cities with high explosives and phosphorus. German soldiers were surrendering more readily, often hailing the British and Americans as deliverers from the Russians. Maxwell for one did not quite feel that way. And nor did all the Germans. They brought an entire new parachute army into action, and strafing attacks were being made by an unexpected new weapon: the jet aircraft.

As ever, the most intransigent were the SS units. They had been given the toughest rearguard actions to fight. It was the turn of the Germans to talk of carrying on the war from a final redoubt, as the French had considered, perhaps in Austria or Bavaria. In the town of Sudweyne, five miles outside Bremen, on 8 April there was a last battle which, in the later telling, added something to Maxwell's reputation for bloodthirsty and aggressive leadership. The battalion found itself opposed by boy soldiers of the 20th SS Training Division. Maxwell, by now promoted to lieutenant, led 7 Platoon in a brisk attack. He yelled to the young Germans to surrender. They answered with rifle fire. It was less than a year since he had been confronted with the deadly SS Babies in Normandy. He ordered up machine-guns.

Years later, in 1969, a *Sunday Telegraph* reporter asked Maxwell if it was true that his fellow-officers had regarded this episode as unsporting and even un-English. Maxwell's reply was unequivocal. 'One or two people may have said: "It's near the end, why be so keen on killing Germans?" I was just against the Germans. They'd killed my people and they threatened this country. I was good at it . . . killing Germans. Fascism? I was too young to know what it meant.'

On another occasion Maxwell explained that the SS men had fired after showing a white flag. The regimental history records that incident as happening to another company. The history is straight-faced about the slaughter at Sudweyne: '7 Platoon (Lieutenant R. Maxwell) alone killed 15 SS and took 14 prisoners.' And it concludes: 'It had been a very good day for 5th Queen's . . . twenty seven prisoners taken at a cost of five men killed and eight wounded.' Fucking krauts.

Maxwell could hardly have been certain at that time that the Germans had killed his family – although it must have seemed highly probable. But nor does it seem likely from subsequent operations that his fellow-soldiers would have been in the least worried about a last-minute reduction in the SS population. (They were anything but squeamish. A couple of weeks further on, in Buchholz, only 37 kilometres from Hamburg, the battalion came upon a Nazi civic shrine. The Queen's brought up the Crocodiles and torched it.)

On the last day of April 1945, Hitler shot himself. It was to be years before the Allies were satisfied that this was true, but within a week the war was over. On 3 May the 5th Queen's rolled in to Hamburg and installed their brigade headquarters in the still sumptuous Vier Jahreszeiten Hotel. The adjutant, Captain R. G. Newell, ran up the regimental flag on the town hall.

The 5th Queen's were given the task of rounding up stray German soldiers and herding them into vast prison compounds near Kiel. Once again Maxwell's languages were in demand to try to comb out SS officers and others who might be charged with war crimes. He also began trying, via the Red Cross, to discover what had happened to the rest of his family. It was to prove a lengthy task. No one could have told him then that Mechel Hoch had been taken from a prison camp which lay in the path of the Russian advance and, with thousands of fellow-sufferers, jammed aboard one of several ships which took them westwards down the Baltic. Only a couple of days before the end of the war, quite near Kiel, some of the ships had been set on fire and many of the wretched prisoners machine-gunned. It seems likely that Mechel died then.

Whether the stoicism in which Maxwell encases himself and the total absorption he was soon to display in pursuing his objectives might be compensations of some kind for having escaped the sickening fate of his parents is a clinical question. But where young Hoch and Du Maurier had been genial personalities the most noticeable impression Captain Maxwell – as he was soon to become – made on people who met him in Germany was of an implacable brooding determination.

As so often in Maxwell's life, the closing of one door coincided with the opening of another. Once again his birthday was near. Leave arrangements were generous, and he flew to London for a reunion with his bride. When he returned to the battalion, now quartered in comfortable houses at Bad Segeberg, near Lübeck, Elisabeth – although she was yet to make the discovery – had conceived. A new generation was on the way to replace the lost.

If the crossing of the Rhine was the great symbolic feat of the Allied armies, there was still another achievement for which the British, especially, longed. Berlin had been taken by the Russians on 2 May. It now lay deep within the Soviet-occupied zone of Germany (soon to become the German Democratic Republic). But it had been agreed that the city would be jointly governed by the victorious powers, and it was time for the Western Allies to show their flags there. On 4 July the advance party of the 5th Queen's, including the newly promoted Captain Maxwell, drew five days' rations and set out along the autobahn in their lorries. It was not a particularly triumphant entry; at the city limits a stern Russian military policewoman held the convoy up while she telephoned ahead for approval.

Two days later, though, Maxwell had an unforgettable taste of triumph. Indifferent to cold rain and the glum ragged watchers, the 5th Queen's, bayonets fixed and colours flying, paraded along the Charlottenburger Chausee, the broad avenue down which newsreel watchers the world over had so recently seen Hitler's legions pound their vainglorious stiff-legged way. Now – apart from the Russian sector – Berlin belonged to them. It was a new world, if a slightly bewildering one. Only twenty-four hours earlier the architect of Britain's victory, Winston Churchill, had been voted out of office. Anthony Eden, too. Lajbi's heroes had been over-thrown by the Labour Party.

THREE

I do not hate as I did during the war; but I cannot forget and forgive.

ROBERT MAXWELL

THERE HAS NEVER BEEN A PLACE to compare with Berlin in the immediate aftermath of the war; it is unlikely there ever will be. The devastation of the huge imperial metropolis awed even those who had inflicted it. Visitors who had known the city well when it was a showcase of German fashion and prosperity could not even find the streets in which they had stayed or shopped or disported, although William Shirer, the American newsman author of a famous account of the war's beginnings, *Berlin Diary*, noted that the only building left habitable on the Budapestrasse was a famous bordello.

By the time the Queens got there bulldozers had cleared the main thoroughfares of the debris from the endless air raids and the final, devasting Russian artillery onslaught. The rubble, stacked two metres high on every side by gangs of women, would eventually become great grassy hills where none had stood before. But on the Wilhelmstrasse, where Goebbels's Propaganda Ministry, Ribbentrop's Foreign Office and Hitler's Chancellery had stood, it was to be six months before two cars could pass abreast.

The city had been divided into four sectors, reflecting the zones of occupation into which the entire country had been split. A *Kommandatura* on which Britain, the United States of America, France and Russia were represented governed through the remnants of the city council. The Russian commandant was, appropriately enough, Marshal Georg Konstantinov Zhukov, who had planned the final offensive.

In all four sectors the more fortunate survivors lived in the cellars or in blasted and burned-out apartment-buildings. The less fortunate, including hordes of refugees from territories under Russian control (most of the Sudeten Germans among them), slept where they could amid the rubble and by day roamed the wreckage of the Tiergarten and the Unter den Linden looking for food. 'Between these embankments where the proud Wehrmacht had marched', wrote Lieutenant-Colonel W. Byford-Jones, one of Montgomery's staff, 'were hundreds of ex-Wehrmacht prisoners, unshaven, unshod, filthy, tattered, empty food tins tied to string that girt their waists, their eyes empty. Like an army of Zombies they moved silently, their feet bound with sacking, as if propelled by some external power.'

The splintered trunks of trees were covered with scraps of paper, impromptu notice-boards on which people appealed for news of their lost.

And from beneath the devastation the hundreds of thousands of dead continued to make their presence felt. The stench of decomposition hung over the city like fog.

Many more Berliners were doomed. Ravaged Europe would not produce enough food and fuel to get them through the next winter, and the conquerors had little left over from their own needs. With the water-supply and sewage services destroyed typhoid, typhus and other epidemic diseases were spreading fast. The British ordered vaccine, quicklime by the ton and coffins by the thousand. Curfew came early at first, and across the vast silent city came the plaintive roars of the starving animals abandoned in the zoo.

But there was life amid the ruins. Even as early as that June the Fräulein Question had begun to disturb the folks back home in Britain, America and France. So many young German men had been killed or captured that nubile women outnumbered their equivalents many times over. It was a warm summer, and in her skimpy dress and wedge-heeled shoes the long-legged German *Mädchen* discovered by the New York and London tabloids looked anything but war-weary. Montgomery had issued a non-fraternization decree intended to drive home to German civilians the detestation in which the world held them for supporting the Nazis. The term 'frat' was soon a euphemism for the most commonly used obscenity in the Anglo-American forces.

There were riches, too – based, for want of anything more stable, on the currency of the cigarette. The price of the average German legal food ration, plus rent, amounted to about 100 Deutschmarks a month. An ordinary British soldier was issued with 120 free cigarettes a week. The black-market rate for these fluctuated between DM7 and DM10 each. A flourishing industry grew up in recycling butts, and the privilege of emptying ashtrays in Occupation messes was something a German would fight for.

For a hungry homeless *Fräulein* the equation was simple. One frat = one packet of twenty cigarettes = one week of necessities, even – when winter came – of life. The venereal disease rate soared, and a German police official consulted by Byford-Jones lamented: 'Even nice girls of good families, good education and fine background, have discovered their bodies afford the only real living. . . . I find myself wondering about my two daughters.'

The purchasing power the occupiers could wield was overwhelming. Even the Russian soldiers, many of them raw peasants from parts nearly as remote as Ruthenia, had money to burn. Some of them had collected two or three years' back pay in currency that they would not be allowed to take home. The Russians bought clothes and trinkets galore from the British and Americans, but from the Germans they simply took whatever they fancied, including the *Fräuleins*.

At first the British and Americans, too, 'liberated' plenty of German possessions. Few of them could see why they should not since their governments were engaged in the wholsesale dismantling of German industries in the name of reparations. But as things became more orderly it was less effort to trade or sell their plentiful Chesterfields and Players. The British could convert at DM40 to £1, the Americans at DM10 to $1. In the first four months of the occupation American military personnel in Berlin sent home $11 million more than they drew in pay.

The Occupation forces sold a lot more than cigarettes. Some of them even turned to cattle-rustling – shooting cows in the countryside and selling the carcasses to black-market restaurants. Berliners were in the market for food of all kinds, for fuel, clothing, vehicles, soap, documents, medicine. In addition to *Fräuleins*, the invaders lusted after gold, jewellery, paintings, silver, furs, furniture, cameras – Operation Plunder had been well named. The feverish underworld economy soon supported the largest community of rogues, desperadoes and opportunists ever assembled. Plenty of them wore Allied uniform.

Many of Maxwell's fellow-officers were ready to get out of the city, if not yet out of the Army. The oppressive effect of the devastation and the corruption of those who stayed for any length of time was hauntingly described by a member of the American war reparations team.

> *The whole situation was such that it gnawed at all men's character like maggots. On first arrival one would refuse to believe what he heard. Then, as he began to see for himself, it was necessary to struggle with his own conscience, his own integrity, to determine to what extent he would permit himself to be dragged into the cauldron. No one could escape the completely disillusioning conditions. Morale was low at all times among Military Government personnel in Berlin.*

That did not quite apply to Maxwell. For all its surreal squalor Berlin was his kind of town. His time in Berlin, he was to tell many people years later, was a far more profound emotional experience than the war itself and one that changed him for life. There is no denying that Berlin gave him an entirely new view of himself. How others saw him at this time is evident from a 1946 photograph. The young captain has grown a moustache that was plainly modelled on the one sported by his hero, Anthony Eden. The stained battledress of the winter campaign has been replaced by a beautifully tailored tunic with a row of campaign ribbons, the tin hat by a peaked cap bearing the Lamb and Flag badge of the Queen's. He stands in the back of a 'liberated' Mercedes tourer, holding an Alsatian puppy up to the camera while his companion, a major, grins admiringly. It is the very image of a virile conqueror.

It was about this time that his old Czech comrade-in-arms and protector, Lou Rosenbluth, got his last glimpse of Lodvik Hoch.

'In 1945 I went to a tea dance in the Regent Palace Hotel in Piccadilly. I was sitting there with a young lady and suddenly I felt a tap on the shoulder. I looked around and there was this captain with a swagger stick in his hand. Lodvik!

'I jumped up. I was so pleased to see him, just like I had been when I saw he was going to get on the ship at Sète.

'In a posh accent he says to me: "Don't I know you from somewhere?"

'I got so annoyed. I was so pleased to see him and he says that to me. I said to him, "If you don't remember – don't bother," and I sat down.

'I often think about it. Maybe I was sensitive because of the young lady I was with. But he must have known who I was.'

Maxwell's languages were soon in demand. Spared from regimental duties, he became an intelligence officer. For a while he was posted to an interrogation centre at Iserlohn in the Rhineland. If he could not kill Germans any more, he would grill them. The hard-core Nazis he questioned there and at similar centres gave him a lot to think about. 'No matter how hard you pressed them they would never crack,' he remembers.

In fact he did not do much of the hard pressing. The Army's interrogation technique was the standard two-man Mr-Nice-alternating-with-Mr-Nasty method. 'I was always Mr Nice,' says Maxwell.

There was general agreement among the occupiers that the Germans might be sorry they had lost the war but not at all sorry that they had started it. Beginning with those he interrogated, Maxwell began to form a less simple-minded view of his hated enemies. Fucking krauts, he might still consider them, but he was deeply impressed by the toughness of the Germans and their unswerving pursuit of an idea.

By the time he was transferred back to Berlin, Maxwell was beginning to be preoccupied by the problem of making a living in a world of which he knew no more than he had been able to glean during his few years of army training in Britain and which, he could see, would be completely changed by peace. He had a feeling that he might find the answer in Berlin, and by the time the fearsome winter was in sight and the Queens were due to be taken back to guard factories in the Ruhr he had got his eye on something guaranteed to keep him there.

There was a desperate hunger for reading material among the Germans; world affairs – of which the Germany of that time was the centre – obsessed them, and there was no other source of entertainment. Despite a worldwide shortage of newsprint all the powers had started up newspapers as soon as they had taken over. Although many German journalists had worked on them (Shirer found a former assistant to Goebbels as managing editor of one), they had been firmly directed by Occupation personnel. Now, with the first postwar election planned for 1946, it was proposed to license new German-owned newspapers and radio stations and to make paper available for magazines and books. The first licence to publish books was issued on 1 January 1946 to the firm of Springer Verlag.

To keep the hearts and minds of German readers – and journalists – on the right democratic track the Allied Control Commission set up an outfit known as the Public Relations and Information Services Control and cast around for German-speakers. At the upper end of the scale Colonel Sefton Delmer, the witness to the invasion of Ruthenia, was given charge of Deutsche Press Dienst, the wire service set up in Hamburg to provide the papers with news. Well down at the other, Captain I. R. Maxwell, MC, won an appointment, at the beginning of 1946, as head of the press section of the relatively small PRISC office in Berlin.

Maxwell's proclivity for reconstructing the past seems to have convinced him that this was the moment at which he became a newspaperman. In 1985 he recalled for Tim Brooks of *Media Week* that at the age of twenty-one he was 'editing an official British newspaper with a circulation of 750,000'. In 1987, making a farewell presentation to a *Mirror* executive, Mike Taylor, who had been, among his other distinctions, the youngest night editor in Fleet Street, Maxwell could not allow the challenge to pass; the limelight to rest on another. 'I was the youngest editor,' he insisted boastfully. 'At twenty-one I was editor of *Der Telegraaf* in Berlin.'

Der Telegraaf was the first licensed paper in the British sector of Berlin and the most successful. It soon achieved a circulation of nearly half a million and gave vigorous support to the Social Democrat Party. Its editor was Arno Scholtz, who had been the chief journalist on its predecessor, *Der Berliner*, which had been directly run by the Military Government. Maxwell had readily recognized the influence that could be exerted. The news the paper printed – the opinions it expressed – was soon a hot topic in every sector. This was something to which he instinctively responded. But his own association with it was the very antithesis of Scholtz's. He was its censor.

'Licensees were required to print nothing which might bring the Allies into contempt or interfere with the execution of Allied policies,' wrote M. Balfour and O. J. Mair, the principal British historians of this fascinating experiment.

> In practice, however, close control proved quite impossible to exercise. Although German speaking officers were as far as possible used for press duties, there were too few of them and they had too many other duties to allow of their reading every issue of each paper immediately after publication. Even if they did see something which they thought questionable, they could not apply sanctions without consulting the head of their unit, and perhaps even headquarters. Consequently offending articles were seldom brought to judgement until they had been published for several days and in such circumstances the decision was nearly always to let the culprit off with an admonition.

Proclaim first, explain later and you would very likely get away with it. But if reading German newspaper stories that he could do little to influence was Maxwell's overt function in PRISC there were also others at which he was far more effective. 'Bob was a censor,' recalls Colonel I. C. 'Ted' Edwards, who was second-in-command of PRISC. 'But he was also an intelligence officer. He used to make his reports to me.'

The Iron Curtain had not yet been rung down, but the first chill of the Cold War was wafting through Berlin. Civilians and military alike could move freely between the different sectors, but the powers had agreed among themselves that their intelligence agents would go about only in uniform. Says Edwards: 'Bob would go down to the Russian sector and come back with anything he found interesting. They were beginning to hold trade fairs and so on.'

It was not, however, Maxwell's command of German and Russian, or his proficiency in English, that launched him in the industry that was eventually to be the making of him. It was the wholly unofficial role he played in juggling newsprint and other paper supplies – the surest form of control over the German publishers who came grovelling to him. In doing it he brought to bear all the arts of bargaining, compromise and barter that had been instilled in him beside the River Tisa. And more.

A PRISC colleague recalled the dawning of Maxwell's business acumen for Insight.

'Almost nothing was available on the open market. So to keep the officially sanctioned newspapers going (by mid-1946 there were thirty-five in the British Zone) the various branch offices of PRISC had quotas of everything supplied by the Control Commission. Inevitably one branch office would turn out to need something it couldn't get on quota, while it had a surplus of something else. The problem was matching up all these needs and surpluses. Maxwell was marvellous at it.'

When Insight first established how crucial Maxwell's part had been in keeping the Berlin presses rolling he was anxious that it should not be overstated. 'If a publisher came along and said he was short of paper, say for an election campaign, I would make a few telephone calls.' Having spoken to people who had watched him at work, the *Sunday Times* reporters were not going to let him get away with such uncharacteristic modesty. Maxwell, they concluded, was 'a natural virtuoso of barter trading'.

As for the book publishers, none was more grateful for the help Maxwell was able to give than Springer Verlag, licensee number one. Insight got hold of a 1959 memo in which one of the firm's executives reviewed the part he played, as a member of PRISC, in getting them back on their feet: 'It was a time when there was no telephone and no petrol and no spare parts for printing machinery or other vital things that were necessary. Captain Maxwell always knew the answer, solved the hardest problems. . . . It was largely attributable to him that the road to the reconstruction of the business was cleared.'

This appreciative German had touched upon one of the critical factors in Maxwell's adaptation of infantry tactics to commerce. If he was a virtuoso of barter, he was soon to become a maestro of the telephone. The only working system in Berlin belonged to the Control Commission, and the practice Maxwell put in on it, hour upon hour, as he pulled off his many-sided deals, made him the master of the instrument he is today. Maxwell is rarely without a telephone in his hand for more than a few minutes during his waking hours, bellowing demands, well-aimed bonhomie or insults to and from the ends of the earth at any hour out of the twenty-four, inducing high blood-pressure in executives spending Sunday morning at home, summoning editors to his private apartments so that his dinner guests can watch the great publisher scan the proofs of his newspapers. 'Maxwell', says Joe Haines, 'is a telephone terrorist.' There was another discovery, too, of far-reaching significance. Books were not simply the implements of information and self-education that Maxwell had used them as until then. They were valuable commodities.

There has, obviously, never been a time when Maxwell was indifferent to money, however little he might want it for himself. Nevertheless, he insists that he was never tempted by the Berlin black market or by bribes. 'Everything was in short supply,' he said long after he had become rich as a civilian. 'I could have made a fortune but I was too honest. I'd been brought up that way. I never took a penny. One businessman did try to bribe me but when he came back for another meeting I said, "Come this way", and handed him over to the Military Police.'

Even though they were an essential part of Maxwell's duties, his visits to the Russian sector and his distinctly un-English knowledge of the language deepened the aura of mystery which had always surrounded him in the Army. None of his fellow-soldiers was to know that the contacts he made in Berlin were to be the eventual making of him or, rather, of Pergamon. A shattered landmark for the rendezvous he kept was even to provide him with a name to give to his first great success: the ruins of the Pergamon Museum. Pergamon is a variation of Pergamum, the ancient city thirty-five miles from Izmir, in Turkey, founded by the Greeks in 283 BC and handed over to the Romans 150 years later. It had one of the most splendid libraries of antiquity until Mark Antony liberated all 400,000 volumes and gave them to Cleopatra.

What his familiarity with the Russian sector and its denizens did do was make him the acquaintance of fellow-practitioners in the intelligence community which he was to put to use when they, like him, were back in civilian life and on the make.

In 1968, before Maxwell was forced to abandon an attempt to take over the *Sun*, he made an extraordinary boast to another old Berlin hand, Geoffrey Goodman, whom he was interviewing for the job of deputy editor. 'One of my secret jobs was to find out what the Russians were up to in stripping East German industries. We knew there were plans in Zhukov's office. My job was to get hold of them. I had a close friendship with a Red Army colonel who knew the set-up and the combination of the safe. Between us we managed to get the plans, photograph them and return them.'

Goodman was flabbergasted. 'I can't believe that, Bob,' he said. But Maxwell insisted it was true.

In time Goodman came to accept the veracity of Maxwell's story.

Another of Maxwell's favourite tales from this period is of how he was thwarted in a great reparations coup on behalf of his foster-country. 'I nearly got Volkswagen for Britain,' he has told many listeners. 'All the dies and casts from the Volkswagen plant were crated and ready to ship. But the authorities vetoed the shipment. Can you imagine it? If they'd given me the go-ahead, Britain would have had the VW.'

The story of this missed opportunity is well known, for the British government did indeed decide that it did not want Volkswagen; but, if the Government did not listen to the experts it had sent to Germany to advise it, it is difficult to see why it should have paid any attention to a young intelligence captain, assuming he might be in a position to offer a view.

By the time he knew he could expect demobilization in mid-1946 Maxwell was beginning to divine how he might put the experiences of the last two triumphant years to good purpose. Even before the Queen's got as far as Berlin he had seen brother officers go back to stand (or fall) in the British election, usually for the Conservative Party. The idea that such a possibility could be open to men whose equal and more he had certainly proved himself made a deep impression. He had paid close attention to the stream of VIP visitors from London which passed through the PRISC office, and it was clear, as he liked to put it, that 'They used toilet paper, just like me'.

Maxwell had, in short, got a glimpse of the possibilities open to a young man with an acceptable accent – with which he was fast replacing the echoes of Birmingham – and what the British of that time liked to call a Good War behind him. He had also found, or sensed, somewhere in the dark corners of the ravaged city, the seeds of his fortune. When in the mess one day talk turned to the future, Maxwell made a declaration of intent that was a good deal broader than the boyish one he had made before his fellow-Czechs. 'I am going to be', he told a fascinated audience, 'two things. A Member of Parliament and a millionaire.'

Recalls Colonel Edwards: 'Here he was, a fledgling captain without a penny to his name – so far as anyone knew. You can imagine the response he got.'

                                   One of the possibilities Maxwell entertained of earning a living in a world of peace was to become a regular soldier. In London to discuss the possibility at the War Office it was discovered that he was still not a British citizen. Speedy naturalization was arranged – Maxwell says 'nationalization', one of the slips that show he has not yet forced an unconditional surrender from the

English language – with the approval of a patrician namesake, Sir Alexander Maxwell, Permanent Under-Secretary at the Home Office. (It would have meant nothing to Maxwell then had he known that in 1942 Sir Alexander had supported Home Secretary Herbert Morrison in a warning to the *Daily Mirror* that if it continued to criticize the war effort it would be banned.)

Flattered though he was at being wooed by the Army, Maxwell was already responding to the scent of the market-place. As a soldier he was still poor. He had installed Betty in a cramped freezing little flat rented for 12s 6d (63p) a week in Little Brick Hill, near Bletchley, North Buckinghamshire, and it was there he visited her when he came on leave. Their few miserable cement-floored rooms were in the corner of a building called the Clock House, originally the stables and servants' quarters of the local manor house which had been turned into a prison for German officers.

Maxwell was deeply interested in German prisoners, of whom there were many thousands still in Britain. He saw them less as former enemies than as future readers of the German newspapers in whose production he was now deeply involved. Soon he was to set up his first commercial operation: to supply them with papers for which the British government paid and which the German publishers supplied free.

It was from the squalid lodgings near Bletchley that Betty went to Queen Charlotte's Hospital in Hammersmith, London, to give birth, on 11 March 1946, to the poor doomed first of their children, Michael Paul André. For every subsequent birth she went home to France. Whether because she found her first British hospital unsympathetic, or because of some lingering exile caution, or simply, as she has sometimes explained, because her sister, by then an obstetrician, had come to own a clinic at Maison-Lafitte in the Paris suburbs, every living child of the man who was to make a public career out of his adopted Britishness was born to a French passport.

On Michael's birth certificate there was no mention of Du Maurier, the name in which his parents had married. The father was given as R. Maxwell. However, uncertainty lingered on about what to call himself. Maxwell still ran across people who remembered him as Lodvik Hoch. Everyone in the Army had called him Bob. But in the early 1950s, when he first began to attract attention in London, he displayed the flexibility towards names, either for himself or for his companies, that has always been a notable feature of his methods by reverting to Ian.

Nor, when he was demobbed three months after becoming a father, did Maxwell seem to know what to do with the rank of which he was so proud. There has always been a type of Englishman, usually a regular army or navy officer, who long after becoming a civilian insists on being addressed in the style to which he had previously been accustomed. But after 1945 most junior officers, at least, were happy to forget their military labels. Not Maxwell. His captain's three 'pips' and the MC were a far more precious token of acceptance than his naturalization certificate. And of power. Springer Verlag were happy to acknowlege that what he was able to do for them was entirely due to 'his drastic and exceedingly successful methods as a captain of the English Army (with an MC)'.

Whatever he ought to have been called in the spring of 1946, when he came to the Clock House on leave to inspect his firstborn, he told Betty that he would not be home for good just yet. He showed her what he had brought with him. Not the usual frivolous stuff from Berlin of cameras or Russian furs but densely printed journals and typescripts in German over which he worked late into the night, translating.

As usual, Maxwell had his priorities right. He was far more likely to become an MP as the result of becoming a millionaire than the other way around. And with gratifying, almost celestial justice he seemed to have stumbled on a way that the same Germans who had slaughtered his family and driven him from his homeland were going to make him into one.

His first priority after being demobilized was to get back to Berlin for long enough to bring off his next move. The Control Commission was operated by the Foreign Office; servicemen like Maxwell had been seconded to it. Now, as demobilization thinned the service ranks, civilians had to be found to take over the jobs they had done. But at least half the replacements were newly discharged military personnel, many of whom simply took the badges off their uniforms (but kept their medal ribbons) and went on with the same job.

This was what Maxwell decided to do. He was gratified to find how easy it was to talk the panel that interviewed him into paying him the top rate of £1,150 a year rather than the £750 they had wanted to. Waiting around London for his appointment to be confirmed, he haunted the Austrian Club in Bryanston Square. The Strassers, his old Czech comrades-in-arms, played poker with him there. 'He was a snobbish fellow by then, a captain,' Freddie Strasser remembers. 'He used to stay in a small room on Little Venice. He was still only halfway to being a big shot. But you know what? When he came back from Berlin he drove a Cadillac.'

Maxwell had already discovered that if he was going to do business on his own behalf he needed a company to protect him from any mistakes he might make. As indeed companies he has owned have, many times over. The principle of limited liability – that, in most circumstances, an individual shareholder is only liable for a company's debts to the extent of his investment but is entitled to its profits in proportion to his shareholders – may have been the most important revelation of Maxwell's existence. How to lose money but stay rich.

It was the beginning of a lifelong love-affair with a vast world of companies, his own and others, yet unborn. In no time at all he would have learned to juggle share issues and balance-sheets as expertly as any auditor and know his way around the Companies Act as surely as he had led his platoon through its battles. Making their first report in 1971 the Department of Trade inspectors, on whom Maxwell disdainfully walked out after contriving to prolong their investigations for three years, paid him an unintentional compliment. 'He has an unusually acute appreciation of financial and accounting matters and is not afraid to enter into agreements of far reaching effect without legal advice.'

On 12 September 1946, Maxwell took up ninety shares in a small trading company called Low-Bell which had been set up in London in December 1945 by a Czech acquaintance, Arnos Lobel, as manufacturer, wholesaler and retailer of fancy goods and kitchen utensils. A month later he took up three hundred more shares and became a director. The company documents described Maxwell as a merchant – which remains the best description of him to this day. He gave his address as 11 Stanley Gardens, London W11, the corner house of a Victorian terrace near the Portobello Road. Gentrified in recent years, the area at that time was a dingy peeling slum, barely an improvement on the better-off parts of Berlin. But it was the first of a string of addresses around which Maxwell was soon to weave a wondrously complex array of activities. The number of companies around the globe which Maxwell now controls is incalculable. There are hundreds. But Low-Bell still exists as Maxwell Scientific International (Distribution Services) Ltd, the foundation-stone of something that was eventually to become known as the Maxwell Family Interests.

The name to which Maxwell changed Low-Bell (beginning as he was to go on, it had been changed once already) reflected the hopes he was placing in the suitcase-load he had brought from Berlin. Others may have dredged the ruins of the Third Reich for Russian sables, grand pianos or Volkswagens. His association with Springer Verlag, who had been Germany's largest scientific publisher, had led Maxwell to a cache of loot that, handled skilfully, would be even more precious, value for weight, than the caviare for which keeping company with the Russians had already given him a lifelong taste.

Before the Nazis took power German science and scientific industries were the most advanced in Europe. German was the second language of scientists everywhere, and the stream of textbooks, learned journals and papers that flowed from the presses of firms like Springer Verlag – now so dependent on the wiles of 'a captain in the English Army (with an MC)' – nourished scientific communities all over the world. Nazi corruption of many scientists – weapons like the giant rockets and the jet fighters had been unwelcome demonstrations of the ability of some of them – put an end to the flourishing export trade of Germany's scientific publishers, and their output was sorely missed.

At the war's end there was immense curiosity among academics and research scientists everywhere about what had been going on in Germany in the years she had been cut off from civilization. Their counterparts elsewhere knew that, as well as doing whatever they had for the war, German researchers would have continued to plod methodically after the secrets of blood chemistry or the pulmonary system of the flea. Where were their findings? Scattered all over Germany, as it happened, many of the documents squirrelled away by Ferdinand Springer, the firm's head, to avoid confiscation by the reparations-seekers.

As Maxwell came to grasp what Springer Verlag had been, he recognized – or someone had pointed out to him – that they were in a situation of which any merchant worthy of the name must dream. Out there in the world were a host of greedy consumers in pursuit of a cornered market. Information, it seemed, was just as much of a commodity as newsprint or penicillin. All that needed to be done was to match the supply to the demand. And set the price.

On 15 March 1947, Maxwell resigned from PRISC. He told Insight – and he has reported since – that he resigned because he objected to the extent the Russians were carting off German industry (he did not mention Britain and Volkswagen) and that his superiors 'did not care' for the anti-Soviet line that emerged from the papers he was censoring. The superior with whom Insight checked offered a different version. Maxwell, he said, had been 'encouraged' to go because not enough of his energy was being spent on PRISC business. In December, having set up an office in London, Maxwell signed a contract with Springer Verlag and became their agent.

The founding firm had now become, for the moment, Low-Bell & Maxwell Ltd, the first appearance the name of Maxwell made in British commerce, lettered upon the door of a poky office overlooking Trafalgar Square. At least it would have overlooked it had the only window not been entirely blocked by a huge hoarding for Ivor Novello's musical *Perchance to Dream*.

London in the late 1940s and early 1950s was almost as full of intrigue and opportunism as Berlin, crowded with men who had discovered that the years they had spent at war were no preparation for peace, clutching at any connection they could find to catch up with real life. For those who had been officers most of the jobs on offer seemed menial. There were plenty of bright ideas around, but very little money to finance them.

Maxwell at least had scraped together a small start-up fund. He had collected an army gratuity of £300, some of which went on a good blue suit. Betty had weighed in with a modest dowry, and some relatives in America, who had been told about the Springer prospects, had loaned them something. The rent was £2 a week. There were two desks, at one of which Betty, not yet pregnant with her second child, Anne, sat at the only typewriter. At the other sat Maxwell the merchant beneath a huge picture of Montgomery the field marshal pinning the MC on Maxwell the captain.

Springer Verlag's agent was, to be exact, the resoundingly named European Periodicals Publicity and Advertising Corporation whose plate was also on the door. Maxwell had registered this company in Berlin a week after leaving PRISC. It was EPPAC, he told people in London, including the Registrar of Companies, that was to supply newspapers to the German prisoners, of whom by then there were hardly any left. But in Berlin one of the purposes of EPPAC had been described as selling scientific literature in Britain and the United States.

EPPAC did import German newspapers, although most of them seemed to get no further than the office. It was usually jammed with bundles of them. To help distribute them Maxwell enlisted Victor Sassi, who was to become owner of the Gay Hussar, the Soho restaurant that is still a favourite haunt of well-fed left-wingers. Sassi had just emerged from an internment-camp himself. 'I took the stuff and sold it for waste paper,' says Sassi. Years later Sassi was standing at the door of the Gay Hussar when Maxwell got out of a cab to go into the Warner Brothers building opposite. 'I'm in the movie business now,' he said to Sassi. 'Can you lend me ten shillings to pay for the taxi?'

Each of the two companies represented a distinct side of Maxwell's operation, but both relied heavily on contacts he had made in Berlin. While EPPAC concentrated on Springer, Low-Bell & Maxwell Ltd wheeled and dealed in anything and everything those days of shortage and – because of currency restrictions and exchange controls – barter brought to Bob and Betty's humble but promising door.

In 1948 the Control Commission put an end to the confiscation of German commercial property, which until then had been official policy for the Allied governments. Whatever was wanted from Germany had to be paid for at rates of exchange negotiated with a Joint Export Import Agency. Through EPPAC, Maxwell negotiated a deal for some Springer documents on behalf of His Majesty's Stationery Office (making, incidentally, his first contact with Oxford through the Bodleian Library, which participated).

Respectable as the transaction was, it was also extremely profitable – for Maxwell. He was somehow able to persuade the JEIA to allow Springer material to be exported at twenty-four Deutschmarks to the pound rather than the thirteen set for other publications. He got the Stationery Office to advance £7,000. He borrowed £5,000 from the Westminster Bank. Springer was paid £12,000 for the documents. Maxwell charged HMSO £20,000. 'Without me,' Maxwell boasted to Margaret Laing, 'they would have had to pay £10,000 more.'

The hugely favourable Deutschmark rate that Maxwell had negotiated was applied to all his future scientific literature transactions. Springer's export trade in their extensive backlist of books flourished at the expense of their rivals who had barely got started up again. The commission Maxwell earned from the exclusive right to handle them was welcome, but he had already come to look on it as small change. By 1949 he had got his hands on rather more than a suitcaseful of promise: a huge cache of wartime and prewar Springer scientific journals that had been hidden away in Austria – seven railway wagons full of them, which he parked beside an old pickle factory in Newington Butts. As Maxwell was to tell the men from the Department of Trade: 'These back numbers are like wine. Their value increases with age.' He was about to sell off the cellar.

Maxwell saw that in order to exploit the lip-smacking exchange rate he had wrung from JEIA for the Springer books as well as journals he was going to need an established sales set-up. He looked around and decided that Butterworth & Co., a publisher of medical and legal textbooks with a worldwide sales network, might be open to a proposal. Its managing director, Major J. W. Whitlock, another former intelligence officer as it happened, referred him to their financial advisers, Hambros Bank.

Then, as now, Hambros was one of the most prestigious establishments in the City. But then it was smaller, and it was not too difficult for Maxwell to get a hearing – Captain Ian Maxwell, MC, not yet thirty, with his military moustache still in place, his regimental tie and crisp white shirt ironed by Betty in the kitchen.

In Sir Charles Hambro, a veteran of the wartime Special Operations Executive, Maxwell found a man whose vision matched his own. The encounter became a City legend. Sir Charles listened to him for no more than twenty minutes before ringing for a retainer to whom he introduced Maxwell and said: 'He is to have a cheque-book. He can draw up to twenty-five thousand pounds.' A year would pass before the arrangement was committed to paper.

In fact, in the year after Sir Charles had shown him how easily it could be done, Maxwell borrowed more than a million pounds from various sources – a far more daunting sum then than it is today. Hambro believed he knew a winner when he saw one. And not just at making money. He was a stalwart of the Conservative Party, which was on the lookout for likely prospects to range against Labour at the next election (and likely contributors to Tory funds).

Hambro telephoned Butterworth and told Whitlock to expect a visit from his new protégé. Subtle as a Tiger tank, Maxwell bowled into the Butterworth boardroom a few feet behind the messenger who was taking in his card. The proposal he delivered to the bemused directors was to lead, in April 1949, to the formation of a subsidiary company, Butterworth-Springer Ltd.

'None of us knew anything about him,' Whitlock recalled, describing the event a few years later. 'But within fifteen minutes we knew we were dealing with an important personality. The next day we lent him a great deal. He paid back every penny.' It is therefore to Hambro and Butterworth that Maxwell, in effect, owes everything. For it was Butterworth-Springer that in 1951 he was to take over and rename Pergamon.

But in 1949 Maxwell was already acting on one of the principles that was to guide his commercial life – the more companies you have, the more they can do business with each other. In September 1949 another brick in the growing structure of the Family Interests was set up to trade as stationers, office equipment suppliers and booksellers: Lange, Maxwell & Springer. Maxwell put £13,000 of the Hambros stake into it. But the new company, which was, in effect, Maxwell's own, was also appointed sole distributor in the United Kingdom for Butterworth-Springer/Pergamon.

In fact it was soon doing much better business than Butterworth-Springer, in which Maxwell merely had an interest. Advance payments for the Springer journals it was selling – payment in advance was another firm principle of Maxwell business practice – poured in, £50,000 in the first few months. In 1950 LM & S had a turnover of £250,000; in 1951 it was £600,000. In 1955 the company name became I. R. Maxwell & Co., and in 1963 Robert Maxwell & Co. Ltd.

Not everything Hambros did for Maxwell had such a happy outcome. The first LM & S figures were yet to be declared when a figure appeared from the shadows of the wartime espionage fraternity to steer Maxwell from the fringe of the publishing industry to its centre – and to his first catastrophe. An elegant old spy of Belgian descent, Count Vanden Heuvel, who had ostensibly been a British diplomat in Switzerland during the war, was now working in a capacity almost as mysterious for the bank. In the American Bar of the Savoy Hotel one evening at the beginning of 1952, Vanden Heuvel introduced Maxwell to Arthur Coleridge, chairman of Simpkin Marshall Ltd, the venerable book wholesalers who were a pillar of the British publishing establishment.

No mention of Simpkin Marshall now appears in any of the versions of Maxwell's life that he has authorized. The names (Messrs Simpkin and Marshall were the successors of the 1779 founder, Benjamin Crosby, a Yorkshire bookseller) mean nothing to the present generation of British publishers. But the firm had provided an indispensable service to the book trade for 150 years. A retail bookseller might occasionally order a large batch of the one title direct from its publisher; but for the most part bookshops depended, for speedy delivery, on the huge wholesale resources of the Simpkin Marshall warehouse. 'If it's in print it's in stock,' was the firm's confident slogan. Their only competitor was W. H. Smith, which flourishes to this day – and which Maxwell would dearly love to own.

But, like much else in Britain at that time, Simpkin Marshall was not what it had been. The German bombs of 1940 destroyed 4 million books in its stacks. After the war a consortium of publishers headed by Sir Isaac Pitman & Sons Ltd had put the pieces together again, not from any altruistic motive but because such a clearing-house seemed essential to efficient distribution.

When Maxwell first heard of it Simpkin Marshall still kept some 125,000 titles in stock and turned over at least £1 million a year. But it was an onerous and unprofitable business. For all that they needed it and wished it well, the majority of publishers refused to increase the traditionally slender wholesale margin on the price of their books. The company owed Pitman alone £268,000 and they were desperate for someone to take the burden off their hands. How, with Hambros help, Maxwell did so, charging into the dusty old firm as though it were full of kraut machine-gunners, could be seen as a blueprint for much of his future business strategy.

The transaction depended less on what Maxwell could pay than on how much Simpkin Marshall owed its backers. It was agreed that Maxwell would take over £160,000 of the debt to Pitman. The remaining £108,000 would be discounted to £79,000, payable in instalments. Maxwell paid Pitman £50,000 cash – all he ever did pay, directly, to control Simpkin Marshall – and undertook to come up with the remaining £110,000 over nine years. In the Simpkin Marshall company accounts Maxwell was put down for a £160,000 credit, even though he owed that £110,000 to Pitman.

Thus, in October 1951, Maxwell became managing director of Simpkin Marshall and overnight a central figure in British publishing. The new blood was warmly welcomed; everyone wanted to see the old firm prosper so long as it was not at their own expense, and Maxwell looked interesting even if, as Betty had first seen him, a little raw. But times were changing, and Maxwell set out to make them change faster still. His seizure of Simpkin Marshall displayed all the characteristics that were to become typical of later Maxwell operations. First the avowal that there would be no untoward changes in the business. 'Mr Arthur Coleridge will remain as chairman,' the press was told. Eighteen months later Coleridge was gone into the Outer Darkness.

'There will be no change of policy,' the press release added. There immediately followed a blizzard of book-keeping, board meetings and dealings with other Maxwell-owned or -dominated companies and large-scale shifting around of premises. Maxwell was everywhere, cajoling, persuading, travelling in spectacular style, tossing off grandiose pronouncements, not all of them to be fulfilled.

Simpkin Marshall's stock was moved to 242–4 Marylebone Rd, NW1, which became the first Maxwell House. I. R. Maxwell & Co. and the other Family Interests stayed at 4–5 Fitzroy Square, W1. Another important Maxwell business principle was established at Fitzroy Square: where Maxwell worked, Maxwell ate and Maxwell slept. A small apartment was set up on the top floor. Butterworth-Springer was no more by this time. Butterworth had seen no future in keeping up a company that was, in effect, competing with another wholly owned by one of its own directors. They handed the company over to Maxwell on condition that he call it something else.

Pergamon Press Ltd as Maxwell – and of course Betty – chose to name the company of their dreams was to be the vehicle of an even greater disaster than Simpkin, but also of a truly astonishing revival.

Although he was so visibly active on behalf of Simpkin Marshall, it was the future of Pergamon, pearl among the Family Interests, that was now closest to Maxwell's heart. It was evident to him that if it was to fulfil the hopes he was beginning to have it would need a base of operations in the United States. But it was a period of galling government restrictions and currency controls in Britain. If capital was hard to find, it was even harder to export. It was about this time that another discovery emerged to match the possibilities offered by limited companies – and which, in the end, was to prove as great a stumbling-block.

•

The second Hoch sister to have survived the war now lived in the United States; her married name was Natkin. 'We wanted to set up the trusts in America,' Maxwell has explained. 'But the paperwork would have taken too long.'

In the early 1950s Liechtenstein had not begun to take full advantage of its potential as a tax haven. But Switzerland had. Two trusts were set up there, the beneficiaries of which were to be Mrs Natkin's children or, should they unfortunately die without heirs, the Maxwell children. To ensure that there would actually be something to inherit, the trusts became the owners of two companies in New York State which mirrored the most important Family Interests established in Britain but were distinguishable by the American suffix 'Inc.' instead of 'Ltd': Pergamon Press Inc. and Maxwell Scientific International Inc. The change of name without which no Maxwell transaction is complete was not left out. MSI Inc. had originally been registered as Pergamon International Inc.

In 1964, when Pergamon was preparing to go public in Britain, Maxwell's infatuation with complexity had become evident in its ownership. Ninety per cent of the company's shares were owned by the Swiss trusts, although they were actually held on their behalf by three Maxwell companies: MSI Inc., Robert Maxwell & Co. Ltd (as I. R. Maxwell had then become) and the Maxson Investment Co. Ltd, a minor Interest. Maxwell himself owned all but three of the remaining Pergamon shares, and those were held by one of his principal associates of the period, Cecil Clark, the deputy chairman of Pergamon, as his nominee. In the United States the trusts owned Pergamon Press Inc. completely.

On the day the public share offer was made in London, however, these old Pergamon shares were redistributed in a way that gave Maxwell himself and RM & Co. 55 per cent of the equity and MSI Inc., on behalf of the trusts, 44 per cent. When the Department of Trade inspectors asked Maxwell about this generous concession on the part of trustees who were supposed to be acting in the best interests of Mrs Natkin and her children Maxwell told them that 40,000 £1 shares had been held by Maxson, rather than registered as belonging to MSI Inc., because he did not wish to advertise the fact in Britain that Pergamon was effectively an American-owned company. Subsequently, he said that the Maxson shares were really intended for a trust for his own children in Britain.

His questioners found both explanations 'surprising'. MSI Inc., together with other foreign companies over which, on paper, Maxwell himself had no control, was largely out of reach of the Department of Trade inspectors. They could not question their officers directly or inspect their books. But whether the foreign companies were subject to Maxwell's legal control or not, the inspectors' report concluded, Maxwell always exercised 'considerable influence' over their affairs.

Maxwell zeroed in on the British Book Center in New York, another venture undertaken by British publishers to market their products that had been well meant rather than well planned. The Center was the sole distributor in America for books from about fifty British firms. The largest investor, B. T. Batsford Ltd, had recently sold its controlling interest to another adventuring British hero – and another decorated Member of Parliament – Captain Peter Baker, MC, whose acquaintance Maxwell had already made. At the beginning of 1952, finding himself short of cash, Baker had borrowed £13,000 from Maxwell against a personal IOU. Lucky number thirteen for Maxwell, if not for Baker.

When, soon after this, Maxwell told Pitman that he wanted Simpkin Marshall to buy the Book Center they refused – as was their right while Maxwell still owed them money. Maxwell then set out to renegotiate his equity in the company. As an infantryman develops an eye for protective terrain, so Maxwell had come to recognize the value of a short burst of cash in the right place, the need for plenty of shares as ammunition and the good cover to be afforded by a nice big book debt. Instead of the £110,000 over nine years that Pitman had originally agreed to accept he persuaded them to take £98,000 – £90,000 immediately and £8,000 a year later. These sums were both duly paid – not by Maxwell, however, but by Simpkin Marshall itself, helped by a £40,000 overdraft which Maxwell arranged. Simpkin Marshall's debt to Maxwell was reduced to £62,000. He had still put up no more than his original £50,000. But now he controlled the company.

In May 1952, Maxwell returned the IOU to the sorry Captain Baker – who in 1954 went to prison for financial offences – in exchange for Baker's 1,215 shares in the Book Center. Maxwell then controlled the Center, too. For good measure he gave Batsfords £7,000 for the £28,000 the Center still owed them and another £3,000 for their remaining shares.

Largely supported in one way or another by Simpkin Marshall, 122 East 55th Street became Maxwell's New York headquarters. To safeguard his operation there Maxwell installed a Hungarian named Ladislaus Majthenyi, known to all as Mr Martini, who also took over the administration of the trusts. The building was modest by Manhattan standards, a five-storey converted brownstone with external fire-escapes, described by a later visitor as looking like a Tennessee Williams film set. Just the same, it took a lot of persuasion to convince its proud new owner that in a land of coffee-drinkers renaming it Maxwell House as well would only get him in hot water. He could not resist for long, however. Pergamon Inc. expanded to warehouses in dingy Long Island City, then to Elmsford, just beyond Manhattan in New York State. In that suburban location a Maxwell House now stands.

British publishers were mightily impressed by the tornado of activity Maxwell was creating on their behalf. They were delighted to hear from him in Rio de Janeiro that he had persuaded the Bank of Brazil to release a frozen £73,000 to pay for book imports. They were mildly bemused to be told that at the same time Maxwell was negotiating with the Brazilians for 7,000 tons of cotton goods worth £250,000. If they had known what other activities Maxwell the merchant managed to fit in while carrying off his gentlemanly Simpkin Marshall tasks, they would have been awestruck. There was more to Maxwell's hyperactive life than books, but until Insight published the results of their researches more than a decade later most of it went unsuspected.

Lunching with his old harness-mate in Butterworth-Springer, Major Whitlock, at the stately Athenaeum Club, Maxwell had been introduced to a successful German refugee chemist, Dr Kurt Wallersteiner. It was said of Wallersteiner, who owned a string of chemical companies in various countries, that to get around currency shortages and other restrictions he had developed international barter into a sporting skill.

Wallersteiner was clearly a man after Maxwell's own heart. They kept in touch. Wallersteiner had good reason – or thought he had – to be interested in Whitlock and Maxwell, or anyone like them who seemed to have contacts with the security services. He had begun to trade in chemicals with East Germany and Communist China – which, while not illegal in Britain, was frowned upon in the United States in the 1950s. Wallersteiner thought that at some point he might need the help of people who knew their way around intelligence circles.

A year later in the boardroom at Hambros – where Wallersteiner, too, was a client – it was agreed that Maxwell would become managing director of Wallersteiner's British operation, the Watford Chemical Company – the first time Watford came to mean anything to Maxwell – in exchange for 20 per cent of any future profits. Maxwell said later that it was not the thought of profit alone that motivated him. 'I would be able to control him and prevent him from doing any unsavoury business in Iron Curtain countries.' But that noble sentiment was expressed in a letter written long after Wallersteiner, like Maxwell, had lost a vast amount of money as a result of the joint venture.

It had also been agreed that Wallersteiner would lend Simpkin Marshall £50,000. One of the first things Maxwell had done, with the assistance of Hambros, was to issue 100,000 new £1 ordinary shares in the company. He took up 54,891 of these himself. And the company paid him back £54,891 of the £62,000 still owing to him on the books. But Wallersteiner did not take any shares at this time. His £50,000 was an unsecured loan. Hambros were not quite so trusting. They got a charge on the company's assets against whatever Simpkin Marshall owed them, which on 1 October 1952 was £74,000.

Wallersteiner and Maxwell soon spread the fame of Watford Chemical far beyond the East End where its modest premises were located. The wondrously convoluted transactions the pair of them brought off read like the script of one of the Ealing comedies that were the regular cinema entertainment of the era, the import–export equivalent of a bedroom farce. As well as sending a vast shipment of indigo dye from East Germany (which the Soviet zone had by then become) to China they shipped anything they got to hear about – babies' bottles to Argentina against frozen pork bellies to Holland swapped for prefabricated wooden houses to Canada. At one point Wallersteiner invented a country – Oceania – with which Austria was induced to sign a solemn trade agreement. The crowning deal was a shipload of East German cement which, for some reason, was refused admission to Britain. The barter boys decided to send it to Canada as foundations for the wooden houses. But the old freighter in which it was being carried took in too much water and the cargo set rock hard in its hold.

So well did the brilliant pair of merchants get on that when Maxwell wanted more capital for Simpkin Marshall it was only natural that he should once more turn to Wallersteiner. By July 1953, Simpkin Marshall owed Hambros £320,000, and Maxwell hated to pay the charges that were ticking up. He proposed that Wallersteiner accept a debenture for the sum. It was, Maxwell assured him, amply covered. When, years later, Insight found Wallersteiner living in Paris he told reporter David Leitch that he had only agreed because Maxwell had assured him it 'would help him keep out of trouble'.

But at the time the two men were clearly on the best of terms. They had a Bastille Day celebration dinner at Les Ambassadeurs. At the end of that month, Arthur Coleridge, whom the shareholders had been assured would remain as chairman, resigned. Maxwell became chairman as well as managing director. His most active co-director was Cecil Clark, who, like Maxwell himself, floated free of the foundering Simpkin Marshall to be rescued, at least for the moment, by Pergamon.

On 28 September 1953, Maxwell asked Wallersteiner to cough up another £100,000 as a second unsecured loan. He assured Wallersteiner, as he had on the occasion of the debenture, that Simpkin Marshall was a thriving concern and that his money was safe. When the balloon went up nine months later not even Maxwell's own accountants could agree with such a rosy view. 'The comparative results of the two years ended 31 March 1953', the firm of Chalmers Wade reported, 'is seriously affected by the treatment of sales . . . of books to the value of £105,000 which were sold to an associated company who retained the right of return.'

And return the books of course the company did, once the Simpkin Marshall accounts had included the purported sale. This was the rather clumsy practice that was at the root of eventual Pergamon catastrophe. Doing business with associated companies – or simply switching assets and debts around between them – was to become an established pattern in Maxwell's life. But it was not until the accountants called in on behalf of Wallersteiner – Peat, Marwick, Mitchell & Co. – made their report that it was seen that of £300,000 Maxwell had borrowed, ostensibly on behalf of Simpkin Marshall, up to April 1954 at an average interest of 5¾ per cent £211,599 had been lent to other Maxwell companies at no interest at all. 'The sums involved', said the Peat Marwick report, 'constitute financial assistance as distinct from a normal trading account.'

The meticulous Insight analysis of the last days of Simpkin Marshall suggests that Maxwell felt the need to reassure Wallersteiner. When

Maxwell asked for the £100,000 he offered Wallersteiner a block of preference shares which, up until then, had been held by Hambros in settlement of the original £50,000 loan. Wallersteiner was assured that these carried voting rights. But first, on 27 October 1953, the shares were transferred to Maxwell. During the brief time they were his, on 30 October, Maxwell and Clark held what Insight called 'a truly extraordinary general meeting'. They resolved to increase the voting rights of Maxwell's ordinary shares in Simpkin Marshall. By the time Wallersteiner actually got his hands on the preference shares Maxwell, using his upgraded assets, was able to outvote him four to one.

Still Maxwell had not finished collecting from his partner what he regarded as his entitlement. After a long talk at Maxwell House on 3 May 1954, Wallersteiner, convinced – as Insight put it – 'rightly or wrongly' that it was the only way to avoid some official action that would ruin his businesses, signed an agreement backdated to 15 January that year which gave Maxwell control of Watford Chemical. Later that month Maxwell asked for part of Wallersteiner's holdings in Simpkin Marshall to be signed over to him.

Even as Simpkin Marshall was beginning to settle in the water Maxwell was still selling books at full throttle both for it and for Pergamon as well. He spent the second half of January in Moscow lobbying Mezhdunarodnaya Kniga, the government agency for book import-export. As chairman of Simpkin Marshall he sold the Russians dictionaries published by Eyre & Spottiswoode and Macmillan. But what pleased him more was getting the Russians to agree to take more British books and periodicals on science, technology and medicine – Pergamon specialities.

It finally dawned on the unhappy Wallersteiner that all might not be well with his considerable investment in the supposedly thriving Simpkin Marshall. He told Maxwell he planned to call a creditors' meeting. If Maxwell had already whipped the carpet from under him, now the roof fell in. Maxwell sent his solicitors, Forsyte, Kerman & Phillips – Isidore Kerman was a director of Pergamon and the firm represented it – to Mr Justice Havers to demand an injunction. The judge granted it, and an order was made forbidding Wallersteiner from even speaking to any other Simpkin Marshall creditors.

The injunction, however, could not prevent Wallersteiner, as a major shareholder, investigating on his own behalf. He engaged Peat Marwick, a formidable City accounting firm, to go through the books. By the end of August it had been established that Simpkin Marshall owed £111,335 to the Book Center and £30,889 to International Encyclopaedias Ltd, another Maxwell company.

In November 1954, Peat Marwick further reported that, despite the optimistic picture Maxwell had offered in his affidavit, in the year ending 31 March 1954, Simpkin Marshall had made a net loss of £34,261. To Peat Marwick a sum of £524,813 owed on borrowings had not been taken into consideration, and in net tangible assets over liabilities there was actually a deficit of £12,173.

'Simpkins is acutely short of liquid resources,' the report warned, 'due to the very substantial sums which have been advanced to associated companies.' The auditors also weighed Maxwell's constant complaint that publishers' margins were unrealistically small. True, said the report, there had been a case for supporting such a valuable institution as Simpkin Marshall. 'On the other hand it would not be surprising if the publishers withheld any concession until they could be satisfied that they were supporting only those activities in which they were interested.'

Despite the injunction, word of Simpkin Marshall's plight had soon spread. On 15 June 1955 – five days after Maxwell turned thirty-two – a meeting of some two hundred creditors, most of them from the book trade, resolved to bring in the Official Receiver to liquidate the company. They were told that unsecured liabilities were estimated at £656,000 of which £456,000 was due to trade creditors. The actual debts, by the time the Receiver had completed his work the following February, stood at £556,249.

'It appears doubtful', wrote Senior Official Receiver J. M. Clarke on 23 February 1956, passing judgement on the mess, 'whether the company was at any time solvent. The directors concerned were at fault in acquiring the Marylebone premises and financing the British Book Center at a time when the company was solvent without making satisfactory arrangements for the introduction of sufficient further capital.' The directors, said Mr Clarke, 'should have considered and decided upon liquidation at a much earlier date'. A contribution to the failure, the report concluded, had been the financing by Simpkin Marshall of MSI Inc. and the trusts.

Maxwell received a lot of sympathy over the collapse. The book trade was inclined to praise rather than condemn anyone who had tried to save such a worthy institution. Maxwell told everyone he had lost £250,000, explaining later that at least part of Wallersteiner's investment should be considered his under their 20 per cent agreement.

Long before Insight got on Maxwell's trail, Margaret Laing interviewed one of the accountants who had probed the wreckage. He, too, was inclined to spread the blame among the niggardly publishers rather than see Maxwell bear it all. 'He was in the wrong place at the wrong time. But it will dog him all the days of his life. He is like the rogue elephant of the book trade.' And the elephant was being damned sporting. 'I've come down flat on my arse,' Maxwell told the *Bookseller*, 'but I'm going up again. And I'll stay up.'

Maxwell's main concern now was to save 155 East 55th Street. The Book Center could not pay the £117,000 it now owed Simpkin Marshall. The considerable number of British publishers who stood to lose not only their stock of books with Simpkin Marshall but also any money the firm owed them talked of taking liquidation proceedings in the United States. Eventually one William Curtis, who had managed the Center for Maxwell, showed up in London with a mere £14,830 which he paid over to the Official Receiver. This parting volley of cash drove off the enemy patrols,

and in the end Simpkin Marshall creditors got less than four shillings in
the £. But Maxwell still had the two buildings in London and New York,
he still had MSI and Robert Maxwell & Co., which was soon turning over
£1 million a year. Above all, he had Pergamon.

FOUR

There is always a want of charity when a man is successful.

Mr Fisker in ANTHONY TROLLOPE'S, *The Way We Live Now*

M

AXWELL WAS STILL SOME WAY
from being a millionaire but he was on the right track. He and Betty had
moved out of the Clock House as soon as they could afford it to Esher,
Surrey – what was known as the Stockbroker Belt before stockbrokers
began work at seven in the morning. He travelled incessantly, particularly to Germany and to America where the journals were finding wider
and wider circulation and where Pergamon was becoming recognized as
a very particular kind of publisher.

Once the first wave of demand for the original vintage journals from
Germany had been satisfied Maxwell had looked around for new markets
– Butterworth-Springer had only five regular titles; by 1964 Pergamon
would have ninety; by 1987 more than 300 – and new sources of material.
He found everything he wanted in the new postwar generation of young
and youngish scientists finishing their education after the war or being
released to civilian careers.

One of the keys to progress in a scientist's career is the frequency
with which he or she can get research work published and the speed with
which they can get their hands on the findings that others in their field
have published. The well-established journals had long waiting-lists for
articles and a conservative attitude to their contributors. Many of the
new fields of enquiry opened up by the war were not even covered.

It was a phenomenal captive circular market. Thousands of physicians,
chemists, physicists and engineers inside and outside universities were
clamouring to be published. Usually the sight of their name in print was
reward enough. They did not ask for fees. The same people were in a
position to insist that the establishments in which they worked subscribe
to the sources of information they needed. If Pergamon launched, say, a
Quarterly of Mollusc Biology, every university library in the United
States, if nowhere else, would feel obliged to subscribe, whatever its
price. And Pergamon's terms were payment in advance. It was cash for
the asking.

The autocratic ways that had marked Maxwell's reign at Simpkin
Marshall went unchallenged, if not uncriticized, at Pergamon. Anything
that mattered Maxwell would trust to no one else. At the first international
conference on atomic energy held in Geneva in 1955, a delicate, highly
official affair, he managed to get permission to set up a Pergamon stand
and ran it himself. He also rented a lakeside villa and entertained with

what seemed to some visitors reckless hospitality. But they were, of course, simply seeing another standard Maxwell method of operation. The result intrigued Anthony Harris of the *Financial Times*.

> *By the end of the conference he had a most impressive bag of new authors, translation rights in foreign scientific journals and was on greeting terms (not first names – he is a great man for titles) with a good slice of the elite of the nuclear world. . . . It is all a bit Flash Harry on the face of it, not at all publisher-like. But – and this is what enrages rivals – it works.*

It worked again in 1957 when he was the only British publisher to take a stand at the British Trade Fair in Moscow. The contacts he made gave him a head start in being able to publish material on Soviet space experiments when the first Sputnik was launched and the United States, fearful of falling behind, became desperate for information.

Nikita Khrushchev, the Soviet premier, visited the Trade Fair, and Maxwell got the Minister of Culture to present him. He asked Khrushchev a question that was to remain of great interest to British publishers for years to come: Did the Soviet Union intend to sign the international copyright convention under which foreign authors would be paid royalties? He was assured that the matter was being studied.

Khrushchev, interested by this assertive Russian-speaking foreigner, asked if there was anything else. As a matter of fact, said Maxwell, I should like to visit my birthplace. But when he mentioned Slatina-Selo, now part of the Ukraine, Khrushchev's affability vanished. 'Nyet!' he said, the most familiar Russian word of those Cold War days.

Not for twenty-five years, by which time he had made nearly a score of trips to Russia, did Maxwell find out why he had been refused. Another Minister of Culture asked him if he still wanted to go to Slatina and arranged it. Maxwell took Betty along. 'Regrettably,' says Maxwell, they failed to find anyone who remembered him.

But he can relate the explanation that the chairman of the village soviet gave for Khrushchev's hostility: 'In 1949, when Comrade Khrushchev was secretary of the Communist Party in the Ukraine, some partisans near here took a shot at him. He had bad memories of Slatina.'

Sir Monty Finniston was one of the eminent contributors Maxwell was able to bag in Geneva. He was then head of the metallurgy division at Harwell, Britain's main nuclear research centre, later chairman of British Steel, a distinguished son of Glasgow's Jewish community. Finniston contributed to Pergamon journals for many years and came to consider himself a friend of Maxwell, even though by the time of the anniversary dinner he did so no longer. 'I didn't want to go but I did,' he says. 'I like Betty very much. She's a very admirable woman and probably the only wife he could have had.'

Finniston's disenchantment was due to a double dose of Maxwell's capricious dealings with those he recruits to help him. In 1979, when Maxwell was about to take over the British Printing Corporation, a vital step to his present eminence, he asked Finniston to become chairman of Pergamon so that he could devote all his energies to the new acquisition. Finniston accepted, terms were settled; he and his wife Miriam went house-hunting in Oxfordshire.

Three weeks before he was due to take up the appointment the Finnistons went to lunch at Headington. After lunch Miriam and Betty stayed while the two men strolled across the lawns to Maxwell's office. 'Then he suddenly withdrew the offer,' Finniston recalls.

'He offered me compensation. I refused. I don't know what led him to it. He's a man who if you agree with him he's a friend, if you disagree he'll turn against you.

'Then in 1987 Clyde Cablevision was looking for support from the banks. They wouldn't give it to me, Maxwell said. They would only give it to someone he had in mind.'

Sir Monty was ousted without so much as a chance to address his board of directors.

The man with whom Maxwell replaced him was Sir Ian MacGregor, the septuagenarian former chairman of the Coal Board with whom Maxwell had some dealings after he had taken over the *Mirror* that were both farcical and enigmatic. Months after he had moved in, the little Scottish cable television company Maxwell had acquired as part of his Mirror Group deal was still waiting for its financing.

During his brief spells at home Maxwell did his rather awkward best to fall in with local customs. Like tennis. One of the Esher stockbrokers who played against him never forgot the experience. Maxwell was determined to win, irrespective of the merit of his game. It was not the game that mattered. It was the gamesmanship.

Betty had long since stopped going to the office. She went instead to Maison-Lafitte at regular intervals. There were now three more children: Philip born in 1949, and in 1950 twins, Christine and Isabel.

'Every time Bob *looked* at me I had another child,' said Betty when she had eventually borne nine (and the father of them was no longer called Ian). 'We both wanted a large family, but contraception not being what it is nowadays children came much faster than planned. I had five under the age of four.'

When, a quarter of a century later, the glossy magazines were begging Betty to pose for them in her beautiful couturier clothes, she gave Vicki Woods the features editor of *Tatler* a demonstration of what her life was like at that time: 'Once a week I would go to Kingston market and fill up my little Morris estate with sacks of potatoes, Brussels sprouts, carrots and boxes of fruit for jam. For years I did nothing but feed, feed, feed.' And then she spun around in a circle on her delicate Jourdan heel, miming the long-gone Betty of the suburbs ladling food into those hungry little mouths.

In 1953 she had had a sixth child, Karin. Her seventh, a boy, was not born until 1956 – the longest she had ever gone without a pregnancy. By then the Maxwells knew that the latest little girl was suffering from leukemia. It was not the only intimation of mortality to be forced upon Maxwell in the midst of his high-speed life. Smoking sixty cigarettes a day had had its effect on one of his lungs, and he was told it must be removed. It was not an operation to be taken lightly; nor were the consequences of not submitting to it. He made some solemn arrangements should the worst happen, among which was the decision to preserve his hard-won identity and all it had come to signify by naming the new baby Ian Robert after his now not so new self.

Physically, the main effect of losing a lung was to deepen Maxwell's already gravelly voice yet more and to leave him with a characteristic hacking cough, bursts of which precede him into a room where he is to speak. But the sense that time could be running out recalled the adolescent boasts of Lodvik Hoch and the brash young Captain Maxwell of Berlin.

The first public pronouncement Maxwell made in British politics was: 'Bloody liar!' He bawled it out in the market-place of Lavendon, Buckinghamshire, at Sir Frank Markham, the Conservative Member of Parliament whose seat he was about to challenge and who had just been unwise enough to make some slighting observations about him.

Although it had been Maxwell's intention for some years to stand for Parliament, it was less certain which party he might join. His grey-striped *éminence banquaire*, Sir Charles Hambro, had suggested to him before the Simpkin Marshall crash that he might have a future with the Conservative Party. The entrepreneurial vigour Maxwell exuded fitted the image of the new young hustlers who had rallied to the Conservative banner as it passed from Churchill in his dotage to Anthony Eden to Harold Macmillan who, by the time a general election seemed probable in 1959, had been Prime Minister for three years. Certainly, if his politics had to be divined from his deeds rather than from his words Maxwell would – to this day – be taken for a High Tory.

Sir Charles, a devout Tory himself needless to say, offered to put in a word in the right quarters. Maxwell told him, he has insisted since the question was first raised, that conservative politicians were responsible for his father's unemployment and that he would not be able to bring himself to become one of them. This was, of course, many years before Maxwell had established himself as one of Britain's largest disemployers in the private sector, eliminating some 8,000 jobs in five years.

Maxwell's socialist convictions may be open to question; his credentials as a practical capitalist are not. He does not conceal his admiration for

Margaret Thatcher's methods in private; sometimes not even in public. Nor for Ronald Reagan or, for that matter, General Jaruzelski of Poland who hardly qualifies as a democrat. Jaruzelski is one of the many Eastern bloc leaders who have qualified for the standard treatment that helps Pergamon do business in their country: a paralysingly uncritical – and infinitely unread – biography.

President Reagan received his acclaim verbally at a cocktail-party full of Washington journalists whom Maxwell was out to impress with his plans for expansion in the United States. 'Don't shoot Reagan,' they were startled to hear their host admonish them. 'He's the best thing you have going for you.' An even greater infelicity, however, was due to Maxwell's fatal inability to detect any but the most literal meaning of anything he says or hears. He referred to his American journalist guests as 'hacks', a term he had evidently picked up from *Private Eye*. The Washington press takes itself seriously. The lighthearted British connotation was completely lost on them.

Thatcher is a much more complicated and more relevant matter. When, by the election campaign of 1987, George Gale, the devil's advocate he had planted in the *Mirror*, had taken off for the Outer Darkness, Maxwell appeared on television, ostensibly to argue the case for Labour. But his praise for the Prime Minister was so fulsome that the *Daily Mail*, the newspaper which provides her least critical backing, was able to report:

> *Robert Maxwell, whose Mirror Group newspapers are backing Labour, congratulated Mrs Thatcher for curbing union abuse. He believes that without the Premier's determination to get rid of shop floor tyranny he could never have started a new newspaper this year creating 1,000 jobs. And he reckons the union laws were decisive in ending a crippling dispute at one of his plants.*

This was quite a fair summary. Maxwell did criticize Mrs Thatcher for seeming to want to destroy the unions altogether with laws that prevented pickets from one union interfering with the work of others, but he also observed something that no one who had watched him operate could quarrel with. 'We on the Labour side wish to co-operate, and do co-operate with business.' The least pro-Conservative observation he made was: 'We are wholly in favour of running a capitalist society but not at the expense of the unemployed, lengthening queues in hospitals and poor people. . . .' The Labour Party and the trade unions were flabbergasted. He swiftly redressed the balance with an unprecedented and costly gesture to underline his partiality. He rejected Tory campaign advertising worth £350,000 to MGN.

Despite what Maxwell might have said to Sir Charles Hambro, it seems quite likely that in his early days Maxwell, even without being aware of it, had attracted the attention of Tory recruiters. When, after he was well established as both a millionaire and an MP, Graham Lord, interviewing him for the *Sunday Express* in 1968, put it to him that he had applied to be a Conservative candidate before signing on with Labour, Maxwell snapped back: 'That rumour is baseless and stupid.'

Why, then, asked Lord, was there a Conservative Central Office memorandum dated 1953 that referred to Maxwell as a possible Tory candidate? 'What goes on in Central Office is their own business.'

Maxwell then gave Lord an explanation of why he was a socialist which has remained his standard encapsulated philosophy ever since.

> *I asked my mother why my father was standing around in doorways and not working. She said it was not his fault, he wanted to work and was looking for work, but it was the political system. The poverty, indignity and hunger have engraved themselves on my heart. I am not attached to property and I could be happy without money. I could even work for someone else. I won't do anything unless it's socially useful. Life has taught me that in the end you'll make a profit out of it.*

Even though the published interview gave Maxwell's explanation in full he was clearly hurt by the enforced association with the Conservatives. Next week the paper said:

> *Mr Robert Maxwell MP . . . asks us to state that at no time did he allow his name to go forward as a possible candidate and that any rumour [to the contrary] is entirely baseless. This we accept without reservation and we apologise to Mr Maxwell for any embarrassment that he has been caused.*

For a man who delights in letting it be known that he has a hide as thick as his wallet, Maxwell seemed to embarrass easily. Actually he is utterly unembarrassable. 'My enemies see a man with the skin of a rhinoceros,' he loves to say. 'They hate me for it.' But he can easily be offended: 'Never forget an insult. Pay it back no matter how long it takes.' He was sensitive to the suggestion of being a political opportunist because he had not got into Parliament without a struggle and there were still plenty of people on his own side who thought that, on several counts, he had no business being there.

If ever, in darkest Ruthenia or starkest Agde, Maxwell had a dream of rural England, it would have looked something like Buckinghamshire: rolling green fields, cobbled market-towns, down-to-earth folk with gentle accents. Two of the nation's sainted politicians lay buried within its borders: Edmund Burke the Whig revivalist and Benjamin Disraeli. It had been home, at different times, to literary figures as diverse as G. K. Chesterton, Enid Blyton and Robert Frost. The little town of Olney, scene of his precipitate début, was famous for the collaboration of William Cowper and John Newton on the Olney Hymns of which the best known is 'Amazing Grace'. At either end of Stony Stratford, one of the villages which was eventually to nominate Maxwell, stand two pubs, the Cock and the Bull, immortalized by the rivalry of their bygone clientele in telling the most improbable travellers' tales. He would have got a good hearing in such company.

The late 1950s were not happy times for Labour. After the six postwar years of office that changed Britain for ever – nationalizing coal, steel, electricity, gas, railways; creating the Welfare State and the National Health Service; dissolving the Empire – the Conservatives had been returned to power in 1951 and again in 1955. The country was happy with them. The majority of voters seemed to believe the mythical Macmillan line that became a byword for the time: 'You've never had it so good.'

Maxwell's first venture into politics was to join not the Labour Party but the Fabian Society, a group of socialist theoreticians he would now consider hopelessly effete. He did not become a member of the party itself until 1958. Since there was no local Labour organization in the blue-ribbon Tory stronghold of Esher he founded his own, a bold move that brought some favourable attention from Labour headquarters at Transport House in London. Esher, though, was about to join the Clock House as part of the past. Maxwell had decided that an academic publishing house like Pergamon ought to be where the academics themselves were and by then he was in the process of moving it to Oxford.

But, if Maxwell had it in mind to stand for Parliament, Oxford, a safe Labour seat, was far too precious to be wasted on an aspirant. To be 'adopted' by a constituency for the election that was being forecast for the autumn of 1959 he would have to find a 'marginal' seat and convince the local party organization that he stood the best chance of winning it for them.

The first possibility came to him through Pergamon. One of his new employees at Headington, Sylvia Stratford-Lawrence, had been nominated as the candidate for Aylesbury constituency, twenty-three miles from Oxford, but decided not to stand. Maxwell applied to take her place, but a replacement had already been picked. However, he was told, a vacancy had suddenly opened up in the adjoining constituency of Buckingham where the established contender, Dr Gordon Evans, had been injured in a car accident.

The reservations of socialist officials about a prospective candidate who bowled up for his first interviews in a chauffeured Humber limousine are easy to imagine. There had been fifteen applicants for the seat, who were to be narrowed down to five for the final choice. Several of them were party stalwarts, including Ray Bellchambers, chairman of the Buckingham Constituency Labour Party. 'No one had heard of Maxwell before,' recalls Bellchambers. 'And him getting out of his car claiming to be the son of a Czech peasant didn't ring easy.'

The thought of a socialist millionaire – a description that Maxwell was already encouraging – was bad enough for many of the Buckingham officials, but the most serious objection for the rustic apparatchiks was that he had been in the party for less than a year. Maxwell assured them he was a true believer of long standing who would have joined up formally long before had he not been compelled to live in Esher and travel abroad for seven months of every recent year. He made a heartfelt plea for acceptance, speaking of his affinity with the countryside. 'Farming is in my blood,' he said. He wanted to live in 'this beautiful area', preferably on a farm. In fact he had, once. The Clock House of miserable memory was only a few miles away.

Maxwell told a wary audience of district party secretaries, whose organizations would have to commend him to the constituency party, about his war record and his Military Cross. The pacifists among them were not impressed. He told them about his nine languages. Said a schoolteacher delegate: 'That proves that you couldn't possibly have been born in England.'

The socialist county kingmakers faced a certain ideological difficulty in opposing Maxwell on the grounds of his birth on the wrong side of the Iron Curtain. The rank and file whose prejudice could run free were not given much of a chance to judge him on it at first, since neither the biographical sketch circulated for the selection meeting that August nor the election propaganda which was subsequently prepared made any mention of Czechoslovakia or of Maxwell's previous names. 'Born 36 years ago of a poor farm labouring family,' was all that was said about his birth. And about his upbringing: 'He had no opportunity for formal education but through his own efforts he educated himself.'

Maxwell was later to admit a tactical error in deciding not to confuse the voters with too much information. For his antecedents swiftly became the most significant issue, winning the obscure campaign national headlines – even a leader in *The Times*. 'If the Labour Party had clearly said that Captain Maxwell had been born in Czechoslovakia this campaign of vilification would have been nipped in the bud. . . .'

On 27 August, Maxwell was selected from the shortlist of five. But it took three ballots, and a great deal of rancour remained when they were over. The vice-president of the constituency party, Tom Mitchinson, was so disillusioned that he stormed off to drown his sorrows with the Tories and ended up by putting his name to the nomination papers of Frank Markham, the Tory candidate. More headlines.

The turmoil and confusion that are now the predictable accompaniment to any Maxwell operation were in full swirl, and onlookers already divided into the camps of hating him or loving him that are now as irreconcilable as Labour and Tory. One of his supporters, Bill West of Birmingham, wrote in *Labour Daily*: 'Captain Maxwell is no more a foreigner than Prince Philip. Like him he was born abroad. He came here as a boy and fought for this country and has been working for its interests ever since.' This was widely deplored as bringing the royal family into politics.

Labour's National Executive Committee gave short shrift to most of the objections to Maxwell when it met to approve new adoptions three weeks later, although James Callaghan, a member of the Shadow Cabinet, grumbled about the ease with which 'inexperienced careerist candidates' were getting a chance at marginal seats. 'This sort of candidate ought to be made to serve an apprenticeship the hard way,' said Callaghan.

The NEC gave an airing to the matter of Headington Hill Hall. Maxwell's enemies in Buckingham had heard that he was spending £350,000 on restoring this stately home.

A little wearily – as the *Daily Telegraph* described Maxwell's response – he said: 'It is true that I am a wealthy man, but the fact is that Headington Hall is leased from the Oxford Council for £2,000 a year by the Pergamon Press, of which I am a director. It will be used as business premises and I shall not live there.'

In fact plans were well in hand for Maxwell to instal himself at Headington. All the Maxwells in fact, for by now Betty had made yet another trip to Maison-Laffitte and come back with Kevin, child number eight.

But the socialists of Buckingham were not aware of this glaring discrepancy between what Maxwell said and what he meant when, on 18 September, Ray Bellchambers swallowed his disappointment and, in Bletchley town hall, formally proposed Maxwell's adoption. Three hundred party members rose to their feet cheering. Betty, plucked from her nappy-changing and jam-making, stood beside Bob on the platform, both of them sporting huge red, white and blue rosettes. She was presented with flowers. He presented his audience with the Buckingham Plan For World Nuclear Disarmament, the wisdom of which, he told them, he had already made available to Messrs Gaitskell, Eisenhower and Khrushchev.

This bold and idealistic scheme required that the nuclear powers agree to hold their weapons in trust for the United Nations and undertake to fire them only in self-defence or at United Nations order. Future testing would be banned and no more weapons developed.

More practical plans to give Maxwell some political visibility became the task of Bryan Barnard, the Labour Party's local election agent. He takes some of the responsibility – although the candidate himself obviously concurred – for trying to blur Maxwell's origins and thinks, now, that it probably cost them the seat in 1959. For Barnard soon realized that he had one of nature's campaigners on his hands.

It was just after Maxwell's adoption that they went together to see what the incumbent was up to. They found Markham in the village of Lavendon, standing on a beer-crate addressing about thirty people outside a bus-shelter. Markham was a worthy opponent. He had once been a Labour man himself, breaking away with Ramsay MacDonald's national movement of 1931. He had held the seat for the Tories since 1951 and only a recent trickle of postwar industrial workers into the predominantly rural constituency put him at risk.

Barnard's recollections of the evening of Maxwell's noisy début are undimmed. 'Sir Frank was telling them the Labour Party hadn't been able to find a candidate in the whole country, let alone Buckingham. They'd had to go all the way to Czechoslovakia. "You'll rarely see this poor fellow in the constituency," he told them. "And he'll never even find his way to Lavendon."'

Taken by surprise at Maxwell's sudden appearance and his outburst, Markham stepped down and Barnard took his place. ' "You've got it all wrong," ' I said. ' "That man is here tonight." ' Barnard passed his loud-hailer to Maxwell.

In Barnard's car the challengers followed Markham and his wife to nearby Olney. Seeking a sympathetic ear while Maxwell was repeating his speech, Lady Markham complained to the uniformed chauffeur of a magnificent new Rolls-Royce she found waiting on the outskirts of the crowd.

'Such an awful night. This terrible fellow disrupted our meeting. Sir Frank was so upset that on the way here he bit the end off the pipe he was given by the Parliamentary Party for twenty-five years' service. By the way, who are you waiting for?'

'Captain Maxwell, madam. Come to take him home.'

The Rolls, for which Maxwell had abandoned his Humber (for which he had abandoned the distinctly un-British Cadillac), annoyed the Conservatives as much as it did the Labour people. It was hard for the Tories to attack such a symbol of British achievement but they could not forget it even when Maxwell turned up in a red and white trailer towed behind a land-rover with 'Here Comes Maxwell' inscribed on its front. 'I had trouble persuading him not to have "There Goes Maxwell" on the back,' said Barnard. 'But it was a lovely campaign, the kind every agent dreams of.'

For Maxwell descended on the unsuspecting citizens of Buckingham with the infantryman's *élan* with which he now habitually attacks entrenched positions. The trailer was packed with aids to communication virtually unknown to the primitive electioneering of that day: tape-recorders, duplicators, a portable public address system and – final dramatic touch – a portable spotlight to illuminate the candidate throughout his speeches.

As the gaudy caravan trundled through the autumn gloom from one to another of the hundred or so towns and villages in the constituency typists would transcribe Maxwell's previous address, complete with subsequent questions and answers. At the next stop a motorcyclist would zoom back to where it had been delivered and distribute an edited version to anyone left awake. These handouts were known as Maxwellgrams, an innovation which – together with the loudspeakers – was frequently to reappear in Maxwell situations.

The main themes of Maxwell's campaign were Tory stinginess towards local government and the growing nuclear threat. Maxwell claimed many years later that perils of the nuclear future had been his unswerving concern ever since the first bomb was dropped in 1945. But the Buckingham Declaration, as his message to the world leaders became known in Maxwell annals, fourteen years later seems to have been the first time he made his views widely known. The locals were quite familiar with the subject. It had been the constant preoccupation of Gordon Evans, the unsuccessful Labour candidate in the two previous elections whose mantle and organization Maxwell inherited.

Once the Tories of Buckingham realized that they had a serious challenge on their hands they sent for reinforcements in the form of the Young Conservatives, the party's *Pioneeren*. Hot-blooded middle-class yobbos in the main, a millionaire socialist of foreign origin and uncertain identity soon had them baying for blood. Racial slogans began to appear on weathered stone walls around the county, including the comprehensive 'Bucks People Do Not Need to Be Represented by an Insulting Foreigner so Let's Put a Check on This Overconfident Czech. A Real Englishman as Member for Us.'

Unlike the bucolic Labourites, the Young Conservatives had heard about Simpkin Marshall. With dazzling chutzpah Maxwell went to old I. J. Pitman, from whom he had taken over Simpkin Marshall, and who was the Conservative MP for Bath, for a testimonial. Pitman wrote him a carefully worded letter saying that in the matter of the scientific book trade no blemish attached to Maxwell's name.

But the Tory shocktroops kept hammering away about that and other matters on which, one of their campaign documents claimed, the candidate was very poor at answering questions.

'Every district is asked to see', said this Tory circular, 'that at any meeting he is asked about: a) nationalization b) his experience in the Czech Army c) his name when he received the Military Cross d) does he employ non-union labour?'

From Maxwell's own party's point of view the last question was loaded, since Pergamon was trying its damnedest to keep unions out. His answers were marvellously evasive. And the Tories had confused themselves over his name and how he came by it. He was able to refute the frequent suggestions that it had been changed by deed poll. (It had simply been changed.) He soon developed a diversionary tactic to deal with references to his origins. Arms wide apart, tears streaming down his face, he would declare to the wondering voters: 'I'm one of you!'

Maxwell's decoration irritated the Conservatives as much as his Rolls and chauffeur. Superannuated officers among the faithful were sent on secret missions to the Ministry of Defence to seek assurances that it could not be true. As late as 1967 a Colonel Charles Frederick Howard Gough, himself a holder of the Military Cross, was firmly compelled to apologize over a letter he had written to the *Illustrated London News* inviting the editor to say whether or not Mr Maxwell had actually been awarded one. Not until a month after the 1959 election did the local weekly, the Tory-supporting *Bletchley Gazette*, get around to printing the picture Maxwell had given them of Montgomery pinning the MC on him.

It was, by the standards of the shires, an unprecedentedly dirty campaign. The most unworthy rumours were circulated which Markham, the Real Englishman, refused to disavow. 'Every British elector', he said, 'has the right to ask any question concerning a candidate's history, background or record. Anyone can ask me any question they like, either political or personal.'

Maxwell showed that he could indeed be the Insulting Foreigner of the wall slogans. 'You are a disciple of the devil,' he fulminated at a parson. And not only did he go for the Real Englishman as though he had been an SS Baby but he also opened up on the Markham family as well. One Maxwell attack on a Tory supporter had Lady Markham writing indignantly to the local papers that Maxwell had told the man he could only be supporting Sir Frank because he had his eye on the Markham daughter.

'May I point out that my daughter, Elizabeth, is married?' said her ladyship's letter, adding: 'We have been astonished at the outrageous statements made and the epithets used by Mr Maxwell about Sir Frank and many constituents.'

And heaped on top of the general confusion and un-English display of emotion were the legal threats now perceived to be another indispensable ingredient to Maxwell's progress. When he met Lady Markham in Bletchley on voting day, 9 September, she, perhaps from some misguided notion of truce now that nothing could alter the outcome, offered him her hand. Maxwell slapped a writ for libel into it.

Similar writs were issued to half a dozen other Tories before the results were declared: Conservative 22,304; Labour 20,558. Sir Frank had increased his margin by 1,552 votes, for which, he told his supporters, he had Maxwell to thank. 'He put fire in the bellies of our people.'

'Long live socialism and liberty,' Maxwell responded defiantly. He declined to shake hands with Sir Frank for the photographers. Betty by his side looked as limp as her rosette.

Losing, however, had not taken the fight out of Maxwell. In less than six months he had got himself recognized as a politician. He had seen how things were done. And he knew there would be a next time. He told the constituency party that he would stick with them if they still wanted him and try again. They did. In October he went to Scarborough to give the annual Labour Party Conference the benefit of his reflections on the handling he had received in Buckingham: voters did not want nationalization but a mixed economy. In the New Year he and Betty were back in Buckingham, dancing the Gay Gordons at the party hop. On 19 March 1960, still less than a year after Buckingham had heard of him for the first time, four other candidates, including Ray Bellchambers, withdrew their nominations for the presidency of the constituency party and Maxwell was unanimously elected to the post.

If Maxwell had turned himself into a political grandee in Buckinghamshire, in Oxford he had become a commercial squire. During the 1959 campaign the Maxwells had rented a token house in High Street, Bletchley. But now they abandoned all pretence of not living at Headington. Crimson wallpaper went up in the vast double drawing-room with its ceiling-high dividing doors. The parquet floors were sanded and polished, the ornate moulded ceilings restored, the balustrade of the superb central staircase renewed, heavy Empire furniture installed, the walls of fake books assembled. Plans were drawn up for a circular swimming-pool and a flock of peacocks bought to strut the grounds. There was no finer council house in Britain. On the front door a brass plate proclaimed a new style: Robert Maxwell, MC. No more Ian. No more Captain. 'I have decided', he said, 'that from now on I prefer to be known as plain Mister. This is an expression of my belief that military power on a national scale is outdated.' Like most Maxwell avowals this was to be reversed a few times. When he took over Mirror Group Newspapers (where he changed the title of the *Daily Mirror* to *The Mirror* and then changed it back again) his letterheads proclaimed him Captain once more.

Maxwell still had his offices in Fitzroy Square and the flat, but to house Pergamon prefabricated buildings were put up among the Headington trees and soon four hundred employees were working in them, most of them well paid, not all of them happy. 'There was a lot of fear in the air,' recalls a designer.

Of all the deals Maxwell has ever made, leasing Headington Hill Hall may have been the smartest. He – or, rather, Pergamon – leased it from Oxford council in March 1959, six months before he assured the Labour Party it was intended only as business premises, for twenty-one years at £2,400 a year, a little more than Maxwell has been ready to admit to. The mansion was built by a family of local brewers, the Morrells, one of whom, Lady Ottoline, conducted something of a literary salon. It had become derelict during the war, and the council, having taken it over, invited tenders for it.

In 1962 the lease was extended to seventy-five years at £3,000 a year, increasing as buildings were added to £5,050 in 1965. One of the buildings was sub-leased to Iraq Petroleum, who occupied it for nine years. When, in 1977, Pergamon wanted an even longer arrangement the council became uneasy. There were heated debates, and proposals were exchanged for months on end. Finally, in 1978, Iraq Petroleum departed, and Pergamon paid a premium of £10,000 and a rental of £10,000 a year for the first ten years of a ninety-nine-year lease that will eventually increase to £20,000. In 1980, Pergamon assigned the lease to All Centre Property Ltd, a wholly owned subsidiary.

The Buckingham campaign had given Maxwell a taste for the microphone. He installed a public address system through which the workers could be exhorted or admonished. The neighbours complained that his amplified booming was worse than the screeching of the peacocks.

But for long periods the loudspeakers were silent. Like one of the new satellites that had brought a fresh dimension to science, Maxwell constantly circled the world to spur Pergamon on. By 1962 he had been to Russia eight times, bringing back, among other scientific accounts, details of the latest Russian space experiments.

Pergamon had begun to make serious money. In 1962 it published 250 book titles and 90 journals, ranging from *Annals of Occupational Hygiene* to *Insect Physiology*. By 1963, while it was still to all intents his personal property, the company claimed a turnover of £2 million and a profit of £140,832. Not only were prices of all its products high; librarians were beginning to complain that they were fooled into buying some of the publications twice, once as a journal and later recycled in a hardcover book. Maxwell agreed to end this profitable practice. Spurred by an extraordinary deal with the American publishers Macmillan – no connection with Prime Minister Harold and his family firm in Britain – Maxwell was confidently predicting an enormous increase in business. He had somehow convinced Macmillan to agree to take up to 40 per cent of the print run of new titles that Pergamon produced. This in itself, Maxwell would disarmingly admit, was twice the number of books his company needed to sell to break even.

Maxwell was also a regular visitor to the other communist-bloc countries. In several of them printing could be done much more cheaply than in Britain – and without the danger of union-inspired difficulties and delays. But the Cold War was at its frostiest, and the printed pages had to be brought to Britain for binding so that they could be presented to the American Customs as British products. Maxwell was beginning to think of himself as a printer as much as a publisher. To be a Member of Parliament as well. . . .

Even before there was a new election in sight Maxwell confidently assumed a political persona, taking it for granted that his views and values were of interest both in Britain and abroad. From the days of the one good suit he had seen that a generous splash of high life was a natural accompaniment to the pursuit of power. He soon picked up the scent that led him to the watering-holes frequented not just by the rich, but also by the beautiful and, above all, the influential. He has come to avoid restaurants now, resenting their prices, preferring to entertain under a corporate roof. But in the early days of Pergamon he was an open-handed host not just at Claridge's, the Savoy and 'Les A' but also at the 21 in New York, the Hôtel George V in Paris. He had a weakness for yachts long before he could dream of anything like *Lady Ghislaine*, chartering them whenever he could. He invited George Brown, the Foreign Secretary, for tea in Greece on a 150-tonner named *Sister Anne*; for another voyage his vessel was *Shemara*, the flagship of a frequently headlined couple of the period, Sir Bernard and Lady Docker.

One stockade of the privileged to which Maxwell was particular drawn was the Round Hill Hotel on the north-east coast of Jamaica. Often he would fly down there with or without Betty and move into one of the deceptively simple whitewashed cabins. The neighbours might be Clark Gable, John and Jackie Kennedy or a couple of top-drawer international hookers, but there was never a dull moment. John Pringle, whose creation Round Hill was, remembers Maxwell's visits. 'I thought he was fascinating. Sinister, you know, but always terribly well informed about everything.' Soon the Maxwells had become regular guests at the nearby house of Dolly Burns, the daughter of Lord Duveen, who was one of a doomed but hard-dying breed, the international 'society hostess'. Her collection of old politicians, some of whom had crossed the divide into statesmanship, made an invaluable strand in the network of contacts Maxwell was beginning to weave for himself.

But far more often than not Betty was left behind when Maxwell took wing. Frequently she herself would head for France while he was away to keep in touch with her family and cultivate the children's French. Anne by then was very much the senior child, helping to herd the others along. 'There seemed to be long long periods when we never saw my father at all,' she remembers.

Maxwell, still in his thirties, cut an impressive figure on these and future travels. There was only the slightest sign of the bulk that has now accumulated on his powerful limbs; his hair was as dark as it is today, without the aid of the colourist, wavy and as long as a man who wanted to be taken seriously dared to wear it. Plenty of women found this tall, dark, suave and ... *mysterious* stranger irresistible. However he became cavalierly brusque if he felt that women wanted more from him than he felt like giving. The reason Maxwell has offered for his achievements is that 'duty is more important than love'.

When on 'Desert Island Discs' Michael Parkinson asked him respectfully (listeners were not reminded that Parkinson was also a *Mirror* columnist) if there was a trick to making money Maxwell delivered a homily on salesmanship and dedication. 'Whatever you do you must give it total concentration and commitment. If you are out selling and it's five o'clock and you have a date with your girl but if you stayed on and walked a further mile you may talk with a customer and fulfil their requirements then you'd better do that than going on your date.'

In his thirties just as in his sixties, time was what Maxwell most begrudged. Work always came first just as it did as he approached sixty-five. Long after his dinner companions had gone to sleep and long before they awoke, Maxwell would be on the telephone, restlessly burning up the lines to some other part of the world where office hours had not yet run out, firing off letters and telexes. Sometimes his travels were shared by a secretary (today it could be an entourage of a dozen). The girls soon became resigned to their duties extending well beyond the normal working day.

It was into this high-speed round-the-clock orbit that young Jean Baddeley was swept in 1962, recruited as a secretary at Headington. It was a fateful choice both for her and for the Maxwells. Betty first took her in hand, putting her to work on constituency matters and, although none of them could have envisaged that the relationship would last for more than a quarter of a century, setting out to shape her for the other tasks that would in the end make her virtually an honorary Maxwell. Working inside Headington itself as much as in the offices, Baddeley soon had her own room there. She became as familiar to the children as though she had been one of them – she was barely older than Anne – or, perhaps, a slightly bossy young aunt. As adults, the children still regard her with affection but no longer as the equal they once might have; Maxwell family doctrine does not allow for equals. Kevin especially is not as dependent as she would prefer, often neglecting to return her calls.

Baddeley speedily passed out of Betty's hands to become Maxwell's most trusted helper. Which is not saying all that much. Although she is a peerless keeper of secrets and as loyal as the Brigade of Guards, she is frequently taken by surprise when she discovers what he has been working towards. But in the end it is Baddeley and no one else who, flushing scarlet with stress, stays late into the night to process the most confidential of documents; Baddeley whose word is second only to Maxwell's own when it comes to giving orders; Baddeley who can be found kneeling by the side of Maxwell's chair as he watches the television news before going out to a diplomatic reception, murmuring her report of the day's events into his ear and straightening the Ruritanian array of decorations on his evening coat.

Even now, although he does not hesitate to put women in well-paid jobs and treat them as indifferently as anyone else he employs, Maxwell's attitude to them is distinctly rough and tumble. He would often insist on leafing through the piles of semi-nude pinups his tabloid newspaper empire accumulated. When he appeared on a television talk show conducted by Robert Kilroy-Silk, another former MP, to defend the immortal right to flood the popular papers with flesh some of the women on the production side tackled him about it in the hospitality room. 'Why do you object to them?' he bellowed at one. 'Is it because you haven't got the equipment yourself?' And when he first discovered an apartment in the *Mirror* complex that he had previously not known about his eyes lit up and he asked: 'Could I take a girl there?'

W~hen~ Maxwell returned to Headington from his travels the children got their share of his attention. The house was always packed, especially for Sunday lunches, with professors and politicians of all nationalities, and the children were expected to play their full part in the conversations. The brash self-promoting salesman of the world outside gave way to an affectionate but firm father out to instil commercial wisdom into them in a more systematic fashion than he had acquired it himself. Maxwell devised a regime for the children that seemed to have been based on some form of business training manual and he imparted it in the form of the three Cs: Consideration, Concentration, Conciseness.

One of these caused Betty herself some problems, she confessed long after the children were grown. 'I am irritated by some of Bob's mannerisms. He has the most irksome habit, in his impatience to get on, of interrupting a conversation with me by saying, "Next? . . . Next?" I know then that I have failed to use one of his three Cs: Conciseness.' To this folksy system of self-improvement Betty added another C – for Courtesy. The children were all impressively well mannered and well behaved, the little girls even curtsying to visitors.

Then there was WWHW, a mnemonic intended to help answer examination questions: What? Why? How? When? 'Now that they are grown up,'

Betty wrote in *She* magazine, 'the children tell us that these basic tenets have remained their anchor and mainstay.'

But it was Maxwell himself who first spelled out for a mesmerized Margaret Laing in 1964 the principles of wisdom he wished to instil in his young:

(1) Look for your questioner's motive before you decide on an answer.
(2) Everyone, however wretched, old, stinking or poor, has something to teach you.
(3) Point out whatever is of personal advantage to the other person in any suggestion you make. Remember it is right that there should be a selfish advantage.
(4) Remember that techniques are useful things.

Maxwell was also adopting an innovative attitude towards the children's formal education. Michael and Philip, the two eldest boys, were at Marlborough College and were destined for Oxford. Ian and Kevin were to follow in their wake. The other children were sent to the kind of schools he decided they might best benefit from. By 1967 there were still two boys at public school, but two other children were at grammar schools and three in State schools. Education reformers in the Labour Party frequently questioned Maxwell about his views, which appeared to be entirely pragmatic. The ones most likely to profit from a public school education – the boys – were the ones to get it. Neither Ian nor Kevin enjoyed school or university, although both did well. They were impatient to get to work.

The last Maxwell child, the beauteous Ghislaine, was born in 1961. But that was a year of unequalled family despair. The first of the new generation, Michael – handsome, personable, a natural leader – out to learn the ropes of the business in which his future lay, was being driven along the Oxford–Bicester road by a Pergamon driver when the car collided with a truck. Michael suffered terrible head injuries. For the next seven years, until he died, he was to lie in a coma in Churchill Hospital, spastic, dumb and totally helpless. For the first year Betty visited him every day. 'I believed he would wake at any moment. It took a long time to accept that he wouldn't. I thought I would die of grief.'

As Philip's tribute at the anniversary party showed, Michael remained a presence in the family long after he had disappeared from Headington and indeed from life. Even those of the children too young to have any recollection of him are at home with his memory, as is Betty, who had taken her firstborn home to the chill squalor of the Clock House after the war with such hope of the world in which he would grow up. 'He was the sun child, the others revolved around him.' The one person who never speaks of Michael is his father.

But in 1965 Maxwell established a grant of £2,000 a year to Oxford University for research into brain damage for as long as Dr W. Ritchie Russell, who was in charge of Michael's treatment, held office as a lecturer in neurology. And long after the glum obligatory proceedings of suing for an insurance settlement were over the driver of the fatal company car, Samuel Swadling, was kept on the Pergamon payroll as a caretaker.

Betty responded to Michael's tragedy and Maxwell's long absences by hurling herself into the effort to ensure Maxwell's chances in Buckingham at the next election. So enthusiastic a manager did she eventually become that many party workers soon learned that it was she rather than Bob who was to be cultivated or feared. Eventually the vigour of her efforts brought a stern admonishment from party headquarters for 'meddling'.

A new Maxwell headquarters was set up separate from the party's own in the Wharf House, a rebuilt eighteenth-century house facing a canal, in the part of Bletchley called Fenny Stratford. Betty started things – an old people's club in Wolverton, a playgroup for working mothers in Bletchley which flourishes still and of which she is justifiably proud. But, most important, she was given charge of mustering the postal vote, a crucial task in a constituency where every vote counted. 'Between 1959 and 1964, the year of the next election, we had one of the finest organizations in the country,' says Barnard, professional pride ringing in his voice. 'We carried out a hundred-per-cent canvass from which we got ninety-seven per cent identification.'

The first of many ugly clashes over people who did not see eye to eye with Maxwell rule in the constituency occurred in February 1961. Ray Bellchambers, who had remained the rallying-point of opposition, was expelled from the General Management Committee for 'conduct unbecoming to a member of the Labour Party'.

One of Labour's best-known figures of that time, brawny Bessie Braddock, the MP for Liverpool Exchange, was sent to Bletchley to hold an inquiry. She did not find Maxwell at fault but she urged the local party to reconsider Bellchambers's dismissal. The NEC upheld his appeal and, against Maxwell's repeated opposition, Bellchambers was reinstated. Nevertheless, Maxwell had little difficulty in being reselected in 1962.

Maxwell had grasped the part of the local political boss as though born to it. Even before he had any real influence in the constituency he flattered future voters with carefully calculated favours and patronage, sometimes finding jobs for the most useful of them in the various businesses he was beginning to acquire. Ray Thomas, a lecturer in economics at the Open University who challenged Maxwell's selection in a later election, says that when he first arrived in Buckingham, 'I kept thinking of Tammany Hall, you know, the political machine that operated in America when there was a huge immigrant population looking for leadership. Maxwell would deal with supplicants personally, get things done by intervening with the right people. It solved some problems, all right. And it won votes. But other people in the Labour Party would say that this did not go to make the people themselves responsible or reactive. It just made them appeal to this one powerful man.'

Maxwell's street smarts, his gift for the vernacular, floored intellectuals like Thomas, who could not understand what he was talking about when he heard Maxwell warn a meeting about the dangers of getting into debt and falling into the clutches of 'the bums'. But the working-class audience knew that in this context 'bums' meant bailiffs – a threat Maxwell himself had faced more recently than most of them with Simpkin Marshall. Thomas had never seen anyone dominate a gathering so completely. 'The emotional tension this man generated was extraordinary. It was very difficult to withstand.'

Maxwell energy and the amount of Maxwell money that had gone into his first campaign impressed the Labour leadership. But he now did something that endeared him to Transport House for years to come. It would have been completely out of character for Maxwell to go on financing his own political career, and he had no intention of doing so. Once he got charge of the constituency party he came up with a plan that was to transform the fortunes not only of Buckingham but also of local parties all over the country. Just as characteristically, it had started off as someone else's idea.

Although the National Fund Raising Foundation has always been associated with Maxwell's name, it was in fact Bryan Barnard who suggested that it be started up in Buckingham. Taking advantage of newly liberalized gambling laws, it was a simple lottery with a first prize of £100. People bought tickets, and the results were published each week in a sheet that was also a Labour newsletter. 'We were getting into thousands of homes each week,' Barnard recalls. 'The draws were held at Bletchley, ping pong balls in drums. Lots of people would come around. The prizes were drawn at two-thirty p.m. and the winning cheques were ready at four-thirty.' In the first year of operation the Buckingham party collected £30,000 and made a profit of £10,000.

Many other constituency parties found gambling as a source of funds distasteful; Labour supporters had a broad puritanical streak. But when they saw the amount of money that could be raised with such ease they usually went along. The simple effectiveness of this competition still lingered in Maxwell's mind years later when he was masterminding *Mirror* bingo. And he was betting that the punters would not win. For Maxwell is an uninhibited gambler. He was already taking advantage of the new gaming laws himself, making late-night appearances in the casinos whose spinning roulette-wheels were transforming London's nightlife.

Bryan Barnard filled in the wait for the next election as secretary to the National Fund Raising Foundation; Maxwell in convincing Hugh Gaitskell and the rest of the party leadership that he was good for more than filling the coffers. He certainly impressed Richard Crossman, whom he had persuaded to let him contribute to some policy-making on science. Crossman's published diary for July 1963 is an absorbing example of the mixed regard in which entrenched Labour figures held Maxwell at the time.

Our old friend Captain Bob Maxwell suddenly rang up from
Bletchley, where he had been rained out of a fete. He asked whether
he could come over on his way to Oxford to discuss my speech.
Maxwell is a strange fellow – a Czech Jew with a perfect knowledge
of Russian, who has an infamous reputation in the publishing world
as the creator of Pergamon Press. Throughout this work on science,
where I regretfully let him set up a group of very powerful scientists,
he has been unfaulted. I can't find him putting a foot wrong. The
paper he and his group have produced is by far the best of the four.
When he came over I ran right throught the speech with him and he
was in fact more helpful, constructive and sensible in his criticism
than I had thought possible.

Influential British socialists were included ever more frequently in the
gatherings at Headington, and so were the journalists an ambitious
politician must cultivate and who were becoming intrigued with this
mysterious *arriviste*. Some of these guests had got wind of Maxwell's new
ambition. No longer satisfied to become a mere Member of Parliament, he
had come, occasionally, to hint of himself as a future Minister of Science,
or Foreign Secretary. Even Prime Minister.

The attraction was mutual and, for Maxwell, contagious. The journalists carried an infection every bit as pervasive as the AIDS virus which was
later to obsess him. Maxwell has never expected people to believe what
he says but he has a self-educated man's faith in the power of the written
word. If he could own a profitable publishing house, why not a newspaper
as well? One that would make him indispensable to the party he was
courting?

Maxwell's first attempts to exert some leverage in national journalism
were made in 1963. One was of modest scale and linked to his growing
presence in Oxford where he had been so bold as to open a bookshop to
challenge the near-monopoly of Blackwell's. *Isis*, the university's political
'rag', had fallen on hard times. Maxwell stepped in with plans to turn it
into a national student publication distributed throughout the growing
network of provincial universities – even at Cambridge.

The experiment spluttered on for several years without really taking
wing. At first a bunch of rather sombre-minded radicals were set up in
an office in the basement of Maxwell's, the bookshop. When Philip
became a student at Balliol and Anne at St Hugh's their father launched
a family tradition by putting them on the staff, his son as business
manager, his daughter in an editorial job. Showing a firm grasp of
Maxwell values, Philip promptly issued an unblinking denial: 'It certainly
isn't nepotism.'

Somewhat more in the mainstream, Maxwell set about seeing if his
new-found role of printer could open a door into the national newspaper
scene. Preferably, in keeping with Maxwell business practice, at someone
else's expense. While the Labour movement could usually depend for
support on the *Daily Mirror*, the party's viewpoint had been unwaveringly
supported since before the First World War by a second left-wing

national, the *Daily Herald*, for the very good reason that the Trade Union Congress owned 49 per cent of the paper's stock. Effectively the *Herald* was an official party publication and, in recent years, a very dull one. Costly, too. By 1961 its owners were paying out millions of pounds to keep it afloat.

The 51 per cent majority share was held by Odhams Press Ltd, the publishers who actually produced the paper. They had just been taken over, in the first of the expansionary waves later to engulf the British newspaper industry, by the group that owned the *Mirror*, headed by Cecil Harmsworth King. The TUC was bought out. The new company planned to convert the *Herald* into a renovated left-of-centre daily, the *Sun*.

These machinations were not universally welcomed. In fact the merger met opposition from all quarters far more vociferous than any newspaper takeover has attracted since. Would-be rescuers surfaced in shoals, Maxwell among the smaller fish. His suggestion of how the *Herald* might be saved was imaginative, though. At the TUC Brighton conference in 1963, by which time Maxwell had set up his first printing ventures, he told George Woodcock, the general secretary, that all the printing work generated by the TUC's 182 affiliated unions should be handed over to him.

The Government – perhaps the Labour government they both hoped was imminent – would then set up a plant in some suitably deprived area to handle these contracts. Maxwell forecast a profit of £750,000 a year which could be used by the TUC to continue to publish the *Herald*.

Long after the *Sun* had been launched Maxwell persisted in trying to get the TUC to let him revive the *Herald*, even spending £6,000 on a survey of former readers. 'I fear very much that the *Sun* is not likely to succeed,' he said. And in that he was right, at least (as the famous fictional press baron that all real ones seem to come to resemble was often said to be) up to a point.

People not acquainted with the principles by which Maxwell operated wondered why he did not start a paper of his own. He could afford to. When Pergamon had been floated as a public company in 1964 after the redistribution of stock Ansbachers, at the outset of a long association, paid £942,000 to Maxwell and the Family Interests for 29 per cent of the shares, which were then put on the market. The offer was over-subscribed nineteen times. That made the holdings still in family hands worth about £3 million. If Maxwell had not been a millionaire before, there was no doubt about it now. Pergamon shares became an immediate 'hot stock'. An Ansbacher director, Bruce Ormrod, explained the appeal of the shares: 'He doesn't run Pergamon like a publishing house. He runs its much more like a factory.'

One of a handful of small businesses in different places Maxwell had bought up was C. A. Layton. Another was Bletchley Printers. He was now a local employer. To emphasize this useful advantage he renamed part of these interests Buckingham Press Ltd and made it a subsidiary of Pergamon.

With Pergamon listed on the Stock Exchange his mastery of the company game moved into a new dimension. There were now three categories of company through which money and book entries could be juggled and which could do business with each other: public Pergamon, the trust-owned American companies and the various private Maxwell companies in Britain, of which the most important were RM & Co. and MSI(DS). In case this should not be sufficiently intricate a second Maxwell Scientific International was set up in Britain by Pergamon, distinguished from the original by the addition of '(1964)'.

The offer document under which Pergamon had gone public in Britain had not even mentioned the existence of Pergamon Press Inc., which at that time was wholly owned, as was MSI Inc., by the Maxwell trusts in Switzerland. But by December 1964 Pergamon had bought it (for Pergamon shares) not from the trusts but from RM & Co. and Mr Martini acting for the trusts. In 1968 PPI, too, went public.

The first transactions of the many upon which the Department of Trade investigation was later to turn a questioning eye took place almost immediately after the Pergamon flotation. On 22 July 1964 a board meeting of MSI(DS), attended only by Maxwell as chairman and the faithful Clark as secretary, recorded an arrangement by which MSI Inc. would deposit with MSI(DS) the £770,000 it had received for the Pergamon shares with which it had parted. The money was to be used, said the carefully formal correspondence between one kind of Family Interest company and another, for payments on behalf to Pergamon – or for anything else that MSI(DS) wished, provided interest of 7 per cent a year was paid. The money was used for investments and became, the inspectors were to recognize, one of 'the two principal sources from which the cash resources of Mr Maxwell and his family are derived'.

The second practice to which the inspectors were to take exception – or, rather, the earliest instance of it – was also applied without delay. Maxwell described the first year of his public chairmanship, to October 1965, as 'the most successful year in the history of Pergamon. Group profits before tax amounted to £848,084, an increase of some £293,000 or 53% over those for 1964.'

The inspectors commented:

What Pergamon's shareholders were not told was that nine days before the end of that financial year, Pergamon invoiced MSI Publishers in sum of $364,857 for books which had not been delivered to MSI Publishers in New York. All these books were from that part of Pergamon's stock which had a written down value of nil. The effect of this invoice was to increase Pergamon's profit in the year to the 31st October 1965 by the sterling equivalent of $364,857 or £130,306.

Four years later the books had still not been delivered. This practice of taking a profit on a transaction that would not be completed until long afterwards, if at all, was to become a hallowed Business Practice.

The object of Pergamon Press acquiring PPI Inc. was to take the job of distributing Pergamon publications in the Western Hemisphere out of the hands of Macmillan. The inspectors questioned whether it had been in the best interests of Pergamon shareholders to end such an advantageous arrangement. They also noticed that one of the results had been greatly advantageous to MSI Inc.

When the Macmillan arrangement was ended Pergamon had already declared as profit the sale of the books that Macmillan had been holding in stock. If the books were now to be taken over by PPI, a wholly owned Pergamon subsidiary, that entry would have to be reversed. To the rescue came the three MSI companies, who bought the stock from Macmillan and sold them on PPI's behalf, thus preserving the profit. In a not untypical example of Maxwellian book-keeping, on 31 October 1965 PPI was owed $471,612 by MSI Inc. and $526,629 by MSI Publishers; PPI owed Pergamon $345,029 and Macmillan $97,106.

Transactions of this kind did not, of course, escape the notice of Pergamon's auditors, Chalmers Impey. On 7 February 1966 they fired a polite warning shot.

In our view it is undesirable that there should be a trading relationship between a public company and another company which, while not a subsidiary, is subject to any measure of common control, so as to leave room for the suggestion that the profits of the public company might be inflated or deflated as a result of such control.

That was equivalent to showing the cat a saucer of cream and ordering it not to drink any. What were companies for?

When the election was held in October 1964, Labour had a new leader, Harold Wilson. Hugh Gaitskell had died in January 1963, suddenly and somewhat mysteriously. He had been due to go to Moscow for a meeting with Khrushchev but fell ill of a virtually unheard-of disease of the organ tissues called disseminated lupus erythematosis.

There were rumours then – recounted in Peter Wright's *Spycatcher* – that this could have been the work of the KGB, who wished to see Gaitskell, a moderate right-wing socialist, replaced by Wilson who had already challenged him for the leadership. Wilson, the conspiracy theory went, would be in some way susceptible to Soviet influence.

Gaitskell's death was a considerable setback to Maxwell's ambition. His efforts had earned the leader's patronage, and his manifest familiarity, through Pergamon, with scientists if not necessarily with science had persuaded Gaitskell to appoint him chairman of a working party set up to study the relationship of industry and technology to government. He could expect a seat on some of the all-party committees that would be formed in the new Parliament, should he be elected.

The new leadership, however, took an acute interest in Maxwell. Buckingham had emerged as an important seat strategically, one of a handful Labour could win and swing the balance. The compliment was returned. Pergamon brought out a flattering pictorial biography of Harold Wilson in time for the election campaign.

Nor were Maxwell's prospects dimmed by a singular prosecution launched by an upright citizen named Edward Cole who found himself tootling along behind Maxwell's Rolls as the candidate was driving it down to the constituency in July. 'He swerved and then bent over to the left,' Mr Cole told the magistrates when his account had been converted into a charge of careless driving. 'For a few seconds I didn't see him at all. Then he got up again and put his left hand to his face.' Maxwell, said Cole, had been shaving with an electric razor. 'If something had been coming the other way there would have been no chance for him to take avoiding action.'

The accusation did not surprise anyone familiar with Maxwell's habits at the wheel. Spurred by his uncontrollable impatience, he has been known to drive, hand on car horn, up the wrong side of a jammed street or ignore one-way signs when they did not take him in the right direction. Even when chauffeured he is an incessant back-seat driver. One driver was made to stop by the roadside and told to find his own way home, while Maxwell drove off by himself.

Maxwell was eventually found guilty of the heinous shaving offence and fined £25. But he contrived three adjournments so that the case was not heard until after polling day. Meanwhile, as well as Betty, Philip, now fifteen, was called in for support. Demure group photographs of the other children were distributed as evidence of the dependants waiting back home while their father did battle. A barrage of Maxwellgrams raked the constituency; every likely voting prospect who had experienced birth, death, marriage – even the loss of a job – got one.

In the village of Castlethorpe, Maxwell personally led a party of skirmishers to squat on the London–Crewe railway line in protest against the closing of their station under a Conservative rationalization. At every stop on the campaign trail Maxwell demonstrated how to turn an enemy attack to advantage. 'I chose this country,' he would say. 'Did you?'

The design staff of Pergamon were ordered to produce a daily news-sheet. When they asked how he wanted it to look their commander, feet on his desk, telephone to each ear, rasped: 'Like the *Daily Mirror*.'

Sir Frank Markham had already made his retreat. The new Conservative candidate, Mrs Elaine Kellett, a widowed barrister, fought bravely, but the well-drilled enemy troops overwhelmed her. Buckingham had the highest turnout of voters in all of Britain: 86.5 per cent. By 1,481 votes, a margin as transparent as a campaign promise, Maxwell became its Member of Parliament, one of Labour's precarious overall majority of four.

Peter Thompson

Souvenir Menu for the Maxwells' fortieth wedding anniversary party held at Headington Hill Hall, 7 June 1985, showing Elisabeth and Robert Maxwell – Betty and Bob – on their wedding day in Paris, 15 March 1945

Inside: the menu covering their courtship and Maxwell's military career

Gala Dinner and Dance
to celebrate

Bob and Betty Maxwell's
40th Wedding Anniversary

Headington Hill Hall, Oxford
Friday 7 June 1985

Dancing to the Music of
Joe Loss's Ambassadors

MENU

Terrine de Homard Normandie
Meursault-Charmes 1979

•••

Selle d'Agneau Cancellier
Panaché de Légumes Versaillais
Nuits Saint Georges 1978

•••

Le Plateau de Fromages Parlo

•••

Bombe Glacée Queen's Royal
Moët et Chandon Brut

•••

Gâteau du 40e Anniversaire

•••

Café et Liqueurs

Lieutenant R Maxwell, M.C., (seventh from the right in the back row) with fellow officers of the 1/5th Battalion of the Queen's Royal Regiment before the crossing of the Rhine

Maxwell during his days in the Occupying Forces in Berlin

Maxwell making his bombs[bid for the *News of the Wo[* October 1 (© The Press Association I[

The victor: Rupert Murdoch (right) shakes hand with Sir William Carr, chairman of the *News of the World*, after their deal in January 1969
(© The Press Association Ltd)

Saul Steinberg, head of Leasco, and Maxwell shake hands on the takeover deal that almost ruined Pergamon
(© The Press Association Ltd)

343.   We regret having to conclude that, notwithstanding Mr. Maxwell's acknowledged abilities and energy, he is not in our opinion a person who can be relied on to exercise proper stewardship of a publicly quoted company.

OWEN STABLE
2 Crown Office Row,
Temple,
London, EC4Y 7HJ.

RONALD LEACH
11 Ironmonger Lane,
London, EC2P 2AR.

The DTI Inspector's conclusion in their first report in June 1971

Maxwell with Tiny Rowland of Lonrho after their breakfast meeting
at Claridge's to discuss the fate of the *Observer*
(© The Press Association Ltd)

DAILY Mirror

£25,000

BINGO

EYES DOWN
ON PAGE 2

Nigeria
expels
British
envoys
over
kidnap

Koo's royal coup

Tories
get
the
jitters

**MAXWELL
BUYS
THE MIRROR**

A pledge from
**ROBERT
MAXWELL**
Publisher,
Mirror Group Newspapers

DAILY Mirror

8, 1984 FORWARD WITH BRITAIN ★★★ 17p(EIRE 23p)

GUARANTEE THAT ONE OF

DO YOU SINCERELY WISH TO BE RICH?
£MILLION GUARANTEED

PLUS THE CHANCE TO
DARE TO WIN
£1,000,000

HOW TO PLAY AND WIN

A Sign this card and keep it in a safe place until we announce soon the great start in the Daily Mirror, Sunday Mirror and Sunday People.

B Then check in the Daily Mirror and/or Sunday Mirror, Sunday People, whether the numbers and the blocks printed in our newspapers match those printed on your card.

My personal numbers are

**CARDHOLDERS
SIGNATURE** ....

| Mirror | Sunday Mirror | People |
| $1 MILLION | ONE MILLION POUNDS | WDW |

| 38 | 26 | 60 | 49 | 53 | 40 | 17 | 59 |

THE Mirror Group is going to
make one of its readers a
certain millionaire. And possibly two.

That is my personal and abso-
lute GUARANTEE.

Today, we are launching a sensational new game—NOT Bingo—which
will find that winner.

EVERYONE over 18 can play WHO
DARES WINS, the "Win a £ Million"
game. £1,000,000 in the top prize in
this instant money game which also
offers prizes of £50,000, £5,000, and
hundreds of £100 prizes.

Unlike other newspapers' games.

PLEASE TURN TO PAGE 5

OUR READERS WILL WIN £1 MILLION

THE WIN A £MILLION GAME

WHO
DARES
WINS

A second £ million CAN be
in the 50-1 lucky-dip chanc

A pledge from Robert Maxwell. . .

Maxwell hits his own headlines when he buys the *Mirror* in July 1984
© The Press Association Ltd)

Bob Edwards: he departed from Mirror Group in October 1985

Tony Miles (left) and Mike Molloy

Right-hand woman: Robert Maxwell with Jean Baddeley at the
London Daily News launch party in February 1987
(© The Press Association Ltd)

Despite the circulation wars
and law suits, Viscount
Rothermere (left),
Rupert Murdoch (centre) and
Robert Maxwell meet at
the Reuters annual lunch,
May 1987
(© Paul Popper Ltd)

The balloon goes up: Maxwell
launches the ill-starred
London Daily News
(© The Press Association Ltd)

Maxwell, with broken ankle, in the *Mirror* helicopter en route
to save the Commonwealth Games
(© Brenard Press Ltd)

Maxwell makes the front cover of *Newsweek*, November 1987. After
Harcourt Brace Jovanovich fought his takeover bid with a near fatal
'poison pill', America is watching him closely
(© Newsweek, Incorporated)

(over) The Flying Tycoon: one of Maxwell's helicopters ready for
take-off in the grounds of Headington
(© Business Magazine)

Maxwell and Elton John enjoy the soccer action as Watford play Oxford
United at the time of Maxwell's £2 million bid for Watford
(© The Press Association Ltd)

FIVE

Mr Maxwell's dealings since he emerged from
the mists of Ruthenia after World War Two haven't always
favoured shareholders.

'BILLY JO' JOVANOVICH

MAXWELL

THE NEXT FIVE YEARS were the most successful and fulfilling of Maxwell's life. But at the end of them he faced ruin. And, throughout much of them, ridicule of a particularly English kind.

The reserve expected of a new arrival at the Palace of Westminster was as alien to him as many of the other hallmarks of British life still seemed to be. David Wood, political correspondent of *The Times*, wrote:

> Maxwell swept into the Commons on Labour's turning tide in 1964 and gave every impression to the old hands that he was mounting a takeover bid for the place. He was loud and thrusting and probably no MP came new to Westminster so little awed by the surroundings.

It was easy to see what Wood meant. Bryan Barnard takes some of the blame for what happened on the very first day of the new Parliament. 'We ran into Dr Horace King, who was Deputy Speaker, in the Central Lobby and I introduced Bob. To my amazement Bob said, "How do I go about making my maiden speech, Dr King?" '

King delivered the standard counsel to new members: be polite and respectful, attend regularly, listen carefully, wait for a familiar subject to be raised. It was not the sort of thing Barnard's errant charge wanted to hear. 'I didn't come here to be a rubber stamp,' said Maxwell. 'I want to make my maiden speech this afternoon.'

King must have had a sense of fun. He strolled away with his hands behind his back, then turned. 'If you're serious, Mr Maxwell . . . I'll assume the chair at approximately four-thirty p.m. Catch my eye.'

It was then 2 p.m. For all his forwardness Maxwell had no speech ready to make. He and Barnard retreated to Fitzroy Square and tried to compose one. 'About eight minutes long and nothing controversial,' Barnard kept muttering.

Driving back to the House in his Rolls, Maxwell rehearsed what they had written. It was well over time. 'He tore the pages up and chucked them into the back seat,' says Barnard. 'He stood up without any notes and made a tremendous speech.'

Struggling for some last hold on the conventions governing a parliamentary début, Barnard had insisted that Maxwell include a tribute to Frank Markham. Maxwell obliged with that, then went on to rehash his election arguments about inadequate roads in his constituency, rail closures and pollution. Then he turned to technology and science, making a profound impression, especially upon Members who knew nothing whatever about either.

He made the first of several Commons attacks on the Concorde supersonic airliner, a project which the new government had promised to review after growing criticism of its cost. There did not appear to be 'any real social or economic demand' for the plane, Maxwell said. Once Concorde was flying, however, he seemed to be hardly ever off it.

Maxwell was marking out a patch of territory he intended to make his own. Soon Harold Wilson, whose own commitment to 'the white heat of technology' was at its peak, did put him on a committee and he was able to help steer the Clean Air Act of 1968 on to the statute-book. It is an achievement of which he is proud to this day and justifiably – although a few other Members did help. With the noxious smoke and fumes that spouted from a million chimneys cut off, the skies of London turned back to a blue not seen since Canaletto painted them and Britain became a far better and healthier place to live. It even had an effect on the process of evolution. A moth whose habitat is the industrial Midlands had developed black spots on its white wings as the grime of the Industrial Revolution multiplied down the years. When the skies began to clear in the wake of the new legislation the spots faded away once more.

After that first opportunity to give the House the benefit of his views there was no stopping Maxwell. Before the end of the month the *Sunday Express*'s acerbic political columnist, 'Crossbencher', wrote:

> *Who is the biggest gasbag in the Commons? Here comes Labour's newest backbench millionaire – publisher Robert Maxwell. This handsome, debonair 41-year-old made the first maiden speech of the new Parliament. And he has scarcely sat down since. Questions to Ministers and points of order cascade from his lips. Seldom a speech is made by anyone else without Captain Maxwell popping in to interrupt. After only four weeks in Parliament already he is becoming one of its greatest bores.*

But, as Maxwell was later to become fond of suggesting about so many of his accomplishments, they had not seen – or heard – anything yet. His disdain for the traditions of the House was refreshing. The year was ending in a welter of dramatic events abroad. In Moscow the hope of unpaid British authors, Nikita Khrushchev, had been deposed. In Peking the Chinese had announced the testing of their first atomic bomb, something that, had it been known about earlier, might have given the election to the deterrent-promoting Conservatives. The foreign affairs debate set down for 16 December was to be the first big day of the Labour-dominated Commons, the new Prime Minister's moment to unfold the policies that Britain, as a socialist major power, intended to pursue. Most important, Harold Wilson was to announce that Alexei Kosygin, the new Soviet premier, was to visit Britain in the New Year.

The House was packed, all the galleries filled with dignitaries and diplomats, the world's press. On the order paper were the usual preliminaries, a few items of routine business to be nodded through before the main event could begin, one of them the Winter Supplementary Estimates. But when a clerk read out the heading of this fiscal formality Maxwell reared ponderously to his feet.

This monstrous solecism united the House in indignation. Labour, Liberal and Conservative Members all shouted to Maxwell to sit down so that they could hear what Harold Wilson had to say. They had a better chance of trying to stop Big Ben overhead from striking. Maxwell spoke for nineteen long minutes, deaf to the chorus of protest. This time it was the House that should not allow itself to be used as a rubber stamp. His target was the Foreign Office, on which his Berlin days, he plainly believed, had made him an expert. 'I am extremely disturbed that it is not implementing speedily or energetically enough recommendations relating to the need for our diplomats to do a great deal more to promote British exports,' he said. Meaning books. No one among Maxwell's reluctant listeners was angrier than Wilson himself. The delay meant that his speech missed the main editions of the evening papers.

When Winston Churchill died in 1965, Maxwell behaved in much the same way. The leaders of the three parties were ready with their ritual tributes. But Maxwell decided that the carefully orchestrated occasion would not be complete without a final few words from the Member for Buckingham. 'I could see the Members on either side of him trying to pull him back down into his seat,' remembers political journalist Terry Lancaster.

Maxwell's readiness to argue endlessly over minuscule details also tried the patience of his parliamentary colleagues. He detected an error in the reporting of a debate. The previous Conservative Minister for War seemed to have used the word 'detached' rather than 'attached' in referring to the number of men in an infantry battalion – something Maxwell certainly knew about. It turned out to be a shorthand-writer's error, but Maxwell turned it into a squabble that lasted for three tedious days.

However, back in his constituency Maxwell was a far more effective MP than he seemed to be in Westminster. Labour's perilously small majority meant that there would have to be another election before very long, and he plugged away energetically at all the local causes: housing, hospitals, inadequate rail and bus services, billing himself as the Man Who Gets Things Done and threatening to sue the Transport Minister, Barbara Castle, who also happened to be the Labour Party's chairman.

Get things done Maxwell did when it came to bullying the local councils, getting a roof mended, fixing someone up with a job. 'He was a first-class constituency MP,' says Barnard. 'It annoyed the Tories that he could play the squire better than anyone they had.'

During a Labour Party meeting in Bletchley the steward of the local Conservative Club – who must have had a highly developed sense of public relations himself – burst in, begging for assistance. He had been sacked and was being evicted from the flat that went with the job. Maxwell immediately stormed around to the club, challenged the

embarrassed Tories – and made sure the national newspapers heard all
about this head-on confrontation amid the grass roots in defence of the
underprivileged. Especially since the steward himself was a member of
the Conservative Party.

'You have to understand', said one of the Buckingham officials, 'that Mr
Maxwell needs to be needed.'

Maxwell could see the need wherever he looked, either as politician or
as publisher. One of the controversial censorship cases of the day was
over the importation into Britain of *Last Exit to Brooklyn* by Hubert Selby.
In his capacity as a distinguished publisher he appeared as a witness for
the prosecution. The book, he said, was 'brutal and filthy'. No, he said, he
had not read James Joyce's *Ulysses*.

Betty played her part just as assiduously. Labour's great weakness had
been analysed as its lack of appeal to women voters, and she and the fast
growing-up family were always ready to be trundled forward. At
Christmas-time sackfuls of cards went out, pictures of the Captain – for he
now wished to be called by his old rank once more – plastered all over
them.

Maxwell's skill at attracting attention
was as highly developed as his commercial instincts. But despite his
indefatigable pursuit of publicity he had difficulty in getting others to see
him quite as he saw himself. Particularly as a master of multimedia, for
instance – a concept that was, in fact, beyond the grasp of many Britons in
the 1960s. A lot of them were still getting used to colour television.

The earliest film production in which he became involved was a worthy
but uninspired version of an opera, Mozart's *Don Giovanni*, staged at the
1954 Salzburg Festival. In 1957 the first visit to Covent Garden by the
Bolshoi Ballet inspired another film venture which demonstrated Maxwell's capacity for acting on impulse. Before dawn of the morning after
the performance Maxwell had made his plans. As soon as his Moscow
contacts were in their office he was on the phone to them.

Astonishingly, he was given permission to film this historic event if it
could be done without disturbing the Bolshoi's schedule, which included
a Command Performance. The whirl of activity into which he threw
himself, for a distinctly disappointing result, was a vivid example of
Maxwell's tendency to get an idea acted upon before taking time to think
about it properly. Startled old friends from his Soho days helped drum up
a film crew, and the Russian dancers, not daring to argue with anyone
whose wishes seemed to mean so much back home, were made to leap
and caper through most of the following night while the conductor waved
his baton to taped music. Maxwell had not included the orchestra in his
budget.

Another ballet he played a part in filming in 1968, *Swan Lake* with
Rudolf Nureyev and Margot Fonteyn, was vastly superior. But the Bolshoi
was a first – of a kind. So was a television cartoon series called 'Dodo the
Kid from Outer Space' which Maxwell also co-produced. So were his

efforts to back playwright Arnold Wesker in a plan to turn the Round House, a former British Rail engine shed in North London, into an arts centre. So was the appeal to Americans that he launched on one of his trips to contribute to the preservation of a house in London where, in the name of science, Benjamin Franklin had once electrocuted a duck.

That most of these relentlessly publicized adventures – especially those connected, roughly speaking, with the arts – came to little set a certain tone in the reporting of Maxwell's non-stop activities. He rejected any suggestion that he cared whether he was acceptable to British polite society or not and, when the stained-glass window at Headington was unveiled (later than expected, since the Israeli artist Nehemya Azaz accidentally dropped a hammer through his first attempt), that the idea of a Samson doing away with the gates might be in some way symbolic. 'I have no inferiority complex,' Maxwell told his friend William Davis, another literary émigré who then worked for the *Evening Standard* and is now head of Maxwell's embryonic magazine division. 'In any case the fact that the Establishment may look down on you acts as a spur to success.'

Even his next setback was converted into useful publicity. Maxwell had been persuaded by a fellow-MP, John Binns, to make a fourth in a syndicate investing £200,000 in the Craven Insurance Company which sold policies mainly to motorists, especially London cabbies. No sooner had the four put their money in than the firm began to exhibit unhealthy symptoms. Maxwell quickly took over as chairman and called for Price Waterhouse to go through the books. Liquidation was the only answer. 'My worst disaster yet,' said Maxwell, although the shareholders and creditors of Simpkin Marshall might not have agreed. It is probably the only occasion on which he has been sold an outright pup. Because of the cabbies, and because a number of other people were also involved, he got a sympathetic press; and £101,000 of the loss went down in the books of MSI(DS).

When it came to attracting attention to his political activities Maxwell's methods became uncompromisingly direct. Although far less influential than the *Daily Mirror* itself, the *Mirror*'s Sunday sisters, the *Sunday Mirror* and the *People*, also generally offered Labour a sympathetic portrayal. Logan Gourlay, then a *People* columnist, still laughs about the proposition the new Member for Buckingham made to him. 'If I would mention him every week, said Maxwell, he would double what I earned. I said, jokingly, that he had a lot of companies overseas. If he would pay me a quarter of a million through one of those it was a deal.'

Private Eye, later to become the target of the only libel trial in which Maxwell has ever succeeded – as opposed to suits in which the respondents have admitted defeat and settled – was at the height of its viperish power. Gourlay told his story at one of the weekly lunches at which the scurrilous magazine's informants gathered, and it was printed. 'Maxwell phoned me and said that I must deny it. I could hardly do that, I said. I had told the story myself.' Maxwell's response, says Gourlay, was: 'Then, I'll say that if you had asked for half a million I would have known you were serious and I would have given it to you.'

The editor of the *People* in 1966 was Bob Edwards, a friend of Maxwell in and out of politics. He asked Maxwell to write an article about how a millionaire would run the Labour Party and, since the final copy needed attention, handed it to Terry Lancaster, his political editor, to be cut and polished. Maxwell was delighted when Lancaster showed him the result. He pulled out his cheque-book and asked: 'How much?'

'No, no, Bob,' said Lancaster. 'We pay you.'

The overseas companies to which Gourlay had referred now included, in addition to the Pergamon operations in America, recent acquisitions that Maxwell believed would take Pergamon to a new level of profitability. Pergamon's first year as a public company had rewarded the shareholders' faith in the Knowledge Market. Pre-tax profits of £848,084 were 53 per cent ahead of 1965, and a dividend of 70 per cent was being paid. In 1966, Pergamon had carried off the Queen's Award for Industry for selling 80 per cent of its products abroad – in 123 countries to be exact. In addition the shareholders were given the chance to enjoy the great new opportunity their chairman's vision had provided: the purchase of George Newnes subscription book business for £1 million, including its subsidiary companies in Australia and New Zealand and – the true prize – rights to the fifteen-volume treasure-house of knowledge, *Chambers's Encyclopaedia*. Three heady years were to pass before it became evident that this coup was to be the ruin of them. Although not of Maxwell.

In the days immediately before and after the Second World War, thousands and thousands of modest British homes held an incomplete set of *Chambers*. For one reason or another, usually Depression poverty, householders had stopped paying the instalments which kept the volumes coming. Many of them rued the day they had answered the door to the salesman's knock. When they failed to keep up the payments the company pursued them doggedly through the courts, squeezing what few shillings it could out of people who had enough difficulty feeding themselves. The unscrupulous methods of encyclopaedia-sellers provided an evergreen exposure story for the popular newspapers, and when at the beginning of the 1960s the Mirror Group acquired Odhams and its subsidiary, George Newnes, it was disconcerted to find it had also become the owner of a company whose selling methods had often come under attack in its own titles.

Cecil King, the group's chairman, gave Newnes a patrician brush-off. The subscription book business, he was to tell the Department of Trade inspectors, could only be run profitably 'by methods that could not be countenanced in private or defended in public. In the case of *Chambers*, for instance, at any one time there were large numbers of cases outstanding in the county courts, forcing people to pay their instalments on very expensive books they did not want.'

King's scruples, however, did not stop him selling Newnes to Pergamon (strictly, to Buckingham Press) in 1966 for a neat £1 million. Only months later the fifteen-volume fourth edition of *Chambers* was launched, dedicated to the Queen. Maxwell placed newspaper advertisements proclaiming: 'I'd like to give every child in this country the freedom to learn from the world's greatest storehouse of knowledge.' Another storehouse that came with the deal was a venerable children's encyclopaedia, *Pictorial Knowledge*, soon to be retitled *Maxwell's Pictorial Knowledge*.

Maxwell had been almost indecently keen to get into the 'subscription book' business. Since the late 1950s RM & Co. had been agents for *Encyclopaedia Britannica* outside the United States and the United Kingdom. Another company that had been set up in France, with Betty on its board at one time, Librairie des Science Techniques Françaises et Etrangères, had been given the French agency. He had seen how profitable this kind of selling could be.

Others felt differently. Chalmers Impey (as they now were) the accountants who reported on Newnes, were discouraging. The obvious drawbacks were the rate at which bad debts could pile up and the difficulty of keeping the door-to-door salesmen under control. The salesmen's commission usually became due when the sale was made, so the eventual ability of the encyclopaedia-buyers to keep up the instalments was of secondary interest to them. Ansbachers, too, whose advice Maxwell was supposed to be heeding, warned him against Newnes. But, as Bruce Ormrod told the inspectors: 'We were more or less told that Maxwell was the organ grinder, we were just the monkeys and that he knew what he was doing.'

No one else's view mattered. Maxwell alone signed the Newnes deal. The inspectors noted in their report:

> There is no record in the minutes of Pergamon and Buckingham of either board having formally approved the acquisition in principle or the terms of purchase, nor do they record that Mr Maxwell had been given authority to enter into the agreement on behalf of Pergamon or Buckingham.

In any case, the inspectors observed, apart from Kerman the solicitor and the ubiquitous Clark, the directors of Pergamon were really just managers who had been given a seat on the board. Maxwell was not interested in the way anyone, even the courts that stood behind the Companies Act, thought he should run things. Public company Pergamon might be, but in essence it still belonged to him. And to the Family Interests. Which, in every sense but the strictly legal, belonged to him, too. This did not mean that Maxwell was unwilling to see Pergamon pass out of his hands if the price was right. It was soon to become evident that he wanted nothing more. But first – since he had now discovered, to his delight, that companies were as likely to be bartered as bought – he had to see what he could make the company appear to be worth. No, first the obligatory name-change. Buckingham became known as Pergamon Subscription Books Division.

In his first year in the encyclopaedia business it seemed as though Maxwell intended to sell most of the sets himself. He worked his way through airline timetables as though trying to set a record for being in the most places in the shortest possible time but, aided by his capacity to work on the wing as well as on the run, still managed to get re-elected in the 1966 election that increased the Labour majority to a more comfortable ninety-seven and be in the House for much of its important business.

On 22 February 1967 he returned from the first of the three world tours he was to make in the next couple of years and called an expertly stage-managed press conference at the Dorchester, public relations wheedlers pressing liquor and handouts on reporters, an imposing podium labelled 'Robert Maxwell'. It was Maxwell as super salesman and statesman. He had covered 70,000 miles, he announced, visiting Hong Kong, Japan, Australia, Mexico, the United States, Barbados and Canada. He dropped a few morsels of gossip from Washington, discoursed on the Japanese economic miracle and analysed the leaching of Chinese communist funds into Hong Kong. Then he told his audience why he had asked them there. On this momentous trip he had personally sold 7,000 sets of *Chambers*, worth £1 million, a dramatic singlehanded contribution to Britain's foreign-currency balances. In addition he had firm orders for another £1.5 million worth and for a similar amount of Pergamon products. A list was handed around: 1,500 sets in the United States; a similar number in Japan; 500 in India. . . . By 20 May he reported another 2,000 sets of *Chambers* sold in Britain.

The figures that Maxwell read out at the conference had actually been compiled by someone who had just begun to work with him, Philip Harris, recently appointed vice-chairman of Buckingham. As Maxwell had cabled back these orders from every stop on his itinerary Harris became more and more excited. At this rate they would be in danger of running out of stock. Since reprinting *Chambers* would take about twelve months he decided to put the preliminary work in hand. The moment Maxwell was back the reprint plans were cancelled.

Yet another storehouse of knowledge was being peddled door to door around the world, the *New Caxton Encyclopaedia*, and was selling better than *Chambers*, its only serious competitor. Its salesmen had an even worse reputation. 'Steel caps on their shoes,' said Ormrod. Just the kind of men Maxwell wanted. He wanted their firm, too. He planned a full-scale frontal attack on Caxton Publishing Company Ltd, whose chairman was Hedley Le Bas, grandson of its founder.

Maxwell knew a great deal about Caxton's affairs, particularly in South Africa where about 25 per cent of its business was done. A former secretary of Caxton, Leonard Shilling, now worked for Buckingham – or, rather, for yet another subsidiary Maxwell had created to process the encyclopaedia trade's bad debts, Pergamon Reports and Surveys. The inspectors did not believe Shilling when he told them he had never disclosed the details of Caxton's South African business to Maxwell. They did believe him, however, when they asked him to describe his new boss's character.

> *He is tough: hard. Whatever he wanted he went after – a very difficult man to work for, inclined to run everything under his own aegis. It*

was very difficult to make a decision at any time without seeing him.
He was a very difficult man. One never knew quite what was behind
some of the decisions he made and he never said.

Wherever Maxwell got his information from, it was, according to Philip
Harris, that Caxton suffered from

a rather precarious financing arrangement in South Africa whereby,
as I recall, if their sales fell below a certain level for a period of time
guarantees fell due in London, which they would not be able to meet,
and this would put the final squeeze on them, which would enable
Maxwell to buy them for a song.

The Caxton franchise-holder in South Africa came to London to see
Maxwell. Harris and Shilling flew out to sign up the whole Caxton sales
and office force for Buckingham.

Then it was Mr Le Bas's turn. In March 1967, Maxwell made an offer for
Caxton shares well below what they might have been worth had the
South African operation still been intact. Le Bas turned to the British
Printing Corporation, with whom Caxton had arrangements for printing,
confident that they would rescue him. But Maxwell had got there first.
BPC was a company – a collection of printing and publishing companies,
really – in which he had long taken an interest. He liked the idea of a
British Printing Corporation. Besides, he saw that the whole organization
might be got cheaply.

BPC could not fail to be impressed by the success Pergamon appeared
to be having with *Chambers*. The subscription book division was claiming
a profit of £757,000 for the first nineteen months of its operation. BPC
agreed to join in a partnership to buy out Caxton and to sell both encyclopaedias and various other subscription books.

The new company into which Caxton was turned, in July 1967, was
called the International Learning Systems Corporation. Maxwell became
its chairman and chief executive, Le Bas managing director. The Consumer Council was called upon to endorse the Robert Maxwell Code of
Conduct for Direct Sellers. 'The success we have had in selling *Chambers*
under this code shows there is no need for foot-in-the-door methods,'
proclaimed the Code's sponsor.

Maxwell let BPC know that he was interested in a much closer relationship, but for the moment the ILSC deal was enough for them. Determined
to expand in some direction, he turned his attentions to Butterworth, his
original springboard.

Pergamon were already beginning to experiment with electronic data
retrieval, and the endless forms and precedents lawyers require – most of
which were published by Butterworth – were perfectly suited to such a
service. Infoline, to be developed first by Thomson the trade magazine
publisher and the Department of Trade, would work in much the same
way. Butterworth had suffered some reverses in its American operations

and looked shaky. But 52 per cent of its shares were controlled by the man who was now its chairman, a waspish and energetic solicitor, Mr Richard Millet, one of the few people in London who seemed prepared to act on the doubts he had about Maxwell's methods. Millet sent a cable to the Standard Literature Company of Calcutta, to which Maxwell claimed to have sold 500 sets of *Chambers*, asking for confirmation of the order. The reply was: 'No order placed.' Scornfully, Millet refused to recommend 'Pergamon paper' to his shareholders, and Maxwell's boarding attempt was repelled there, too.

When ILSC was being investigated endless hours were spent trying to establish just how many sets of *Chambers* Maxwell actually did sell abroad as the best-known encyclopaedia salesman in the House of Commons. Chaotic book-keeping made an accurate figure unattainable, although one director worked it out at fewer than 700 sets. Some 1,600 had also been sold in Britain. The inspectors decided that the 1,500 supposed to have been placed in the United States were actually 1,400 that had been sold to MSI Inc. and that those sets had been invoiced, although not actually delivered, before Maxwell left on his first sales trip. The same went for another 500 which had been invoiced to Libraire des Science Techniques Françaises et Etrangères in Paris. These were never delivered, the invoice being subsequently reversed. Maxwell could never have sold anything like 7,000 sets 'if the normal meaning of the word "sold" is applied'.

But the inspectors had no doubt about the purpose of the premature invoicing. It was intended to get the sale of the sets on to the books of Pergamon to boost the profits at a time Maxwell was anxious to impress BPC.

> *The history of Pergamon Subscription Books Division is a history of the overstatement of its normal trading profits and of exaggerated claims of the sales of Chambers's Encyclopedia. Both are in our view serious matters because both must have had a material effect on the value of Pergamon's share in the stock market: both must have had far reaching effects on BPC and its shareholders and both must have played a significant part in bringing the shareholders of Pergamon to their present unenviable plight.*

But the ploy had worked at the time, and Maxwell was to have no hesitation in using it again. At that moment in 1967, however, it looked as though he had been dead right in believing that subscription books were the way to the future. Or at least to the next step: profits that would either make Pergamon an impressive partner for any important acquisition he might try to bring off or irresistible bait for any well-heeled predator interested in taking the company over. Pergamon shareholders were told they had an investment of £1 million in ILSC; the forecast profits from it for 1968 were a healthy £100,000. For the group as a whole they were £2.5 million.

Maxwell had already tried to interest other people who made a living from print in participating in ILSC. He wanted partners for the more distant territories in which the storehouses of knowledge were being peddled. In Sydney he had got in touch with an up-and-coming young publisher by the name of Rupert Murdoch. Of all the doors in which he might have stuck a foot during his restless travels he could hardly have picked a worse one. Rupert Murdoch has caused Maxwell more chagrin and frustration than anyone else he has ever come up against, and taking him for a colonial soft touch has a lot to do with it.

Twenty years later the rivalry between these two media empire-builders, a feud that is both financial and personal, had permeated three continents, decided the ownership of five national newspapers in Britain and shaped the course of most of Maxwell's ambitions. Everywhere Murdoch led in the later phase of his carefully calculated expansion Maxwell has followed, or tried to, move by move, although usually without the dazzling sense of timing Murdoch invariably displays. It was Murdoch's apocalyptic confrontation with the Fleet Street print unions in 1986-7 – based on the Tory anti-picketing laws – that allowed Maxwell, along with every other newspaper publisher, to reduce ludicrous overmanning and operate profitably once again. For all that he has been ready to take on unions himself, as he was to show when he finally got his hands on BPC, Maxwell could never have backed such a brutal confrontation and maintained any connection with the Labour Party, let alone still claimed to be a socialist.

The rivals are on speaking terms now; for a long time they were not. 'Rupert won't even look at me,' Maxwell mused after a dinner at the Grosvenor House Hotel in 1984. 'I don't know why he hates me.'

Murdoch does not hide his views. Sitting back comfortably in his Manhattan stronghold at 210 South Street beside the East River, he speaks frankly about his old adversary. 'He almost physically loves the feel of power. He's a business brigand, but both all the good and bad things that means.'

Murdoch has a characteristic gesture of splaying his hands with opposing fingertips together and pressing until his knuckles click. 'I don't bear him any malice.' Click. 'There was for a time undoubtedly some sort of paranoia about me. Now, I doubt it.'

Nobody who worked for Maxwell doubted it. 'He has a fixation about Rupert,' say more than one of the executives who have worked for both men. It is in the nature of publishing that talent is hired back and forth between the two camps. Maxwell grills the defectors from News International in true Mr Nice fashion. They, conscious that they may be back with Murdoch any day, are apt to feed him misleading titbits. Lord Rothermere, an interested and informed spectator since the match first began, has no doubts, either. 'Rupert has always got the better of Bob, and I'm sure it rankles deeply. Rupert is his real target.'

Maxwell's attempt in 1968 to buy the *News of the World*, which Murdoch frustrated to achieve his own first foothold in Fleet Street, is usually regarded as the outset of hostilities. Rather, it was, as a *News of the World* headline-writer might have it, Rupert's Revenge.

The two men had met twice since their first encounter in Sydney when Maxwell, the globe-circling encyclopaedia salesman, first aroused Murdoch's resentment by beating him at poker. Maxwell remembers his arrival in Sydney that time in terms of the first-class standard of the Australian airline. 'I asked for a brandy and cigar after dinner,' he said. 'I lit the cigar and tasted the brandy. Then I dropped the cigar into the glass.' A stewardess, accustomed to mere Australian varieties of uncouthness, displayed her puzzlement. 'They deserve each other,' Maxwell told her, laughing as he recalled the moment.

Maxwell's status as an MP and his angloid posturing made Australians take notice. He was anything but a 'reffo', as they were wont to call their own European immigrants. But neither was Murdoch, for all his whipcrack accent and shirt-sleeved ways, unaccustomed to first-class standards himself. He was the son of a celebrated First World War correspondent turned newspaper boss; he had been to Oxford and worked as a sub-editor on the *Daily Express*. At thirty-six he had already pulled off several coups which had parlayed the one newspaper his father had left him in Adelaide into a nationwide group which was now threatening the market leaders. He went regularly to London and was on first-name terms with most of the Fleet Street proprietors, something Maxwell could not claim at the time.

'He sought me out to invite me to be a partner in his business,' Murdoch relates. 'He was proposing to have a separate company for Australia and South-East Asia for all Pergamon's publishing business. He offered me a fifty-per-cent interest in it.'

Murdoch took Maxwell home to dinner. They played cards. Maxwell expanded on his plans for ILSC and the prospects for *Chambers*. 'We had quite long talks in Sydney, once in Los Angeles and once in London. I quickly discovered that he was proposing to put a value of a couple of million dollars on the encyclopaedias, just the ones to be consigned to Australia. I found out in London that IPC had written them off their books years ago as being of no value.'

American flags, testament to the citizenship Murdoch adopted in order to become a television power in the United States, flapped outside in the brisk autumn breeze as Murdoch recalled the discovery. He looked past them down the East River to the Brooklyn Bridge, the furrows in his tall forehead deepening. 'I was probably naïve to let it pass me even once. I simply realized that the deal was one-sided and I was pretty lucky to find out. I don't mean Maxwell was crooked about it. But he probably would have made a very good profit.'

Among the many wonders of the British newspaper industry the *News of the World*, controlled by the Carr family since 1891, was unequalled. It was, at that time, a broadsheet selling, in 1968, 6 million copies every Sunday. It had once sold 8 million.

The winning editorial formula was a kind of music-hall mix of patriotism, prurience and piety.

Yet another National Institution among newspapers, this valuable property had become vulnerable because a singular member of the family, remote from its management, Professor Derek Jackson, decided to sell his 25 per cent legacy in the company. Jackson, who now lived in Switzerland, was worth a story in the *News of the World* himself. He was much more colourful than the errant vicars, sex maniacs and fallen débutantes who crowded its pages beneath a figleaf of more responsible journalism. Derek Ainslie Jackson, OBE, DFC, was a war hero, a wing commander and Chevalier de Légion d'Honneur. He was a scientist, the inventor of the tinfoil 'chaff' scattered by RAF bombers to confuse enemy radar. He had had six wives, the first of whom was Pamela Mitford, the fifth Barbara Skelton, novelist and playmate of, among others, King Farouk and George Weidenfeld.

His cousin Sir William Carr, chairman of the *News of the World* for sixteen years, was appalled at such treachery but eventually offered Jackson 28s (£1.40p) a share, a fraction above the market price. Jackson declined and placed his holding with N. M. Rothschilds to sell to the highest bidder on the open market. Maxwell's grapevine picked up the scent when Rothschilds contacted Robert Fleming, a merchant bank which also did business with Pergamon. Here was yet another chance to apply the leverage that the soaring value of Pergamon shares provided, as well as unlocking the door to Fleet Street. On 16 October 1968, Maxwell offered Jackson and the other shareholders 37s 6d (£1.88) a share – in 'Pergamon paper' – if he gained control: a bid worth £26 million.

It was essential that Pergamon shares, which had been doing extraordinarily well on the stock market, were not allowed to cool off during this critical period and thus become less appealing to *News of the World* shareholders. To see that their price did not fall Maxwell asked Flemings to buy some 200,000 against his guarantee that he would buy them back at the price they paid, a perfectly legitimate device, duly declared according to Stock Exchange rules. Other measures he took to keep both price and profits high were eventually to attract the attention of the inspectors.

October 16th was also the day Soviet Premier Kosygin flew into Prague to sign a treaty authorizing the 'temporary stay' of Russia's invading troops in his homeland. Maxwell, who had flown back from holiday in Yugoslavia for the Commons debate on the Czech crisis, described the Soviet forces dismantling the liberalized Czech state as 'Russian barbarians'.

Maxwell's own one-man assault on the *News of the World* redoubt in Bouverie Street, just off Fleet Street, was made with all the vigour that his admirers now expected of him. It met with stiff-upper-lip resistance. Sir William called his bid 'impudent', the board called it 'completely unacceptable' and shareholders were advised to hold on to their shares in the Stock Exchange scramble that was bound to follow. Maxwell was evasive about his motives: 'I am a businessman, an industrial manager, not a Fleet

Street proprietor.' His main aim, he said, was to fit the *News of the World*'s spare press capacity and the Liverpool gravure plant of Eric Bemrose, a subsidiary, into a European Publishing Corporation he now wanted to assemble since he had got nowhere with the British one.

Betty was less than keen on the paper. 'I have never read the *News of the World* until last Sunday,' she told writer Jillian Robertson. 'I had heard it was a scandal sheet with nude pictures and I like serious reading. Personally, it is not a newspaper I would like in the house with young children and young girls.'

Maxwell walked in on the interview, and Betty confessed: 'Darling, I hope you won't be cross but I said I have never read the *News of the World*.' Whether Maxwell himself had read it or not, he declared that he was willing to give up his Commons seat to run it.

The London bureau of Murdoch's newspapers was only a few steps from the Red Lion pub in Red Lion Court, just off Fleet Street. The publican had thoughtfully installed a Press Association teleprinter in the bar so that his clientele need not feel out of touch.

The deputy bureau chief, Frank O'Neill, a tall rangy figure who had once ridden a horse across Australia from north to south, had been instructed to stay on Maxwell's trail. After spurning the offer to get into harness with ILSC the Australian group had been looking into the sales methods the encyclopaedia salesmen were using out there. When the PA machine hammered out word of the *News of the World* bid he swallowed his beer and loped back to his office to contact Sydney.

'I'd never thought of taking over the *News of the World*,' said Murdoch. 'I didn't know much about it. But when I saw the takeover bid, knowing Bob, I instantly knew there was a place here for a white knight.' Through his British financial adviser, Lord Catto of Morgan Grenfell, Murdoch offered a partnership to Carr. Carr, a sick but determined man, responded favourably. Anyone, it seemed, was preferable to Maxwell.

Murdoch slipped into London unnoticed on Sunday, 20 October, while Fleet Street was occupied with a merger worth rather more than he or Maxwell had in mind: the marriage of Jacqueline Kennedy to Aristotle Onassis on the Greek island of Skorpios. Catto had contacted him in Australia to warn that a new bid from Maxwell was imminent. Murdoch was plucked from the racecourse in Melbourne where he had gone to watch the Caulfield Cup. He missed the race but spent much of the thirty-hour flight to London on a Boeing 707 working out takeover odds.

Catto was at Heathrow with the latest: Jackson was publicly urging Sir William to accept Maxwell's offer, but a leading article in that day's *News of the World* showed how the Carr family felt. Editor Stafford Somerfield, describing his newspaper as 'as British as roast beef and Yorkshire pudding', wrote: 'I believe Mr Maxwell is interested in power and money. There is nothing wrong with that but it is not everything. This is a British newspaper, run by British people. Let's keep it that way.' It was just as bigoted in its way as the slogans on the Buckinghamshire walls.

The deal Murdoch was proposing to prevent Maxwell from getting the 50 per cent minimum stake he was after meant that the company would soon be about as British as kangaroo-tail soup. For 35 per cent of the *News of the World* voting equity, Murdoch was offering *Truth*, his Melbourne-based weekly specializing in sex and sport, *New Idea*, a women's magazine, *Best Bets*, a slick racing guide, and local newspapers in Victoria and Queensland including the *Dandenong Journal*, the *Frankston and Peninsula News* and the *Surfers Paradise Mirror*. 'Small bait to catch a big whale,' Maxwell called the package contemptuously. As it happened, while Murdoch was booking into the Savoy, his wife Anna back in Sydney was telling callers: 'He's gone fishing.'

This was the biggest scheme Murdoch had yet embarked on. He was far from his own turf and distinctly edgy. He changed his hotel room because he feared it might be bugged. 'I was certainly being followed. No doubt they were trying to keep track on our movements – which banks we were going to and things like that.'

Anyone following Murdoch's tracks would have found that he was moving fast and flying high. He dined with members of the Carr family, breakfasted with Sir William and visited Lord Thomson, Vere Harmsworth – as the present Lord Rothermere then was – and Hugh Cudlipp the MGN editorial director, men who between them controlled much of Fleet Street. On 24 October, Hambros, acting for the *News of the World* this time, announced that the board 'and their associates' had gained control of the voting rights.

Even in this opening skirmish so much heat was generated that the Stock Exchange suspended trading in *News of the World* shares. Maxwell dispatched a party of marauders to Australia to reconnoitre the enemy base. He sued News International in the Australian courts for £1 million over the encyclopaedia exposés. He approached Leonard Goldenson, president of the American Broadcasting Corporation of New York, about 625,000 shares his company held in News Limited. Goldenson turned him down. Sir Frank Packer, last of the maniacal gang of newspaper barons known as the Wild Men of Sydney and a Murdoch rival, and Lord Thomson were sought in vain as allies. 'He was thrashing about to see if he could take over our company,' said Murdoch. 'There was never any question of it.'

Maxwell raised his bid. His second and final offer of £34 million, or 50s (£2.50) a share, set off a frantic scramble for *News of the World* shares. 'We will not give up,' said Maxwell. 'This is a disgraceful affair.' Murdoch, with whom he had been so keen to join forces in the Knowledge Market, was now 'a moth-eaten, empty-pouched kangaroo whose tactics might go down well in Australia but shareholders here will condemn them in no uncertain terms'.

'He said a lot of pretty rough things,' said Murdoch. 'He said we were trying to steal it for nothing. But right up to halfway he was only offering shares in Pergamon. We went out and worked very hard to show that Pergamon was worthless: the result of a lot of creative accounting.'

Who was to be seen as the villain of the noisy piece and who its hero varied from day to day. Maxwell was better at manipulating the financial press, which, for the most part, lined up behind him. 'They saw him as Modern Man, Modern Management, Modern Britain,' said Murdoch. 'But the banks, of course, had had experience of Bob over Simpkin Marshall and there was a lot of score-settling going on – no doubt about that.'

Farce, as ever, was never far off. Maxwell inspired three *News of the World* pensioners to seek a High Court injunction ordering pension fund trustees to vote against the Murdoch deal. The pensioners argued that it was their 'clear duty' to accept the better financial bid – the Pergamon bid. Refusing the order, the judge described the litigants as pawns in Pergamon's game.

The takeover panel of the Stock Exchange started an ineffectual inquiry to determine whether its code of conduct had been broken. In a speech at the Guildhall, Harold Wilson threatened action unless the City cleaned up its act.

The adversaries finally came face to face at a shareholders' meeting at the Connaught Rooms on a cold Thursday, 2 January 1969. Maxwell made an odd impression, not like roast beef at all. He wore an astrakhan cap as though he had just flown in from everyone-knew-where.

'He came over and the TV cameras were going,' said Murdoch. 'He made some fairly loud remarks – I mean loud enough to be heard.'

Carr, now chronically ill, addressed the meeting of 500, some of them loyal employees turned into shareholders by being issued with shares for the day. 'Pergamon has no experience of newspapers and the unions regard their proposals with dismay,' he said. 'We have no faith in Pergamon shares. Mr Murdoch has enjoyed great success in Australia and he will bring new blood and energy to our organization.'

Murdoch paid tribute to Sir William and described the assets he was putting into the *News of the World* as 'first class'. 'I would not be putting my reputation on the line if the deal was unfair or did not have exciting prospects.'

Then it was Maxwell's turn. Stafford Somerfield, in his book *Banner Headlines*, recalls: 'There is a hiss and a boo and shouts of "Sit down." Maxwell stands his ground.'

Maxwell attacked the company's profit performance, challenged Carr's claim about the unions and pressed the Pergamon cash alternative. 'It is lamentable that you have to be rescued by Mr Rupert Murdoch,' he said. 'Go back to the Old Vic,' someone shouted.

It was a lost cause. When Carr called for a vote, it was carried easily on a show of hands: 299 in favour of the Murdoch merger, 20 against. 'We both knew the result beforehand,' said Murdoch. When the shares were counted, the margin was rather more in favour of Maxwell: only 4,526,822 to 3,246,937.

'The shareholders did extremely well by us,' said Murdoch. 'If they'd taken Pergamon, they would have been wiped out.' Maxwell went down with all guns blazing. 'Our defeat is entirely due to the failure of the Take-over Panel,' he said. 'We are back to the laws of the jungle. We played according to the rules while the other side treated them with cynical disregard.' He added a wry postscript, borrowed from Benjamin Disraeli: 'I'm on the side of the angels.' He thought about that and added: 'Amazing!'

Maxwell's turn to explain some of the transactions he embarked upon during the *News of the World* takeover did not come until June 1971 when he appeared before the Department of Trade inquiry. He was asked about purchases by MSI(DS) of Pergamon shares worth £1.1 million during October, November and December 1968. The shares were close to the highest price they were to reach, and at the time the company – Maxwell's own save for Betty's 5 per cent and a token three shares held by Clark – did not have enough money to pay for them. A sum of £200,000, which helped, was handed over to it by MSI(1964).

The inspectors' questions to Clark left no doubt what they were getting at.

> *That appears to us to be a breach of Section 54 of the Companies Act, by Pergamon: on this ground, I think, that MSI(1964) was a subsidiary, but MSI(1964) was lending money to a third party to buy Pergamon shares . . . if in fact Pergamon or a subsidiary of Pergamon makes a loan to a third company with knowledge that the third company is asking for a loan in order to buy Pergamon shares then it seems to me Pergamon in making that loan is in breach.*

Clark:

> *Yes, on the face of it, I think. But there is this difference surely: that these shares were being bought not for anyone's benefit but for the general assistance of Pergamon in its bid and one cannot put a worse picture on it and say 'Look, someone was hoping to make a lot of money out of this.' It was really done in the terms of the bid situation.*

Maxwell's own responses were of such length, complexity and inconsistency with the accounts of Clark and an accountant concerned that the learned inspectors were almost defeated. But they hung in there, pursuing the elusive £200,000 through the confusing books of company after company under Maxwell management. No charges were ever laid under Section 54.

If Maxwell never did get the true measure of the clubby House of Commons, the reverse was not necessarily so. His campaign slogan in 1966 had been 'The Man Who Gets Things Done'. His colleagues took him at his word. The catering arrangements of the House were in an appalling state. The kitchens were archaic, the service primitive rather than traditional and the food unspeakable. Even though, while the House was sitting, Members, staff, journalists and guests ate and – rather more to the point – drank at all hours the catering department had lost £33,000 the previous year and had a £61,000 overdraft. Persuaded that only a businessman of his calibre could succeed in a task essential to the comfort, dignity and efficiency of the parliamentary community, Maxwell took over as chairman of the Catering Subcommit-

tee and promised a profit of £20,000 for 1968. He then set out to shake
things up – to spectacular effect.

Maxwell's determination to create a profit against all odds is still
remembered with awe. Application of the Business Principles was only
the beginning. He raised some instant operating capital by selling off the
splendid wine-cellar – the only commendable thing about dining at
Westminster – at bargain rates. Cases of Bollinger Special Cuvée champagne were off-loaded on to eager Members and journalists at a saving of
£2.40 a dozen. He sat on payments to suppliers to conserve money and
speeded up the cash-flow by raising prices, dunning MPs to pay their
overdue bills. He raked in even more by getting the Treasury to increase
its already generous subsidy. The inspirational address he delivered to a
mass meeting of cooks, waiters and kitchen-hands on his first morning
was described as worthy of Montgomery on the eve of Alamein. They
called him Chairman Ma. 'He's got to make a profit,' Roy Jenkins, then
one of Labour's luminaries, told reporters. 'He's the only person who has
ever gone around the tills at night stuffing banknotes in instead of taking
them out.'

Mischievous fellow-Members took full advantage of the obligation to
respond to parliamentary questions that went with Maxwell's appointment. In the longueurs of the House they would bedevil him with provocative demands for free-range produce and complaints that it now cost an
extra fourpence for the pink in a pink gin. Literal-minded as ever,
Maxwell would produce lengthy, solemn, detailed replies. 'The average
daily consumption of œuf en gelée during the summer', he reported, 'was
approximately twelve per day.'

The optimistic forecast for 1968 was soon modified to £7,000 and eventually, when the accounts were submitted to the Exchequer and Audit,
only £1,787 was claimed. Even this would have been no mean feat. But
Maxwell had used a unique system of book-keeping. The Treasury
subsidy had been included in the profit figures, and certain mandatory
deductions had not been made. Calling these 'errors of substance', the
auditors revised the modest profits into a £3,400 loss.

Well before the inspectors went to work Insight held up this episode as a
microcosm of Maxwell business methods.

> It displays all the classic movements in the Maxwell repertoire – the
> Amazing Leap from the Wings with loud promises of Modern Effici-
> ency; the Masterly Treatment of Accounts; and the Rapid Dis-
> appearance just before the audience starts to throw things.

Of everything that Insight was subsequently to write about him, criticism
of his efforts in the legislative kitchens seemed to wound Maxwell particularly. He took his complaints to the Committee of Privileges, Parliament's junta for looking after its own, but was told that the articles raised
'neither the question of privilege nor that of contempt [of Parliament]'.

The interpretation of this opinion that Maxwell intoned to The Times
was as masterly as his handling of the accounts. 'I note that this senior

committee of the House of Commons has unanimously decided that my conduct as Chairman of a Select Subcommittee was entirely proper, and it follows that there was no truth in, nor justification for, the *Sunday Times*'s personal attack on me in this regard.' When he abandoned his legal proceedings against the *Sunday Times* and he was invited to offer a counterbalancing account, the final of the only four points Maxwell chose to make was about his reign as the House's head caterer.

The effects of Maxwell's improvements in the feeding habits of the House were enduring. Probably the most memorable of them was to abolish tipping and to reopen Annie's Bar – named for the original barmaid – which had been closed since the war. Members had been forced to drink in the Strangers' Bar where Lobby correspondents were also allowed. Maxwell wandered in there one night when Lena Jeger, a spirited representative of the relatively small number of women Members then in the House, and now elevated to the Lords, was talking to Terry Lancaster.

'Captain Maxwell!' Jeger greeted him jovially. 'Would you say that you were the richest man here?'

Maxwell did not need to look about him to agree. 'I suppose I've got a couple of bob.'

'Well, then,' said Jeger. 'Why the hell don't you buy us a round of bloody drinks?'

Which Maxwell graciously did. After he had gone, Jeger said to Lancaster: 'What do you think of him?'

'An extraordinary character,' said Lancaster, meaning it.

They fell to discussing the various gossipy theories about Maxwell that circulated around the lobbies. Misgivings that the high-profile financial style associated with him might somehow embarrass his fellow-socialists have never come to anything. On the contrary, by private donation, by the constituency lotteries, by sound financial counsel, Maxwell has, over the years, considerably enriched the Labour Party – and, by professional patronage, certain of its members. Nor have the inevitable malicious rumours thrown up by his business contacts with the Eastern bloc. 'They say my money comes from Russia,' he complained to one of his editors. Told that the editor had heard it was East Germany, he guffawed hugely, obviously enjoying the distraction it provided for his enemies and others. Kevin Maxwell, too, has learned to deal with this recurring suggestion. In the course of the rights issue he responded to a questioner at a meeting who seemed to be hinting at a sinister connection: 'This is "Is Russian gold financing Pergamon?" No!'

Even Rupert Murdoch, who loathes all forms of socialism, does not believe that Maxwell's relations with the Eastern regimes go beyond the mutually advantageous commercial. 'He does adulatory books on Brezhnev or Gorbachev or a page in the *Mirror* on some thug in Bulgaria. In return they buy a lot of his books at very high prices and give him the result of all their research to publish, which is the basis of the material for all those journals, at nil cost almost. It's a very narrow, interesting business he's carved out there. Very profitable.'

The commercial benefit to Pergamon has been evident for many years, and it would be extraordinary if Maxwell's highly public shuttling to and from communist countries all through the Cold War had failed to attract the attention of the security services. Sir Tom McCaffrey who went to work for Maxwell after finishing his stint as Prime Minister James Callaghan's press secretary, resigning over Maxwell's drastic treatment of some of his less resilient managers, scorns the idea that Maxwell's florid patriotism could be anything other than it seems. 'I would say he is a good deal more patriotic than the average native-born Briton.'

It certainly seemed that way when in the first few days of 1968, a time when the inefficiency of British industry under Labour was receiving more than its usual share of attention, Maxwell set out to bestir a startled nation with a bid for its attention that could not possibly be ignored. The 'I'm Backing Britain' campaign, with which his name became indelibly associated, was, like the constituency lotteries, someone else's idea. But, as so often, Maxwell reckoned that he deserved it more because he knew what should be done with it.

Brenda, Christine, Valerie, Joan and Carolann, five ordinary typists, began it all in that bastion of English ordinariness, Surbiton. To the delight of their ordinary employers, Colt Heating and Ventilation Ltd, they proclaimed a joint New Year resolution. They would do their bit for a better Britain by working an extra half-hour a day for no more pay. Harold Wilson read of this ingenuous proposal and invited the girls to lunch at the Commons. They were taken aback by the traditional sprawl of the Front Benchers. 'That George Brown with his little flesh-coloured socks.'

A grateful press enlivened the post-holiday doldrums by turning them into national heroines. Jingoistic echoes rang from near and far. The Governor of Tasmania sent a cable saying that all there regarded it as the finest feat since the Battle of Britain. Colt, so overwhelmed by attention that no one there could get any work done at all, beseeched the Government to take things over, and a small independent organization, the Industrial Society, was handed the job of shaping an I'm Backing Britain Movement.

Maxwell, however, decided that he was the Only Man to get this thing done. 'I had the idea virtually as soon as the typists,' he said. And he went charging out to deploy his own version, under a slogan that took some people back to the early 1930s: Buy British. In no way, he replied to puzzled enquirers, did this contradict his support for Britain's membership of the Common Market. But he decreed that in the Commons dining-room Camembert and other French cheeses would no longer be served. And the same went for Headington, said Betty loyal as ever.

The Industrial Society, with its low-key even-handed ways, was overwhelmed. But Maxwell had no time to waste. 'I'm the hit-and-run bandit in this affair,' he told Mark Wolfson, then in charge of the campaign. He planned to be into it and out within six months. Holding the Society off with one hand, Maxwell picked up the telephone with the other and speedily assembled a battery of big guns – most of whom had something to sell – to pledge money and support for his ideas: Billy Butlin of the holiday camps, Michael Sieff of Marks & Spencer, Joe Hyman of Viyella. He even got Jim Conway, secretary of the Amalgamated Engineering Union, along to one meeting when the union had already told its members at Colt to put the skids under the whole idea.

An advertising hotshot of the day, David Kingsley, whose agency had produced Labour's slogans in the past two elections, was commissioned to think up one for this occasion. Kingsley had a fixation on the concept of 'crankiness'. 'There is a new kind of crankiness abroad in this country,' he mused, '. . . that nothing can be done about our problems.'

Maxwell then made a takeover bid for the Industrial Society's efforts. 'You're all trying to be virgins,' Maxwell barked triumphantly at director John Garnett. 'Whiter than white. I've succeeded in raping you all along.'

Garnett was bullied into a compromise by which Maxwell took over the task of impressing consumers while the Society concentrated on industrial production. There were, in effect, to be two campaigns. 'It's not so much that Maxwell will not take no for an answer,' Garnett said despairingly. 'One wouldn't mind that. It's that he seems to be able to convince everyone, including himself, that you never said no.'

Plenty of people were having second thoughts about whatever they might have agreed to. One of the great advantages Maxwell enjoyed was his friendship with David Frost (table E1 at the fortieth anniversary) on whose interview show, once the campaign was under way, he appeared with Joe Hyman. But no sooner were they on the air than Hyman launched an attack on the Buy British aspect that Maxwell was so keen to plug. It could only attract reprisals abroad and damage exports, he said. For good measure Hyman said the same thing again in a letter to *The Times*, adding that he did not want to be associated with anything so jingoistic.

Maxwell replied resoundingly, but his letter made a mention of the Common Market. This in turn drew a blast of dissent from another departing supporter, Sir Max Aitken, whose *Daily Express* group was delighted to Back Britain but loathed the idea of Europe. The *Express*, retorted Maxwell, simply wanted to hijack the campaign.

There were a few days of calm while Kingsley perfected the series of newspaper advertisements that were to serve as a manifesto. Maxwell went on selling his ideas to anyone he could lure to the Commons: Great Universal Stores, Littlewoods, impresario Bernard Delfont, Bowaters the paper manufacturers and United Newspapers, a wealthy provincial group. Then on 7 February the first advertisement appeared, a full page in *The Times* and the *Daily Telegraph* headed '100 Uncranky Suggestions of Ways to Help Your Country – and Yourself'. The suggestions themselves were fatuous but harmless. One was that children might renounce free milk at school. What led to the massive defections among Maxwell's supporters was that hardly any of the sponsors listed had any idea of what was to be published in their names. Sighed Delfont (table H3): 'It shows what happens when you let people run amok.'

Several newspapers had already displayed their misgivings. The *Observer* noted that the Buy British campaign of the 1930s had also been promoted by someone who was not a native, Lord Beaverbrook. There was an uncharacteristic tinge of prejudice in its editorial view.

> *The mysterious Captain Robert Maxwell has at last achieved his ambition . . . with his totally misguided campaign and his string of TV appearances – looking like an impossibly successful stall holder in Petticoat Lane – he has contrived to emerge as a National Figure.*

Now even the true blue Tory *Telegraph*, which had been happy to take the advertisers' money, felt moved to speak out. What was happening was a massive diversion of attention from real causes and culprits. 'Mr Maxwell's campaign should be laughed into the oblivion it deserves before it does real harm.'

Maxwell was unrepentant. He explained that he had merely rushed the advertisements into print in time for a meeting of the National Economic Development Council. 'If it only served to make people aware of our problems then the campaign would have served its purpose. All I want is for this great country to stop the retreat.'

None of Maxwell's loquacious critics seemed aware – and he did not tell them – that, while the disastrous advertisements were being put together in London, in Oxford the six-year agony of Michael Maxwell came to a merciful end. He died on 27 January, aged twenty-one.

What the reporters assigned to throw some light on the restless activities of this parliamentary maverick in the 1960s had the most difficulty with were exactly the same contradictions that Maxwell was flaunting twenty years later. Harris of the *Financial Times* had already been keeping an eye on the phenomenon for ten years when he wrote, in October 1968, that Maxwell's glaring ambiguity was actually the secret of his success. Harris recalled a famous remark by Charles Wilson, a recent American Secretary of Defence, who had said that what was good for General Motors – of which Wilson happened to be president – was good for America. Like Wilson, Maxwell drew no line between public interests and self-interest. When he said, 'I am primarily concerned with social need,' he meant almost the same thing as when he said, 'I am very market-oriented'.

Others wrestled dutifully to reconcile Maxwell's pronouncements with his activities. 'What you don't realize', Maxwell told Allan Hall of the *Daily Express*, 'is that I have no sense of property. I am not interested in ownership.'

'It is not just success that makes Maxwell unpopular,' wrote Hall. 'He's so damned virtuous.'

Some simply confessed their bewilderment. 'He has not been a Westminster success,' was the judgement of David Wood. Maxwell, he wrote, would never understand the art of winning men. But after four years in the Commons, added Wood, a lot of people had come to understand him. 'Maxwell can be a warm and emotionally sympathetic friend; and there is no contradiction between his millions and his socialism for he never forgets the refugee boy who was harried across Europe.'

Almost all the journalists who saw Maxwell regularly, particularly the financial writers, became used to his telephone calls at odd hours, a habit that persists to this day. Usually the tip he wishes to offer is advantageous to one of his myriad projects but none the less newsworthy, sometimes, for that. They became rather inured to suggestions, usually from Maxwell rivals or people he had shouldered aside, that his affairs might reward a little investigation. Nicholas Tomalin, who had first likened him to Beaverbrook, wrote in 1968:

> *Almost every day of the week some indignant publishing rival will whisper some innuendo of appalling financial corner-cutting – but no one ever discovers a really damaging publishable fact behind the rumours. The conclusion must be that though behind Robert Maxwell the Super Patriot there is a dashing financial pirate, he is seldom as bad as his enemies make out. Furthermore, anyone who gets to know Maxwell will find that beneath his brash pushingness, his over-eager salesmanship, his appalling ignorance of the done thing in publishing, politics and public life in general, he is a charming operator who has been so successful in convincing himself that he is supremely patriotic, efficient and effective that he often is so.*

However, it was soon to be seen that some of those indignant publishing rivals may have known a thing or two that Tomalin did not.

Maxwell resigned from the catering committee in 1969. Momentarily his attention was diverted to some other shortcomings of the House. Hurrying to vote one night he slipped and twisted his left knee. The first-aid room to which he was taken and its equipment, he complained, were lamentably out of date.

At the same time Maxwell was getting ready to use the performance that he claimed ILSC was putting up in the Knowledge Market to boost the share price of Pergamon on the Stock Exchange he was also kicking off the deal that the inspectors identified as the second transaction upon which the family's wealth was based. It also provided a fine example of two more habitual Business Practices: intercompany dealings and the 'mingling' of funds belonging to the public and private companies.

In 1966 RM & Co., on behalf of MSI Inc., purchased two warehouses and the land on which they stood in Wolverton, Buckinghamshire, from

British Rail for £355,000. The money was scraped together by the various family companies in Britain, but always, Maxwell insisted, on behalf of MSI Inc., the American family company. In 1969 the property was sold for £1,052,500. For some of the time MSI Inc. owned it, two of the buildings were leased to Pergamon for storage. Asked why RM & Co. had made the purchase rather than Pergamon itself, particularly since Pergamon was admitted to be short of space, Maxwell explained that it had not been in his capacity as chairman of Pergamon that he had heard about the opportunity and he was therefore not obliged to tell Pergamon about it. His counsel was able to convince the inspectors that there was nothing incorrect in this contention.

The distribution of the profits from the Wolverton sale was even more complicated than the assembling of the purchase price. The money, together with some other funds that became celebrated under the label of 'Spanish Translation Rights', did not reach America until Maxwell was about to be removed from the board of Pergamon and the company was in danger of collapse. MSI Inc. actually owed the amount and a good deal more to Pergamon, and the directors who replaced the sacked board set out to get it back. They never did, entirely, but when a settlement was finally worked out they found that Maxwell had created yet another company, Maxwell International Microforms Corporation (that soon had its name changed to Microforms International Marketing Corporation) to deal with the matter.

Sir Henry d'Avigdor-Goldsmid, who became the first interim chairman of Pergamon after Maxwell had been deposed, said to the inspectors regarding MIMC: 'It was a company with no accounts, balance sheet, directors or even any address . . . my own feeling was that his incurable inventiveness couldn't allow him to make an agreement between a company in which he was directly interested and another company in which he was interested – he had to invent a third company.' He subsequently wrote to Maxwell's solicitors: 'I think I ought to have made it clear to the inspectors that MSI's creation of MIMC was a device approved by Pergamon's then legal advisers with the object of protecting funds in transit between MSI and Pergamon from being blocked or a tack by Leasco who had refused to give an indemnity in respect of them . . . this device was for the benefit of Pergamon as much as Bob Maxwell. . . .'

But Maxwell had plans for MIMC. Big plans.

SIX

People have such strange ideas. They think he has the
money in little suitcases.

ELISABETH MAXWELL

MAXWELL

THERE WAS A NOTICEABLE STIR in the usually austere atmosphere of the Pergamon offices at Headington in the spring of 1969. Maxwell ordered a warehouse to be cleared out and the contents shipped to a distribution centre he had set up at Wembley: the Book Centre – a sort of small-time Simpkin Marshall. The space was turned into a large open-plan office, the desks divided by elegant bookshelves hastily put up by Sam Swadling, who was also the firm's carpenter. The employees who were moved there from other, far less gracious surroundings were forbidden to add any of the homely touches they were used to or make their surroundings untidy in any way. To the bafflement of his editors Maxwell insisted that some of the educational literature, particularly the audio-visual, of which there was little, be catalogued with American references, 'High School' substituted for 'O Level'. American visitors, of whom there had always been a number, became more frequent around the impressive new layout. Many of them were from a company called Leasco Data Processing Corporation, including its founder and chairman, Saul P. Steinberg, and its president, Bernard Schwartz, both of Brooklyn.

Steinberg was one of the archetypcal space-age prodigies that the United States produced in the early Computer Age. At the University of Pennsylvania he had written a thesis, 'The Decline and Fall of IBM'. His father, who owned a rubber factory, staked him with $25,000. He borrowed more, bought IBM computers wholesale and leased them – something that had not occurred to IBM itself at that time. At only twenty-nine he was already many times wealthier than Maxwell. In fact he enjoyed the distinction of having made more money faster than anyone else under thirty in America. He spread it around in tearaway style. He had bought a place on Long Island: '. . . a modern palatial mansion just like any other kid of twenty-nine. You know, twenty-nine rooms, tennis court, two saunas, six or seven servants, a couple of chauffeurs. I've learned to live with the burden of my wealth.' Getting married for the second time, he had his secretary bring several million dollars to the register office in a shopping-bag to settle an alimony dispute with his first wife.

To keep up its momentum and win more clients Leasco, already worth £250 million, depended on an ever-widening range of applications for computers. They had the retrieval systems which were still only a dream to Maxwell; Pergamon, because of the scientific journals, had the data.

And Pergamon was – at least, at first glance – a flourishing concern besides, one of the great British success stories of the 1960s. The predator's nostrils twitched.

There were sound reasons why a company as dynamic as Pergamon should offer itself for sale. Two attempts to expand had been frustrated by BPC and Rupert Murdoch. It was not in the nature of Maxwell, unquestionably the moving spirit behind its success, to sit back and consolidate, and a new owner might be willing to allow him to share the journey towards new horizons. But the best reason of all was that all the shareholders would get rich. Especially Maxwell and the Family Interests, who between them owned 34 per cent of the stock.

The trouble with Pergamon was ILSC. Even when Maxwell had been most deeply preoccupied with the struggle for the *News of the World* he still insisted on giving all the orders at ILSC. Now he had become absorbed in collaring yet another newspaper, the *Sun*, into which the Mirror Group had transformed the old *Daily Herald* but which had failed miserably and was now being jettisoned. As soon as he heard the *Sun* was to be shut down Maxwell started to canvass his plans. He wanted to print it on the presses of the *Evening Standard*, which were idle during the evening. It would be a sort of *Daily Worker* for the élite, half a million circulation, low advertising volume. The description read like that of the *London Daily News* eighteen years later. Richard Crossman noted in his diary: 'Maxwell is a strange, roguish man and I can't really believe he is going to make this thing a success.'

But the *Sun* was yet another distraction that led Maxwell to ignore the alarm signals which were now being set off at regular intervals at ILSC as it became apparent that the company was in a mess. How much of a mess was something no one seemed capable of assessing since no one had any clear idea how many encyclopaedias had been sold in the various territories, paid for, returned, discounted; how much the company was owed or where the money was. All this had an importance beyond ILSC itself, because Pergamon – Maxwell – had signed a warranty that, if ILSC were to make less than £500,000 profit from the part of the business that did not originate with BPC, Pergamon would make up any shortfall. Pergamon had assured its shareholders that such a thing was improbable; they still looked forward confidently to the £500,000 or so the partnership would contribute to their company's 1968 profits. Above all, Maxwell the aggressive salesman MP, champion of British commerce and cheerleader for science and popular education, had convinced the world at large that ILSC was a hero among companies.

There had already been a threat of shortfall in the accounting period that ended 30 June 1968, held off temporarily by a resort to backdated orders. In New York, Mr Martini had now been replaced by Laszlo Straka. Straka had had an extraordinary escape from Hungary as a child. His father had been a director of the Hungarian National Bank, and when the Russians began to move in at the end of the Second World War the country's gold reserves were put on a train and, accompanied by most of the bank staff and their families, taken into the American zone of Austria. Straka obligingly doubled to 5,000 his orders for sets of the *New Caxton* for PPI (which ILSC, in any case, did not have the stock to meet). This was transformed in the ILSC accounts into a sale worth $350,000. The first part of Straka's order was dated 25 June 1968. The second, dated 26 June, was stamped in the ILSC office 'Received 20 December 1968'.

The confusion at ILSC was almost entirely of Maxwell's making, although the directors of BPC deserve blame for allowing him to get away with it. By the middle of 1968 there was no one left in the company who understood the Knowledge Market. In the eighteen months that followed no fewer than five different company secretaries were appointed. One of them later described his duties: 'To carry out Mr Maxwell's instructions to the letter and to do nothing more.'

Most of the executives who did not jump ship Maxwell sacked anyway, beginning with the hapless Le Bas whose undated resignation letter he had kept in his desk since the company had been set up. He was later to accuse Le Bas of being 'too fond of liquor', although the DTI report refers to him as being, at the time, a total abstainer. This turmoil did not go unobserved in the City, and the hitherto uninterrupted ascent of Pergamon shares began to falter. But Maxwell was confidence itself, always on display, always ready to discuss his plans for the new *Sun*, full of hints about the great developments imminent at Pergamon.

In April 1969, just when it became imperative that Pergamon get together an impressive set of accounts for Leasco, Maxwell was warned by Chalmers Impey that given the state of the ILSC books it was impossible to say if Pergamon would have a liability under the warranty or not. On 15 May 1969, Maxwell tried to persuade an ILSC board meeting to let him assure Pergamon shareholders – and therefore Leasco – that there was no question of a warranty claim. But the BPC directors insisted that Pergamon might have to come up with £100,000 or perhaps £150,000. The danger of this was not the money, which Pergamon could easily afford, but the revelation that ILSC, far from being the money-spinning miracle Maxwell had promoted it as, was a failure.

Maxwell tried to get the other directors to agree at least to a statement that the business was 'at present profitable'. But BPC had at last decided to acknowledge the dangers ahead. They would have difficulty, its directors averred, 'in joining him in this assertion'. One thing they all agreed about was that there was no hope of the accounts to the end of December 1968 – which included the last warranty period – being ready before September 1969.

However, when Pergamon's 1968 annual report was published on 22 May 1969, Maxwell took the opportunity to make a unilateral statement boosting ILSC. He claimed it was running to forecast with £7.5 million sales in its first eighteen months of business and had a 'bright and profitable future'. The delay in completing the accounts was due simply to the 'usual' difficulties associated with trading in forty different countries but because of it the warranty must still stand. 'However, in the opinion of your directors, no liability will arise.'

Maxwell certainly had no intention of letting Leasco discover otherwise. Two days after the ILSC board meeting he had sent Bernie Schwartz ILSC's 1969 first-quarter management accounts and profit forecast 'prepared on the most conservative basis'. 'You will see that the company is running well,' he wrote. The difficulty with BPC, he told Schwartz in this letter (which also contained the accusation against Le Bas), was that the men who ran it had been in fear of him since his takeover bid and were trying to depress the value of ILSC in order to buy it cheap. That in turn had brought down the Pergamon share price. In fact the BPC directors were about to conclude that life with Maxwell was impossible and that the best solution was to sell out to him.

The courtship between Leasco and Pergamon passed into its serious phase on 17 June 1969. Steinberg assured Maxwell personally, pending the drawing-up of a formal offer document, that he would be taking over all the issued shares of the company, which then stood at 37s (£1.85), or a trade of Leasco stock. Maxwell and the Family Interests would get £8.5 million for their 34 per cent holding, £2.5 million of it in cash. Maxwell would become deputy chairman of Leasco and, with an equity of 2.5 per cent, would be the second-largest shareholder.

Maxwell, for his part, did some more warranting, among which he assured Leasco that Pergamon did not and would not have any liability in regard to ILSC. More important, he affirmed that the level of business Pergamon and its subsidiaries were doing was essentially that reflected in the 1968 annual report and he undertook to inform Leasco if there was any change. On the following day ILSC's exasperated parent companies, each for its own reasons, made a deal which, when exhumed by the inspectors, was labelled as the Secret Agreement. BPC, seeing the prospect of getting out of the onerous partnership, allowed their original agreement with Buckingham/Pergamon to be altered retrospectively so that the warranty no longer applied.

The inspectors made a point of letting everyone know what they thought of this:

> Whilst we appreciate the desire of directors to keep information confidential which might affect the welfare of their companies, the history of ILSC, with regard to what is disclosed, is a series of suppression of information and of optimism verging on recklessness with the occasional statement which was untrue and calculated to mislead.

But for the moment the agreement stayed secret, even from Maxwell's advisers in the Leasco transaction, Robert Fleming, a merchant bank renowned for its probity and conservatism. Leasco were represented by the no less prestigious N. M. Rothschild.

As soon as the glamorous takeover proposal was unveiled Pergamon was catapulted from the finance sections to page one. Whizzkid Steinberg was a glittering figure to the London financial establishment, and the idea of the notoriously ebullient Maxwell, the flamboyant politician-salesman just turned forty-six, playing second fiddle to him gave headline writers plenty to work with. Would Maxwell put the money into the *Sun*? Would he use it to buy a bigger piece of Fleet Street? No, said Maxwell. His newspaper interests were being financed by his private resources. Pergamon shares shot from 27*s* 6*d* (£1.32) to 37*s* 6*d* (£1.88), subsiding to 35*s* (£1.75). Maxwell would not be the only one to get rich. Richer.

There were still details to be attended to. Maxwell and Steinberg met frequently on both sides of the Atlantic. On 7 August 1969, in New York, Maxwell agreed, at Leasco's insistence, to end the cosy and profitable agreement under which MSI Inc., the instrument of the family trusts, had the extremely profitable right to reprint Pergamon journals. Pergamon would pay MSI Inc. $1.6 million compensation.

But, unknown to the enthusiastic audience applauding the lustrous merger, Maxwell still had a major problem. Up to this point Leasco had been under the impression that the pre-tax profits of ILSC were running at more than £500,000 a year, making an important contribution to the £2.5 million profit forecast for Pergamon. If this was not the case – and it certainly was not – Maxwell was bound by his personal warranty to Leasco to disclose it to them, wrote the inspectors.

> *An element of desperation is apparent in Mr Maxwell's actions at this time. He seems to have solved his dilemma by escaping from the frying pan in the hope that the fire could be quenched when he landed in it.*

On 12 August 1969, acting as chairman of Pergamon, Maxwell wrote three letters without the knowledge of any other director. The first was intended to purchase *Maxwell's Pictorial Knowledge* from ILSC for £200,000 – well in excess of the auditors' valuation. The second reduced by £114,895 the sum ILSC was being charged for taking over Reports and Surveys. The third gave ILSC back £42,000 of the amount Pergamon had charged ILSC for use of the Fitzroy Square offices. Even with these sums added to the credit side of the ledger the joint auditors of ILSC, persuade, cajole and storm as Maxwell might, were only prepared to concede that the company had made a trading profit of no more that £40,000 in its eighteen months of existence. That was the figure Maxwell had to send to Rothschilds, incorporated in his letter of recommendation to Pergamon shareholders that was to accompany the Leasco offer document.

In those days the City was a somnolent place in August, its denizens spending their gains on Mediterranean beaches or, after the Glorious Twelfth, off shooting in Scotland. But a few days after Rothschilds received Pergamon's documents rumours began to percolate.

Maxwell was doing all he could to save the deal. He argued for hours on end with Rothschilds, who had now got some inkling of the true state of affairs. If they would only look at the figures his way, he insisted, they meant something entirely different. Reported the inspectors:

> *The fact is that at this stage the truth about ILSC was most unpalatable. Its records and accounts were in a shambles. The crisis had been reached.*

In a last-ditch concession, Maxwell told Leasco that provided other share-holders got the full offer price he would accept only 18s 6d (93p) for his holding and the balance after the profit forecast had been realized.

There was steady dealing in Pergamon shares, and the price was sustained at 35s (£1.75). Curiously, in a takeover situation, Leasco kept on buying. They were later seen to have built up a stake of 38 per cent. Then MSI Inc. was suddenly reported to have sold about a million shares belonging to the Swiss trusts, realizing £1.75 million. On 21 August, Maxwell was summoned to the Takeover Panel to answer questions about this. 'The trust is a distant family interest,' said Maxwell blandly, repeating to reporters the explanation he had given. 'The trustee is entitled to do what he likes with the shares. There is no suggestion that I have behaved improperly.'

That afternoon Steinberg announced 'with regret' that he did not intend to proceed with the takeover. It was sensational news. the mating of Pergamon and Leasco had caught the country's imagination. Thousands of small investors had been counting on comfortable profits.

The Takeover Panel was aghast. It demanded that the Stock Exchange suspend dealing. Its chairman, Lord Shawcross, was recalled from his yacht in the Adriatic and explanations were demanded from both sides. Leasco cited the plight of ILSC which had belatedly been disclosed and the machinations of MSI Inc. Bitterly, Maxwell accused Leasco of having negotiated in bad faith. They did not have enough money to conclude the deal, he alleged. Their share-buying showed they had been out merely to gain a controlling interest. The acrimonious exchanges between the two companies – or, rather, between Maxwell and Steinberg, for it quickly became a personal feud – showed that neither had ever really trusted the other.

At first City opinion had rallied behind Maxwell. Perhaps he was something of a rascal, but he was *their* rascal. But the façade was crumbling. The auditors withdrew even the modest forecast that Maxwell had wrung from them. Robert Flemings withdrew their services. The Leasco disclosures about MSI Inc. were the first many people had heard of the secretive Maxwell trusts. Even the *Sunday Telegraph*, whose financial pages have always given Maxwell a noticeably warm press, was unhappy about them. 'What are the amounts, who are the beneficiaries, who are the trustees?' The same questions were still being asked nearly thirty years later.

After the Takeover Panel had considered matters for a while it decided to let the corporate gladiators slug it out between themselves. What concerned it more was the attitude Pergamon – and BPC – had maintained towards shareholders during the ILSC episode. This, the Panel decreed, should be the subject of an investigation, and on 9 September 1969 the Board of Trade appointed to the task a distinguished accountant, Sir Ronald Leach, and a barrister, Owen Stable, QC. A week earlier Maxwell had withdrawn his offer to buy the *Sun*. SOGAT, the print union on whose backing he had depended, accused him of 'public gimmickry'. The paper's journalists had challenged him to put up or shut up. Rupert Murdoch moved in and grabbed the title and those who wanted to go on working for it. Said Hugh Cudlipp: 'This is obviously the end of Mr Maxwell's dream of being the proprietor of a national newspaper.'

On 10 October 1969 an extraordinary general meeting of Pergamon shareholders removed Maxwell – who still owned 28 per cent of the stock – and the rest of the directors. They were replaced by directors appointed by Grindlay's Bank, who were Pergamon's financial advisers, the 'institutions', as the various funds and insurance companies which had invested were known, and Leasco, the largest single shareholder. The 2,800 known small investors were supposed to be represented by three non-executive directors. The general idea was that Pergamon was still fundamentally sound as a business and that as soon as a grip could be got upon its unruly affairs Steinberg would be happy to make a bid for the rest of its shares. Said Maxwell: 'You can't expect me to be other than very, very sad. I am going away for a few days' holiday.'

While the Leasco deal was still in the making, but long before there was any suspicion that Maxwell was about to go down yet again, taking a lot of shareholders with him, he was understandably disconcerted to find that reporters had begun to ask questions rather than just take note of his pronouncements. The *Sunday Times* had a new editor by then, Harold Evans. But its principal journalistic asset had been firmly in place before he arrived. Then in its heyday, Insight, jointly commanded by Godfrey Hodgson and Bruce Page, was so prestigious that if a project was sufficiently important (like the thalidomide scandal, a major insurance fraud or the DC-10 disasters) it could ransack any other section of the paper for expertise. The most egocentric of by-lined specialists were usually ready to contribute under its rule of collective anonymity. But not even the thalidomide story which Insight pursued to the House of Lords could be compared for breadth, depth or endurance to the excavation Page and Hodgson embarked upon once it became clear that there was a lot more to Maxwell than anyone had yet seen.

It was little more than the improbable profits Pergamon kept claiming – for a publisher whose books were only rarely seen in Britain – that first aroused Insight's curiosity. The first reporters assigned to ask questions soon discovered that they had strayed into baffling territory. Few people who knew Maxwell were ready to talk about him (something that is just as true nearly twenty years later). Many of those approached were quick to let Maxwell know that Insight was on his trail. Maxwell himself had only just been approached, and the Insight executives yet to be convinced that there was something worth investigating, when the first rumblings of resentment were heard and the subject himself appeared in the *Sunday Times* office in a state of considerable dudgeon. He had no intention of speaking to reporters, even to Hodgson or Page. He had come to see the editor.

Evans had established a policy of inviting anyone who complained about his staff to come and do it personally. He knew that Maxwell had gone to Denis Hamilton, the editor-in-chief of Times Newspapers, who contrived to keep him at arm's length while Evans made his judgement.

Every editor must be ready for legal confrontation; none welcomes it. Evans had to balance the probable achievements of Insight against cost, time, aggravation. Anyway, he wanted to be fair. Neither he nor the Insighters had ever known anyone to react like Maxwell. They were nearly overwhelmed. Maxwell was, after all, a Member of Parliament. He was also loud, aggressive, verbose and persistent in his accusations of dishonesty and malice and threats of legal action. At one stage in the noisy wrangle Maxwell turned on Hodgson, an urbane and deceptively gentle-mannered operator, and said: 'Did I hear you call me a lobster? You're insulting me. You're calling me a lobster.'

'No, no, no,' Hodgson assured him. 'I said you reminded me of the story about the lobster.' Maxwell listened suspiciously as he explained.

'Just recently I ordered a cold lobster in a very expensive restaurant. When it came it didn't look right to me. It looked, actually, as if the poor old lobster had been dressed up, not with chef's own hand-made mayonnaise and the usual little bits, but with something out of a bottle. Heinz's Russian Salad for instance.'

Maxwell allowed some of Hodgson's scorn for this unworthy substitution to be reflected in his own expression.

'So I complained to the waiter, who came back and said the chef insisted that it was the real stuff. I asked the waiter to get the chef.'

Such a forthright reaction was clearly correct in Maxwell's eyes.

'Well,' Hodgson continued, 'a few minutes went by. Then out of the kitchen burst this wide-eyed figure waving his arms about and demanding to know who was calling him a liar.'

'Yes?' said Maxwell, plainly baffled by this lengthy parable.

'Well, don't you see?' asked Hodgson. 'I wasn't sure whether it had been Heinz's Russian Salad at all when I asked to see the chef. I might easily have been wrong. But when I saw the man come charging out like that, waving his arms and protesting, then I knew, Mr Maxwell. I knew it had to be Heinz's Russian Salad.'

The investigation that Insight then launched into Maxwell and his affairs was epic, involving dozens of reporters in Britain, on the Continent and in the United States. They tapped many a rich source, including Rothschilds who had been outraged to discover that one of the Waller-steiner adventures had been called the Rothschild Investment Trust. Maxwell fought them for every inch of ground, counter-attacking tirelessly. There was talk of anti-Semitism, laughable to Hodgson whose wife and two children were Jewish, wounding to Page, a dedicated liberal.

The only concession Maxwell was able to extract from Evans was that before the *Sunday Times* went into print with the two-part profile of him that the months of labour produced it would be submitted for his comments. It was, since his life even up to that point had been so mysterious and improbable, an immensely complicated account. 'Maxwell argued over every comma, every adjective,' Page remembers. 'We came to realize we were dealing with a man who did not have a commonplace perception of what might constitute a fact.'

·

The investigation that Sir Ronald Leach and Owen Stable conducted into Maxwell's affairs was another of the more extraordinary inquisitions of modern British life. It took them from November 1969 until the end of 1973 to complete, during which, as one of the judges who had to be called on to enforce it said, Maxwell put 'every conceivable obstacle' in their way. In this he was ably supported by his solicitor, John Silkin (table E2), who had to engineer the course of the torrent of litigation Maxwell unleashed to avoid answering questions or having information revealed. The inspectors estimated that Maxwell's efforts prolonged their task by two years.

Three reports were finally issued. Much of the compilation was done by Price Waterhouse, whom Maxwell had ordered in for impartial research. They came to 664 pages in all with huge appendixes of evidence in addition, and they are shattering documents.

But, if the distinguished inspectors with their meticulous minds and manners got the measure of Maxwell, Maxwell with his chess-player's gift of staying several moves ahead had begun to outsmart the men who had been put in to run Pergamon – before they were given the job. Even while the Leasco negotiations were at their most promising he had evidently grasped that the probability of a collapse once Steinberg realized the true state of ILSC was very high.

On 12 June 1969, the same day he met Steinberg to arrange the buyout of MSI Inc.'s privileged relationship with Pergamon, Maxwell also journeyed up from Manhattan to Maxwell House at Elmsford. In his capacity as chairman of PPI he presided over its annual general meeting.

Kerman and Clark were the other two Pergamon directors who were also directors of the American subsidiary. Kerman later swore that he knew nothing about what happened and that Maxwell had been delegated by the board to deal with PPI. Clark had given Maxwell a proxy for his vote. The Elmsford meeting resolved to drop a set of bylaws containing a provision under which the secretary of the company was bound to call a special meeting of the company at the request of stockholders owning a majority of the stock. Thus, when the new Pergamon board took over at Oxford they found that in New York Maxwell was still chairman and president of a 70 per cent owned subsidiary company at a salary of $40,000 a year and there was nothing they could do about it. 'Would you regard it as unduly offensive', inquired Mr Stable of one of the new Pergamon directors, 'if I said that they'd pretty well got Pergamon over a barrel?'

Maxwell was able to produce an affidavit from an American lawyer saying that the change in the bylaws had been suggested by his firm and that it had never been anticipated that the two managements would come to loggerheads. Nevertheless, despite spending £200,000 in applications to the American courts, the furious British caretaker board could not get any control over PPI.

At the very beginning of the investigation Maxwell was a model of co-operation. In person and in writing he assured the inspectors of his anxiety to see the affairs of ILSC clarified as soon as possible so that it could go on to greater achievements. The companies' severe problems, he told Stable and Leach at his first meeting with them, had been largely caused by publicity, 90 per cent of which was untrue. But when Maxwell was asked to give evidence he told them that he expected certain undertakings on how the inquiry was to be conducted.

By this time Leasco, while still talking of making a bid for the whole company, had filed a $22 million breach-of-contract suit in the United States, and Maxwell argued that the disclosure of some of his affairs might assist them with it. Since the inspectors considered that they held a clear brief from the Department of Trade under section 125(b) of the Companies Act 1948, they, not surprisingly, refused to do things his way. Maxwell therefore would tell them nothing except to state that he was a Member of Parliament and give his name, rank and MC.

The inspectors applied for a court order to compel Maxwell and other Pergamon directors to answer their questions. The directors appealed and, after a delay that Maxwell, at least, was able to put to use, came up against the no-nonsense figure of Lord Denning, who gave them a dressing-down in his soft Hampshire accent and warned them they were risking contempt of court if they did not speak up. 'It would have been far simpler for the appellants,' he admonished, 'as men with high positions in the business world, to show a sense of responsibility to the public interest instead of raising points which were premature and ill founded.'

Meanwhile, Maxwell had been chucked out of Parliament as well.

Not only did Maxwell lose the election that was held in June 1970, but he – and Betty – also began to lose the grip he had established over the local Labour Party organization. It is doubtful if the Leasco affair meant much in Buckingham. The villain at that particular moment was Steinberg. The main concerns of the constituency stemmed from the decision to build the new town of Milton Keynes on Bletchley's doorstep, which Maxwell had backed in Parliament, and the prospect of a new international airport being built at Wing, which at least had the right address. But there had been a new agent, Jim Lyons, for the last couple of years who had made the mistake, in Maxwell terms, of trying to do things in his way.

When the election was called the Maxwell family moved in, just as before – Betty and Philip, too, backed up by Jean Baddeley. They swept aside the arrangements Lyons had made and set up the crucial register of supporters that had been compiled under Bryan Barnard not at Bletchley but at Headington Hill Hall where it was all but inaccessible to anyone not in their inner circle.

The machine that had worked so well in 1964 and 1966 ran just as smoothly. This time the land-rover that took Maxwell through the lanes with his loudspeaker was a bright socialist red. He had a hatch made in the roof through which his head, encased in a socialist cloth cap, protruded like a tank commander's. He was as avuncular as ever to the faithful and as crude and rude in response to anyone who attacked him in the name of the new Tory contender William Benyon.

In Wharf House the red and white telephones were never quiet. The outflow of Maxwellgrams never stopped. They even went to victims of traffic accidents whose names appeared in the news. Every day began with a press conference. 'Maxwell almost dictates the copy, including headlines,' noted one of the reporters, Geoffrey Moorhouse. Giving Moorhouse a lift back to Oxford, Maxwell confided one of his secrets: 'Different techniques for different situations, that's the way to do it.' It was not the way so far as the voters were concerned. Benyon the Tory won by 2,521 votes.

Maxwell's defeat was the end of Labour's prospects in Buckingham and the start of a spectacular if sporadic display of acrimony. But, even though it soon became evident there would be challenges for the candidacy in a new election, the Maxwells defended their territory and the rights they had abrogated like feudal barons.

Geoff Edge, later the Labour MP for Aldridge-Brownhills, had just been appointed as a lecturer at the Open University which was being set up in Milton Keynes when Maxwell was defeated. He moved into a house in Bletchley and asked Lyons if there was any party work to be done. Mischievously, Lyons invited him and Jean Thomas, the wife of another lecturer, to start a party branch in a ward which, unknown to them, contained Wharf House. 'I went along to the first town party meeting not knowing anybody,' said Edge, 'and found myself being abused by this woman with a French accent.'

Dedicated as Betty was to Bob and his destiny, she had some plans for herself now that Pergamon, in which she had been taking an increasing interest, was out of their reach for the moment. In emulation of her father, Betty, at forty-six, decided that she, too, would go after some academic rewards for herself. She enrolled at St Hugh's, where Anne had been, to read for a degree in modern languages. Despite the inevitable upheavals and distractions of life with her unpredictable husband she finished her studies and in 1981 upgraded her degree to a doctorate with a thesis on 'The Art of Letter Writing in France at the Time of the French Revolution and the Napoleonic Era'.

St Hugh's was one of Oxford's five original women's colleges with something of a reputation for sportiness. Not that that was what attracted Betty. 'I would get up at 5.45 a.m., drive to my digs in college to study, then attend lectures and tutorials before driving back to Headington.' Could she have done all this without money? she asked herself. 'Obviously not, but the greatest advantage money brings me is that it buys time and the support of a wonderful staff.' Few students would disagree. But, academically speaking, Betty's honours were well earned. She worked under the guidance of a notoriously hard-to-please woman don, Vera Daniels, who had nothing but praise for her.

The conduct of the Maxwell campaign had raised so many hackles among the new generation of Labour activists, who had an innocent belief in democratic principles, that the Buckingham party had inevitably split

into pro- and anti-Maxwell camps. The National Executive Committee
had to hold an inquiry. Lyons was criticized for lack of preparation. Both
Maxwells and the party officers closest to them were censured. There had
been 'undue influence and interference'. Reported the NEC:

> Whilst it is encouraging to see the wife of a candidate taking an
> active interest in the affairs of a constituency party, a difficult
> situation can arise if such a person holds senior office and becomes
> over-involved in the direction of organizational work.

And involved Betty remained, right up to 1975 when Maxwell, having
tried since October 1974 to find another constituency and having failed,
gave up for the time being. She even won the admiration of Jean Thomas
who, together with Edge, the Maxwell faction tried repeatedly to get
expelled from the Labour Party. 'She was a tremendous worker. If we'd
been on the same side I'd have thought she was great. Wherever she went
her personal maid and chauffeur went with her. The chauffeur, of course,
voted Conservative.'

When Edge was elected as secretary of the Bletchley party he went to a
meeting chaired by Betty. Item 6 was 'Accusations Against a Member for
Anti-Party Activities'. He was alleged by a Maxwell supporter to have
pocketed a £1.20 subscription. Edge was able to survive this slur and went
on to be elected MP for Aldridge in 1974. 'It's important to remember', he
says,

> that the people who were anti-Maxwell embrace the political
> spectrum. It wasn't Left versus Right. It was the right of party
> members to say what they wanted and have free choice in selecting a
> candidate. Maxwell expects total obedience. He expects people to
> do whatever he tells them. The way he behaved was deeply counter-
> productive to his own interests. If he had behaved differently I
> suspect he would have been reselected anyway.

Maxwell eventually appeared before
the Department of Trade inspectors seven months after he had first been
summoned. In any case it took that long for the accounts of ILSC to be
completed. They showed a trading loss for its brief life of £3.68 million.

The investigation was held in private. It was informal, even conversa-
tional, in tone, although the witnesses who attended were sworn in and, if
they wanted it, allowed legal representation. Sometimes one or another of
the inspectors or their assistants would oblige busy witnesses by calling
upon them to take their evidence.

During the sittings that Maxwell and scores of other participants –
including Rupert Murdoch and Godfrey Hodgson – attended between
September 1970 and June 1971, Maxwell brought into play every facet of
his incomparable talent for complication and concealment. But he had
met his match in these two shrewd and unimpressionable interrogators.

With grave courtesy they disregarded his blusterings; with infinite patience they sifted his irrelevancies; and with unfailing suspicion they tested everything he told them against their other sources.

In selecting Sir Henry d'Avigdor-Goldsmid as the new chairman of Pergamon, Grindlay's Bank showed a certain amount of subtlety. He was everything Maxwell was and more: an MP, although a Tory one; a major as opposed to a captain, he also had an MC. But he had a DSO as well. Above all he was a Jew. There were to be no rumblings of prejudice this time, and Leasco nominated the deputy chairman, a Dr Kalinski who was inspired by the righteous wrath of Steinberg, the wonder boy from Brooklyn who had taken Maxwell's misrepresentations as personally as had Rupert Murdoch. For the first eighteen months of an interregnum that was to last more than four years Goldsmid and Kalinski devoted themselves singlemindedly to getting Maxwell and other representatives of the Family Interests to release enough of the money owed to Pergamon to keep the company out of the clutches of the National Westminster Bank to which it owed £1 million and to keep it in business.

Once that was done Goldsmid resigned to become chairman of the Israeli Bank, handing over to one of the non-executive directors, Sir Walter Coutts, a vigorous and upright public figure who had, among other things, put in a spell as Governor of Uganda. Keeping Maxwell in line was just the job for a man whose last adversary had been Idi Amin.

From the beginning Coutts and Alastair Thomson, the other Grindlay's nominee, had the bracing chore of running Pergamon day by day. Most of the 400 employees in Oxford were, on the whole, glad to see them. They feared the company would go into liquidation unless Leasco took it over. But Coutts and Thomson, mindful of the plight of the small shareholders as well, were determined to keep it going. Pergamon had been rather neglected during the ILSC saga, but it was capable of a turnover of £3.5 million a year even in its present condition – even if, with no money behind it, it had to be run parsimoniously.

Maxwell's view, however, was known far and wide. He was the Only Man who could run Pergamon. He was not alone in this opinion, and the new directors were beginning to be made aware of it. As soon as the election was over Maxwell picked up a thread of the self-perpetuating academic network that bound Pergamon together. He was awarded a Kennedy Fellowship to the Harvard Institute of Politics. For a few months in early 1971, while Coutts was trying to disentangle his doings and Company Squad detectives riffled through the Pergamon files, he took Betty and five of the children on a visit to Boston where he delivered a series of lectures on the subject of productivity and earnings. He also set out, working the telephone like a maestro, to plan his campaign to win Pergamon back.

Harvard was one of the many academic centres where people who had first been able to draw attention to themselves in Pergamon journals were now in positions of influence. Editors and contributors who heard Maxwell's version of events began to make Coutts aware of their resentment. Maxwell was the man they had always dealt with; Maxwell was the man they wanted to go on dealing with.

'They felt just like he did,' Coutts remembers. 'Pergamon was Maxwell's baby. He'd created it from the bottom. He'd done an extraordinarily good job, particularly on the academic journals, and when it went out of his control he did absolutely everything to try to get it back.'

Two difficulties loomed above everything else, so far as Coutts was concerned. First, the Stock Exchange was cool, to say the least, to the idea of giving the company back a listing so that its shares could establish a price. Only when the Department of Trade report, unpredictably delayed by Maxwell's tactics, was delivered might that change. Second, when Maxwell was not in America, he returned to Headington Hill Hall and took up residence on the very doorstep of the Pergamon offices. He had no difficulty in finding out exactly what was happening under the new management on the other side of the lawn.

Among the conditions of the settlement the new board worked out between Pergamon and the Family Interests, particularly MSI Inc., were that Maxwell would resign from PPI and that he would be allowed to rejoin the Pergamon board as a non-executive director. Maxwell enhanced this acknowledgement that he – or at least his expertise – was indispensable by letting it be known that if Leasco were not going to go ahead and bid for Pergamon he was well able to do so himself, which came as something of a surprise to people who had heard him complaining about the immense losses he had so recently suffered.

By this time he had withdrawn his legal actions against the *Sunday Times*, and on 2 May 1971 an article in the paper's Business News section said: 'The *Sunday Times* has offered this remarkably resilient businessman the opportunity to express his point of view and describe his plans for Pergamon in the future.'

Disarmingly, Maxwell conceded that ILSC had been 'a real whopper – the one element in Pergamon I really regret. I trusted people and I was let down.' Before turning to the Commons catering episode, he blamed the encyclopaedia salesmen he had gone to such lengths to acquire rather than the principle of door-to-door sales. 'Next time I would be very careful about training and put a high premium on honesty. The people would be on salary, not commission, where the temptation – as we found out – is to sell encyclopaedias to the names on the tombstones in the nearest cemetery.' The sales of convenience to MSI and the French company, not to mention the figure for 'the public', were forgotten.

'But now I am back,' Maxwell continued in statesmanlike manner. 'We are out of our period of crisis . . . a force to be reckoned with.' None the less, he had no intention of making a bid to regain control of the company until it had fully recovered. 'Were I to make a bid now it would have to be at a very low price, most unfair to any shareholders who bought at higher levels in the past. I am not prepared to risk the accusation that I am trying to buy Pergamon back on the cheap.'

A few days later the Department of Trade sent Maxwell the first part of the inspectors' report. This was the section that ended with the frequently quoted conclusion:

> *Notwithstanding Mr Maxwell's acknowledged abilities and energy, he is not in our opinion a person who can be relied upon to exercise proper stewardship of a publicly quoted company.*

Stable and Leach based this stern judgement on twenty-one examples that they gave of the ragamuffin way ILSC had been run, ranging from the sabotage of Caxton to the various 'Misleading Statements'. And, although the other Pergamon directors got a contemptuous passing rebuke, the inspectors had no doubt where the true blame lay.

> *Mr Maxwell maintained that he left financial and legal matters to his professional advisers. This we cannot accept. He has an unusually acute appreciation of financial and accounting matters and is not afraid to enter into agreements of far-reaching effect without legal advice. The evidence we have received convinces us that no major decision on financial or business policy was made in ILSC or Pergamon without his approval and they were usually his decisions.*

They also nailed down the Pergamon share-price support effect that resulted from inflating the profits of ILSC: 'We are also convinced that Mr Maxwell regarded his stewardship duties as fulfilled by showing the maximum profits which any transaction could be devised to show.'

More than twenty years later their piercing assessment of Maxwell is still valid:

> *He is a man of great energy, drive and imagination, but unfortunately an apparent fixation as to his own abilities causes him to ignore the views of others if these are not compatible. This is very evident in the recurrent (and frequent) changes of personnel in ILSC which were one of the factors that contributed to the disaster. Neither his fellow directors, his professional advisers, nor his employees were able to sway his views and actions. The concept of a Board being responsible for policy was alien to him.*

The explosive report was not made public for another month, when the Department had decided that publication would be in the public interest. No one had imagined the fault that was found would be so extensive or damning. Maxwell's return to the Pergamon board was now out of the question. Both Leasco and the institutions threatened that if he came back they would immediately call an extraordinary general meeting and dismiss all the new directors. But the board was still anxious to use Maxwell's talent so long as he could be insulated from Pergamon's affairs. A powerless advisory panel was established on which he sat as 'publishing consultant'. He was paid a salary equivalent to the $40,000 he had got at PPI, which worked out at £16,666.

Because of the painful slowness with which Maxwell had compelled them to proceed, the inspectors dealt with their ILSC findings first and promised more about Pergamon in a later instalment. From the time Maxwell saw the interim report, the inspectors noted in a later one, 'we experienced great difficulty in obtaining information from him, so much so that we believe Mr Maxwell has been determined to obstruct the course of our investigation and to delay its completion for as long as possible'.

Not only was Maxwell enraged by the first report. He was threatened. The inspectors' brief had been widened to look into the affairs of Robert Maxwell & Co and MSI(DS) as well. He immediately took out writs against Stable and Leach personally and against the Department of Trade – the first instance of such a challenge to the Department's right to look into the behaviour of rogue companies – to prevent the inquiry continuing or any more findings being published.

Seething with indignation, he told a press conference the report was 'a smear and a witch hunt'. The 'so-called City establishment' had got off lightly, he claimed, whereas by a Star Chamber procedure he, Maxwell, had virtually been barred from making a living. With the £16,000 they were paying him in mind, this caused a certain amount of wry amusement among the new directors.

Maxwell was convinced he could contain the damage. John Silkin's QC brother, Sam, was sent into court in his wig and gown to argue that because the inspectors had not presented Maxwell with their findings before publishing them and given him a chance to rebut them he had been denied 'natural justice'. The inspectors replied that if a person was aware that he might be criticized and was given the opportunity to deal with the criticism of other witnesses he had been given a fair hearing.

On 29 September 1971, Mr Justice Forbes, who heard these applications, ruled that the inspectors probably had erred in their procedure, that the error could indeed amount to a denial of natural justice which might invalidate their report. But he declined to stop the inquiry because even if the Appeal Court, which was the next stop, agreed with him the inspectors would be bound to give Maxwell an opportunity to deal with the criticism. In fact he urged the inspectors to press on and deliver their report. 'My decision', he said, 'most emphatically does not mean that the inspectors have been unfair as the term is often used. It merely means that in my judgement it is likely that at a trial of this action they may be found to have taken a wrong decision in a field where the landmarks are few and the terrain confused.'

Confused terrain was Maxwell's natural habitat. Wrote Stable and Leach:

His failure to obtain interim relief from the court did not prevent Mr Maxwell from behaving towards us from the time he instituted pro-

ceedings as if the court had given him the relief he sought and had included the inspections of the affairs of RM & Co. and MSI(DS) in its order for good measure. . . . By January 1972 it was obvious to us that if Mr Maxwell was unable to prevent us from disentangling the affairs of Pergamon, RM & Co. and MSI(DS) from the puzzling skein which he has woven about them, he was determined to delay our doing so for as long as possible.

But it was getting harder for Maxwell. By that time the keenly anticipated second part of the report had been issued and rich detail on the inner workings of Pergamon revealed. One of the questions that had been put by the inspectors touched delicately upon one of the Business Principles. Pergamon had claimed a profit of £145,000 on a sale to ILSC. They asked Maxwell if he really believed a company could claim to make money by selling something to itself, as it were. To a company of which it owned half. Maxwell's reply was relished by all who remembered the inspectors' earlier acknowledgement of his financial astuteness. 'Well, there I am out of my depth,' he had told them. 'And I can only put that down to my lack of training and knowledge of accountancy principles. I have a blind spot in my business knowledge in this area.'

Years after they parted company with Maxwell the men who worked to salvage Pergamon had one dominant recollection: Maxwell's awesome ability to reach them on the telephone no matter what time of day or night it was or where in the world they or he happened to be. Only when his Rolls was out of range, for the car phone system then was primitive, were they safe from his probing, nagging, wheedling, bullying intervention.

'We never really had a moment's peace,' says Coutts. 'Maxwell was doing something all the time either to subvert us or to interfere. Very often I'd be rung up between six and eight in the morning about something, probably inconsequential, that he wanted to talk about – but it was all harassment.'

While the echoes of the interim report were still reverberating through the City, Maxwell and Coutts went to the United States to confront the academic contributors and editors who by then were in open rebellion, threatening to withdraw their services if Maxwell was not reinstated, which would have been the final blow for the crippled business.

Maxwell had arranged meetings in New York, Boston, Chicago and Los Angeles. He had also orchestrated, Coutts is convinced, the hostile grilling the Americans gave the new chairman who, it was obvious, they took for a 'Steinberg man' out to turn Pergamon over to Leasco. Coutts came to believe that Maxwell was out to demonstrate that if he was not taken back on to the board of Pergamon he could easily set up an alternative operation in America, wrecking the attempt to refloat Pergamon.

The showdown came after a lunch Maxwell had arranged in the John Hancock building in Chicago. As soon as the meal was over the entire company of professors and doctors turned on Coutts while Maxwell sat back smiling. 'They absolutely hammered me until about four o'clock in the afternoon,' Coutts remembers. 'Most of it was fairly unpleasant.'

'I had never imagined a crowd of men could be so vicious,' said Lady Coutts, who sat next to the most aggressive questioner. Maxwell ought to have known better than to pull something like that on a man who had faced up to Idi Amin. Next morning Coutts called him in his hotel room. 'Never do that again. I have enough contacts in the City of London to sink you as far as you'll ever go. And you'll never come up again.'

In Los Angeles, the next stop, a huge bouquet of flowers awaited Lady Coutts. 'Maxwell was grovelling,' she said, 'but we knew Pergamon was paying for the flowers.'

'Most of my arguments with Maxwell were about his personal expenses,' said Coutts. Consultant Maxwell was as expansive and self-confident as Chairman Maxwell had been – even more so since someone else was responsible for the accounts, it seemed to the other directors. Not only was he still the squire of Headington; he was soon once more the toast of Claridge's and the master of an elegant town house in Knightsbridge, 27 Montpelier Square, rented at £85 a week. There had to be an appropriate setting, he argued, to entertain Pergamon editors and contributors who were otherwise rewarded merely by seeing their work published or by the occasional cash handout.

Between April 1971 and 31 August 1972, Maxwell submitted expenses of £6,071.85 to Pergamon – an average of £357.16 a month. Coutts slashed them nearly in half, approving only £3,523.50, and that grudgingly. He would only permit Maxwell to charge £5 a head for dinner and £4 for lunch for guests entertained at Headington. But Maxwell was incorrigible. Claridge's bills arrived, in addition to those he paid there himself, over £1,000 in all during his consultancy; he insisted on charging 20p a mile for driving his Rolls rather than the 10p Coutts was prepared to allow; and he wanted to charge £16 a night for staying in Montpelier Square – his rented house – when in London on Pergamon business. So far as Maxwell was concerned the money was spent in a good cause. He and Pergamon were indivisible.

Despite the hard time he had been given, Coutts had been impressed by the support Maxwell had been able to muster. Although he did not believe it was desirable to have Maxwell back on the board, at least yet, he gave him his due when he explained to the inspectors the difficulty of running Pergamon without him. 'I maintain that he has a computer brain in that he can read things, particularly in the scientific magazines, which he will store away and that at the right moment of time it will come out of the computer and he will be able to talk to those people in the same language that they talk among themselves.'

The analogy of the computer brain has struck almost everyone who has come in contact with Maxwell for any length of time. The same innate ability by which he has picked up his languages enables him to absorb what he reads – and, above all, what he hears – with no apparent effort and to retrieve the data with exceptional speed. It is an accomplishment of memory rather than of reason, but none the less impressive for that, and it is what allows him to exercise such near-simultaneous control of different situations.

It is, of course, a well-established resort of politicians, stand-up comics and other habitual public speakers to adapt whatever comes their way in the shape of material. But the speed with which Maxwell can absorb and recycle something he has been told is startling. It may also have something to do with his inclination to fantasy. The replays, while instant, are not always accurate. And the reinterpretation usually enhances Maxwell's position. Tell him a story and he may tell it back in no time at all with himself in the lead role. The garbage-in garbage-out rule of computer programming also applies to the phenomenon. Once Maxwell has filed away an imperfect or inaccurate impression it is difficult to erase it.

Something else that people had noticed during the hearings was the frequency with which he would – as he still does – refer to himself in the third person, often as *Mr* Maxwell.

Maxwell worked incessantly on everyone he could reach to get his hands back on the switches at Pergamon. On 2 May 1973 he wrote to Lord Aldington, the Grindlay's supremo who had brought in Sir Walter and Alastair Thomson:

> *If you want to help Wally [Coutts], his colleagues and me to restore Pergamon to its rightful place then I appeal to you to accept that the time is more than overdue for my return to the Board, and please do not ask me for any further delays or allow anybody to prevent my return on the claim that 'this may injure the chances of the Company's shares being requoted'.*
>
> *What possible justification could the Stock Exchange Council have for penalizing shareholders in this way? Surely it is not being suggested that the Council would want to be beastly to some 2,000 Pergamon shareholders on the grounds that they are part of the City Vendetta against Maxwell or that they accept that I am guilty of any misconduct, solely on the uncorroborated and biased DTI reports which, because of the Inspectors' failure to comply with the rules of natural justice, are in any case likely to be declared invalid.*

Christmas 1973 arrived without the long-promised Leasco bid materializing, although Rothschilds had started negotiating directly with the institutions and it appeared that they might get control without actually making a bid. Pergamon was balanced up and trading profitably, but the Stock Exchange would not consider allowing the company to be quoted until the final Department of Trade and Industry – as it had now been renamed – report appeared.

Somewhat to the surprise of a few people who had followed the hearings, John Silkin had been appointed one of the non-executive directors. But the impartiality he displayed impressed his fellow-directors, and he certainly understood the workings of Pergamon. Presumably at his client's urging, he did point out that the present situation could actually be held to be in Maxwell's favour since it was his unfitness to administer a 'publicly quoted company' that the inspectors had questioned and Pergamon was now a non-quoted company. Writing to the Governor of the Bank of England in December 1973 to ask him to head Rothschilds off, Coutts called it all a 'dreary farce'.

The hearings dragged on until July 1973 when the inspectors finally called Maxwell's obstructive bluff. They had tried to get him to comment, for the record, on the analysis of Pergamon's financial position that Price Waterhouse had delivered back in 1970. He said he would now like to have all the papers looked over by 'a distinguished professor of accounting'.

Incredulous, Leach pointed out that it could take a year for someone to go through the mountain of documents. He reminded Maxwell that he himself had appointed Price Waterhouse as independent accountants. Said Stable: 'I do not mind telling you I simply think you are filibustering.'

'Well, Mr Stable, I think this is most undeserving and unfair . . .,' replied Maxwell. A week later his solicitors informed the inspectors that Maxwell would answer no more questions unless directed to by a court.

Maxwell issued yet another writ to try to stop the final report being published, but it was dismissed and the inspectors signed the report in August 1973. It was rough stuff. It provided chapter and verse of what, to the shareholders, was the most galling revelation: that in 1968 one-third of Pergamon's £2.1 million profit was derived from the sale of back issues to only two companies, one of which was Maxwell's own RM & Co. and the other MSI Inc., owned by the trust. When Pergamon stopped trading with the Family Interests it had had to write off £1.16 million in their favour. Overall losses suffered under Maxwell's direction now stood at £4.52 million. Not only had Pergamon shareholders not been given sufficient information about the company's transactions with MSI Inc., it said – the question the inspectors were originally appointed to answer – they particularly had not been given sufficient information about the extent to which profit forecasts depended on transactions with the Maxwell family companies in general.

> Having now investigated a large number of transactions between Pergamon and the Maxwell family private companies we have come to the conclusion that until the Leasco deal foundered the real purpose behind the transactions on which we have reported was to increase the value of Pergamon's shares in the stock market. The Pergamon saga and Pergamon's reputation as an exceptional 'growth stock' could not have been established without the network of related private companies and without undertaking transactions

such as the ones on which we have reported in this report and this purpose is discernible through all Mr Maxwell's conduct with the regard to Pergamon. It runs like a thread through all he did up to the time when the Leasco deal went off.

The inspectors drew attention to the alacrity with which, unknown to the other Pergamon directors, Maxwell had, at the last moment, thrown off the lines which tied the Family Interests to the sinking Pergamon ship – and assured them of generous compensation.

From the time when the Leasco deal foundered part of his energies switched to ensuring that as far as he could arrange matters the private companies were relieved of some of the special transactions into which they had entered. This change of purpose can be seen in his cancellation of the transaction involving the purchase of the so-called Australian debts for £45,213 and the cancellation of the transaction involving the purchase of the other debts for £110,000 both by MSI(DS) and the purchase of the Spanish Translation Rights for £104,166. It can be seen in the terms of settlement with the private companies which Pergamon was obliged to accept in 1971.

The inspectors let Chalmers Impey off the hook, saying that they did not believe the accountants were in any way party to any of the 'ingenious transactions' involving the Family Interests.

In considering Chalmers Impey's position it should be remembered that up to the time of the Leasco transaction Mr Maxwell enjoyed an enviable reputation in the City of London and in the political world and seems to have been able to overwhelm almost everyone with whom he had dealings by the force of his personality.

The inspectors had been surprised that Goldsmid and Kalinski had been ready to wipe the slate clean with Maxwell before the final Department of Trade report had been delivered. When they mentioned this to Coutts he gave it as his opinion that an agreement at that time was vital to save Pergamon. Interest on the National Westminster overdraft alone was a crippling £350,000 a year.

Stable: *Presumably these agrecments were negotiated at a time when you didn't know whether Mr Maxwell could have malfeasance against him or not?*
Coutts: *Yes, indeed.*
Stable: *If as a result of our final report it becomes perfectly obvious that he has, does this agreement preclude proceedings of malfeasance against him?*

In the end, although the inspectors had no doubt that there had been breaches of the Companies Act, no one was ever charged with 'malfeasance' of any kind. Neither they nor anyone else had little doubt that Maxwell would soon be back at the helm of Pergamon. From the way he was behaving most people assumed he already was. The drama had gone on so long even the newspapers seemed to have forgotten how it had started. Pressure from the academics seemed irresistible, and it was doubtful if the company would ever flourish again without his help. The inspectors were philosophical. Two highly critical reports on Maxwell's activities had not 'to outward appearances abashed him or affected his fixation as to his own abilities'. Why should a third?

The takeover bid for Pergamon came not from Leasco (which by 1974 had changed its name to Reliance, but was still suing Maxwell and Flemings) but from the mysterious company 'without accounts, balance sheet, directors, or address', which Goldsmid had scorned, now called Microforms International Marketing Corporation. Triggered by the realization that the institutions were on the point of succumbing to Steinberg's ploy, Maxwell 'persuaded' MIMC to bid eleven pence a share for all Pergamon shares. He then launched a one-man offensive on the exhausted Pergamon board to get it accepted.

Since John Silkin was finding it difficult to spend as much time on Pergamon affairs as they demanded, Maxwell had been allowed to become an 'alternate' director to attend meetings when he could not. On 14 January 1974, Maxwell turned up in Silkin's place at the crucial meeting in the boardroom of the Grindlay's subsidiary where Thomson properly worked, at which the MIMC offer was to be discussed. But so did Silkin, who had warned Coutts only that he would be late. Already irritated by Maxwell's direct approaches to various stockbrokers and accountants concerned, the board insisted that Maxwell withdraw. The following day Coutts wrote to him:

> I would be grateful if you would cease these activities immediately and play your proper role presently which is to remain completely dormant until the bid has been considered by the board and ultimately decided upon.

Indignantly, Maxwell replied: 'I am sick and tired of being harped at and criticized about my ostensible improper behaviour.'

Tempers were short. The others had been wrestling with Maxwell now for more than four years. The same day Coutts wrote back:

> I asked Alastair Thomson, as a favour, to allow our meeting to be held in his Board Room. If you cannot see that your behaviour in using one of his offices and his telephone as if you owned the place and being determined to take part in a discussion bang in the middle of a bid situation was embarrassing to me, I find it difficult to explain what is proper behaviour. I am equally sick of being told that the only person with know-how, the only person who knows anything at all, indeed the only person in the world upon whom the sun never sets is R. Maxwell.

In the end the shareholders accepted twelve new pence (2s 6d) each for the shares for which Leasco had offered 37s 6d (£1.88). Reliance were the last to agree, but well before they had Maxwell was back in the chair of Pergamon. His relentless counter-attacks and elephantine charges had overcome all opposition. 'I have shot Mr Maxwell through the forehead seventeen times,' said Nat Rothschild, one of the bank's partners, after Reliance, too, had thrown in their hand. 'But he just kept on coming.'

In his selective replays of the past Maxwell now manages to make it seem as though the scarifying Department of Trade reports were about someone else. In August 1986 he wrote a letter to his old supporter the *Sunday Telegraph* arguing that the courts had discredited the Stable–Leach report. He took to quoting Judge Forbes's ruling to counterbalance the findings of the investigation. 'It was all wrong,' he told a television interviewer, threatening that he would not continue if questions on the subject were pursued. 'I was exonerated.' He said the same thing to the *Wall Street Journal* in 1987. But the *Journal* had to note, after it had printed Maxwell's statements 'That wasn't precisely the case.'

He was not exonerated. When the 'natural justice' claim was actually tried in December 1972, Mr Justice Wein dismissed his contentions. That decision, too, ended up before Lord Denning in the Court of Appeal in January 1974 and was upheld. 'This is nothing more than an attempt by Mr Maxwell to appeal from the findings of the inspectors,' said Denning. An associate judge sitting with Denning, Lord Justice Lawton, commended the patient cross-examination technique Stable had used with Maxwell. 'I can but admire the way he dealt with a witness who tended to be verbose and irrelevant.' Denning himself praised the inspectors for their 'conspicuous fairness'. 'Having done their work so well,' he said, 'they should not be harassed by this attack.'

Coutts was living in retirement in Perth, Western Australia, when Maxwell's letter appeared in the *Sunday Telegraph*. He wrote to the paper himself.

> *Once again Mr Robert Maxwell has forgotten that: a) The mess in which Pergamon Press found itself in the late Sixties was entirely of his own making. b) Had it not been for the hard work over four years of three independent directors appointed by Grindlay's bank and a dedicated staff at Headington Oxford, Pergamon Press would have been declared bankrupt, handed over to a receiver and disappeared with Mr Maxwell into oblivion. c) Because of that hard work Mr Maxwell was virtually handed on a plate in 1974 a firm base on which to build the business about which he now boasts. Whatever the DTI inquiry did or did not do is irrelevant as the above are the facts. Some of us, including the original smaller shareholders, have long and somewhat bitter memories.*

Maxwell disputed all of this, and the inspectors couldn't say much. Sir Ronald Leach, retired to Jersey, and Owen Stable, now a Crown Court judge, are unable, by the terms of their appointment as inspectors, to comment. 'I feel quite neutral,' said Leach. 'The report speaks for itself,' said Judge Stable. But it is true that the Department of Trade modified the procedures, following the Pergamon case, to ensure that anyone crici-tized was given an opportunity of rebuttal before the findings were published.

Coutts suffers no inhibitions. 'Maxwell has an ability to sublimate anything that stops him getting what he wants. He's so flexible he is like a grasshopper. There is no question of morality or any conscience. Maxwell is Number One and what Maxwell wants is the most important thing and to hell with anything else.'

It was Lady Coutts who got the last word in when it was all over. Maxwell insisted they go to dinner at Headington. Afterwards he was saying goodnight to his guests in various languages. She responded in one he could not even recognize. 'I said to him in Swahili: "Kwaheri ashante sana sitaki kukuona tena. Goodbye. Thank you very much. I don't wish to see you again." '

SEVEN

This is obviously the end of Mr Maxwell's dream of being
the proprietor of a national newspaper.

Hugh Cudlipp, 1969

THE *Daily Mirror* always loved a party. Almost as much dedication and ingenuity went into planning some of them as into producing the issues that won the paper such a special place in British life – the one, for instance, that was so broadly parodied in a special edition for the great Hugh Cudlipp farewell on 1 December 1973. HUGH! DON'T BE SO BLOODY RUDE! the front-page headline read. The *cognoscenti* remembered a message in those terms being delivered by Cudlipp to Khrushchev on page 1 thirteen years earlier. Now it referred to his decision to retire at the relatively early age of sixty. Considering the way things were going at the *Mirror*, this was a wise decision. But it was not going to be a gracious departure.

Hugh Kinsman Cudlipp was one of the immortals of popular journalism, the 'biggest, brashest, boldest, best' of his day. He was also mischievous, vain, arrogant and no less convinced of his infallibility than Robert Maxwell. Although he had twice been editor of the *Sunday Pictorial* (before it became the *Sunday Mirror* in 1963), he was never editor of the *Daily Mirror*. He simply ran it – and all the group's other titles, first as editorial director and finally as chairman.

Cudlipp had joined the *Mirror* on the August Bank Holiday of 1935, thirty-two years after Alfred Harmsworth, later Lord Northcliffe, launched it as a daily newspaper for women, a publishing experiment which, he admitted, was 'a flat, rank and unmitigated failure'. The first front page contained only advertisements, six in all, selling dresses, robes, furs, automobile toilettes, a new corset and Tiffany jewellery. The all-female staff, including the editor, were sacked soon after. 'It was like drowning kittens,' said Hamilton Fyfe, who had been brought in to relaunch the paper as the *Daily Illustrated Mirror* ('the first halfpenny daily illustrated publication in the history of journalism').

In the new format the *Mirror*'s fortunes revived dramatically. Harmsworth made a 'full and frank confession' that his mistake had cost him £100,000. 'The faculty of knowing when you are beaten is much more valuable than the faculty of thinking you are not beaten when you are,' he said. 'Some people say a woman never really knows what she wants. It is certain she knew what she did not want. She did not want the *Daily Mirror*.'

Ten years later, Northcliffe sold the restored publication to his brother the first Lord Rothermere. The issue proclaiming the outbreak of the First

World War sold over 1.7 million copies and the *Mirror* became 'the Forces' paper', a tradition renewed in the Second World War. After its criticism of the conduct of the war Herbert Morrison told Parliament: 'A watch will be kept on this paper and the course which the Government may ultimately decide to take will depend on whether those concerned recognize their public responsibility and take care to refrain from further publication of matter calculated to foment opposition to the successful prosecution of the war.'

The fighting classes loved the *Mirror* just the same. Jane, its scantily clad cartoon pinup, was the period equivalent of page-three 'crumpet'. The *Mirror*'s circulation, and the pro-Labour political influence it provided, soared after the war until in 1965 sales peaked at just over 5 million. Everything the *Mirror* touched seemed to sing with success.

In the history of the *Mirror* there were three indelible names: Harry Guy Bartholomew, who pioneered banner headlines and heavy black type; Cecil Harmsworth King, who created the IPC empire out of the newspapers' earnings; and Cudlipp. 'And how did they get on, this happy few, this band of brothers?' wrote Terry Lancaster, reviewing Cudlipp's book *Walking on the Water*. 'Well, Bartholomew sacked Cudlipp, then King sacked Bartholomew and rehired Cudlipp, and eventually Cudlipp chaired the board meeting which sacked King.' Betrayal of one kind or another was so much a part of life at the *Mirror* that most of the staff had forgotten that the office pub was really called the White Hart. It was universally known as the Stab in the Back. The Stab.

In the days of Cudlipp's editorial domination Cecil King had, by and large, been happy to leave the contents of the papers to him while King went about fulfilling his own imperial vision. When Cudlipp took over he showed no desire to expand the frontiers King had mapped out; the vast domain was already unwieldy enough. Nor did he have much appetite for the task of fighting off the numerous marauders who saw in the wealthy but unruly IPC realm the prospect of considerable plunder if the share price drifted. Murdoch, for one, was looking it over.

One of the states of the confederation was Reed, the prosperous paper and newsprint group whose board had the respect and confidence of the City's bankers and investors. An unusual merger was arranged whereby IPC, which had originally had a controlling interest in Reed, became a Reed subsidiary instead. The papers were given, at Cudlipp's insistence, a formal guarantee of editorial autonomy.

'IT WAS YOU who taught us the art of combining this kind of night with the serious business of making newspapers,' read the mock *Mirror* produced for the great farewell. 'IT WAS YOU who represented the *Mirror* spirit across years too long to remember. IT WAS YOU who could thunder one night and make the magnificent gesture next morning. Because of that, and so many other things, we are here to wish you thanks for the memories.'

Among the river-steamer load of *Mirror* staff absorbing these sentiments – prepared by the man who was to succeed Cudlipp, Tony Miles – together with a great deal of champagne on the way down the Thames to the Trafalgar tavern in Greenwich there were many who did not agree. Whatever Cudlipp's achievements in the past he had made one spectacular, irrevocable and, to the *Mirror* men and women, unforgivable mistake. He had sold the *Sun* to Rupert Murdoch. He had believed, wrongly, that the *Mirror* was unassailable and that Murdoch would fail. (It never occurred to any of them to wonder what might have happened if he had sold it to Maxwell.)

For his part, Murdoch thought little of Cudlipp and the *Mirror* executives and even less of their recent attempts to tilt the paper's readership profile up-market. Innovations such as 'The Inside Page', a skilful and informative diary, and 'Mirrorscope', a pullout section on politics, current affairs, even the arts, had left a lot of readers behind – as many of the journalists were aware. When the *Mirror* had been the only national tabloid worth considering it could set its readership net at whatever level it wished. The higher the *Mirror*'s intellectual aim, the more space left below the trawl. There were plenty of fish still to be found in the lower depths, even if some of them were a little strange. Two months before the new *Sun* first appeared, in November 1969, Murdoch's henchmen were spreading the doctrine: 'Rupert is going back to the *Mirror* of the fifties. He thinks the *Mirror* has gone too far too fast.'

Cudlipp's reaction, after flicking through the first issue of the Murdoch *Sun*, which had blatantly cribbed many of the *Mirror*'s – of *his* – old ideas was: 'We've got nothing to worry about.' But the *Sun*, edited by Larry Lamb who had been one of Cudlipp's young lions at the *Mirror*, had some new ideas, too. It forged 'page-three girl' as a universal synonym for bare-breasted 'glamour' and spread the Permissive Society from the West End of London to every working-class town in the country. Sex was fun, and anyone with the price of the paper could join the party.

Four years later when Cudlipp, who, fortuitously, had always let it be known that he would quit at sixty, was departing MGN the *Sun*, propelled by soft porn and sub-populism, had streaked past 3 million copies a day and the *Mirror*'s supremacy was crumbling fast. Plenty of people drinking their way down the river were ready to forget that Cudlipp had been the making of them; they blamed him for being the breaking of the *Mirror*. The adulatory speeches fuelled their resentment, and when Cudlipp stood to respond he was jeered and pelted with bread rolls.

Cudlipp toughed out the sorry spectacle. Like Maxwell he was sustained by an unnerving self-confidence and a contempt for anyone of lesser attainments. He waved his big cigar disdainfully and went off to accept his peerage. When the Social Democratic Party was formed he resigned from the Labour Party to join it – something more that the *Mirror* held against him.

One of the guests, however, had viewed the events with mounting disbelief. Alex Jarratt, a civil servant mandarin who had become managing director of IPC as a division of Reed, was appalled by what he saw and heard and the disharmony and rancour it suggested. A decade into the future he had learned a good deal more of the *Mirror* and its profligate ways – even its friends called it 'the mink-lined coffin' – but memories of that night were still with him.

Ten years later the newspaper titles
had been organized into Mirror Group Newspapers, a wholly owned
subsidiary of Reed International, and an increasingly burdensome and
unprofitable one. The 1984 forecast was for a paltry £5 million profit on a
turnover of more than £250 million. Reed's magazine operation, IPC, was
far more profitable, partly because they now let Maxwell print their
publications and thus did not have the intractable print unions to wrangle
with. The labour problems which bedevilled not only MGN but every
Fleet Street title seemed insoluble. Besides newsprint, Reed produced
cardboard boxes, rolls of wallpaper and tins of paint by the million. The
Mirror Group papers were a blot on the prospectus, and before it became
any bigger Jarratt, now Sir Alex and chairman of the Reed board,
resolved, in October 1983, to impose independence on this troublesome
outpost of the otherwise prospering empire.

In order to honour the original undertakings and to avoid obstruction by
the Labour Opposition in Parliament – and to fulfil their hope of raising at
least £100 million – Reed decided that instead of selling it to the highest
bidder MGN would be floated on the Stock Exchange in the first half of
1984 and, in tune with the Thatcherite doctrine of privatization, sold
mainly to small shareholders. That, at any rate, was the folksy sales pitch
propagated in the *Mirror* itself: anyone with a few pounds would be able
to own a piece of this famous newspaper.

But in the end Reed broke that and every other undertaking they had
made either publicly or in private. 'We will be able to ensure that no one
will have a major controlling shareholding in the company,' Jarratt had
said. No individual or company would be allowed to take over the group
because that would jeopardize 'tradition, character and independence'.
Quite how the *Mirror* was to be protected was not made clear. Nor were
the paper's tradition, character and independence defined in any way.
Jarratt did, however, assure the nervous staff: 'The Mirror is a good
company with a strong board and a good bunch of assets to see off any
predators.'

But all too soon, inside the Holborn stockade, Maxwell could be heard
roaring in the jungle. The sound spread alarm among both journalists and
printers. At loggerheads for many years, one of the rare matters on which
the two main divisions of the industry might agree was that they did not
want to work for Maxwell.

The printers had the most to fear. Bullying them – or at any rate their
'brothers' in the big plants outside Fleet Street that he now controlled –
outwitting them, outfacing them, firing them in droves when he could and
closing down operations when he could not was what had made Maxwell
a serious commercial force in the ten years since he recaptured the
Pergamon chair. It had also made him much more money than Reed
imagined.

The British Printing Corporation had
really never recovered from the ILSC partnership with Maxwell. After

that, its directors trembled every time they heard his tread. The company was in trouble anyway. It was more a conglomeration than a conglomerate, its various components some of the formerly great names of British printing: Purnell, Waterlow, Sun Printers, Hazell Watson & Viney. Their original owners had become shareholders in the Corporation, hoping to benefit from centralized management that had never successfully been established. BPC plants could take on virtually any printing job imaginable, but costs had become so great that publishers had turned to Continental, even Far Eastern, alternatives.

Uncoordinated, decrepit, overdrawn, besieged by greedy unions, disorganized, BPC had lost £11.3 million in the year 1980 and was sinking fast. Its bankers and the Government doubted that it was worth saving. To Maxwell, it looked like a golden opportunity. In 1981 BPC shares were down to 25p. Maxwell had just been bested once again by Murdoch over Times Newspapers, a contest he had no hope of winning from the start but which he could not prevent himself from joining. He took out his frustration on BPC. In a well-timed dawn raid, Maxwell raked in 29 per cent of the bargain-basement shares for a mere £3 million. Demanding a seat on the board, he proclaimed: 'I am the only man who can deal with the British print unions.'

He was about the only man the terrified BPC directors were not prepared to countenance, the 'frozen dead rat' they were to be forced, in the end, to swallow. Searching for protection, they turned to a distinguished scientist and former chairman of Courtaulds, Lord Kearton of Whitchurch (table F1). After sizing things up he told them: 'The man you need here is Bob Maxwell.'

Maxwell had found yet another influential patron. Kearton had headed one of the hopeful instruments forged in Harold Wilson's white heat, the Industrial Organization Corporation, and had known Maxwell as an MP. Maxwell had tried to get the IOC to finance in the early 1970s the concept of information retrieval he was to bring to fruition in the late 1980s as Infoline. Kearton had seen that the time was not yet ripe and turned him down. But he had been impressed by Maxwell's abilities. 'He's not an easy man,' he says now, 'but he's as near to a genius as we've got in this country.'

Kearton, then aged sixty-nine, agreed to become chairman of BPC and undertook to persuade the Bank of England, the National Westminster Bank, which also held the BPC accounts, and the shareholders that despite the Department of Trade report they should put their trust in Maxwell. 'Part of my job was to go around saying that in my view he *was* a fit and proper person to run a public company,' Kearton recalls. It was a job which he did for nothing. 'That was my subtle weapon with Bob. I never took any pay from him or even expenses. He found that very odd. I still had the idea that one had a certain public duty. Not so popular now.'

Under the umbrella of Kearton's chairmanship Maxwell had first proposed to complete his acquisition of BPC by pledging advance subscriptions to the Pergamon journals amounting to £10 million. Charles

Williams, the chairman of Ansbacher who were advising him, looked around for allies. Sir Robert Clark of the much larger firm of Hill Samuels was prevailed upon to use his influence with Sir Gordon Richardson, the Governor of the Bank of England. Convinced that saving BPC was a worthy cause, he in turn intervened with Robin Leigh-Pemberton, now Governor of the Bank of England himself but at that time chairman of the National Westminster Bank who had most to lose if BPC collapsed. Maxwell was able to raise his stake to 77 per cent of BPC's equity with an investment of £11 million. He telephoned Leigh-Pemberton and asked: 'Who prints NatWest chequebooks?' Soon it was Waterlow, BPC's security printers. Maxwell could afford it. The shares were now half the price he had paid for his first batch. A distinctive Maxwell negotiating concept emerged: Take it or leave it. Under this principle, novel to British trade unions, he imposed a Survival Plan by which 26 per cent of the workforce – 4,000 printers and managers – eventually were made redundant and 10 plants closed down. He even went out looking for plants to close. Reed were only too happy to sell him their huge Odhams roto-gravure plant at Watford in return for an undertaking to print their magazines wherever he liked. He told its staff: 'Your option is not to deal with Reed but to deal with me or the Receiver.' Then he shut the plant down and sold half the land to a hypermarket.

Maxwell warned striking printers at the Park Royal plant where *Radio Times* was produced that if they did not go back to work the plant would never reopen. They did not believe him. They should have. 'I don't have any committees to consult,' said Maxwell.

Kearton left after a year, and Maxwell became chairman as well as chief executive. He put in the 'C' for Communication to mark the visions beyond printing. The usual comic sideshows flourished. Maxwell was discovered lurking in the changing-room of one print works to see if the printers began their shifts on time. Negotiating sessions at the South London office of SOGAT, the main print union, were interrupted by Maxwell storming out in the early hours of the morning only to be found outside waiting to be persuaded back in. Printers on a picket line tried to throw ink over him; avoiding it, he took a fall.

Pergamon made full use of the huge tax-loss advantages it acquired with BPC. But that was nothing beside the new value it could soon put against BPCC. The holdings that had been acquired for less than £15 million in 1980 and 1981, said the annual report for 1984, were now worth about £200 million – 'a massive appreciation in response to their vastly improved performance since Pergamon gained control'. Of the £37.86 million profits for the year, £15.61 million came from property sales. But even those familiar with the Business Practices of old who harboured suspicions about Maxwell's ways with a balance-sheet could not deny that it was a remark-able achievement and that BPCC was now an admirably run company – even if it, like Pergamon before it, was still a one-man band. 'I've shaken this place up,' Maxwell boasted on the eve of a trip to Moscow to receive an Honorary Doctorate of Science from the State University. 'I sure as hell have got control and everybody knows it.'

Maxwell was a deft judge of when to exchange the stick for the carrot, or something rather more toothsome. The printers would have been surprised to see him sweeping into the Savoy Grill to meet Bill Keys, the General Secretary of SOGAT, and another union chief, Teddy O'Brien, who, seeing no need to wait for him, had already started on their second dozen oysters and the back-up bottle of Chablis. Impatient as ever, Maxwell had jumped out of his Rolls in the forecourt without bothering to stop it properly, leaving Sir Tom McCaffrey petrified in the passenger-seat. Private discussions concluded, the union men went off in a cloud of Maxwell cigar smoke.

But when Maxwell wanted a result he would try to get the union men to Maxwell House, now a charmlessly functional building in Worship Street on the fringes of the City, where he could pull off a ploy that did a lot to enhance his reputation for high-powered dealings and durability. Meetings with two, three or even more groups would be set up simultaneously in different rooms with Maxwell shuttling between. He would courteously excuse himself from one discussion to join another, then do the same with the second and third, leaving each batch of participants to their own devices until he returned. The consultations might go on all through the night, union representatives growing more and more haggard while Maxwell appeared to thrive on the overload, brighter and more alert at every reappearance. Well he might be. When each group of union negotiators thought he was with another he had often retired to his flat for a refreshing nap, a snack or a few phone calls. 'He would emerge bathed, shaved and scented,' McCaffrey relates, 'and wade into them.'

One of the companies Maxwell had acquired with BPC brought him into contact with a kind of publishing very different from Pergamon: Macdonald Futura, already flourishing then under the direction of Tim Hely-Hutchinson. Macdonald was getting ready to publish *The Magic Garden* by Shirley Conran. Hely-Hutchinson invited Conran to dinner at Langan's Brasserie to meet the new proprietor.

Maxwell was enchanted by Conran, a woman more often to be found discussing her own success than listening to someone else telling her about theirs. He persisted, however, in confiding to her the secrets of his rise. 'Always sign every cheque yourself', was the dominant one. So taken was he with what Conran managed to convey about herself in return that he told Hely-Hutchinson. 'We must publish this lady's next book, even if it costs. . . .'

Pausing to decide upon a sum that would impress Conran, Maxwell found that his dealings with Pergamon authors did not offer much in the way of guidance. 'Even if it costs £100,000.' Gamely, all present agreed. *Lace*, Conran's last book, had made her a millionaire. Once, however, he had come to terms with the facts of competitive publishing and the huge sums staked, Maxwell's gambler's spirit was aroused. In 1982 he tried to buy a majority interest in Collins, the largest publisher in the country. Yet again Rupert Murdoch beat him to it.

·

The shockwaves Maxwell created at BPCC had faded long before reaching Fleet Street. In 1984 the wealthy and coddled printers of the national papers were still defying every attempt of owners and managers to get them under control. What the MGN 'chapels' (as the local branches are known, after their earliest meeting-places) particularly feared about Maxwell was that he might be tempted to repeat a success he had had only a few months earlier when closing down one BPCC company, Waterlows Security Printers. Using the despised new Tory anti-picketing legislation, he had prosecuted SOGAT and the other print union, the National Graphical Association. They had been heavily fined. This had introduced an entirely different spirit into Maxwell's relations with the union leaders, many of whom he had treated not only as cronies but – however incongruously – as socialist comrades. Capriciously, Maxwell decided to pay SOGAT's fine. But SOGAT had chosen a new leader, Brenda Dean, to succeed Keys on his retirement. She was so incensed with Maxwell's resort to Tory law that she wrote to the Oxford branch of the Labour Party, to which he now belonged, asking for his membership to be reconsidered.

Maxwell and Dean, a handsome statuesque woman, were not destined to dine out. 'Brenda is a wanker,' he would say ungallantly. Thereafter he always treated her with elaborate courtesy to her face and petty disdain when she was out of sight. Sitting with printing executives in his MGN office, he dialled her private number. 'This is an absolutely confidential conversation, Brenda. I am on my private line. There is nobody else here.' Then he switched the call to an amplifier and grinned at his audience as he talked to her.

Significant though Maxwell's achievements with BPCC were, they had, if anything, served to keep him out of the headlines for the previous ten years. Regarding all printers as grasping, malignant, unpredictable Luddites, Fleet Street preferred to avoid writing about them, even about their discomfiture. The public eye, as it was focused by the national press, still held the image of Maxwell imprinted on it by his parliamentary performances and the inspectors' report.

The occasional feeble lunges he made whenever a newspaper group seemed to be for sale had come to look like the reflexes of a dying ambition. When 'Tiny' Rowland suggested he might sell him the *Observer* and the two of them had a well-publicized breakfast at Claridge's (chicken livers for Maxwell – pink inside) the gossip columnists took it more seriously than the City writers, particularly when Maxwell said he would have sacked the editor for publishing a story the *Observer* had carried about Mrs Thatcher's son Mark.

There was not much more interest when, in April 1984, Maxwell bought 10 per cent of Express Newspapers, the old Beaverbrook group, from another corporate raider, Robert Holmes à Court. To anyone who had suspected that Maxwell might go for the *Mirror* that seemed to make it unlikely. In May, Pergamon was involved in 'a major event in public and political life' in Britain – at least, according to Moscow Radio. The publication of the English-language edition of the collected speeches of Soviet leader Konstantin Chernenko was celebrated at a glittering reception at the Soviet embassy in London. Tass noted that the leading figures in British life among the guests included Ray Buckton of the engine drivers' union – an old Maxwell ally from the Buckingham hustings – and Sir Harold Wilson.

There is an unexpected witness to events in Maxwell House in the weeks before Maxwell made his one-man raid on the *Mirror*. Derek Jameson is now one of Britain's better-known television and radio 'personalities'. Then, however, he was an unemployed newspaper editor, having been fired from the *Express* by its chairman of the period, Lord Matthews, and later from the *News of the World* by Murdoch. He was also flat broke. A libel suit he had brought against the BBC for slighting his literacy and his East End background had misfired and he was left with costs of £75,000. Maxwell, whom he knew only slightly, telephoned him to sympathize.

'He said he knew exactly how I felt,' Jameson remembers. 'The same thing had happened to him. He had been wrongly and unjustly accused and it had taken years for him to clear his name. That's when he was judged unfit to run a public company. I knew about him from Pergamon and all that. Now he was still very much a technical publisher, not connected with newspapers at all.'

Maxwell asked Jameson to work for a media committee he had been asked to head to help the National Society for the Prevention of Cruelty to Children. He gave him an encouraging hug. 'It will get you back in the land of the living,' Maxwell told him.

'He's a very avuncular figure,' Jameson says. 'There's no way you can say no to Robert Maxwell, whatever he asks. I went out stirring up things, organizing, producing stories and pictures. I was rubbing shoulders with the Duke of Westminster, Gerald Ronson the boss of Heron Industries, people like that, all in the name of Robert Maxwell. He paid me out of his own pocket, literally. Just kept giving me – oh, perhaps a couple of thousand pounds because he knew I needed it.'

During the tentative approaches Maxwell was making to the *Express* he was called on by Lord Matthews. 'Your friend has been in,' Maxwell told Jameson one day. 'We didn't get very far.' Jameson says he told Maxwell: 'Never mind the *Express*, Bob. It's the *Mirror* you want to go after.'

'Stone me!' Jameson recalls. 'Within days he had forgotten the *Express* and was deeply immersed in the battle to get control of the *Mirror*. I'm not saying it was anything to do with me, but it was a strange coincidence.'

The journalists at MGN might, like Jameson, have come to regard Maxwell as being, in their terms, little more than an ambitious and noisy dilettante. But a bizarre episode after he had got Pergamon back ten years earlier made them only a little less apprehensive than the printers.

One other noteworthy event of 1974, in addition to Maxwell's restoration, had been the decision of Express Newspapers to close the *Scottish Daily Express*, a paper which, because of his own Scottish ancestry, had been Beaverbrook's particular pride. The 2,000 jobs that went with it were a cruel blow to Glasgow, a city already suffering high unemployment and hardship. The rump of the workforce under Allister Mackie, a forty-five-year-old printer, set about forming a co-operative to take over the *Express* building in Albion Street and bring out their own paper, the *Scottish Daily News*. It was a bold plan, born of desperation but destined to end in grief.

But the Scots had only themselves to blame. They asked him. The works committee had already approached Tony Benn, the Labour government's Minister for Industry and a ubiquitous champion of the proletariat. Despite the natural resistance of his departmental civil servants Benn offered help of a sort. For every £1 the workers raised the Government would put in £1. The Scots handed over their payoff cheques, but the fund was still short of its target. Sitting in Trafalgar Square watching the pigeons, a delegation from the works committee cast around for a backer. Maxwell's name came up.

Maxwell invited the Scots to Headington. He was not long back from a cruise in *QE2*. There had been a strike of cabin crew as he and Betty boarded. Cunard had declined his offer to mediate. The Scots outlined their plans. Maxwell pledged £100,000 to the cause. 'All I'm interested in,' he told them, 'is the political mileage.' The visitors were delighted but they noticed one thing. Everyone was drinking tea from the same monogrammed crockery. But the cup Maxwell was given was twice the size of any other.

As the deadline for the workers' fund to close grew near they were thousands of pounds short. Unless the money was raised the government loan would not be activated. Maxwell joined the campaign, attracting plenty of attention but no more contributions. 'I'll bridge the gap,' he offered the other members of the co-op. 'However, I have to control the paper.'

'The works committee agreed verbally at the time,' said Ron McKay, one of the journalists who worked on the *Scottish Daily News*. 'The money was raised and the paper saved. Then, to some extent, the committee reneged on its agreement with Maxwell, though he remained as co-chairman.'

However, Maxwell had considerably more than a foot in the door, and as the broadsheet *Scottish Daily News* was launched so did his dreams of becoming a newspaper proprietor float to the surface once more. 'From his actions it was clear that he wanted to take over the paper; to get it on the cheap,' says McKay.

The 500 members of the co-op soon found that Maxwell, his frequently avowed socialist principles notwithstanding, was a hardline autocratic capitalist when it came to running a business. As sales slipped, he took important decisions without referring to the committee or anyone else. Without consultation, he cut the cover price. 'He didn't appear to understand the economics of the operation,' says McKay. 'He thought: If I cut by twenty per cent, I'll have to sell twenty per cent more papers. In fact, he had to double the circulation.'

Maxwell was everywhere, even if not in person. His voice boomed out over a loudspeaker system he had discovered, exhorting the workers to greater efforts: 'We must meet deadlines. If page five isn't ready, go without it.' He meant it. The paper often appeared with blank holes in the pages. As friction grew between Maxwell and the works committee, his broadcasts included personal attacks on its members, Mackie the chairman especially. Threats of legal action failed to silence him. 'Mackie and the others are out to ruin your jobs,' Maxwell would thunder at midnight. 'Don't let them get away with it.' Then, in one of his mercurial switches of character, he would be found in the canteen cooking the sausages and hamburgers for the workers' supper.

A meal prepared by Maxwell can be expensive. After he had moved back into Pergamon, Dr Horst Benzing, a representative of the German publisher Bertelsmann, came to collect some £10,000 in Deutschmarks which Bertelsmann considered they were owed. Maxwell invited him to spend the night at Headington.

In the morning Maxwell cooked them breakfast and introduced Benzing to a nifty business practice. He had made out a cheque for £5,000. 'You can either take that in full payment,' Maxwell told Benzing, 'or you can sue me.'

'I took the cheque,' says Benzing, 'and said: "Thanks for the breakfast." '

In Albion Street an essential item of crisis equipment was sent for. A large bed, so that the Scots could see that Maxwell was merely snatching a few hours' sleep between editions. But once all was quiet he would slip out to the Albany Hotel where he was really staying.

Sixteen months into the Scots' courageous effort the works committee collapsed in disorder. At the final mass meeting Maxwell called them 'incompetent fools and malcontents', and when Mackie tried to speak he led the booing. Although the paper had an elected editor, Fred Sillitoe, Maxwell's influence was now unfettered. In a last attempt to save the paper it was relaunched as a tabloid.

'I got a story about a children's home in which children were being locked in cells, beaten and neglected,' said McKay. 'As I was writing the follow-up the next day, Maxwell sat down beside me, put his hand on my knee and said: "This is the way you have to write it." '

The struggle to keep the paper alive lasted another six months before the Receiver was called in. Maxwell walked away from it, blaming his old enemy Insight, which published yet another devasting exposé of his performance at the *Scottish Daily News* and his tactics in banishing its founding fathers. The report quoted this exchange:

Mackie: *You really claim you're a Socialist?*
Maxwell: *Yes, I am.*

Mackie: *If you were an honest man you'd tear up your Labour Party card and join the National Front. At heart you're a Fascist.*

Maxwell just grinned at Mackie's accusation, Insight reported. But Sillitoe fired off a telex of protest to Harry Evans. Both Evans – and Sillitoe – were taken aback to read the article described as 'the shittiest and most disgraceful piece of journalism in the history of British newspapers'. Maxwell had dictated this additional paragraph and ordered it to be sent under Sillitoe's name. As usual, Maxwell sued the *Sunday Times*. As usual, nothing came of it. After he had resigned Maxwell reminded Glasgow: 'The bulk of my family was annihilated by the Nazis and the last thing you can throw at a person like myself is the epithet of being a fascist.'

The MGN journalists lost no time in letting it be known that Maxwell would not be welcome. The most vocal opposition came from Joe Haines, the *Daily Mirror*'s chief leader-writer. Haines had put in seven years as Harold Wilson's press secretary. He joined the *Mirror* after the paper had serialized his book *The Politics of Power*, which Wilson described as 'a dedicated hatchet job'. He knew Maxwell from his Downing Street days and told everyone at MGN who would listen: 'The man is a monster.' And he would elaborate at great length about what he knew of Maxwell through Number 10.

After he had retired as political editor of the *Daily Mirror*, Terry Lancaster encountered Haines at the Gay Hussar.

'Saw you on television, Joe,' said Lancaster heartily.

'"Question Time"?' asked Haines, who had just appeared on that current affairs programme.

'No, the nine o'clock news. You were carrying Maxwell's bags at Glasgow airport.'

The great mistake Reed made – if indeed it was a mistake – was to give such lengthy notice of their intentions. The response of City underwriters to the proposed flotation had been somewhat underwhelming, and the chances of getting as much as they had hoped for the company was fading. By July 1984, the point at which Reed had said the operation would be under way, a firm date for it had yet to be announced.

To champion the cause of the flotation to the small investors they hoped to attract Reed had recruited Clive Thornton, head of the Abbey National building society, as MGN's new chairman. The only previous dealings Thornton, a self-made solicitor proud of his working-class Geordie roots, had had with newspapermen were confined to financial writers in the placid backwater of the home mortgage market. Tony Miles stood down and became deputy chairman as well as editorial director. The other MGN directors rallied around Thornton. The only people who did not behave as they were supposed to were the Reed directors – and Maxwell.

Thornton had lost a leg in a tramcar accident early in his life, and the slightly uneven gait his artificial one imposed quickly became familiar in the MGN corridors. He began in a refreshingly innocent way to come to grips with the alarming world into which he had been pitchforked, talking to unhelpful union officials as though they were mortgage holders behind in their payments, spurning the comforts of his private dining-room to eat in the greasy canteen with press hands and bundlers. He had come across Maxwell only eighteen days after arriving at MGN when they were both invited to the centenary lunch of the Parliamentary Lobby, the secretive cabal of journalists in the House of Commons which is allowed to mix with Parliamentarians in their own domain provided they write only indirectly about what they hear or see.

Maxwell swooped. They shook hands. Thornton looked up from his awkward stance, a short bespectacled figure with a quirky smile that gave warning of an unexpectedly sharp wit. Maxwell, gold-toothed grin glinting beneath the chandeliers and sleek blackened hair glistening, towered over him, Scotch in hand. 'Mr Thornton! I wanted to meet you. How is the flotation going?' Watching a television programme about the subsequent *Mirror* takeover, critic Nancy Banks-Smith was reminded of 'a salivating, handsomely-ruffed wolf' descending on a 'perspiring, City-suited pig'

Thornton parried by switching the subject to Oxford United. Still to distinguish themselves, Oxford were due to meet mighty Everton, the Merseyside team with a strong Catholic following, in a vital tie of the FA Cup. 'I'm taking the precaution of consulting Cardinal Heenan,' said Maxwell, 'and asking for his blessing.'

'That will be an interesting conversation,' said Thornton, himself a serious Catholic, flashing his little smile. Heenan had long gone to his reward. Perhaps Maxwell meant his successor, Cardinal Hume? Maxwell laughed good-naturedly. Thornton had won the first round. He did not win any more.

As the weeks went by Reed reiterated their stand time and again. The various merchant banks involved – S. G. Warburg for Reed – went on preparing the flotation. Maxwell kept uncharacteristically quiet, although he did maintain one particular link he had always enjoyed. The editor of the *Sunday Mirror* was now his old friend Bob Edwards, a Labour Party stalwart who had never lost touch with Maxwell during the wilderness years. He was a frequent guest at Headington where he would tell the Maxwell children present: 'I'm very fond of your old man. But I don't think I would want to work for him.' Edwards provided Maxwell with a small but flattering service. The paper's newsdesk had a standing order that every Saturday night someone was to phone Headington and read Maxwell the headlines of the various Sundays. Ever more avidly, Maxwell watched the progress of the flotation plans. He had not needed Jameson to tell him to go after the *Mirror*. He was close to sixty-one, a year older than Cudlipp had been when he quit. His need to own a national newspaper had become like an itch he could not scratch.

Bob Edwards was one of the editorial group which as well as attending MGN board meetings – all the editors were directors – conferred with Reed's chief executive, Leslie Carpenter, at a monthly lunch. The others were Mike Molloy, editor of the *Daily Mirror*, Richard Stott, editor of the *People*, and Tony Miles. Almost every time they met while the flotation was being worked out Carpenter assured them there was no prospect of any single proprietor, let alone Maxwell, taking over the group. Reed, Carpenter reminded them, had contracts with Maxwell's printing companies that were worth millions to him and that those would be used as pressure to fight him off. In any case, he said, Reed did not believe that Maxwell had the money to buy MGN.

More worrying to Reed, although Carpenter took good care not to say it, was whether or not they could still attract enough investors to take up the MGN shares. The long delay had seen the stock market drift lower. One of the important assets of MGN had been a stake in Reuter, which was now seen to be worth less than its original valuation. Uncertainty about the group's future had hit the sales and advertising of its titles and, naturally, MGN's various rivals were incessantly critical of its performance. By the beginning of summer the original forecasts had been revised sharply downwards. The Reed board were beginning to wonder if the flotation ought not to be called off.

Meanwhile, out in the jungle, word had reached Maxwell of something no one outside the two boards was supposed to know. Under the plan Thornton had prepared no single holder would be permitted to own more than 15 per cent of MGN shares during the two years following the launch. Maxwell had to pounce before either the float took place or it was postponed. The phone call Alex Jarratt had hoped never to receive came on 3 July.

Maxwell was not alone in his fortunate timing. A short while before, the *Guardian* had sent Mike Molloy a recently reissued classic work on the British press to review for its media page: *Dangerous Estate* by Francis Williams. Molloy was – is – one of the more remarkable figures of the popular newspaper industry. Except for a brief detour to the late *Daily Sketch* in the 1960s he had worked for the group since he was fifteen; he was now forty-three and had been editor of the *Mirror* for nine years.

Looking, by his own description, 'like an overweight Robert Redford', he was the last of the mythical breed who had started out as humble tea-makers and worked their way up to the editor's chair. Even more remarkably, Molloy had done it without ever having been a journalist in the usual sense of the term; he had never been a reporter or subeditor, never sat on the 'back bench' where the news pages were made up nightly. Until he became an executive Molloy was a make-up man, a craftsman in production and design, master of a tabloid skill essential to the successful presentation of the efforts even of inspired pamphleteers like Cudlipp. Many of the great *Mirror* front pages for which Cudlipp enjoyed credit had been designed by Molloy; in fact it was the 'look' that Molloy, over the years, had imposed on the *Daily Mirror* which, in a wide range of imitations and corruptions, came to govern the appearance of the whole present generation of British tabloids.

Accident had thrust Molloy into the editor's chair in 1975: the illness of Michael Christiansen whose deputy he had become only three months earlier. It was not a *Mirror* tradition for deputies to succeed. Nor, for that matter, for editors to edit. The deputy was there to run the paper while the editor was receiving instructions from the editorial director or performing ceremonial duties of one kind or another. In Cudlipp's time he, as editorial director, had been, in effect, editor-in-chief of all the titles. He took little notice of the daily or weekly bolting-together of the papers, but all the editors knew better than to make any moves of consequence without consulting him or taking his known views into consideration. This principle was preserved by Cudlipp's successor, Tony Miles, whose prejudices were rather less predictable.

If the years in Cudlipp's shadow had made a skilled courtier of Molloy, a long association with Miles had refined his corporate cunning. Apart from a preoccupation with British party politics that many readers thought showed to excess in the *Mirror*, the two shared one overruling resolve. They were determined not to miss out on any of the opportunities for vicarious participation in the life of the nation that came with their jobs. And these were many and varied: first-class travel to America, grand receptions at the annual Labour and Tory conferences, Ascot and the Derby, lunch at Buckingham Palace, dinner at 10 Downing Street. Molloy, who had gone to the Ealing School of Art in the suburb in which he still lived, particularly enjoyed the Royal Academy dinner each year and invitations to High Table at an Oxford college.

When the occasion demanded – publishing the Haines book was but one – Molloy could show admirable nerve and determination. But, lacking the usual burning curiosity of the calling where news was concerned and having little taste for dealing with the daily tabloid grist, Molloy was usually happy to leave the contents of the paper to subordinates and concentrate his efforts on its appearance. Since its policies were largely in Miles's hands the paper was, in effect, edited from the rear. Nor, it seemed, could the complacent and ineffectual management tolerated by Reed stave off the growing pressure from rivals, particularly the *Sun*. Catastrophic managerial misjudgements over production equipment had crippled the paper's ability to compete. The unions – including the journalists – were behaving like anarchists. The circulation had drifted down from 4 million when Molloy had taken over to nearer 3 million. There being little Molloy could do about any of this on his own, he spent more and more time on his private interests. He had an easel moved into his office so that he would be able to paint if the mood took him. He began to write thrillers. And, on a beautiful mahogany card-table with felt inlays and chip-wells, he offered a stimulating game of poker to anybody who wanted one.

When he sat down to review *Dangerous Estate* a poker game was the metaphor Molloy chose for the state of Fleet Street, deploring the wasteful folly of proprietors who, rather than look for genuine market-gaps, preferred to launch publications intended to bulldoze competitors out of business altogether. A lot could be said now that could not have been said before.

Since Cecil King was deposed and ownership passed into the hands of Reed International the Mirror Group has lacked the kind of auto-

*cratic player who can take his seat in the Fleet Street poker game.
Consequently, we have reacted to market forces rather than created
them. After the flotation of the Group things will change. The benign
but distant rule of Reed International will be over and power will
once again return to the ninth floor at Holborn Circus.*

When news of Maxwell's offer to Jarratt got about – and he put it about
immediately, himself – reporters roared around to Worship Street. Among
them was John Edwards, star writer of the *Daily Mail*. 'I'm going to get it,'
boasted Maxwell. 'You'll soon see' On his desk lay a copy of the *Guardian*,
open at Molloy's piece. Maxwell slapped his palm down on it. 'That's the
kind of man I want to be editor of the *Mirror*.'

'He *is* the editor of the *Mirror*,' said Edwards.

Jarratt knew Maxwell well. As well
as he wanted to. Once both of them had been flying the Atlantic on
Concorde. Maxwell had buttonholed Jarratt as he was trying to visit the
toilet and demanded that Reed sell him Butterworth, which by then Reed
owned. 'It's not for sale,' said Jarratt, squeezing hurriedly by.

He said the same thing when Maxwell told him that Tuesday, 3 July, that
he wanted to make a bid for MGN. A bid would not be welcome. Jarratt
would prefer that Maxwell did not make one. Maxwell asked if he might
come to see Jarratt. He was told no. 'I'll send you a letter,' said Maxwell.

The letter was a bid of £80 million. By the time it arrived at Reed House
in Piccadilly, Maxwell had already told the media that he was prepared to
go higher, perhaps to £120 million. Jarratt replied, reminding Maxwell of
Reed's public intentions but saying that he would submit the offer to the
board which, coincidentally, was due to meet. The board turned Maxwell
down. But already some of the members were weakening. The estimates
of what might be raised by the flotation were even more pessimistic than
before. Others were scornful. Maxwell did not have that kind of money.
He would try to pay them in Pergamon stock.

Never before had the media been so enthralled by a story about one of
its own elements. The *Mirror*'s unique place combined with the Maxwell
Factor made it irresistible. A swarm of reporters followed Maxwell everywhere. He was at his expansive, competitive, exhibitionist best. Sue
Cameron of the *Financial Times* jumped into the back of his Rolls. At a
traffic light they pulled up alongside a Porsche. 'Think he'll beat us?'
Maxwell asked. As the light was about to change he wound down the
window and shouted to the other driver that something was wrong with
his rear wheel. The driver pulled into the kerb to investigate. The Rolls
roared away from the light.

The men at Reed only had to switch on a television set or pick up a paper
to know that Maxwell was not taking no for an answer. He announced
that he now intended to raise his bid to £100 million. He was making the
offer publicly, he said, because it was impossible for him to obtain any
information from Reed to assess the true value of the company. All Reed

had to do, said Maxwell, was to sign a copy of his most recent letter and they could have his bankers' draft immediately. Reed, actually, had difficulty in understanding the letter. They wrote back asking for clarification. But they were backed into a corner, and it was time for desperate measures. Little as they wanted Maxwell, they could no longer refuse to recognize his offer. Their last hope seemed to be the Labour Party from whose ranks a groundswell of protest was emanating.

Carpenter knew that Neil Kinnock, the Leader of the Opposition, was a neighbour of Molloy's in Ealing and a close friend. Would Molloy go to him and try to rally Labour to oppose Maxwell? Miles passed on the plea and Molloy, moving with the same secrecy in which Reed was operating, arranged a meeting with Kinnock in a private room at Brown's Hotel on Friday, 6 July. He acted with some trepidation. In the slightly slapdash way of the *Mirror* he had never been given a contract as editor. Kinnock's office was notorious for its leakiness and sooner or later word of the meeting could be expected to reach Maxwell. If Maxwell did get the *Mirror*, he could not be expected to take kindly to anyone who had tried to prevent him.

Nevertheless, Molloy stated the case against Maxwell as strongly as he could. He had a receptive audience. Unlike Molloy, Kinnock had actually met Maxwell, if fleetingly, at party conferences. He knew him as an important contributor to Labour funds. He had also heard from him quite recently.

Kinnock's deputy Roy Hattersley had a closer acquaintance with Maxwell. Hattersley was a friend of Charles Williams of Ansbachers (Lord Williams of Elvel and a financial adviser to Maxwell by the time he got to table E2). When Maxwell needed someone to convince Kinnock that it would be in the best interests of Labour *not* to oppose him it was to Hattersley he turned.

The argument that Maxwell wanted pressed home to stifle opposition from the Labour benches was that, whatever objections there might be to him, he could be counted on to support the party in the next election. If the flotation went ahead, if Thornton's starry-eyed plans were carried out, there was no telling what the *Mirror*'s policy might be at that time. There might not even be a *Mirror* by then. The party could be without any national press backing at all. 'And he has kept faith with them about that,' Molloy points out. 'The *Mirror* supported Labour to the hilt when the election came. More strongly even than it had ever done before.' Even to the extent of depriving itself of £350,000 of advertising revenue.

On the morning of the day Maxwell's first bid was announced, Hattersley had called on Kinnock in his Commons office. Kinnock was already preparing a statement that Labour did not believe Maxwell was the right owner for the *Mirror*. Hattersley argued against it. Kinnock was swayed.

A few minutes after Hattersley had left a red telephone on Kinnock's desk rang. It was his private line, the number known only to his close associates. 'Fuck me!' yelped Kinnock, skittering into his outer office. 'I've just had a call from Robert Maxwell.'

What the implacable nemesis of the telephone had said was: 'I'm glad you have listened to the advice you have been given.'

Back at the *Mirror* journalists and printers alike huddled feverishly in union meetings during the next few days. Wary of Thornton's idealistic 'open-mouth management', Reed had long since banned him from making any kind of public statement. The only information that passed between Piccadilly and Holborn was that nothing had changed. Not nearly as many people believed that now. 'I got to the point where I couldn't trust the Reed board,' Thornton said mournfully afterwards. 'I tried to avoid saying I was betrayed but I found a great deal more frankness, honesty and integrity around Fleet Street's union leaders than I have in the Reed board.'

Maxwell, in his press conferences, had openly discussed what he planned to do with MGN. 'My first direct action will be to start a London evening paper by September 15.' Well, he did not say which September. What would he be like as a proprietor? The reply was what he had told Tomalin sixteen years earlier. 'I would be a Beaverbrook type – but without the vendettas.' Then Maxwell flew off to France to negotiate for an Infoline database.

On the very day Molloy had met Kinnock, the *Mirror*'s industrial editor, Maxwell's old acquaintance Geoffrey Goodman, had drawn the strands of resistance together for page 1.

> *The strongest opposition came last night from the largest of the print unions, SOGAT, whose general secretary-elect, Brenda Dean, declared 'total opposition to Mr Robert Maxwell – or any other one individual person – acquiring control of the company'. SOGAT, backed by the National Union of Journalists, urged Reed International to resist the Maxwell bid and his typical manoeuvrings. The SOGAT–NUJ statement said: 'All unions dealing with Mr Maxwell have found great difficulty in negotiating in good faith with him in the past. Undoubtedly he will insist on manning reductions as part of any deal to take over MGN, not only in London but in Manchester and Glasgow as well.'*

David Thompson, a political reporter who was head of the *Mirror*'s NUJ chapel, said: 'If he comes in here, it will make his past rows look like squabbles in kindergartens.' Said Haines, still the most vociferous opponent: 'I will walk out the back door as he walks in the front.'

By the following Thursday, 12 July, Reed had a revised bid from Maxwell to which they were going to have to respond. Until that moment no one from Reed had been ready even to talk to him face to face. Jarratt still was not. But they could no longer refuse to deal with him. Warburgs had assured them that Maxwell had the bank credits ready. 'Reed has not turned down my offer,' Maxwell was trumpeting in the streets. 'They *can't* turn down my offer.' Whatever Reed might have thought – or hoped –

until then, he had the money. Jarratt gave the task to Carpenter, the man who had kept up the assurances to MGN that this moment would never come.

Carpenter had a reputation for tough dealing. An accountant who used to play the horses in his youth, and a magazine man most of his life, he, too, knew Maxwell of old. He had been at Newnes when Maxwell bought *Chambers's Encyclopaedia*. Later he had negotiated the sale of Odhams Watford to BPCC. What he had learned about Maxwell then was to guide his actions now. That and the need for some dramatic justification of Reed's action in breaking its pledge.

A favourite Maxwell gambit, Carpenter believed, was to agree a deal, announce it to the world and then try to improve the terms on negotiating the fine details. 'With Odhams, Maxwell and I had quite quick discussions and reached agreement easily,' Carpenter remembers. 'But then we spent bloody ages nitpicking over the contract afterwards, him trying to chip away at everything. I didn't give in, but it was tedious and time-consuming.'

Carpenter phoned Maxwell and told him that if there was to be a deal it would have to be completed on the day they met. There had to be cash on the nail. 'No warranties, no agreements to pay on a certain date, nothing. We would hammer out the details. He would hand me the money. I would hand him the share certificates.' It was an unprecedented method of going about a transaction of such size, but one that appealed to Maxwell as much as to Carpenter.

Reed did not want Maxwell to come to the Reed offices. Carpenter had no intention of going to Maxwell House. He suggested a meeting at the Ritz Hotel on the other side of Piccadilly. Maxwell took a suite. Baddeley and her assistant Debbie Dines were sent along to set up their type-writers and lay out the food and drink for a marathon negotiating session. Carpenter said he would be there at 4 p.m. when the clock would be set running. Jarratt put the Reed board on standby and retired to his office. He had no intention of speaking to Maxwell again, or even of seeing him.

Once he had got the *Mirror*, Maxwell would regularly boast that he had bullied Reed into selling by threatening to make a takeover bid for Reed itself. 'I told them that if they didn't agree I'd make a bid in the morning.'

'He certainly did not say that at that time,' says Carpenter. 'Neither do I believe he could have done it by a bloody mile.'

It took no more than two hours for the men to come to terms. Baddeley typed them up in a two-page letter, and that was it. Maxwell had arrived with his cheque, drawn on the faithful National Westminster Bank, already made out. But it would not do. He had overlooked the debts that came with MGN, the ordinary financial obligations that remain when a company's trading is stopped dead on one page of the ledger. They came to another £23.4 million. It was, in fact, money that Reed owed MGN and would be refunded. But if the deal was to be made on the spot it must be 'clean'. Maxwell had to pay the extra sum as part of the purchase price, £113.4 million altogether. And he did not have enough money. The credits he had arranged were £6 million short.

'He claimed it was only because the banks were closed and I'd sprung this on him,' says Carpenter. For a while it looked as though they were in trouble, Carpenter tripped up on his own condition that the deal be made before the day was over. He took Maxwell's letter back across Piccadilly where the Reed board were waiting. The latest estimate of what flotation might raise had dropped below £50 million. So anxious were the wallpaper manufacturers to get out of the newspaper business by then that they offered to lend Maxwell the £6 million.

Maxwell waited at the Ritz until 9 p.m. for a cheque-book to arrive from Maxwell House. Then, at last, he was invited to Reed House – not to Carpenter's office but to the boardroom – for the final scrutiny of contracts and other documents on which herds of lawyers and bankers from both sides had been working through the evening. The signing took place just before midnight. Maxwell borrowed his £6 million at 2 per cent over the bank rate and paid it back soon afterwards. Reed gave him back £23.4 million, leaving them with £90 million. They got Maxwell's cheque cleared first thing the following morning. The bank returned it to him. He had it framed.

As Maxwell was leaving, Reed executives remembered something else from the Odhams Watford experience. Sam Silkin had still been in the office going over the contracts when Maxwell took a helicopter down to Watford, climbed up on a trestle table and started telling the troops their fortune. He had warned the printers a lot of them were going to lose their jobs. 'I do that sort of thing rather well,' he had said afterwards. Mindful that the presses at the *Mirror* would now be running and that the following day's editions depended on keeping them running, Carpenter's parting words were: 'Don't go down there tonight, Bob.'

'I won't,' said Maxwell. He went back to the Ritz and made a couple of phone calls. Then he got in his Rolls and drove straight to the *Mirror* building.

The night was right for melodrama at Holborn Circus. Lightning cracked around the windows of the directors' suites on the ninth floor of the *Mirror* building, and the splendid view across the City was overshadowed by a bank of dark cloud. Thornton and a couple of others knew something was going on at Reed; there had been telephone calls long after the time anyone was usually to be found in the Piccadilly office. One had been from Jarratt to Miles assuring him that nothing of consequence would happen that night. The *Mirror* men had no inkling of what was going on at the Ritz or even that Reed had decided to negotiate with Maxwell. Loyally following the assumption that the flotation would go ahead, Miles, the retiring chief executive Douglas Long and his successor Roger Bowes were giving dinner in one of the private dining-rooms to two candidates for the non-executive directorships that were part of the structure Thornton envisaged. Thornton himself, not feeling well, had gone home to his London flat.

After the first edition of the paper had been sent to press Molloy came up from his third-floor office to have a drink with the departing guests and stayed on to talk to the others. They told him of the puzzling calls from Reed and about another from Thornton. About 10 p.m. Thornton had been rung by the convenor of the group's NUJ chapels, Revel Barker, who had heard something through his own sources. Why was Reed having a board meeting? 'I tried to phone them,' Thornton told Miles plaintively. 'Now they won't even take my calls.'

At midnight the *Mirror* men had all decided to call it a day. One minute into Friday, 13 June, the telephone rang in Miles's office. Jarratt broke the news. 'It's the best thing we can do,' he said.

'OK,' said Miles. 'That's it.' They were all flabbergasted. In his flat off Tottenham Court Road, Thornton answered the phone to Carpenter. 'He said he was very sorry, the *Mirror* had been sold. I was out of a job.'

One of the calls Maxwell made from the Ritz was to Bob Edwards's *pied-à-terre* in Notting Hill Gate. 'I'm your new boss,' he said. 'Come down to Maxwell House and have a drink.' The other was to the *Mirror*. Molloy went out to answer the phone on the secretary's desk. 'This is Robert Maxwell. Let me speak to Tony Miles.' But Miles did not want to talk to Maxwell. He had been at the *Mirror* for thirty years, rising from feature writer to editor on his way to the chairmanship. He doubted he would be there much longer. 'Tell him I've gone home.' Jarratt had said that Maxwell was on his way back to Worship Street. Tomorrow would be time enough to welcome the conqueror. And home Miles went.

Maxwell had hung up by the time Molloy returned to the phone. Minutes later he was introducing himself to the astounded doorman at the dingy side-entrance to the building. There had never been a chance that Maxwell would be able simply to drive past the building which now embodied the dream of a lifetime, his on the 13th for £113 million. 'He's gone up the editorial floor,' the man told Molloy on the phone.

Molloy and Long looked at each other. They felt like the defeated garrison called upon to surrender the fortress. 'It's my duty as editor to go and meet him,' said Molloy. 'Quite right,' said Long, putting on his jacket. 'I'll come with you.' As they were heading for the lifts one opened and out swept Maxwell, Pergamon financial director Richard Baker in the rear. To hell with the editorial floor. Maxwell knew where the action would be.

Long invited them into his office. Not that Maxwell needed inviting. He headed for Long's drinks-cupboard and poured himself a serious Scotch. 'Anyone else like a drink?' Whose Scotch was it anyway? A reporter and photographer came in. This was a *Mirror* exclusive. Maxwell's rapturous grin outshone the flash of the camera.

Baddeley and Dines arrived with a slightly sheepish Edwards who had been found waiting on the doorstep of Maxwell House. The women looked around wide-eyed at the splendours of the ninth floor. Long's office was several times larger than the best Worship Street could offer. Roused by Long, company secretary Ken Hudgell had been telephoning around. Other directors began arriving. Miles came back.

Then the inevitable happened. Production manager Roy Cooke rushed in. Just as Carpenter had feared, the printers were expressing their view of the new proprietor by stopping the presses. Maxwell told Baddeley to find herself a typewriter. The message that went down to the bowels of the building was something that had never been heard down there before: if the paper was stopped that night, it would never come out again. Never. It was a gesture Maxwell could afford, and the better-informed of the printers' leaders must have known it. He had got the papers for a song. With the £23.4 million cash he was to get back from Reed, together with the Reuter shares and the value of the buildings, he could close down the titles, sell the property tomorrow and still, probably, make a profit. The paper was produced to schedule, on page 1 a large box headlined 'Maxwell Buys *Mirror*'.

'You see, gentlemen,' rumbled Maxwell. 'Instant decision-making. Now we will have a board meeting.' He proposed himself as chairman and chief executive. Nobody voted against him.

It was daylight before the gathering broke up. Maxwell went back to Worship Street briefly, but by 7 a.m. he had moved into the most storied office in the *Mirror* building, the vast space overlooking the Old Bailey and St Paul's Cathedral where, in the pre-Reed days of 1968, Cecil King sat before the Adam fireplace he had whimsically had fitted between the steel girders and wrote the front-page editorial that became his professional obituary. In the grip of *folie de grandeur*, the occupational disease of newspaper magnates, King (according to *Spycatcher*, an MI5 agent of long standing) tried to use the *Mirror* to unseat Harold Wilson's government and replace it with a government of national unity which would include, of course, himself. His directors deposed him – he owned only a few shares – and Cudlipp moved in. It had been the chairman's office ever since. Miles furnished it with a vast partners' desk that had belonged to an early saviour of the *Daily Herald*, Lord Southwood. On it stood the pink marble casket in which the old Odhams company had preserved his lordship's ashes. Miles used it for his cigars. Clive Thornton arrived, as was his habit, at 8 a.m. Reporters were waiting for him when he left again soon afterwards. Had he seen Maxwell? 'I could hardly miss him. He was sitting at my desk.'

The first thing Maxwell had said to Thornton was: 'I was being tipped off about your every move.' It was true. Carpenter had been disconcerted to discover the extent and accuracy of Maxwell's intelligence about MGN. The prime suspect, of course, was Edwards. A man of nervous demeanour, prone to repeat himself, Edwards constantly assured even those who would not dream of asking that he had not been the mole. 'I know what they're saying, but it wasn't me,' he said over and over. He was still saying it long after the Outer Darkness had enfolded him.

Nor was Edwards the mole. The Reed board had enemies within. A copy of the still-secret prospectus was slipped to one of Maxwell's advisers. Maxwell was only allowed to read it in the intermediary's presence, but that was long enough for him to find out about the 15 per cent share limit and an even more crucial piece of information: the magnitude of the MGN pension fund. The fund was so flush with contributions and profits that Maxwell immediately saw that the leverage it could give him justified a much higher offer for the group than he might otherwise have been able to make.

Thornton let himself be persuaded by a photographer from the *Evening Standard*, Mike Moore, to summon up a big grin for the camera and have his picture taken tearing a copy of the *Mirror* in half. The result was not pleasant. The *Guardian* commented:

> *Mr Thornton may not, of course, have at that moment perceived himself in the business of symbolism. He may have felt tired and betrayed and out of a job. But there is still something chilling – something terrible – about the gesture itself; and especially about the smile.*

All round, the *Guardian* seemed to feel far more badly about things than most people at the *Mirror* in fact did by the end of that momentous Friday. Its diary named 'the brothers Silkin' as possibly being an additional influence in muffling Labour objections. But the leader continued:

> *If there is blame and recrimination in this affair – and there is by the bale – then most of it should be dumped squarely on the doorstep of Reed International, of Sir Alex Jarratt and Mr Leslie Carpenter. They made an awful, febrile botch of things. The opposition to Maxwell had glass jaws and putty backbones.*

But to an increasing number of people at the *Mirror* it seemed that, at least, they were now in the hands of someone who cared for the papers. Maxwell had not started out by jumping on a trestle table. Both in the shirt-sleeved conviviality of the early-morning hours and the series of appearances he made on the Friday he said a lot of things that people who were the true bone and muscle of the papers – and not just the journalists – were ready to listen to. Above all, he told them that it was his intention to beat Rupert Murdoch and put the *Mirror* back in its rightful place ahead of the *Sun*.

The flab the *Mirror* had accumulated was another matter. Despite the warnings he must have received about the number of passengers the group carried, Maxwell could not hide his wonder when he summoned the senior executives of every department to the ninth floor. There were so many they could hardly fit into the huge office. Not only was Maxwell seeing them for the first time. Many had never laid eyes on each other. Nocturnal creatures of the editorial floors in crumpled ash-flecked suits crowded up against space-peddling hucksters in Gucci loafers with no idea who they might be.

Maxwell singled out some subjects to interrogate. Why did *Sporting Life* lose £2 million a year? A good question, considering it had a monopoly. Why were there so few women among them? Another good question – although four years later there were not many more. Spotting Roger Bowes, who until the clock struck twelve the night before had been the new chief executive: 'What's your name again?'

Then Maxwell went to confront the lower-echelon executives, hundreds of them. They had been waiting for some time, speculating on their

fate. He put two fingers in his mouth and gave a piercing whistle. 'That's
how we get attention at football matches,' he explained.

'Courtship, pure and simple,' was the admiring description one of his
audience offered for the twenty-minute wooing that followed. But when he
met the *Mirror*'s small army of chapel 'fathers' – and 'mothers' – whom
he had kept waiting for the three-quarters of an hour that everyone soon
discovered to be his standard he demanded: 'Do you think I'm just on an
ego trip?' 'Yes!' they all bawled back. He told them defiantly: 'I am the
proprietor. I am the boss. There can only be one boss, and that is me.' Asked
afterwards how such a pronouncement could be made by a socialist,
Maxwell made his most enduring proclamation. 'They have their job and I
have mine,' he said. 'I love them as brothers, but business is business.'

At lunchtime, Maxwell took Miles, Molloy, Edwards and Stott, to the
Royal Suite at Claridge's. He ordered champagne. Miles asked for a gin
and tonic. Maxwell frowned. 'This is where all the crowned heads stay,'
he told his guests. 'Have you been in this suite before?'

'Henry Kissinger invited me here,' said Miles. There was a silence.
Then Maxwell pronounced the first of the slogans by which the new
Mirror and the other titles were to be run. He was well aware how the
editors resented the richly padded layers of minor and middle management that soaked up the papers' earnings. 'From now on, gentlemen, it's
going to be journalists on top, management on tap.'

'Less welcome axioms Maxwell had made his own down the years were
soon to become harrowingly familiar: 'Don't try to reinvent the wheel'
usually meant that Maxwell wanted something done the way he had seen
it done in another paper. 'He who will not be guided by the rudder will be
taught by the rocks' meant that Maxwell's way was the only way. Any
proposal beginning with 'If' was likely to evoke 'If my grandmother had
balls, she'd be my grandfather'. 'I'm not a member of the Salvation Army'
was another favourite. It meant the same as 'There's no such thing as a
free lunch'. Especially at Claridge's.

At 4 p.m. they gathered again for a media conference. Maxwell, aglow
with pride and sincerity, had never performed better on the hustings. He
read, without seeming to read, a statement written by Tom McCaffrey.

> *Under my management, editors will be free to produce their news-
> papers without interference with their journalistic skills and judge-
> ments. I shall place only two strictures on those who have editorial
> responsibilities. One, the papers must retain their broadly sym-
> pathetic approach to the Labour movement. They will continue to
> use their intelligence, their dedication and inventiveness to fight for
> the return of a Labour Government at the next election. Two, the
> papers must and will have a Britain First policy. I want to inform
> Britain, entertain Britain and boost Britain.*

Miles and Molloy sat on Maxwell's right. Neither smiled. Over the previous night's drinks Maxwell had been talking in general terms about
editorial policy. Molloy said he assumed it would be subject to con-

sultation and discussion with the editors. Miles had noticed Maxwell frown. After they had returned from Claridge's, Maxwell had asked Miles: 'Why didn't you take Mike Molloy to task for that remark about editorial policy?' Miles replied that it had seemed a fair point. 'I will make editorial policy,' said Maxwell.

That being the case, Miles left amicably a couple of weeks later. 'Of course he likes to get people to do what he wants,' says Miles, who is now in charge of a tabloid publishing group in Florida. 'He tried to get me back on cigars, which I had given up a year earlier. One day he pushed one into my breast pocket. "You'll smoke that cigar," he said. Well, I didn't. When I cleared my office out all that was left on the desk was that cigar.' The only thing Miles had wanted to take with him was a painting from his wall, by Ruskin Spear, of a deck-chair with a *Daily Mirror* lying on it. 'No,' said Maxwell when he mentioned it. 'I'll leave it to you in my will.'

Maxwell's 'Forward with Britain' manifesto covered the *Mirror*'s front page the next day under his own by-line, the trimming on his newspaper crown.

> *I am proud to be the proprietor of this group which holds such an important place in the life of the nation. The* Daily Mirror *and I already have one thing in common. We have supported the Labour Party in every election since 1945. That support will continue. But the* Mirror *has never been a slavish paper. It will not become a Labour Party organ now. We treasure our independence.*

There were other pressing considerations. How was Maxwell to be addressed? In the first encounters the editors, naturally enough, referred to him as 'Mr Maxwell' – just as he referred to himself. Baddeley, they noticed, called him, with simple reverence, 'RM'. But newspapers are a first-name world. Edwards had always called him 'Bob', and the others followed this example. After a brief, narrow-eyed pause, Maxwell accepted it. Now, as what was he to be referred to in the papers? Proprietor? Publisher? 'What's wrong with Owner?' asked Maxwell. But he settled for Publisher, particularly after he was compelled to distinguish between what he did not own and what the *Hinterlegt* did. 'RM', however, is the favoured form of his personal, as opposed to editorial, cadre.

During the trial of his libel action against *Private Eye* in 1986, Maxwell was asked if he had actually written the manifesto. 'Virtually all of it,' he replied. 'I had some assistance.'

In fact there had been a certain amount of difficulty in getting anybody to write it. Normally, such editorializing would have been produced by Haines in his capacity as leader-writer. But not only was Haines, a man of regular habits, off that day since there was normally no editorial in a Saturday paper, but also everyone remembered the bitter opposition to Maxwell he had reiterated only days earlier, first at a chapel meeting then in the aftermath of a lunch in Miles's office.

Terry Lancaster, who could always be relied upon for a swift and pithy piece, recalls: 'It was suggested that Joe should come in on his day off and write the piece, but Tony Miles said: "We do not want a row the first day. Joe's going to come in here and storm out. Will you write it?" So I wrote it. It appeared roughly as I wrote it. The major amendment was that I said Maxwell wanted to revive the old *Mirror* slogan, "Forward with the People". He changed it to "Forward with Britain". It was typed by Tony's secretary and Tony took it to him.'

However it was written Maxwell was back in politics once again, and far more potently than any mere MP. During his first day at Holborn the Labour Party of which he spoke had broken its long silence. So restrained was Kinnock's only comment that in the thunder of self-acclaim coming from Holborn it went almost unnoticed. 'The history of single proprietor ownership of newspapers in Britain is not a happy one,' Kinnock noted, as though he had heard of the goings-on by mere accident. 'Mr Maxwell could be the exception to the rule.'

'Neil despises Maxwell,' said one of the journalists plumbed in to Kinnock's office, 'but he can't turn his back on such a powerful source of support.'

Whatever the two might have thought about each other in private, Maxwell, as Molloy noted, was as good as his word when the election did come in 1987. Not only did he give Labour the ungrudging support of all the Mirror Group titles; he endorsed Kinnock personally. In a speech prominently reported in the *Mirror* of 18 May he said: 'He will make a first class Prime Minister. I know Kinnock well. He is a decent man and he is his own man. He is dictated to by his own conscience, no one else's.'

Once again the ninth floor seethed with excitement until dawn. The editors still had misgivings aplenty, but they and a lot of other *Mirror* men who had reeled through Maxwell's intoxicating first day were beginning to have high hopes. The champagne flowed, the cigars were handed out, Maxwell hugged everyone in reach and they all guffawed over his horoscope in the *Evening Standard*.

> *Although the coming months will at certain times be demanding, not for a second should you think you are doomed to fail. Far from it. A career change must add to your long-term security.*

Nobody, the astrologer Patric Walker included, realized exactly what they were witnessing: a wheeler dealer born again, aged sixty-one.

EIGHT

There would be more and prosperous British
newspapers if their publishers contracted out their printing
and left that to the experts.

ROBERT MAXWELL before the launch of the
London Daily News

Never again will I launch a newspaper on presses
I do not own.

ROBERT MAXWELL after the close of the
London Daily News

MAXWELL

NOBODY WHO HAD EVER SEEN Maxwell at the gaming-tables would have been surprised at the many-handed game of grab on which he launched himself as soon as the Reed cheque was in its frame. With the new credibility – and creditworthiness – he won along with MGN he started to put down chips on an astonishing variety of chances. Down at Maxim's Casino Club in Palace Gate, W8, that was just the kind of action they were used to.

Gambling was in Maxwell's blood. Had been ever since he learned to play poker back in Agde. Even when he first began to play roulette in his Westminster days, Maxwell was a high roller. Then he was most often to be found in the private room at Ladbroke's Casino. He would settle in for the long haul, among the sharks from Las Vegas and the reckless Gulf Arabs, a pile of chips worth £250,000 or more at his elbow. 'He enjoys that side of life very much,' says Rupert Murdoch, who was always interested to hear if Maxwell was winning or losing. 'It explains a lot about him. But he's not a compulsive gambler.'

He is a determined one, though, going at it, as he does at everything, at full throttle. By the time he had moved into the *Mirror* Maxwell preferred to take his money to Maxim's, a richly discreet little establishment near the Kensington Gardens Hotel run by the brothers Barrett, formerly of the Casanova Club. There are card games on the ground floor and roulette, which he prefers, upstairs. Impersonal good cheer pervades the atmosphere, combined with a certain respect for those who are about to do themselves out of a fortune. Whenever Maxwell arrives, usually after midnight, the well-controlled tension increases sharply. So does the noise-level. One wheel does not spin fast enough for him. He will bet on two, sometimes three, simultaneously, striding from table to table plonking down stacks of £1,000 chips with each hand.

Ian and Kevin share their father's foible. They sometimes go to Maxim's with him. But their gambling is only approved if done under his supervision – or if they do not lose. When Ian, tempted to Molloy's green baize table at the *Mirror*, dropped several hundred pounds at seven-card stud one night his fear that Father would find out made the other players sorry for him. Maxwells were supposed to win. How well Maxwell's own celebrated luck holds up at Maxim's is hard to gauge. But as a Sudanese who has regularly been shouldered out of the way at one of the tables observed: 'If he was winning all the time he wouldn't get such a good welcome there.'

Maxwell also liked to gamble on the two family football teams, Oxford United and Derby County. When Oxford booted its way from the second division of the Football League to the first he raked in £100,000 in bets. Oxford, which had once been known as Headington United, was losing £2,000 a week when he took it over in 1981. Within eighteen months of Maxwell investing £120,000 it was making a profit of £30,000 a year. A lot of people did not like the Maxwell methods: raffling tickets, raising ground advertising rates because of increased television exposure. But the fans liked the results. A new manager, Jim Smith, got the club out of the third division just a few months after Maxwell moved into the *Mirror* (and Ghislaine collected the trophy).

Once he had discovered the visibility that owning a team could bring Maxwell tried to buy his way into the first division. He was ready to pay millions for mighty Manchester United and its famous Old Trafford ground, but Martin Edwards, the principal shareholder, would not listen. Piqued, Maxwell shifted target back to the second, and in the East Midlands where, years before, he had joined the North Staffs bought Derby County, which soon made it into the first division.

Oxford's great success came in 1986 when it beat Queen's Park Rangers 3–0 for the League Cup. Maxwell waved the silver trophy aloft then came down from the stand and, to the horror of Betty watching from the directors' box, broke into a ponderous trot to jog along with the team in a *tour d'honneur*, as proud as though he had scored all three goals himself. Ron McKay, the *Scottish Daily News* veteran, asked Maxwell if he had ever played as a boy. 'Oh, yes,' said Maxwell. 'I was a leftwinger.'

'I'll bet you never passed the ball,' said McKay.

Established as a football mogul, Maxwell went about polishing the image of a lifelong enthusiast for the game. He worked up an anecdote for sports writers about climbing over a fence to watch Manchester United play on a prewar visit to somewhere in Czechoslovakia. His old friend Lou Rosenbluth was puzzled when he heard it. 'Most of the young boys would come to watch when we played football in the Army. But not Lodvik. He just wasn't interested in football.'

The Football League rules would not allow Maxwell to be chairman of both clubs. Regulation 80 forbade a director of a club from having control directly or through a nominee of another club. Even though Maxwell still maintained a shareholding in Reading, with which he had once opened negotiations over a merger with Oxford, no objection was raised when Kevin was made chairman of Oxford and Maxwell himself became chairman of Derby. The malleable League accepted that Maxwell would have no control over his youngest son. And Derby had been heading for bankruptcy. Maxwell paid £1 million to Southampton for a new goalkeeper, Peter Shilton, and the fans started to flock in. 'The profits of trading in warm flesh,' Maxwell called it.

Maxwell soon came to regard himself as the Only Man Who Could Save British Soccer. When Margaret Thatcher came to lunch at the *Mirror* he gave her a lecture on how hooliganism might be controlled. She listened. After all, she was aware that Maxwell himself had lumbered down on to the ground to intervene in brawls. 'I hope you're taking notes, Bernard,' she told her fuming press secretary, Bernard Ingham.

Maxwell's mixed feelings about Thatcher were what led him to offer George Gale a brief that ran contrary to the pledges he made to the Labour Party and to the *Mirror* staff. But when an election seemed imminent and Maxwell bowed to the pressure – from Stott, who had now become editor of the *Mirror*, as well as from Haines – to confine Gale to the *Sunday Mirror* Gale decided that his contract had been breached. He left on cool but polite terms, believing Maxwell had agreed to a settlement. He had not expected they would both resort to lawyers.

'June 11th' said Maxwell in parting. 'That's the election date.'

'Are you sure?' asked Gale.

'She's got to go then. The polls, everything. That's the day.'

'And she'll walk in,' said Gale.

Maxwell smiled and nodded. He was right about the day. And, of course, the result.

The half-year figures for Pergamon Press in September 1984, two months after Maxwell had moved into Holborn, were riveting. Although its turnover remained as forecast at £174 million, its profit before tax had more than doubled to £25 million. Its earnings per share had risen from 64.3p to 145.5p. Pergamon it was which had bought MGN. BPCC, of which Pergamon owned 61 per cent, was also doing well, 62 per cent up on the previous year at £12.5 million. The shares for which Maxwell had paid less than 20p in 1981 were now worth 177p, which provided enormous leverage. By the end of the financial year BPCC profits had risen to £37.8 million from £22.07 the year before. But by then it had become apparent that nearly £15 million of the profits came from the sale of the Watford site.

This kind of optimistic book-keeping had already attracted attention. On 14 December 1984 a *Guardian* financial writer noted:

> *Mr Maxwell has been far from conservative in his accounting methods. In 1982, for example, he took expected 1983 redundancy costs of £19 million as a capital provision set not against profit and loss but straight to balance sheet. This helped boost BPCC's earnings figures.*

The *Guardian* also examined a £6.4 million credit for 'accumulated depreciation released on revaluation and deferred tax provided' which had helped swell the earnings-per-share figure.

> *Where does this latter profit stem from? Very simply, the group has revalued much of its printing equipment on an 'existing use' basis allowing it to write back the depreciation previously knocked off.*

Even though its value had momentarily drifted down during the last days of the Reed MGN the group's Reuter shares – every major British and Commonwealth newspaper publisher had an allocation and a seat on the board – were an important asset. They also landed Maxwell with a difficult test of temperament. For the only time in his maverick career he had to take his place among equals and abide by company rules he had not himself made. He could not do it.

At the first meeting he gave the Reuter management a blast of the boorishness with which he was accustomed to treat minions. His fellow-directors, most of whom could afford a tantrum in their own boardrooms, were appalled. Even Murdoch sat silent. Soon a far more serious breach occurred. Without consulting Reuter, Maxwell transferred a large batch of the shares to BPCC and sold them.

'He announced that he didn't know anything about the dealings,' Murdoch remembers. 'It had all been done by his subordinates.' To anyone who knew how little latitude Maxwell's employees were allowed this seemed surprising.

'The chairman, Sir Christopher Hogg, spoke to all the directors about whether Maxwell should be asked to resign or be reprimanded,' Murdoch continued. 'A public reprimand was issued. He had known all about the discussions and yet he came to the next board meeting, in New York, and made a tremendous fuss about how badly he'd been treated, hadn't been allowed to put his case. But he'd now given instructions that no one should deal in Reuter shares without reference to him.'

Board meetings are simply not Maxwell's style. The Pergamon board always met regularly at Oxford. But the first MGN board meeting that he called within moments of arriving at Holborn was the last for many of the directors. Maxwell soon proposed that the board delegate its authority to an executive committee consisting of himself and the company secretary, and future gatherings were downgraded to management meetings. When an innocent assistant company secretary appeared to take minutes Maxwell chased her out of the room. The serried leatherbound volumes of past minutes going back to the handwritten copperplate of the turn of the century were carted off to join the vast collection of company records at Headington.

But the increasing number of bankers beginning to sit up and take notice of Maxwell were less interested in his masterful touch with a balance-sheet than in the explanation of how he had raised the amount of money that so surprised Reed: £32 million as a seven-year loan, £32 million in short-term loans – including the Reed £6 million. With some respect they noted that he had been able to produce £49 million in cash.

Liechtenstein, the last remaining principality of the Austro-Hungarian empire under which Maxwell just missed being born, has been described as a country with its heart in Austria and its wallet in Switzerland. Sandwiched between the two, this strip of territory twenty-five miles long by six miles across does not even have a currency of its own. But anything that Switzerland, Monaco, Andorra or the Cayman Islands can do in the way of insulating money from tax it can do better. Liechtenstein's principal exports are agricultural products, precision instruments, artificial teeth and secrecy. It is the home of the Pergamon Holding Foundation, the last known resting-place of the shares in MIMC, the family company that bought Pergamon Press. Since 1982, when the company was handed over by a Paris lawyer M. Geouffre de la Pradella, who had become its nominal owner, the Foundation had also owned PPI.

PHF is registered as a *Hinterlegt*, a unique local form of trust so secretive that there is no way of finding out who the trustees are, what its capital or income is or anything else about it. As the legal text has it, there are no 'members, participants or shareholders'. Two Liechtenstein laws of 1960 and 1961 guarantee total secrecy for all bank accounts, but there is not even a public record of the existence of a *Hinterlegt*. If PHF had not been acknowledged by Maxwell – before he was made aware of what a hindrance such an impenetrable device could be to his plans – there would be no way of knowing that it had ever been set up. But, since the *Hinterlegt* has repeatedly turned out to be the trip-wire that brought his carefully shaped ambitions crashing down like a tripped-up goalkeeper, the enigma of PHF is now encased by an even deeper mystery: What does Maxwell have to hide?

The advantages PHF provided to elude the taxes Maxwell detests and shield him from the one form of attention that he finds unwelcome were considerable. No tax is due on the income or profits of a *Hinterlegt*; capital is taxed annually at derisory rates: 0.1 per cent on 2 million Swiss francs; 0.75 per cent on 10 million; over that 0.5 per cent. The one catch is that to qualify for the privilege of establishing such a trust its objective must be charitable. Apart from that, one of the trustees must be a Liechtensteiner, although his or her identity need not be disclosed.

A year before taking over the *Mirror*, BPCC made a takeover bid for John Waddington, a profitable printer and packager best known as the manufacturer of Monopoly. Incorporating aspects of Waddington would ensure a monopoly in certain printing specialities. The bid was resisted by the chairman, Victor Watson, whose family had run the company since 1913. Watson got the full Maxwell routine – no fewer than fourteen separate telephone approaches, he calculated; a proposal that he become deputy chairman of BPCC. He did not like it.

Waddington shares were then 104p. By the time Maxwell was ready, looking up from the *Mirror* takeover in the autumn of 1984 to make use of his new-found financial muscle, he was willing to offer 500p – a payout of £44.2 million. Still Waddington refused to recommend the offer to its shareholders. Worse, Waddington and its merchant bank, Kleinwort Benson, stopped Maxwell even from passing Go. Section 74 of the 1981 Companies Act permitted a public company to ask shareholders about the 'beneficial interest' of their holdings, that is, who got the eventual benefit? If they refused to tell, the shares could be disfranchised.

To the growing audience coming to take a connoisseur's delight in his performance Maxwell decided to make something clear that had not been clear before. He, personally, held less than 1 per cent of BPCC stock and none at all of Pergamon's. Nor was he the proprietor of the *Mirror* and the other papers. 'I am the publisher. Ownership is a separate issue.' He refused to say who the trustees of PHF might be, except for the resident director, Dr Walter Keicher. 'It is a perfectly proper and legal business. But I am not in the business of disclosing other people's business.'

On 15 November, Waddington's company secretary trudged down the fresh snow of Aeulestrasse, the main street of Vaduz, Liechtenstein's only city, and served a notice on Keicher's office at number 5, demanding details of PHF as the beneficial holder of 23.3 per cent of the company already acquired by Pergamon subsidiaries. 'Utterly disgraceful,' protested Maxwell.

Keicher's thin smile soon became as familiar to reporters and bankers as his thin politeness. He acknowledged that he had acted for the Maxwell family for more than thirty years. 'I am sorry I cannot tell you more,' he would say, having told his callers nothing more than how the secrets of a *Hinterlegt* were maintained. 'But that is the point of it.'

Neither did the only declaration that could be wrung from Maxwell, as he tried for once to divert the spotlight, answer the questions: 'Every public statement I have ever made has made it clear that neither I nor my wife nor my family will inherit one penny of all the wealth that I have managed to create.'

Eventually, with Waddington preparing to go to the High Court with an application that Maxwell be ordered to disclose the beneficiaries of PHF, Ansbachers, representing Maxwell, issued a statement that these were 'a number of charities and relatives of the respective grandparents of Mr and Mrs Robert Maxwell not resident in the United Kingdom'.

'Potentially rather a large cast of people,' said Christopher Eugster, a Kleinwort director. For of course it could be taken to mean every Maxwell alive – and then some – depending on where they were resident at the time. The counter-attack worked. Under the fascinated gaze of the financial community, seeing yet another bewildering aspect of Maxwell's financial machinations laid bare, the Waddington shareholders rejected Maxwell's bid.

Plainly, the Kleinwort elixir would keep Maxwell at bay in other situations. The next to resort to it was Lord Matthews, uncomfortable at the thought of Maxwell still holding 15 per cent of his company's shares. In January 1985, after consulting Kleinwort, he wrote to Maxwell demanding to know who were the real owners of his stake. Once again the threat was effective. But not entirely to Matthews's advantage. Maxwell sold his stake to a five-foot-three-inch-tall provincial newspaper-owner with national ambitions, David Stevens. With the help of Maxwell's shares, forty-seven-year-old Stevens soon bought Matthews out. Mrs Thatcher made him Lord Stevens of Ludgate – after Ludgate Circus at the foot of Fleet Street. The nifty double act made him and Maxwell known as the industry's Laurel and Hardy.

Woodrow Wyatt, a former Labour MP, newspaper proprietor and

printer, offered Maxwell some advice in an article in *The Times* headlined 'A Friendly Word for Maxwell'.

> *While adoring massive publicity in many of his activities he has a Howard Hughes type mania for secrecy in others. If he maintains this secrecy he will find himself increasingly blocked when he tries to expand his organization. That would be a pity because there is much good he can do. As I am sure Mr Maxwell has nothing damaging to hide, his not making a clearer statement as to who are the beneficiaries, owners and controllers of Pergamon Holding Foundation is the equivalent of Oxford United deliberately scoring own goals.*

A letter in reply came from Sam Silkin in his capacity as deputy chairman of BPCC. Maxwell was not, as Wyatt had suggested, the only voice that mattered in Worship Street. The Waddington and Fleet shares had simply been sold 'at the commercially logical time'.

> *As to which of Robert Maxwell's relatives or charities will ultimately benefit from the success of the BPCC group, well really, Woodrow, would you not agree that in such matters some degree of discreet reticence is normally the friendliest posture to adopt?*

Now that Liechtenstein had become an issue Maxwell was again in the position of having his very real achievements overshadowed by his impulsive contradictory behaviour. Using the *Mirror* and its assets as a financial Sten gun he was charging through the market-place, capturing objectives right and left, most notably the Philip Hill Investment Trust which he bought for £350 million, dismantled and recycled at enormous profit. By October 1986, after fifteen months in Holborn, he had driven BPCC into eighty-seventh place in the Stock Exchange list of the Top 100 British companies. It was capitalized at £656 million and its shares were worth 260p, a 2,268 per cent improvement under his management. But still the Maxwell Factor prevailed when it came to the most powerful – and conservative – elements of the City. As well as his adamant refusal to lift the curtain on Liechtenstein, the very ingenuity of his share dealings made him suspect. To say nothing of what was happening with the *Mirror*.

The ninth floor was a scene of round-the-clock pandemonium. Within days of Maxwell's arrival it looked as though Marshal Zhukov's men had been through: doors boarded up, walls stripped out, pipes and wires dangling from open ceilings. Maxwell's passion for security and supervision was reshaping everything. There would be luxury there again soon enough – but for Maxwell alone. The EMI 4400 card-key system he planned would admit only those he trusted to the floor. Directors and his other personal staff would soon find they had nowhere to hide; they must work at open desks or in glass-fronted cubicles. A deep-bellied shirt-sleeved colossus straddling un-imaginable disorder, Maxwell dominated the building and everyone in it, his menacing rumble chilling the blood of a thousand time-servers who knew their days were numbered. 'I've only got one lung!' Maxwell would remind the minions who shuffled in and out, clearing his throat with the bark they soon learned to recognize three rooms away. 'Think what I'd be like if I had two!'

He had quickly settled on a strategy to point the circulation graphs skyward once again. The journalists had hoped he would adopt a broad policy of reviving the dormant editorial potential of the papers. Instead, squinting through the telescopic sight of his own gambler's lust, he decided to aim for the weak spot he could envisage in the heart of every prospect: greed. Bingo was the answer. Never mind that the detested game had mesmerized -- paralysed – Fleet Street for years. Never mind that Maxwell had pledged to drop it. The Maxwell version would be different. He borrowed the motto of the SAS to name it 'Who Dares Wins'. (The squire of Maxwell House was beyond any concern about who might have done what first – MGN's new seal and letterhead logo was a copy of the MGM lion of the movies.) There would be a £1 million *Mirror* bingo prize.

It was a staggering amount of money to pay out on top of the enormous cost of promotion and advertising. Better still, said Maxwell. There will be *two* £1 million prizes. Given by his own hand. For it was Maxwell's hand and only Maxwell's that now guided the papers and what went into them: Maxwell's picture, Maxwell's name, Maxwell's admonitions, boasts and bestowals. Buy the *Daily Maxwell*. For a television bingo commercial he was filmed in front of £1 million worth of crisp new banknotes piled up under the nervous eye of guards at Coutts Bank in the Strand.

The matter of the second £1 million prizewinner was successfully evaded. Lord Cudlipp justified the generous fee Maxwell was paying him with one stroke of his seasoned pen.

'Are you really going to give away two lots of a million quid?' Cudlipp had asked, looking over the proof of a front-page announcement.

Mawell shrugged. It was . . . possible.

Carefully, Cudlipp wrote into the copy: 'One and possibly two. . . .'

'I never thought I'd end up sub-editing a bloody bingo blurb for Bob Maxwell,' he muttered.

Until living-quarters could be built for him at Holborn, Maxwell still slept at Worship Street. He would start his telephone onslaught on the world from Maxwell House as early as 6.30 a.m. Long after midnight he would be back there making his own calls again. Around midday, usually, he arrived at Holborn accompanied by Baddeley; Wilson the chauffeur lugging huge rigid document-cases of the kind used by aircrew, she hugging a bundle of data-discs for the Wang computers on which all the Maxwell correspondence and record-keeping was done. Asked how he managed to run both BPCC and MGN at the same time Maxwell seemed surprised. 'Printing is a morning business,' he said. 'Newspapers are an afternoon business.'

In fact he never made any attempt to compartmentalize his increasingly convoluted activities. Morning, afternoon and evening the anteroom to his office was packed solid with people waiting – all with appointments: half the staff of an advertising agency come to make a presentation, an out-of-work peer hoping for a job, a financial journalist wanting an interview, a personnel manager with a hit-list. Some of the visitors waited all day and left in tears or tantrums; often nobody knew why they had been asked there. Others were ushered in after cooling their heels for a mere hour and half and so swamped with charm that they immediately forgot the ordeal. Some of the baffled and constantly growing crowd would eventually be distributed around the ruins rather than shown into the presence. Just as with the union delegates, the presence would materialize for a few minutes of audience with one in a makeshift dining-room and another in the kitchen.

Where Maxwell was the Ericsson telephone system on which he depended as much as he did on his single lung would find him. A discussion about new furniture or Pergamon sales in Latin America would be interrupted by a stockbroker, an MP, the First Secretary of the Bulgarian Communist Party. If there was a takeover deal in the offing, which increasingly there was, posses of bankers and lawyers would be escorted up in the key-operated executive lift and down again, grey-faced, at midnight. As they left, the cavalcade of editors, reporters, circulation, production, transport men resumed its steady flow. Inevitably the streams intermingled. In the middle of a free-wheeling exchange of views around Maxwell about the new bingo promotion, opposed groups of Young & Rubicam marketing yuppies and editorial executives realized that a middle-aged man of stern bearing who had sat, silent and ramrod-straight, through the shouting did not belong to either camp. He turned out to be the East German ambassador.

Against all his expectations Molloy survived. He decided to confess to Maxwell that he had been a messenger, at least, of opposition to him by arranging the meeting with Kinnock. 'I knew about that, of course,' said Maxwell – of course. 'But that's all in the past. I need you here.' Big hug. Molloy was grateful. He had nowhere in particular to go. And he was intrigued. He had never seen a real tycoon in action. He instructed Maxwell in some of the building's lore: Cecil King's wife, Dame Ruth Railton, claimed to be psychic. She dreamed a crack had appeared in the façade. King had authorized a survey costing £10,000 but nothing was found wrong with the structure. It had been King himself who was cracking. He told Maxwell statesmanlike jokes: What do you think would have happened if Khrushchev had been assassinated rather than Kennedy? One thing is certain: Ari Onassis wouldn't have married Mrs Khrushchev. But, even if he was staying,

Molloy knew that he would need all the talent for blandishment at his command if the critical elements of the editorial structure were to be kept from hurling themselves away from the new source of manic energy at the centre into the Outer Darkness.

There were certain to be defections. The new publisher had already stunned some of the notionally independent staff writers by rewriting their copy or dictating the version that he wanted published. 'We must learn to deal with these stories', he had grumbled in one treasured exchange, 'or I'll have to write them myself. What's the use of me spending hours and then we get other people involved and it ends up with precisely the opposite of what we're looking for?'

The Mirror Diary was written by a former actor named Peter Tory who, because he was also a weekend flier, was known to his friends as 'Biggles'. Reference to the heroes of middle-class British childhood were wasted on Maxwell, who in any case found most of Tory's playful items unintelligible. 'Good afternoon,' Maxwell had said, welcoming him to the ninth floor, 'Boggles.'

Maxwell never saw a piece of copy he could not improve. He was no sooner in the building than he pointed to the headline on a long-running rapist story. 'Why do you call this man "The Fox"? A fox is an intelligent animal. Call him "The Rat".' Miles had managed to evade the issue. 'That would be like changing "Jack the Ripper" to "Charlie the Knife," ' he said later.

As the more astute journalists who had to deal with Maxwell came to realize that he was far too hyperactive to read the papers the following day – or to read more than two paragraphs of anything – his whim became subject to interpretation. The leader-writers learned to leave in awkward syntax like 'urgent legislation must be passed' as a signal that the words were not their own. When he occasionally discovered that he was being disobeyed his wrath was thunderous. Savouring the danger, the journalists felt like Resistance workers in occupied territory.

Fleet Street had been trading in warm flesh before anyone realized that a footballer could be worth anything. Keith Waterhouse, the *Mirror*'s star columnist, could name his own price. He was a playwright, scriptwriter, novelist and a freelance under contract who was at liberty to write what he pleased. Any paper that could afford him would be delighted to give space to his idiosyncratic musings. When Maxwell began to take stock of his newly acquired stable, Waterhouse was anxious that this should be understood.

Maxwell did not readily grasp Waterhouse's privileged status. How could anyone be taking his money and not do what they were told? When Molloy told Waterhouse that Maxwell wanted to see him, Waterhouse invited them both to lunch at the Connaught Hotel.

'He doesn't go to lunch,' said Molloy. Not that Maxwell did not *have* lunch. Lunch was a crucial element of Maxwell's day, as was breakfast, dinner and the endless flow of food he consumed in between. No matter how late Maxwell stayed at Holborn, the ninth-floor kitchen was on standby. On Sundays some of the large smiling clan of Filipino maids who provided the domestic services at Headington were driven down to keep up the flow of smoked salmon, matzo, champagne and coffee in a vast basin of a cup Maxwell used, inside the rim of which was lettered 'I Am a Very Important Person'. These tributary vessels had a short life, regularly sent flying off the desk by an extravagant gesture but quickly replaced from Baddeley's stock. In their spare time the Filipinos cleaned the Maxwell shoes.

To Molloy's surprise, Maxwell accepted the invitation. As his guests headed towards the Connaught in the Rolls, Maxwell glued to the car phone, Waterhouse had walked into just the kind of scene he would have enjoyed writing about. Of the reservation he had made days earlier there was no trace. And there were no tables available in the dining-room. So sorry, sir. 'I was frantic. I told them that the man who might be about to buy the hotel from over their heads was on his way,' Waterhouse recounts. 'But what really did the trick was my witty way with a large banknote.'

Overcome with relief, Waterhouse ordered an impressive bottle of wine in Maxwell's honour, a Château Latour of one of the great vintages. 'This is very nice,' said Maxwell, putting down his glass. He looked at the label. Had Waterhouse known Maxwell longer, he could have guessed the next line: 'I've got several dozen of it in my cellar.'

Sure enough, Maxwell had something with him that he wanted Waterhouse to write about.

> He showed me some papers about a union ballot. He wanted me to do a kind of industrial indignation bit, à la Woodrow Wyatt or Bernard Levin. I explained that that was not really my line. I tried to get him to understand my relationship with the paper. My column was like a music-hall act. It could be top of the bill at the Coliseum or at the Palladium. If one place didn't want it – or vice versa – it could move to the other. He didn't quite get that then. But he did subsequently.

Months later, when Waterhouse left the *Mirror* for the *Daily Mail*, Maxwell gave him a big hug and said: 'You can always move back from the Shaftesbury to the Aldwych.'

The helicopter clattering out of a sunny autumn sky at lunchtime was not the kind of thing the Royal Bath Hotel at stately Bournemouth expected, even during a Labour Party Conference. Maxwell had been infatuated with these useful machines since first chartering one in a Buckingham campaign. Denied planning permission to build a landing-pad on the roof at Holborn, he had decided to buy the adjoining building, which already had its own, from W. H. Smith for £17 million. In September 1985 everyone he needed to see had to be delivered to him. Labour and TUC conferences were his favourite arenas in which to parade as a power broker. No way was he going to leave this one before it was over. Neil Kinnock had some more dues to pay for everything the *Mirror* had done to support him in the past year, and Maxwell was going to collect in person. As the chopper hovered over the grounds a guest watched, appalled, as the rotor wash blasted his elegantly cut sandwiches over a wall. Gravel was blown through the dining-room windows like buckshot, spattering everyone there. A clutch of bankers scrambled out and headed for Maxwell's suite.

At the centre of Maxwell's political entourage was the group of *Mirror* men he called his 'politburo': the editors of the papers, Geoffrey Goodman and Joe Haines – who had not, after all, walked out when Maxwell had walked in. Instead, Lancaster, the political editor, did.

Goodman had been summoned only forty-eight hours after Maxwell's arrival at the *Mirror*. 'I am setting up a group to control policy. I want you to join it.' Goodman did not care much for the 'politburo' label, but he agreed. He had a certain difficulty in concentrating on the conversation because Maxwell had fallen on a bowl of fruit and was devouring a pear, spitting the pips on to the immaculate carpet.

Haines was next to ascend to the ninth. Just as he had seen that Goodman's encyclopaedic knowledge of the labour scene made him a valuable asset, not only to the paper but also to his other interests, Maxwell knew that Haines's familiarity with everyone and everything in national politics was indispensable. Maxwell promoted him on the spot to assistant editor; gave him a gratifying rise. He would continue to be the leader-writer. Haines explained that he had not wanted Maxwell as publisher. Warned Haines: 'I won't write anything that I'm not prepared to argue publicly.' Said Maxwell: 'I won't ask you to.' When the time came to prepare the 'Survival Plan' for MGN on the model Maxwell had used at BPCC, calling for 2,000 redundancies, Haines was its joint architect. When the first Maxwellgrams began to fly it was Haines who drafted them.

The politburo lunched together every Tuesday. It was soon evident that the papers' political policy was already well under control. There was to be only one point of view. Nevertheless the politburo were not the only source to which Maxwell turned for advice he was temperamentally incapable of taking. Soon after his reign began he called the editors to his office. 'Let me introduce you to my new editorial consultant. The man who guided the *Mirror* in its first period of greatness.' There stood Lord Cudlipp with a glass of champagne in his hand. The *Mirror* men were astounded. Apart from anything else, they remembered – as Maxwell had not – that Cudlipp was now a member of the despised Social Democratic Party.

Haines's early acceptance of Maxwell was a crucial development. It took the fight out of the opposition. A lot of the journalists who drifted away from the papers were decided by it. But it also convinced many that Maxwell could be kept under control. Haines would resist Maxwell's wilder attempts to inflict his views upon the readers, and Maxwell would allow himself to be curbed. He recognized that if he did not Haines would go. Haines thus became one of the very few people Maxwell took care not to push beyond the limits of tolerance, although with Maxwell's natural contempt for anyone he could buy or hire Haines had to be the more supple.

'You can argue with Maxwell,' Haines would reflect, 'but only up to a point. It's a matter of body language. He makes a little karate chop with his hand and that's it. After that you do what he says. Or you don't.'

Haines's elevation intrigued his former employer. Harold Wilson had not spoken to him since publication of *The Politics of Power*. Maxwell brought them together again when Wilson made his first visit to the *Mirror*. 'Hello, Harold,' said Haines, hand outstretched. Wilson took it as though having trouble recognizing its owner. 'Hello, Joe. You've changed your haircut.' At a dinner some months later, Wilson asked a group of journalists: 'Who's that over there with Bob?' He wanted to draw their attention to the little cameo of Haines, notebook balanced on his knee, scribbling urgently as Maxwell dictated. 'He used to work for me,' Wilson chuckled. 'He didn't move so fast in those days.'

Maxwell was unexpectedly sensitive to where the uncrossable boundaries might lay in dealing with people he would have difficulty replacing; to those he did not, at the moment, need or whose qualities he was unaware of he was brutally indifferent. 'Bob simply never realized how much goodwill there was in the place towards him had he wanted to draw on it,' Molloy lamented, long after the Survival Plan and Maxwell's usurpation of all initiative had drained away much of the *Mirror*'s talent along with the dross. Where Haines might argue for principle, Molloy usually found himself trying to make Maxwell understand the sense of vocation that motivated the better journalists. 'He never took the trouble to distinguish between one man's contribution and another's.'

Whatever the editorial quality now left in the Mirror Group titles, there can be no doubt that the war of attrition Maxwell, Haines at his side, waged throughout the overmanned Holborn buildings saved the group from bankruptcy. Although soon restructured so radically that its past and present performance could not be compared – and although the circulation of the papers rose only microscopically – it was soon showing good balance-sheet profits.

Once again Maxwell's remarkable luck was in. He might never have wrung the concessions he needed from the unions had not Murdoch, just after Maxwell had mounted his own onslaught, broken their power completely. In a ruthless, brilliantly planned coup Murdoch transferred the production of his papers overnight to a barricaded high-tech complex in Wapping, by the Tower of London, where no printers, only electricians and journalists, were needed to produce them. Without even needing to risk his own confrontation with the MGN printers Maxwell swept the winnings off the table.

The first political conference to provide a forum for Maxwell's new persona was the 1984 TUC conference in

Brighton, only seven weeks after he had moved into Holborn. The earlier part of that year had been marred by a bitter miners' strike that kept picket-line violence at the top of news schedules. The miners and the Coal Board had reached the stage where neither had anything to say to the other. Maxwell could not resist the chance of applying the political clout he was confident that ownership of the papers had brought him. He would step in as peacemaker, break the stalemate and bring the two sides together under the gaze of a grateful nation.

His old Buckingham crony, Ray ('of Hope') Buckton, was chairman of the conference. Maxwell spoke to Ian MacGregor, the Coal Board chief (soon of Clyde Cablevision), and *Mirror* writer John Pilger (soon of the Outer Darkness) arranged a secret meeting before the conference between him and the fiery and devious miners' leader, Arthur Scargill. 'Do you realize, Arthur, the damage you're doing to the trade union movement?' Maxwell demanded. Somewhat bemused, Scargill revealed an unsuspected talent for mimicry. He gave Maxwell an account of the talks that had been abandoned, impersonating the voices of MacGregor and Mick McGahey, leader of the Scottish miners, and Peter Walker the Energy Secretary. Maxwell was plainly enchanted by the unexpected performance. But at the end Scargill said: 'I don't think we've achieved anything.'

Maxwell, his conspiratorial instincts aroused, thought differently. He rounded up the miners' men once again. Fearful of leaks at Holborn, he sent an optimistic account of his mission to Maxwell House. It was delivered to the *Mirror* in a sealed envelope. Where the *Mirror* led the rest of the press had no option but to follow. Maxwell strode through Brighton, shaking hands and acknowledging plaudits as though back in the lanes of Buckinghamshire. Spotting his old dining companion Bill Keys, Maxwell hailed him. Keys fled. Maxwell pursued him. 'Bill, Bill, I've got to talk to you.' 'Fuck off, you cunt,' hissed Keys. 'I can't be seen talking to you in public.' But the deterioration into farce and fiasco was swift. Made just as uncomfortable as Scargill had been by Maxwell's intervention, Mac-Gregor backed away. The talks were eventually resumed. But not because of the *Mirror*. 'It was blatant news management,' says Goodman, to whom the task of trying to prop the story up had fallen. 'The paper was making its own news.'

The conviction that he could end the strike stayed with Maxwell long after he had embarked on the other great personal intervention of the early Maxwell *Mirror*. The ghastly Ethiopian famine was plainly a case for SuperMax, the first of dozens of causes in which Maxwell, his thirst for personal attention alloyed with an unquestioned conviction that he was needed, mobilized the power of the *Mirror* to mount an appeal. A visiting Australian editor having his arm twisted for a contribution said: 'The heartfelt plea for the starving would have sounded better if it had not come from a man with a glass of champagne in his hand and a mouth full of smoked salmon.'

Mirror readers stumped up £2 million. Maxwell flew to Ethiopia himself. A line-up of editors and senior executives were summoned to

Heathrow to see him off. He shook hands with them in turn, like Anthony Eden departing on a mission of state. Over the crackling line from Addis Ababa, Maxwell dictated alternately what the miners were to be told and how the *Mirror* should report the tributes to his intervention. 'Make sure to say "The British Embassy thanked Mr Maxwell for his contribution. . . ." ' Back at the *Mirror* he said: 'I always make my own news.' Bob Geldof's Band Aid began to overshadow Maxwell's efforts (eventually raising £78 million), and he was outraged. There must be something discreditable to be published about Geldof's fund, he told the editors. They were not looking hard enough.

But Maxwell's quirkish generosity continued to assert itself. When reporter Gill Pringle was proposed for a job on the *Mirror*'s pop column Maxwell insisted on interviewing her himself. She told him she was getting married soon. Not only did she get the job; she was called back to the presence and given a cheque for £1,000 as a wedding present.

Now, in Bournemouth, Kinnock and his wife Glenys came to lunch. Earlier in the year they had graced the first-anniversary party for the Maxwell *Mirror* after some negotiations that were soon to receive an unwelcome airing in court. But on this sumptuous occasion there was nothing but mutual affection and common purpose. Maxwell spoke first, congratulating Kinnock on a stirring attack he had made from the conference platform on Labour's far-left menace, the Militant Tendency.

In response, Kinnock revealed what he was going to do for his host in return for everything that the *Mirror* papers had done for him. The next Labour government would introduce legislation to ensure that only British citizens would be able to own newspapers published in the United Kingdom. Murdoch, an Australian turned American, would be excluded.

Kinnock's pledge became official Labour policy a year later. When news of it reached the East River, Murdoch just cracked his knuckles. 'My two sons were born in Wimbledon,' he said. 'They are British. They own all the shares in the British operation. I don't think Kinnock has checked that out. Anyway, I don't think he's going to win the election.' Kinnock, of course, did not.

That evening at dinner the politburo was augmented by wives and the other *Mirror* celebrities attending the conference. Maxwell demanded speeches. 'Every time anyone else spoke, Maxwell got up and spoke,' remembers Waterhouse. 'It was like *Toad of Toad Hall*. No matter what the last person said, Maxwell would pop up with something more to say – about Maxwell.'

One of the things no one had expected Maxwell to say was that Bob Edwards would be departing the following month. Although Edwards had always vowed that he would retire at sixty, journalists had come to believe that, as the only friend Maxwell had found in the building when he arrived, he would be asked to stay. Edwards had moved from the editorship of the *Sunday Mirror* on 1 January 1985. 'May I suggest you make me deputy chairman so that no one will suspect you have pushed me out?' he had said then, according to his book *Goodbye Fleet Street*.

Presumably, Kinnock did not realize that the law he proposed would bar any of the Maxwell offspring from running the *Mirror*. The first of the family to inspect the new acquisition had been Betty. Maxwell brought her to the building on the Sunday following the immortal Friday the 13th, driving the Rolls himself and making an illegal U-turn in Holborn to park on the bus stop in front of the building. Ian and Kevin soon followed, both of them instantly recognizable reproductions with the coal-black eyes of the youthful Lajbi but with manners distinctly superior to the better-known Bob.

Ghislaine, however, was more immediately noticeable. Her father put her to work in his outer office from which she could quickly dash to pour a drink for a guest or pose for a photographer in need of some warm flesh. Thus, stories on Oxford United, bingo and a host of other Family Interests were illustrated by her striking raven looks. A picture of her stood on Maxwell's desk. Until the renovation was finished it was the only ornament in his office.

At Oxford, where she read French Literature at Balliol (she did her thesis on the Dreyfus scandal), Ghislaine had been friendly with a group of well-heeled tearaways, including Olivia Channon, a Cabinet minister's daughter who died of a drugs overdose. Such staple causes of the tabloid press as drugs, AIDS and abortion never failed to provoke Maxwell's concern. Ghislaine's picture was a permanent reminder to him of the fears of a million parents, and the *Mirror* inveighed tirelessly against the drug culture. Ghislaine herself seemed more interested in the *Mirror* library, a treasurehouse of clippings and pictures about everyone she had ever known.

Nothing so frivolous was permitted the sons. Every morning at half-past seven they met their father at Maxwell House. Ian had only to walk from the Barbican, a huge apartment complex nearby where he kept a small smart flat. Kevin drove in from a painfully modest house in an ungentrified street near Barons Court Tube station where he and his wife Pandora had moved after their first child was born. Maxwell showed no interest in the young men's life outside the office, so long as it did not attract the gossip columns. 'Where do you live now?' he asked Kevin. 'It sounds awful.'

The truth was that the children lived where they could afford to. The companies paid them a good salary and allocated them a BMW each. Apart from that they were treated even more demandingly than if they had been minions. Ian's first responsibilities concerned BPCC. Later, when the prospect of expansion into France beckoned, he was sent to Paris. He was the second generation's linguist, having put in a year in Japan to learn the commercial language of the future, in addition to his French and German.

Of the sons, it was in Ian that a flicker of waywardness had occasionally shown itself. In addition to being the only member of the family committed, however temporarily, to the Outer Darkness, at thirteen he had teamed up with a cousin in a legendary escapade. The two of them had painted psychedelic white swirls on the newest maroon Rolls delivered at Headington. Out of sight of 'the Old Man' – the euphemism with which the young Maxwells were most comfortable when discussing their father with outsiders – Ian, like Jean Baddeley, developed a taste for the raffish late-night company of some of the *Mirror* men, joining not just the poker games but also the pre-dawn carousing in the West End.

Kevin, by contrast, went home – whenever he was allowed to. Far more than Ian, he shared his father's dedication to profits and acquisition. Even as a schoolboy he had been fascinated by printing, playing for hours with a toy typesetting outfit. When, in 1983, Maxwell, in a mystifying departure from his pursuits up until then, had bought a financially enfeebled office equipment and timber manufacturer named Hollis, he had given Kevin the job of restructuring it. He did it quietly and without too many bloodstains. Since then Maxwell had loaded him more and more heavily with more and more varied responsibilities.

Wan but unfailingly courteous, Kevin would be dispatched to fire a few hundred people here or there, put in an appearance at a charity dinner in place of his father, read a speech that Maxwell did not want to make. If there were questions, an audience might imagine they could snare Kevin into revealing some morsel of information his father would have known how to conceal. They should have known better. Sometimes, however, what the listeners did get was all the more convincing, coming from the controlled and polite young ectomorph who plainly understood what needed to be done with the immense inverted pyramid of businesses Maxwell had erected on his own shoulders.

At a meeting of investment advisers during the 1987 BPCC expansion Kevin, suddenly thrust into his father's place, was peppered with questions about Maxwell management style. One was: Will your father be taking a lower profile? Kevin found the idea as improbable as everyone else. But he took the chance to drive home the point to a lot of people who were still mesmerized by the irrepressible antics of the Old Man, that neither of the men now actually running the printing operations in Britain and America, which were still the financial dynamos of BPCC, was a Maxwell.

Maxwell sits in his office at Headington. Sunday is the same as any other day to him, just as midday is the same as midnight if there is work to be done. And to his staff. He is in deep discussion with a City image-maker, whose expertise would be valuable to someone more accustomed to taking advice. A tall man with a lined face and eyes that have seen happier times enters the room. He waits for Maxwell to notice him. And waits. And waits. Eventually Maxwell does. 'Yes, Peter. What is it?'

'The two deputy premiers say they can't wait any longer, RM. They have been waiting for forty minutes now.'

'How are they going? By train or road? Train? We'll send them in the Chinook. They can wait a bit longer.'

xwell now had his own huge Chinook helicopter, registration
G   IGN. He had bought British Airways helicopter division for £12.5
million, tracking down an old *Sunday Telegraph* contact, deputy editor
Ian Watson, to give him the home phone number of BA chairman Lord
King as soon as he saw it was for sale. He was now chairman of the new
company, British International Helicopters. Rupert Murdoch might have
50 per cent of an airline in Australia, but Maxwell now owned more
helicopters than anyone in Europe.

Maxwell goes back to his conversation. Peter Jay, his £80,000-a-year
chief of staff, a former British ambassador to Washington and ex-son-in-
law of an erstwhile prime minister, returns to console the loitering
supplicants.

Of all the people Maxwell has ever been able to get to work for him Jay
is the least expected. His diplomatic career was not distinguished, tainted
as it was with accusations of nepotism – and anyway the Jimmy Carter
presidency was no time to make an impression on the White House. But
Jay, still only fifty, had been hailed as one of the most promising young
men of his generation: Winchester, Christ Church, President of the
Oxford Union, First-Class Honours degree, economics editor of *The
Times*, a sagacious television interviewer. Why would a man like this
submit to the exhausting, exasperating indignities that working for Maxwell in any capacity entailed?

The unexpected truth was that Jay had always admired Maxwell. Even
back in Maxwell's most controversial period of the early 1970s he had
defended his methods. It was not something on which his wife of that
time, James Callaghan's daughter Margaret, agreed. Maxwell, in turn, had
been a friend of the Jay family since his time in Parliament. Jay senior
had been President of the Board of Trade, as the Department of Trade and
Industry was known before the Pergamon inquiry. As an MP, Maxwell
had aspired to a post under him.

When, in 1983, Maxwell needed help with *Banking World*, a small
publication he had acquired along with its publisher, he hired Jay as
consultant for £20,000 a year. In 1984, Jay became its editor for £35,000.
He was given his present title in 1986. His first task was to reallocate the
spaces in the *Mirror* garage.

When Haines heard of the appointment he sized up the kind of experience Maxwell was assembling in Jay, himself, and other people with
government backgrounds who were being recruited, and recognized the
model to which Maxwell was working. 'He's putting together a Cabinet
Office!'

Jay had other considerations, too, in berthing himself alongside Maxwell. He nurses a particular loathing of Rupert Murdoch and his works.
But people who work for tyrants run the risk of being turned into syco-
phants. Success cannot be achieved on an objective level; it depends on
pleasing the only source of approval – in this case Maxwell. Jay goes
about his duties with an embittered air. At an annual Maxwell event, the
dinner following the Ernest Bevin memorial lecture, he sat long-faced and
unsmiling through a speech delivered by his former father-in-law, now

Lord Callaghan, and conspicuously refrained from applauding.

For all that Jay has to suffer, his haughty Wykehamist manner and the example of the devious Foreign Office functionaries who once danced attendance on him have helped him develop a nice line in obsequious bullying. Maxwell is not allowed to leave nearly as much detail neglected. Also, like Maxwell, Jay is a chess-player, the next move never far from his mind.

A fellow Czech-born millionaire, Ivan Lendl, was the cause of Maxwell breaking his left ankle and contributing a new attraction to the jinxed 13th Commonwealth Games held in Edinburgh in July 1986 – the Foot. Maxwell was boarding G-RMGN to watch Lendl play Boris Becker in the Wimbledon men's final when he slipped and fell. Lendl went on to lose the tennis match, and Maxwell ended up on crutches. The heavily plastered foot that cartoonists invariably drew poking out of his Rolls-Royce became a more appropriate symbol for the crippled Games than the engraved claymore with which the opening ribbon was cut, now on display at Headington.

After two solid years of Maxwell the King of Money-Raising there was really no one else for Scottish Secretary Malcolm Rifkind to turn to when a spreading boycott over South Africa threatened to bring disaster. The Games were £4 million short of the £14.1 million needed. It was a dramatic challenge. Maxwell had to respond. There was all of five weeks before Prince Philip was due to perform the opening ceremony. And as Maxwell said: 'Jerusalem wasn't built in a day.'

But any suggestion that Maxwell might be out to hijack the Games for his own glory was righteously rejected. His newspapers would have no special privileges. His family would not be presenting any medals. Nevertheless, *Mirror* mastheads replaced those of the *Daily Mail* on the electronic scoreboard.

As Mrs Thatcher's refusal to impose sanctions on the Botha regime fed resentment against South Africa, the Commonwealth itself, not just the Games, seemed in danger. One country after another began to pull out. Many of the smaller ones, far worse off for money than Scotland, actually welcomed the excuse. Maxwell sent a personal plea to African leaders: 'I and my colleagues at Mirror Newspapers are working hard at getting rid of Mrs Thatcher because she's been there too long, but we're not using the Commonwealth Games,' he said. 'These Games are too important, too vital.'

The week before the Games opened, Maxwell flew to Edinburgh, supporting his weight on a black cane, a present from an African leader. He wore, as he always did in Scotland, his Maxwell tartan tie. 'She is a tough lady,' he replied to reporters who asked him about Thatcher, 'and I am a tough hombre.' As cameras transmitted his message to the far pavilions of the Commonwealth, he declared: 'These are not Mrs Thatcher's Games. They are the athletes' Games. They are Scotland's Games. They are the Commonwealth's Games. They have nothing to do with her.' As he spoke he thumped the table so hard with his fist that the Foot jerked.

Even after the crippled Games were off and running, Maxwell remained the main event. He held a series of impromptu press conferences outside the press tent, where his office was located. The recurring question was whether his own cash was actually in the till. Tiring of hearing it, he ordered a private corridor built.

The tiresome detail about who was actually paying did not detract from Maxwell's pleasure in presenting a medal to Steve Cram, England's winner of the 1,500 metres. Nor in the company of the various visiting royals. It was only a matter of time before he bumped into Brigadier Francis Coutts, chairman of the Games VIP and hospitality committee and a veteran of forty years in the King's Own Scottish Borderers. Maxwell had not at first realized this was the brother of Sir Walter, the former interim chairman of Pergamon. 'By God, he was sharp,' the brigadier soon found. 'He remembered Wally's wife's nickname straight away: Bones. That impressed me. I took him round my section, but having been army men we both knew the whole inspection thing was a bullshit operation. What he was really interested in was the royals. "How many members of the royal family are coming? How many events are they visiting?" '

Maxwell arrived for the closing ceremony in his Rolls, the Foot emerging first. He stood beside the Queen on the podium. 'He talked to her endlessly,' said Bruce Wilson of the *Melbourne Herald*. 'Once he reached a vast right arm across her back. It was a gesture somewhere between a hug and a pat. The Queen was not amused. She deliberately turned away from the march past and started talking to city officials standing behind her.'

For deliverance from the price of this moment of royal intimacy – the final shortfall was over £3 million – Maxwell turned not to the Commonwealth but to 'one of the world's greatest philanthropists', as the Maxwell press described his old friend Mr Sasakawa of Japan, last encountered when he had come up with £100,000 for Ethiopia. Sasakawa, eighty-seven, was the benefactor of the Great Britain Sasakawa Foundation, a charity founded to promote social, cultural and economic contacts between the two countries. Maxwell was its chairman. Way back in 1931, Sasakawa had founded a fascist party in Japan in admiration of Benito Mussolini which, among other things, caused him to be detained at the Allies' pleasure for three years after the Second World War. He had changed his political outlook since then, Maxwell assured everyone. Actually, old Sasakawa had gone on to promote the Moonies, the World Anti-Communist League and a variety of causes associated with martial arts and right-wing nationalism. What mattered, however, was that Sasakawa was ready to put in £1.3 million. To try to scrape together the rest Maxwell wrote to the defaulting Commonwealth countries asking for money to 'meet losses which unfairly fell on people who bear no responsibility for the policies of the Government of the United Kingdom. They have done nothing to deserve the loss of their money, which in many cases may mean bankruptcy and loss of jobs for innocent people.' Kenya got a bill as did India, Nigeria, Papua New Guinea, Jamaica and the Virgin Islands. A year later firms with a stake in the Games were still being liquidated in the Scottish courts. 'Maxwell's involvement was a gimmick from start to finish,' said Brigadier Coutts. 'But you could say that without him there would not have been any games.'

By the end of 1985 Maxwell was playing on ever more tables at the same time, and the flow of secret paperwork with which Baddeley had to cope was never-ending. Even though she took down Maxwell's letters and memos and processed them over and over again, she often had no real idea what the transactions were in which he was involved. Frequently the sons, too, no matter what else Maxwell may have entrusted them with, were excluded. Complained Kevin when his father had called him in on some particularly delicate negotiations: 'As soon as things got interesting he ordered me out of the room.'

That year Maxwell went to both Russia and China. Asked what he had said to Teng Hsiao-p'ing about world events, he replied: 'I asked him if he knew what would have happened if Khrushchev had been assassinated instead of President Kennedy. . . .'

With the City watching him as cannily as a croupier, he started to dabble in other people's takeovers as only a genius of share manipulation could. Maxwell wanted Extel, the financial and racing service. While the company was fighting off another predator, he had built up a 26 per cent stake. Extel in its turn tried to act as 'white knight' to a middle-sized publisher and printer, McCorquodale, in the face of a bid from Norton Opax. Maxwell had crucial stock. He first backed Norton then switched camps twice. He was just beginning to enjoy himself when he had to go to court to give evidence in the only libel suit of the many he had threatened, begun or settled actually to come to trial.

The case of Maxwell versus Pressdram and Richard Ingrams, publisher and editor respectively of *Private Eye*, was heard in November 1986. The jury of six men and six women had originally been chosen to hear criminal cases at the Old Bailey – 'murder, rape, mayhem or something like that', as the judge, Mr Justice Simon Brown, told them sympathetically. The issue to be decided in court 11 at the Royal Courts of Justice was whether two articles suggesting that Maxwell had acted as 'paymaster' to Neil Kinnock in order to secure a peerage were in fact true.

The offending articles were published in consecutive issues of *Private Eye* in July 1985. The first said that Patricia Hewitt, Kinnock's press secretary, would shortly be announcing that Kinnock was to visit the East African capitals of Dar-es-Salaam and Nairobi, 'though she won't be revealing that Maxwell is acting as paymaster for the trip'. Claiming that Maxwell had already funded Kinnock's trips to Moscow and Central America, the *Eye* asked: 'How many more Kinnock freebies will Maxwell have to provide before he is recommended for a peerage?' The suggestion of bribery, said Richard Hartley, Maxwell's QC, was clear.

Never at ease from the beginning, the jury had to ask the judge to define a peer and his or her duties. It was a sensible question. Few citizens fully appreciated the workings of the British honours system and the manner in which a peerage was granted. A peer, said Judge Brown, was 'no more and no less than a member of the House of Lords. As for duties, well, they are not compelled to do any work as such at all.'

No one would ever take that as a definition of Maxwell, but it was a widely held view that he lusted after a lordship for reasons of vanity. He had denied the *Eye* story. Hewitt backed him up with a letter of her own to the magazine, adding that the trips were paid for in 'the usual way' by Mr Kinnock's own office. The *Eye* repeated the original libel in its second article which told of a problem with the guest-list for 'a glittering, champagne-all-the-way party marking Cap'n Bob's first glorious year at the helm of the *Daily Mirror*'. Kinnock, it said, had not planned to attend. 'Tell him', Maxwell was alleged to have said to Julia Langdon, the *Mirror*'s new political editor, 'that if he doesn't come to my party, the *Mirror* will not be reporting his African tour.'

'Thankfully good sense finally prevailed,' wrote the *Eye*'s own political editor, Christopher Silvester, a dandified Cambridge graduate of twenty-five and grandson of the dance-band leader Victor Silvester. 'Mindful of His Master's Voice, Kinnock duly turned up.'

Maxwell arrived in court to give evidence at 10.14 a.m. on 5 November, the usual bronchial activity announcing his approach. Heads turned. He had chosen a revolutionary red tie, pink-striped white shirt and dark blue suit. The tie and shirt toned in with the colour of his nose. He looked ill.

But he took the oath in a clear voice. No one asked him about religious affiliation or beliefs; he was asked only to swear. He stood erect in the witness-box, hands gripping the top. Even the corridors outside were packed, heads craning over shoulders to hear his answers.

Hartley referred his client to an item in the *Eye* headlined 'Kray Twins' which showed lookalike pictures of Maxwell and Ronnie Kray, one of the notorious East End twins serving life for murder. Asked if he saw anything funny in the comparison, Maxwell replied: 'Not only was I not amused but, far worse, Mrs Maxwell and all our children were utterly shocked to have me, their father, compared to a convicted major gangster.'

Maxwell had sued then, and the *Eye*, on that occasion, had apologized and promised not to smear him again. Thereafter, in its irrepressible way, it adopted the device of signing letters about other lookalikes 'Ena B. Maxwell, Headington Hill Hall'. 'Mrs Maxwell was very upset with me that I settled the action,' said Maxwell.

Hartley then referred him to lookalike pictures of the Duke of Edinburgh and Adolf Eichmann. Immediately, Maxwell lost his composure. Tears welled in his eyes. His shoulders heaved. He stabbed a finger at the postage-stamp-sized photograph of Eichmann on the page in front of him. 'My family was destroyed by Eichmann,' he said, the words partly drowned in sobs. A stunned silence descended. Maxwell pulled out a white linen handkerchief, dabbed his eyes and blew his nose. 'I'm sorry, my lord,' he said. A sip of water, and he had recovered sufficiently to continue. He had another five and a half hours to go in the witness-box.

Had he exploited his position as a newspaper publisher to advance his personal standing with and influence over the leadership of the Labour Party?

'It is not true.'

Was it his personal ambition to be elevated to the Lords?

'Not true. I have no ambition to be a member of the House of Lords.'

What about the guest-list for the *Mirror* party?

'I asked Sir Tom McCaffrey whether Mr Kinnock was coming. I believe I was told by Sir Tom that on the same night there was an event at Mr Murdoch's *Times*. I said words to the effect: "Well, if he won't come to the *Mirror* party, we won't go to his African party." It was, I hope, a funny joke. Certainly everybody else laughed about it.'

Was it a threat?

'Certainly not.'

The jury was never to hear McCaffrey's version of this. After the court adjourned that day Maxwell called him at home. The conversation, McCaffrey recalls, eliminated him as a witness.

> *Maxwell came on and said: 'How are you doing, mate?' Considering the terms on which he and I parted company, I thought that was, to put it mildly, a bit thick. He went on to remind me that Neil's office had said he couldn't come because he had already turned down an invitation to* The Times.
>
> *Private Eye were claiming that on hearing this, Maxwell exploded into saying: 'Tell him if he doesn't come to the party tonight he will not get any coverage for his trip to Africa in the* Mirror.' *I said: 'But Bob, you did say it – in my presence.'*
>
> *'Oh,' he said, 'but I was joking. That was a joke, wasn't it?' Then a lawyer who was listening – Maxwell had told me the loudspeaker was on in his room – came on the line and asked if I would go into court and say all this. I said: 'What exactly do you want me to say?' He said: 'I would want you to say that Mr Maxwell was joking when he said that.'*
>
> *I said: 'I don't see how I could do that because only he knows if he was joking.' At this point, Bob came on again and said, 'Thank you, mate,' and put the phone down.*

It was in the middle of the trial that Maxwell's most spectacular and mystifying plunge into diversification was revealed. Previously placid Hollis made an agreed £265 million bid for AE, a specialized motor components manufacturer. Sir Francis Tombs, chairman of Turner & Newall, who were also after the company, was floored. 'Hollis has no background in engineering or even any experience in the automotive industry,' he said.

Maxwell, hurrying to court, explained: 'I want to build a group based on science and technology.' He failed that time but didn't stop trying. Hollis soon added Stothert & Pitt, the crane-makers, to its industrial portfolio and six months later Ransomes & Rapier, makers of the biggest 'walking draglines' in the world, were 'rescued' as well, although at the cost of jobs.

When the court adjourned after Maxwell had given evidence most of the day, he met successive delegations from Norton Opax and McCorquodale until the early hours of the following morning. He finally chose Norton Opax. But he persuaded McCorquodale's chief executive – John Holloran – to join BPCC. Maxwell, by then forbidden by the Takeover Panel to make a new bid for Extel until April 1987, did what Oliver Hardy would have done in a good mood. He sold the Pergamon Media Trust's 26.8 per cent to Samuel Montagu who sold it to Stan Laurel, now Lord Stevens.

When the *Eye*'s QC, Andrew Bateson, came to cross-examine Maxwell, he rose slowly to his feet and peered over his spectacles. If Maxwell was offered a peerage, would he accept?

Maxwell was ready for that. 'I have been offered it twice before and I have said No.'

When was he offered it?

'Some few years ago by Mr Goronwy Roberts [Labour's deceased deputy leader in the Lords]. He asked me whether I would allow my name to go forward for a peerage, and I said no because I couldn't support the defence policies of Michael Foot. Last year, the deputy leader of the party, Mr Hattersley, asked me if I would like to be considered. I said: "No, thank you very much."'

This caused a certain amount of confusion in the Hattersley camp at the House of Commons. 'Roy has never asked Mr Maxwell if he would like to be a peer,' said a Hattersley aide. 'He has never offered him a peerage.' Maxwell explained that Hattersley had made a remark along the lines of 'I suppose you will want to be the next to go to the Lords?'

'It was at a time when our mutual friend, Mr Charles Williams, was made a peer,' said Maxwell. But, he added, Hattersley had now told him that it was 'jocular and not to be taken as an offer of any kind'. 'Naturally I accept that,' said Maxwell, 'but I took his words seriously and made a serious answer and that answer remains my position.'

Bateson asked Maxwell if he thought giving money to a political party was 'a very good route to a title'.

'Certainly not.'

Mr Bateson referred to a column, 'Straight Talk', written by John Smith in the *People*. He quoted: 'Every tycoon knows that the short cut to a title is to cough up cash to the party in power.'

Smith, said Maxwell, was 'a star reporter with the freedom to express himself subject only to the laws of libel'. He did not say that Smith had accompanied him to Ethiopia where he had found himself subject, mainly, to the laws of his publisher.

When the grilling was over, Maxwell descended from the witness-box and took his seat on the front bench. Nick Grant, one of his assistants, slipped a piece of paper to him. Maxwell bowed to the judge and left. The note had said: 'One of our helicopters is down in the North Sea. There are many people dead.'

At the *Mirror* news of the disaster was flooding in. Forty-three oil-rig workers and two flight crew had been killed as one of the Chinooks of which he was so proud, Foxtrot Charlie Two, crashed on its final approach to Sumburgh airport in the Shetlands. Maxwell sent a message of condolence to the bereaved, then returned to court for the afternoon session.

Before the end of the trial Maxwell, telling only his lawyers, took off for New York to pursue one of the items on his American shopping-list. A *Mirror* insider said: 'He asked for a progress report every three hours. He wanted to be kept in touch with any developments. When he was told that Hartley was summing up Maxwell said: "Tell him to keep talking until I get back. I want to tell him how to finish up."'

Maxwell slipped back into court five minutes before the jury returned to deliver its verdict, smiling and confident of a favourable result. The *Eye* defence had been pathetic; it had failed to produce the key witnesses: its sources. Suddenly the foreman was on his feet. Maxwell was awarded £3,500 for the first libel and £51,500 for the second, £50,000 of it exemplary or punitive. He beamed like a bingo winner.

To consolidate the victory Maxwell produced a leaden newsprint lampoon entitled *Not Private Eye*, designed by Molloy, and a glossy hardcover book on the case, *Malice in Wonderland*, largely written by Haines. The cover of *Not Private Eye* was a large montage showing Ingrams as Hermann Goering poring over a map of Europe with Adolf Hitler. The caption said: 'And if anyone objects we say we were only doing it for a laugh.' Suddenly, the Third Reich and everything that Maxwell had so recently wept over could be funny.

Maxwell's capacity for being disappointed in lesser folk and failed ambitions is infinite. He had done everything possible to build up the *Mirror* titles, and still they were not performing to plan. There were fewer printers, but they had called his bluff. He had threatened repeatedly that if production of any paper was interrupted by a dispute it would never be produced at Holborn again. The printers stopped the *Mirror*. He started it again. He *had* taken *Sporting Life* out of the building in a round of frantic tomfoolery that had Kevin traipsing around non-union East End typesetters in the early hours of the morning. But he had not, as he had pledged, sold it. It was, after all, the Queen Mother's favourite reading.

Editorial executives were delighted when, in one marvellous gesture, he routed the circulation department, an entity more adept at mystery than Maxwell. Between the six-monthly Audit Bureau of Circulation reports the papers' sales were what Maxwell said they were. The journalists were not nearly as thrilled when he brought in a squad of marketing men who referred to the *Mirror* as 'The Product'. They were headed by Patrick Morrissey, formerly of Beechams where he had won recognition as the man who put the pink stripe in a brand of toothpaste. Soon the *Mirror*, too, had its own pink stripe, a twice-weekly pullout on rosy paper.

Molloy, now elevated to editor-in-chief, designed it. But there was only one way Maxwell was going to be satisfied.

'I don't rate anyone on the *Mirror*,' he had complained in the summer of 1985 as the Rolls bore him between Maxwell House and Holborn. Nobody? 'Nobody in the group at all. Not even the journalists.' Then he added pugnaciously: 'I'm going to start a paper of my own.' It would be his own firstborn, not the adopted 'products'.

As usual with Maxwell, the reason he gave was not the only one. The unions believed that Murdoch had used plans for a new evening paper, the *London Post*, as a cover to instal computer equipment in Wapping and train non-printers to use it. Publicly, Maxwell called Murdoch's methods 'anti-British', likening Wapping's barbed razor-wire to Auschwitz. He would bring change the British way, through negotiation. Privately, he began to plan 'a Wapping without the wire'. And, since Murdoch had not, after all, launched his evening paper, then Maxwell would. It would be called the *London Daily News*. That was only the first thing he did wrong.

The editor of the first *London Daily News* that hit the streets in 1846 was Charles Dickens, who quit after only seventeen issues, calling it 'a brief mistake'. His successor 141 years later was Magnus Linklater, a distinguished veteran of the *Sunday Times* and the *Observer*. 'Welcome aboard,' Maxwell said as he shook his new editor's hand in April 1986. 'You've made a decision you'll never regret.' Linklater, wary of Maxwell's hands-on habits, demanded a guarantee of independence in writing. Maxwell gave it to him. Linklater would only be fired if he criticized the royal family, opposed NATO or agreed in print with Labour's unilateral defence policy.

Even so, Maxwell insisted on vetting the staff. Linklater wanted Alan Rusbridger, a former *Guardian* columnist who had often poked fun at Maxwell, as his Washington correspondent. Maxwell grilled him. 'Do you take drugs? Have you ever been a communist? You'd better tell me now. We'll find out in the end.'

Maxwell hired Bill Gillespie, an Irishman with a soft brogue belying a steely resolve, who had masterminded the Wapping operation for Murdoch. Gillespie knew the unions better than any executive in Fleet Street and he set about stepping over their hidden trip-wires to deliver deals in printing and distributing the new paper. He soon found that the 'free hand' he had been promised was not the only one at work. At one point the NGA said to him: 'You don't really understand. That's not what Maxwell told us on Sunday.' Maxwell was having his own secret talks with the unions. Gillespie resigned in disgust after only five months.

Linklater was bowling ahead with his plans when the autumn 1986 launch was suddenly abandoned. The *London Daily News* would now be launched on 10 February 1987. But, Linklater learned to his consternation from an unheralded Maxwell announcement to his staff, it was to be Britain's first twenty-four-hour newspaper: the paper that never stops for the city that never sleeps. This was mistake number two.

But survivors of the *Scottish Daily News* nodded knowingly. Maxwell had done exactly the same thing in the middle of his first newspaper venture. There might have been some justification for morning and evening editions of the same paper in Glasgow – if the proposal had not immediately been defeated within the co-op. But in London, where eleven national newspapers appeared every morning, it was an absurd idea.

Still, Maxwell looked like achieving his peaceful Wapping. The cowed print unions would concede 'direct input' – journalists would be able to operate typesetting keyboards not only on the *London Daily News* but also on the Mirror titles. Just in case they did not, security arrangements were stepped up. The *London Daily News* office, across the street from the main building, could be turned into an electronically protected fortress like the ninth floor.

Mistake number three that Maxwell made – the really fatal one – was to leave out of his considerations the competitive skill and cunning of the third Viscount Rothermere, owner of Associated Newspapers, publisher of the paper the *London Daily News* was most directly challenging, the *Evening Standard.* At sixty-one, Rothermere was the last of the hereditary press lords. Maxwell despised him on that and several other counts. His wealth was inherited, he had a languid upper-class manner and he was a friend of Rupert Murdoch. The link with Murdoch was a family tradition. The founder of the dynasty, Lord Northcliffe, had been so helpful to Rupert's father that Sir Keith Murdoch had been known in Australia as 'Lord Southcliffe'.

Maxwell could never have ruled as Rothermere did. He was a tax exile, able to spend only ninety days a year in Britain where, in his boardroom overlooking the Thames, drinks were served from a cabinet that Nelson had used on board *Victory.* The rest of the year he kept in touch from his Paris flat, his villa on the Côte d'Azur, his Manhattan apartment or wherever else his travels took him.

When a million copies of the *London Daily News* finally rolled off the presses of five printing centres on 24 February 1987, they were accompanied by what the paper itself described as 'a certain amount of hype'. The Life Guards trumpeted a fanfare. Maxwell released 5,000 balloons into the night sky from the *Mirror* building rooftop. He was host at a party for 400 where dancers dressed as robots performed in a suitably high-tech setting. A stretch of the Thames was closed for a fireworks display set off from a barge near Blackfriars. Mrs Dorothy Pasfield, an employee of Citicorp, had her nose broken by debris from a rocket. Margaret Thatcher and Neil Kinnock sent congratulatory messages about the paper.

Maxwell was soon claiming victory. 'After only two weeks, the *London Daily News* is a rip-roaring success,' he said. 'The falling *Standard* boasts its sales over the past few days have been above 550,000. What it doesn't say is that 150,000 to 200,000 are being returned unsold every day. These former *Standard* readers have decided they prefer to buy the *London Daily News.* We know it. They know it. Every wholesaler, retailer, newsagent and news vendor knows it. When Viscount Rothermere, who fights his battles from Paris, declared war on us, he thought he could put us out of business.'

What Rothermere had done was exploit the peril, against which Maxwell had been warned, of including 'News' in the title. Years before Associated Newspapers had shut down the old *Evening News* to give the *Standard* a monopoly. Now Rothermere pulled what he called his 'Lazarus trick'. He relaunched the *Evening News*, in makeshift form to be sure, but the confusion it caused in the minds of buyers and advertisers got badly in the way of the *London Daily News*'s market. There was the usual exchange of writs. While Maxwell was suing the *Evening News* for 'passing off' because of its similar title, the *Standard* went to court over his assertion that it was falsifying its sale figures. Maxwell backed down, unreservedly withdrawing the allegation and apologizing for having made it.

Maxwell's preoccupation with the *London Daily News* was a welcome bonus for the Mirror titles. 'It was like the Battle of Britain,' said Mike Molloy. 'One day the Luftwaffe didn't turn up – and it was all over. One day the phone didn't ring – and Bob was gone.'

But Maxwell was, as always, playing on another table as well and in a far bigger game. He was spending a lot of time in the Presidential Suite of the Waldorf Astoria in New York ($3,000 a day plus 13 per cent tax). For Betty's scrapbook, he had his photograph taken in front of a plaque commemorating previous illustrious occupants. 'Presidents and the Queen have stayed here,' he told the photographer, Mick Brennan. 'Have you been here before?' 'Yes,' replied Brennan. 'I shot Idi Amin standing where you are.'

Maxwell was already well on the way to becoming the second-largest printer in North America. He had paid a total of £310 million for Providence Gravure, Diversified Printing Corporation and Webb & Company in the United States, and a share in papermakers Donohue Inc. in Canada. Diversified added a big asset to the Maxwell Communication Corporation Inc., as his American operation had become: a billion-dollar contract to print *Parade* magazine. While his presses churned out 32 million copies a week, another Maxwell acquisition, AD/SAT, was transmitting advertisements by facsimile to more than a hundred newspapers across America.

He was out to challenge the world leader, R. R. Donnelley, whom he had once shunned as a partner for BPCC, on their own home ground. He had lured away the president of Donnelley's biggest division, Jim Sullivan, to be president of MCC Inc. – the other key lieutenant outside the family besides Holloran. But the rights issue Alexanders Laing & Cruickshank were organizing would bring more than $1 billion into his warchest, and what Maxwell wanted to spend it on was Harcourt Brace Jovanovich. That would put him in publishing as well as printing, where he surely deserved to be.

The $2 billion bid Maxwell launched on 18 May 1987 was not welcome. So much so that HBJ would not even answer the phone to him. He had to send a fax. 'Preposterous both as to intent and value,' the corporation's president called it.

William Iliya Jovanovich, who had added his own name to a venerable house and built it into a citadel of assorted interests, was a fitting opponent for Maxwell. He was a coalminer's son of immigrant stock, born in Colorado. He had worked his way through university – three, actually: Colorado, Harvard and Columbia. That apart, 'Billy Jo' and Maxwell had a lot in common. He, too, was a high roller. 'I play in Las Vegas or wherever I can. It must be my Levantine blood.'

He even sounded a little like Maxwell might if he had chosen America rather than Britain. 'My parents sent me to school to become an American. That is a trust I have kept for forty years of publishing for American schools. I refuse to believe Mr Maxwell can be allowed to preside over the largest education publisher in the United States. His dealings since he emerged from the mists of Ruthenia after World War Two haven't always favoured shareholders – as Mr Sol Steinberg can attest.'

Jovanovich, it transpired, had heard of Kleinwort Benson and their successes in Britain. He engaged them and rounded up a team of investigative lawyers to invoke the Liechtenstein Defence, a tactic Maxwell denies has ever impeded his empire-building. And he kept shouting: 'What can be said about a man whose sources of income are hidden? What can be said about a man who, on receiving a doctorate from Moscow State University in 1983, commented: "I am confident that when the circumstances surrounding the shooting down of the South Korean plane have become fully known, people around the world will understand that the US is deliberately using this as a pretext for stepping up anti-Soviet propaganda?" Mr Maxwell has money but not enough. He has ambition but no standing. He ought to be sent packing to Liechtenstein.'

'Unparalleled personal vituperation,' was Maxwell's lofty response to this tirade. True, he had said that the United States would use the Korean airliner attack for anti-Soviet propaganda, but the Tass report of his speech omitted his strong condemnation of the disaster. Then, persuaded – not too reluctantly, for he has a weakness for funny hats – to be photographed in a baseball cap bearing the names of his New York attorneys, Maxwell belted out a series of court actions, including a subpoena against the HBJ investigators, in an unsuccessful attempt to gain access to their findings.

HBJ went deep into debt with a modified version of a leveraged buyout of its own shares costing $3 billion. 'A typical poison pill tactic,' Maxwell called it. 'We pitched our price fairly and sensibly. They decided to hock the company.' BPCC withdrew its offer and tried in vain to block HBJ's plan to refinance its equity.

Maxwell returned to Holborn, the war-chest intact apart from the lawyers' bill. Restlessly he picked a new target: *Today*, another high-tech low-flying creation of a newspaper which was, however, the only national British daily printed in colour. The sale was agreed with 'Tiny' Rowland and his Lonhro conglomerate which had bailed out *Today* a year earlier. The paper was Maxwell's for £10 million down. His plan was to use its presses for a relaunch of the flagging *London Daily News*. The two lame ducks would learn to fly in tandem as *Today* and *Tonight*.

Mike Molloy was already clearing his desk to take over at *Today*'s offices when Maxwell decided to break the news to Murdoch, who was in California. He wanted to be assured that Murdoch would transfer to him the valuable contract under which *Today* printed a million copies of the *News of the World* each week. And to gloat a little. Murdoch had been interested in buying *Today*.

During the HBJ hunting expedition, Maxwell had quoted a saying he said he had learned from his father: 'Before you sell the bearskin, you better catch the bear.' Murdoch may have heard it, too. As Maxwell talked to him Murdoch realized that the deal with Lonhro was agreed but not yet signed. The next day Bill O'Neill, his new Wapping supremo, put a deal for £38 million in cash on the table in front of Rowland's lawyers only half an hour before Maxwell was due to sign his own agreement. 'Tiny' Rowland gave his consent, and Murdoch, making one of his Concorde day trips to London from New York, tied up the loose ends. The loss of *Today* effectively sealed the fate of the *London Daily News*. Maxwell had publicly pledged that the paper would be given 'two to three years' to establish itself. Speaking on his father's behalf to media analysts, Kevin Maxwell had said: 'I can categorically confirm that the investment in the *London Daily News* will continue.'

At midday on Friday, 24 July, five months to the day after the spectacular launch, the editorial staff gathered in the newsroom believing they were going to hear an inspirational address from Maxwell about the way ahead. Instead he told them what he had told Linklater only half an hour earlier: the paper would close that day. He blamed the contract printers and the distribution system he had set up. Everybody else blamed Maxwell. The worst mistake of all had been to believe that there was room in London for a second evening paper.

Once it was all over, Rothermere sat in his apartment on the Ile St-Louis remembering how much fun it had been, easily worth the piddling £3 million it had cost. The morning sun filtered through the plane trees bordering the Quai d'Orléans and across the Seine to the Left Bank. 'Robert Maxwell is a very good businessman, indeed very brilliant,' said Rothermere. 'But it's fairly obvious he's not really a newspaperman. He seems to act a great deal off the cuff, almost as a man who has so much money he can indulge his whimsies. I couldn't see where the *London Daily News* was supposed to go or what it was supposed to do. Indeed, it became apparent neither did the editor.'

Then Rothermere ordered the *Evening News* laid to rest – until he needed it again. Maxwell had already announced that he intended to launch no fewer than three new publications, one of them a *free* London evening paper. Oh, and one in Montreal too.

However much the October 1987 crash had cost Maxwell – and the shareholders – he still had money to kick around when it came to football. Part of the reorganization that was to stem from the creation of MCC was to confirm the remainder of the old Odhams site at Watford as the headquarters of BPCC. The MGN titles would eventually be printed there (although still edited in Holborn) in full colour. When Elton John, just as improbable a football patron as Maxwell himself, who owned the local first-division team, decided to sell it Maxwell offered him £2 million. Watford would wear BPCC jumpers; John Holloran would run it.

This was too much for many of the game's supporters. Accepting Kevin as chairman of Oxford while Maxwell himself was chairman of Derby County had tested regulation 80 to its limit. Intended to ensure that there would be no curbing of competition in the conduct of matches, the setting of transfer fees or anything else, the rule was uncompromising. 'No official may, at any one time, be involved in any capacity whatsoever, in the management or administration of more than one club.' It had, in fact, often been bypassed in less blatant ways. But if BPCC bought Watford three of the League's twenty-one first-division clubs would be headed by directors of MCC. In addition, Maxwell interests still held a 30 per cent stake in Reading, another club he had once set out to buy. However, the hitherto complaisant management committee of the League did not seem to be in a position to object.

Maxwell was gracious at first. If the League disapproved, he would withdraw from the deal. He tried to set himself at a distance. He would be taking no managerial or administrative role, he said in press statements and letters to the League. But a few days later, when the management committee took legal advice and decided that it ought to resist the proposal, he turned on his opponents savagely, labelling them the 'Mismanagement Committee'. The objections that had now been voiced by the League's president, Philip Carter, were 'childish, scandalous and slanderous'. The deal was set for 8 December. The sports pages of the *Mirror* were loaded up to support Maxwell's newest takeover bid.

On 4 December the League went to a High Court judge for an injunction to prevent Elton John handing over his shares. Neither John nor Maxwell had been notified of the application, said the League's counsel, for fear that the transfer might have been brought forward. MCC might be controlled from Liechtenstein, said Mr David Oliver, QC, Mr Holloran might be installed as the team's chairman, but there was evidence that neither instance would prevent Maxwell's bidding being done. Enraged, Maxwell warned the League that a legal battle could last months and cost 'a very large sum of money indeed'.

The next day Maxwell and Carter met privately and reached a compromise. Maxwell would be allowed to buy Watford if he sold his interest in Oxford and Reading. Maxwell agreed. Watford was what he really wanted now. But the management committee had found its nerve under the storm of insults with which Maxwell was pelting it. It repudiated the president's deal. An extraordinary meeting of all ninety-two clubs in the League was set for 19 January.

Maxwell's fury consumed acres of newsprint. Any pretence that editors or writers controlled the contents of the papers was swept aside. Ferocious attacks on the 'mismanagement committee' and anyone who might share its views erupted from page after page of the *Mirror*. The infelicities deliberately left in the stories were the unmistakable sign of Maxwell dictation. 'Furious Robert Maxwell sensationally revealed last night,' began a front-page piece on 17 December intended to concentrate the minds of the ninety-two chairman soon to convene. The sensational revelation was that Maxwell would quit soccer if his agreement with Carter was not confirmed. So saturated with Maxwell's rhetoric did the *Mirror* become that a sports executive suggested the readers might have had enough. 'It's my paper,' said Maxwell. 'I do what I like with it.'

The extraordinary meeting came to yet another compromise. Regulation 80 was revised to allow a major shareholder in a club to own up to 2 per cent in any number of others. But it was not made retrospective. It meant that Maxwell could keep Oxford, Derby and his interest in Reading but that he could not buy Watford. Maxwell accepted the verdict grudgingly. 'The mismanagement committee are now discredited. . . .'

Until Maxwell turned Holloran into a pawn in his rapacious onslaught on the Football League, a lot of doubters were beginning to be convinced that the one-man band had not simply expanded into a one-man symphony orchestra. They were ready to believe that instruments other than the one Maxwell was blowing or banging at the time stood some chance of being heard. The astonishing and sustained performance Maxwell embarked upon over Watford showed that they had been right in the first place.

Holloran had the reputation of a tough and independent-minded executive, and Maxwell had set out to emphasize the autonomy he was to enjoy. But from the moment hostilities began over the team Holloran was to run the only voice heard on the attacking side was Maxwell's. Holloran stayed firmly in the rear ranks. 'I do actually exist,' he said plaintively on the second match-day that Maxwell, abandoning any pretence of detachment or delegation, was hosing the League down with caustic abuse like an out-of-control Crocodile. But, like the family, he existed in Maxwell's shadow.

The rampaging over Watford was vintage Maxwell. It is doubtful that anything Maxwell had ever done caused him so much damage in the esteem of those he wanted most to impress – City investors.

As Maxwell's sixty-fifth birthday approached, the time that remained to the 1990 deadline he had set himself to achieve the £3–5 billion turnover of his boasts seemed dautingly short. Especially since he had planned to earn half of MCC's profits between now and then by 'Treasury' deals – the balance-sheet label for dealing on the stock market. The Crash made that seem a doubtful prospect which must also unnerve his backers. After all, it was only by a 'fluke' – Maxwell's own word – that he had moved the HBJ war-chest into bonds in time to preserve it.

But the dust of the Crash was still thick in the air when Maxwell charged in again with is shopping-bag. He paid $77 million for a New Jersey printer, Alco Gravure – and said that it was to be his final printing acquisition – £35 million for United Trade Press to bolster his magazine plans and £24 million for a disk storage company. He also began to buy into a company that prints much of the world's money, De La Rue the banknote manufacturers. Even after all this he claimed he had enough left to buy another American company almost as big if nowhere near as glamorous as HBJ, Bell & Howell of Chicago whose name used to be synonymous with movie cameras but which has diversified into the Knowledge Market and information retrieval. His early overtures met with the usual response: the directors hid under their desks and warned shareholders to take the phone off the hook.

Maxwell could have got control of Bell & Howell for about £300 million but in early December 1987 he pulled out of the negotiations. About £100 million of the shareholders' funds from the rights issue had been earmarked for a wrinkle that brought a sigh of relief from admirers who feared he might be losing his touch. MCC, the public company of which the *Hinterlegt* in Liechtenstein owned at least 51 per cent, was to buy Pergamon Orbit Infoline, as it was now known – the business Maxwell had been virtually given by its original owners – of which PHF owned 100 per cent.

The original price put on the package, which also contained Molecular Design, a California electronic publisher, and Pergamon Books, was £111 million. Outlining this forthcoming transaction when the rights issue was being launched earlier in the year, Kevin Maxwell had explained that, the risks of developing Infoline having been borne by Pergamon, it was now a viable business. Even accepting that some of the shareholders who had put their money up when the stated objective was HBJ demurred. The deal was revised to a down payment of £56 million which could be increased to £100 million if future profits were satisfactory. Even so the report by Bankers Trust circulated to MCC shareholders was a model of reserve.

> *Our financial opinion as to the value . . . is based on financial and other information provided to us by Pergamon and its accountants and from other sources believed to be reliable. The estimates of sales and earnings for the years 1987 and 1988 have been prepared solely by Pergamon. No independent accountant has expressed an opinion on these estimates. Furthermore we have not independently verified the financial results. . . .*

The extraordinary general meeting to approve these acquisitions, to which were added the American Maxwell House and other property at Elmsford for $12.5 million, took place at 10 a.m. on New Year's Eve and was over in minutes. The press were kept out. Not enough chairs for them, said Maxwell blandly when he joined them later for some boasting. Besides, there had been too much ill-informed criticism already of this enlightened piece of trading.

The reporters were actually more interested in the most unexpected development of the entire year; Maxwell's apparent reconciliation with Rupert Murdoch. When it first seemed that Murdoch, already badly shaken by the Crash, might be compelled, as a result of Senator Edward Kennedy's sleight of hand with a Senate vote, to sell the *New York Post*, Murdoch came to breakfast in Holborn. Maxwell's wilder dreams include a nationwide American newspaper modelled on *USA Today* which his American plants and satellite set-up might be able to achieve if he had an editorial base. Murdoch let Maxwell's men have a look at the money-losing *Post*'s figures. But when Maxwell came up with an offer Murdoch scorned it as nothing more than a real-estate bid for the paper's decrepit but valuable downtown building.

Every year since 1984 had brought its surprises. Maxwell might not yet have got himself recognized as the Great Communicator he wished to be. But he had certainly got himself recognized. His face and the unmistakable, profoundly caricaturable figure had become familiar not just in Britain but throughout half the world. Prime ministers, kings and presidents took his telephone calls and posed for pictures with him. Bankers offered him the key to the safe. Thirty-five thousand employees jumped at his every growl.

In return he bestowed lordly favours, assuring the French for instance, that if British investors failed to finance their share of the Channel Tunnel he would underwrite it himself. That was to say, for £3 million worth, anyway.

Well into the fourth year of Maxwell's reincarnation the energy, the financial savvy and the sheer monumental truculence with which he forged ahead showed no sign of faltering, even if the boastful predictions still far outstripped the achievements. 'I have been blessed with a powerful constitution,' he assured anyone who had showed concern for his health. 'I will take a lot of stopping.' And if he had brought 1987 to an end with a reminiscent whiff of the old Maxwell he began 1988 the way he so desperately wished to go on, by starting another newspaper. The first adventure of the new year was in Montreal, an English-language tabloid called the *Daily News*. It was to be produced in partnership with Pierre Péladeau, president of Quebecor Inc., and the nearest Canada has to a Maxwell of its own. Maxwell had already shared his 55 per cent of Donohue, the newsprint operation, with Péladeau, which brought him even more than the usual visibility in Canada. In Montreal they called him 'Sir Bob'. Péladeau had denied after the Donohue deal that he planned any more ventures with Maxwell. 'No way in the world,' he said. 'Never.' But if Murdoch could change his mind, then anybody could.

Index

Addis Ababa, 223
Adelaide, 142
AD/SAT, 238
AE, 232
Agde, 51–6, 108, 211
Agence-France Presse, 28
AIDS, 33, 225
Aitken, Sir Max, 151
Alco Gravure, 243
Aldington, Lord, 175
Alexanders Laing & Cruickshank, 16, 238
All Centre Property Ltd, 115
Allied Control Commission for Germany,
    81–3, 86, 89
Allied Welcoming Committee, 64
Amalgamated Engineering Union, 151
American Broadcasting Corporation, 28,
    145
Amin, Idi, 169, 174, 237
Anglo-American Press Club, Paris, 33
Annals of Occupational Hygiene, 115
anti-Semitism, *see* Jews
Antwerp, 67
Ardennes, 67
Argentina, 95
Associated Newspapers, 236
Audit Bureau of Circulation, 235
Auschwitz, 50, 60, 235
Australia, 138, 142, 144, 145, 146
Austria, 37–44, 48, 58, 71, 89, 96, 158,
    214
Austria Club, London, 86
Austro-Hungarian Empire, 37, 39, 44, 214
d'Avigdor-Goldsmid, Sir Henry, 154, 169,
    177, 178
Aylesbury, 109
Azaz, Nehemya, 135

Bad Segeberg, 72
Baddeley, Jean, 16, 29, 117–18, 166, 201,
    203, 218, 220, 225, 229
Baker, Lt M. L., 69
Baker, Capt. Peter, 94
Baker, Richard, 203
Balfour, M., 81
Balkans, 39
Balladur, Edouard, 29

Band Aid, 223
Bank of Brazil, 94
Bank of England, 176, 187
Banking World, 228
Banks-Smith, Nancy, 195
Banner Headlines (Somerfield), 146
Banque de France, 29
Banque Indo-Suez, 29
Barbados, 138
Barker, Revel, 203
Barnard, Bryan, 111, 112, 120, 121, 131,
    133, 166
Bartholomew, Harry Guy, 184
Bastogne, 67
Bata, 37
Bateson, Andrew, 232
Batsford, B. T., 94
Battle of the Bulge, 67
Bavaria, 71
Beaverbrook, Lord, 20, 55, 152, 153, 190,
    191, 200
Becker, Boris, 227
Belgium, 53, 67
Bell & Howell, 243
Bellchambers, Ray, 109, 111, 114, 120
Bemrose, Eric, 144
Beneš, Eduard, 39, 45–6, 51, 56
Benn, Tony, 192
Benyon, William, 167
Benzing, Dr Horst, 193
Berlin, 50, 59, 77–9, 80–4, 86, 88;
    partition, 72, 77; Military Government,
    79, 81; black market, 83
Berlin Diary (Shirer), 77
Berliner, Der, 81
Bertelsmann, 193
Best Bets, 145
Béziers, 52
Binns, John, 135
Birk, Ellis, 14
Birmingham, 57, 84, 110
Blackcock, Operation, 67–9
Blackwell's, 122
Bletchley, 85, 111, 114, 120, 121, 122,
    133, 166, 167
Bletchley Gazette, 113
Bletchley Printers, 124

Blyton, Enid, 109
Bodleian Library, 89
Bohemia, 37, 39, 44, 46, 48
Bolshoi Ballet, 134
Book Center, see British Book Center
Bookseller, 98
Boston, 169, 173
Botha, P. W., 228
Bouygues, Francis, 29
Bowaters, 151
Bowes, Roger, 202, 205
Braddock, Bessie, 120
Brazil, 32, 94
Bremen, 71
Brennan, Mick, 237
Brezhnev, Leonid, 149
British Airways, 30, 49
British Book Center, New York, 93–4, 97,
    98
British Broadcasting Corporation, 10, 20,
    23, 57, 63, 191
British Expeditionary Force, 53
British International Helicopters, 230, 233
British Printing and Communication
    Corporation, 29, 216, 217, 218, 225,
    232; name, 10, 32, 33; image, 16, 32;
    RM's ambitions for, 23, 31, 226;
    investors, 31; American activities, 33;
    value, 188, 213; 'Survival Plan', 188,
    221; unions, 189–90; purchase of
    Odhams, 201; Watford site, 213; bid for
    Waddington, 214–15; RM's stock, 215;
    Harcourt Brace Jovanovich, 238–9;
    Great Crash (1987), 240
British Printing Corporation: RM takes
    over, 105, 139, 140, 141, 158, 186–8;
    and ILSC, 139, 159, 162, 186–7;
    'Survival Plan', 188, 221; Macdonald
    Futura, 189
British Rail, 154
British Steel, 104
Brno, 58
Brooks, Time, 81
Brown, George, 116, 150
Brown, Lt, 60, 62
Brown, Mr Justice Simon, 230
Brussels, 52
Buchholz, 72
Buckingham, 109–14, 115, 120, 126–7,
    139, 166–8, 190, 223
Buckingham Plan for World Nuclear
    Disarmament, 111, 112
Buckingham Press Ltd, 123, 136, 137,
    138, 160. See also Pergamon
    Subscription Books Division
Buckton, Ray, 190, 224
Budapest, 48, 49
Bulgaria, 49, 149
Burke, Edmund, 108
Burns, Dolly, 116
Bury St Edmunds, 59

Butlin, Billy, 151
Butterworth & Co., 90–1, 92, 139–40, 198
Butterworth-Springer Ltd, 90–1, 92, 95,
    103. See also Pergamon Press
'Buy British', 150–2
Byford-Jones, Lt-Col. W., 77, 78

Caen, 60
Calcutta, 140
Callaghan, James, 110, 150, 226, 227
Cambridge, 122
Cameron, Sue, 198
Canada, 96, 138
Cannes, 28, 29, 30, 33
Cap d'Antibes, 27
Carpatho-Ukraine, see Ruthenia
Carpenter, Leslie, 195–6, 199, 200–2, 203,
    204, 205
Carr, Sir William, 142–6
Carter, Jimmy, 226
Carter, Philip, 241–2
Carthew-Yourston, Brig M. A., 59, 70
Castle, Barbara, 133
Castlethorpe, 126
Catto, Lord, 144
Caxton Publishing Company 138–9, 171
Central Television, 23
Chalmers Impey (formerly Chalmers
    Wade), 96, 125, 137, 159, 177
Chalons-sur-Marne, 54
Chamberlain, Neville, 44–5, 46, 54
Chamber's Encyclopaedia, 136, 137, 138,
    139, 140, 142, 201
Channel Tunnel, 244
Channon, Olivia, 225
Charles, Prince, 9, 11, 28
Chernenko, Konstantin, 190
Chester, 57
Chesterton, G. K., 109
Chicago, 173–4
China, 31, 32, 95, 132, 138, 229
Cholmondeley, Lord, 57
Christiansen, Michael, 196
Churchill, Winston, 23–4, 47, 54, 55, 56,
    59, 73, 106, 165
Chust, 40, 47
Clark, Cecil, 93, 96, 97, 124, 137, 147, 165
Clarke, J. M., 98
Clausewitz, Karl von, 11
Clean Air Act (1968), 132
Clock House, 85, 86, 103, 109, 110, 119
Clyde Cablevision, 13, 105, 223
Coal Board, 105, 223
Cold War, 82, 104, 116, 150
Cole, Edward, 126
Coleman, Terry, 58
Coleridge, Arthur, 91, 92, 96
Collins, 189
Colt Heating and Ventilation Ltd, 150–1
Columbia Broadcasting System, 28
Common Market, 150

Commonwealth Games (1986), 33, 227–9
Companies Acts, 86, 137, 166, 177, 215
Concorde, 132, 198, 239
Conran, Shirley, 189
Conservative Party, 26, 84, 90, 106–9, 112–14, 133–4
Consumer Council, 139
Conway, Jim, 151
Cooke, Roy, 203
Cordrey, Jeannette, 12
Coutts, Brig. Francis, 228, 229
Coutts, Lady, 174, 180, 228
Coutts, Sir Walter, 169, 170, 173–6, 178, 179, 228
Coutts Bank, 217
Cowan, Sir Zelman, 15
Cowgill, Bryan, 29
Cowper, William, 108
Cram, Steve, 228
Craven Insurance Company, 135
Crosby, Benjamin, 91
'Crossbencher', 132
Crossman, Richard, 122, 158
Cudlipp, Hugh, 145, 162, 183, 184–5, 195, 196, 197, 204, 218; Walking on the Water, 184
Cunard, 184
Curtis, William, 98
Czechoslovakia, 37–50, 64, 110, 111, 212; National Army, 57; National Bureau, 51; National Committee, 51, 53, 55, 56; Social Democrats, 41, 46

Daily Express, The, 20, 32, 42, 142, 151, 152, 191
Daily Herald, The, 123, 158, 204
Daily Illustrated Mirror, The, 183
Daily Mirror, The, 14, 15, 20, 25, 29, 81, 117, 126, 227, 229, 233; RM's ownership, 11, 23, 105, 149, 198–208, 211, 214, 215, 216–20, 221, 224; football, 23, 234, 242; unions, 24, 189, 190, 203–4, 235; bingo, 24, 121, 217, 218, 225; circulation, 26, 32; support for Labour, 26, 123, 135, 230, 231, 232; and war effort, 85; change of name, 115; RM's apartment, 118; history, 183–4; 'Jane', 184; IPC, 184; Reed, 184, Murdoch on, 185; 'Inside Page', 185; 'Mirrorscope', 185; MGN, 186–208; Margaret Thatcher visits, 212–13; 'Mirror Diary', 219; Harold Wilson visits, 222; Ethiopia appeal, 223; causes, 225; Commonwealth Games, 228
Daily News (Montreal), 244
Daily Sketch, The, 196
Daily Telegraph, The, 111, 151
Daily Worker, The, 158
Daladier, Edouard, 44–5
Dandenong Journal, The, 145
Dangerous Estate (Williams), 196, 197

Daniels, Vera, 167
Davis, William, 135
D-Day, 50, 60, 61
de Bono, Edward: Lateral Thinking, 19
De La Rue, 243
Dean, Brenda, 190, 200
Deferre, Gaston, 29, 32
Delfont, Bernard, 151–2
Delmer, Sefton, 47, 81
Denmark, 53
Denning, Lord, 166, 179
Dennis, L/Cpl R., 69
Department of Trade and Industry: reports, 16, 24, 25, 31, 86, 159, 170, 171, 175–6, 177, 179, 180, 187, 227; interviews, 70, 89, 166, 168–9; trusts, 93; MSI, 93, 124–5, 176; premature invoicing, 140; RM's writ, 172
Derby, Lord 59
Derby County Football Club, 212, 242
'Desert Island Discs', 56, 117
Deutsche Press Dienst, 81
Diana, Princess of Wales, 28
Dickens, Charles, 235
Dieppe, 63
Dines, Debbie, 201, 203
Disraeli, Benjamin, 108, 146
Diversified Printing Corporation, 237
Docker, Sir Bernard and Lady, 116
'Dodo the Kid from Outer Space', 134
Dolly, Cpl, 69
Don Giovanni (Mozart), 134
Donnelley, R. R., 238
Donohue Inc., 238, 244
Dow-Jones, 23
Dracula, 41
Dunkirk, 50, 53
Dunoyer, Gen., 54, 55
Duveen, Lord, 116

Eden, Anthony, 56, 59, 73, 79, 106
Edge, Geoff, 167, 168
Edinburgh, 33, 227–9
Edwards, Bob, 136, 195, 203, 204, 206, 224
Edwards, Col. I. C. 'Ted', 82, 85
Edwards, John, 198
Edwards, Martin, 212
Eichmann, Adolf, 48, 50, 231
Eisenhower, Gen. Dwight D., 67, 111
Elizabeth II, 13, 137, 228, 235, 237
Elmsford, 94, 243–4
Elsevier, 32
Ely, 59
Encyclopaedia Britannica, 137
Esher, 103, 109, 110
Ethiopia, 33, 37, 223, 229
Eugster, Christopher, 215
European Coalition Broadcasting Corporation, 28
European Periodicals Publicity and Advertising Corporation, 88–9

European Publishing Corporation, 144
Evans, Dr Gordon, 109, 112
Evans, Harold, 163–4, 194
Evening News, The, 237, 240
Evening Standard, The, 135, 158, 204, 208, 236, 237
Express Newspapers, 190, 191
Extel, 230
Eyre & Spottiswoode, 97

Fabian Society, 109
Farouk, King, 143
Felvidek, 47
Fenny Stratford, 120
Financial Times, The, 30, 104, 152, 198
Finniston, Sir Monty, 13, 104–5
First Czech Division, 52, 54, 56, 57, 58
Flanner, Janet, 39–40, 47
Fleming, Robert, 143, 160, 162
Foley, Jo, 14
Fonteyn, Margot, 134
Foot, Michael, 233
Football League, 212, 213, 234, 241
Forbes, Mr Justice, 172, 179
Forsyte, Kerman & Phillips, 97
France; Paris Peace Conference (1919), 37, 38, 39; and Czechs, 43, 44–5, 49, 51, 57; guarantee to Poland, 48; Foreign Legion, 51, 52; Germany invades (1940), 54, 55; 7th Army, 54; Vichy, 56, 65; liberated (1944), 60–7; occupation of Germany, 77
Franco, Gen. Francisco, 45
Franklin, Benjamin, 135
Frankston and Peninsula News, The, 145
Frost, David, 151
Frost, Robert, 108
Fyfe, Hamilton, 183

Gable, Clark, 116
Gaitskell, Hugh, 111, 121–2, 125–6
Gale, George, 14, 107
Garnett, John, 151
Geldof, Bob, 223
General Motors, 152
Geneva, 103–4
Geouffre de la Pradella, M., 214
Germany: Holocaust, 33, 38–50, 52–3, 60, 65–6, 231, 234; Sudetenland, 38–50, 77; invades Czechoslovakia, 43, 44, 46, 49, 51, 52; pact with Russia, 47; invades Poland, 48; Gestapo, 48; and France, 54, 55; and Holland, Denmark and Norway, 54; and Russia, 60, 68; Allied occupation, 72, 73, 77–79, 83–4, 88
Gien, 55
Gillespie, Bill, 235–6
Glasgow, 104, 191–3, 194–236
Gliga, Vasile, 15
Goebbels, Joseph, 77, 80
Goering, Hermann, 234
Goldenson, Leonard, 145

Goodmann, Geoffrey, 83–4, 200, 221
Gorbachev, Mikhail, 15, 149
Goronwy-Roberts, Lord, 232
Gough, Col. C. F. H., 113
Gourlay, Logan, 135, 136
Grade, Lord, 15
Grant, Nick, 233
Great Britain Sasakawa Foundation, 229
Great Universal Stores, 151
Greece, 49, 116
Grigg, Sir James, 66
Grindlay's Bank, 66, 163, 169, 175, 178, 179
Guardian, The, 59, 196, 204–5, 213, 235
Guinness, 15

Habsburgs, 37
Haines, Joe, 14–15, 83, 194, 200, 207, 222–3; 228; *Malice in Wonderland,* 234; *Maxwell,* 14, 24, 54; *Politics of Power,* 194, 197, 223
Hall, Alan, 152
Halsall, John, 25
Hambro, Sir Charles, 90–2, 95, 97, 106, 107, 145
Hamburg, 72, 81
Hamilton, Denis, 163
Harcourt Brace Jovanovich, 30, 32, 278–9, 240, 243
Harmsworth, Alfred, *see* Northcliffe, Lord
Harmsworth, Vere, *see* Rothermere, Lord
Harris, Anthony, 104, 152
Harris, Philip, 138–139
Hartley, Richard, 230, 231, 233
Harty, Russell, 16
Harvard Institute of Politics, 169–70
Harwell, 104
Hattersley, Roy, 199, 233
Haut de Forges, 62
Havers, Mr Justice, 97
Hazell Watson & Viney, 187
Headington Hill Hall, 63, 64, 117, 118, 122, 166, 170, 174, 195, 226, 150; 40th anniversary, 9–18, 22–4, 27; stained-glass window, 12, 135; Pergamon moves to, 109, 111, 114–15
Heenan, Cardinal, 195
Hely-Hutchinson, Tim, 189
Henry Ansbacher, 15, 123, 137, 199
Heron Industries, 191
Hersant, Robert, 32
Hewitt, Patricia, 230
Hinterlegt, 214, 215, 240
His Majesty's Stationery Office, 89
Hitler, Adolf, 39, 47, 48, 50, 53, 60, 68, 73, 77, 234; Munich, 44, 45; in Prague, 46, 51, 52; suicide, 72
Hoch, Anna, *mother,* 40, 41, 42, 44, 49, 50, 108
Hoch, Mechel, *father,* 40, 41, 42, 44, 49, 50, 53, 72, 108

·Hodgson, Godfrey, 163, 164, 168
Holland, 33, 53, 57, 67, 95
Hollis, 225–5, 233
Holloran, John, 234, 241–2
Holmes à Court, Robert, 190
Holocaust, see Jews
Holy Roman Empire, 37
Hong Kong, 32, 138
Horthy, Adm. Miklos, 45, 47, 50
Hudgell, Ken, 203
Hume, Cardinal, 195
Hungarian National Bank, 158
Hungary, 37, 38, 40, 47, 48, 50, 66
Hyman, Joe, 151

I. R. Maxwell & Co. Ltd, 90, 92
Ilfracombe, 58
Illustrated London News, The, 113
'I'm Backing Britain', 150–2
Independent, The, 14
Independent Television, 10
Industrial Organization Corporation, 187
Industrial Society, 150
Infoline, see Pergamon Infoline
Ingham, Bernard, 213
Ingr, Gen., S., 51
Ingrams, Richard, 230, 234. See also
    Pressdram *and Private Eye*
Insect Physiology, 115
'Insight', see Sunday Times, The
International Business Machines, 157
International Encyclopaedias Ltd, 97
International Learning Systems
    Corporation: formed, 139; and BPC,
    139, 159, 162, 186–7; value, 140, 153;
    RM's plans for, 142; Murdoch and, 144;
    dissarray, 158, 169, 170, 171, 172; and
    Leasco, 160–1, 165–6; Secret
    Agreement, 160; accounts, 168
International Publishing Corporation, 26,
    142, 184, 185, 186
Iraq Petroleum, 115
Irish Republican Army, 24
Iserlohn, 80
Isis, 122
Isle of Man, 57
Israeli Bank, 169
Italy, 37, 61, 116

Jackson, Prof. Derek, 143
Jamaica, 116–17
Jameson, Derek, 191, 195
Japan, 32, 138, 225
Jarratt, Sir Alex, 185, 186, 196, 198, 200,
    201, 202, 203, 205
Jaruszelski, Gen., 107
Jay, Douglas, 227
Jay, Margaret, 227
Jay, Peter, 13, 227–9
Jeger, Lena, 149
Jenkins, Roy, 148

Jewish Chronicle, The, 14
Jews, 14, 33, 38, 40, 41, 44, 46, 47, 48, 50,
    52–3, 60, 65, 164, 169
John, Elton, 241
Joint Export Import Agency, 89, 90
Jovanovich, William 'Billy Jo', 31, 238–9
Joyce, James: *Ulysses*, 134
Juan Carlos, King, 28

Kennedy, Edward, 244
KGB, 83, 125
Khashoggi, Essam, 27
Krushchev, Nikita, 104, 111, 125, 132,
    183, 218, 229
Kiel, 72
Kildare, Marquis of, 13
Kilroy-Silk, Robert, 118
King, Cecil, Harmsworth, 123, 136, 184,
    197–8, 204, 218
King, Dr Horace, 131
Kingsley, David, 151
Kinnock, Neil: and RM's takeover at
    Mirror, 199, 200, 219, 224; 'despises
    Maxwell', 207–8; RM endorses, 208,
    219, 225; African trip, 230–4; *London
    Daily News*, 237
Kissinger, Henry, 206
Kleinwort Benson, 215–16, 238
Kliske, Private J. K., 58
Klopstock, Dr, 52, 59
Kosygin, Alexei, 132, 143
Kray, Ronnie, 231
Kristallnacht (1938), 46

La Bijude, 61, 62
La Ferte-sur-Jouarre, 54
La Nouvelle, 52
Labour Daily, 110
Labour Party: *Daily Mirror* and, 26,
    123, 135, 230, 231, 232; RM and, 107,
    110–11, 114, 119; NEC, 110–11, 168
Lace (Conran), 189
Lady Ghislaine, 27, 28, 116
Laing, Margaret, 19, 21, 52, 59,89, 98, 119
Lamb, Larry, 185
Lancaster, Terry, 133, 136, 149, 184, 194,
    207, 221
Langdon, Julia, 230
Lange. Maxwell & Springer, 90
Last Exit to Brooklyn (Selby), 134
Lateral Thinking (de Bono), 19
Lavendon, 106, 111
Lawton, Lord Justice, 179
Layton, C. A., 124
Le Bas, Hedley, 138, 139, 159, 160
Leach, Sir Ronald, 162, 165, 166, 171,
    172–3, 176, 179–80
Leasco Data Processing Corporation, 21,
    154, 157–63, 165, 166, 170–9, 238;
    Secret Agreement, 160; becomes
    Reliance, 178, 179

Légion Tchèque, 51–2
Leitch, David, 96
Lendl, Ivan, 227
Les Nouillons, 62
Levin, Bernard, 220
Libraire des Sciences Techniques Françaises et Etrangères, 137, 140, 170
Liechtenstein, 29, 31, 32, 93, 214–17, 239, 241, 243
Lilley, Maj. C. V., 69
Linklater, Magnus, 236, 240
Little Brick Hill, 85
Littlewoods, 151
Liverpool, 51, 120, 144
Lobel, Arnos, 87
Loire, River, 55
London Daily News, The, 25, 27, 30, 32, 33, 158, 235–40
London Gazette, The, 66
London Post, The, 235
Long, Douglas, 202, 203
Long Island, 94, 157
Lonrho, 239
Lord, Graham, 107–8
Los Angeles, 142, 173, 174
Loss, Joe, 24
Low-Bell, 87. See also Maxwell Scientific International (Distribution Services) Ltd
Low-Bell & Maxwell Ltd, 88, 89
Lübeck, 72
Luftwaffe, 67
Lyons, 63
Lyons, Sir Jack, 15
Lyons, Jim, 166, 168

Macao, 32
McCaffrey, Sir Tom, 49, 150, 188, 189, 206, 231
McCorquodale, 230
MacDonald, Ramsay, 111
Macdonald Futura, 189
McGahey, Mick, 224
MacGregor, Sir Ian, 105, 224
McKay, Ron, 192, 212
McKee, Alexander, 60
Mackie, Allister, 191–2, 193
Macmillan, Harold, 106, 109, 116
Macmillan & Co., 97, 116
Macmillan Publishers Inc., 116, 125
Magic Garden, The (Conran), 189
Maginot Line, 53
Mair, O. J., 81
Majorca, 28
Majthenyi, Ladislaus, see Martini, Mr
Malice in Wonderland, 234
Maloney, Mike, 29
Malon, 61

Manchester United Football Club, 212
Marie-Antoinette, Queen, 40
Marie Theresa, Queen, 40
Markham, Elizabeth, 114
Markham, Sir Frank, 106, 110–14, 126, 131
Markham, Lady, 112, 114
Marks & Spencer, 151
Marlborough College, 119
Marne, River, 54
Marseilles, 28–9, 56
Marsh, Peter, 27
Martini, Mr 94, 124, 158
Matthews, Lord, 191, 216
Maxson Investment Co. Ltd, 93
Maxwell (Haines), 14, 24, 54
Maxwell, Sir Alexander, 85
Maxwell, Anne, daughter, 23, 117, 118, 122, 167
Maxwell, Christine, daughter, 23; 105
Maxwell Elisabeth, wife, 49, 89, 92, 103, 169, 237; 40th anniversary, 9, 12, 16, 70–1; and Pergamon, 18, 147; courtship and marriage, 17, 18, 24, 65–7, 70–1; degree, 23; in Cannes, 28–30; family background, 63–5; Allied Welcoming Committee, 63–5; first meets RM, 63–5; children, 72, 85, 86, 88, 106, 111, 119–20; character, 104–5; electioneering, 114, 120, 126, 134, 166, 168; in Jamaica, 116–17; Libraire des Sciences Techniques, 137, 140, 170; and News of the World, 144; 'Art of Letter Writing', 167; QE2, 192; Oxford United, 212; visits Mirror building, 224; and Private Eye, 231
Maxwell, Ghislaine, daughter, 23, 119, 212, 225
Maxwell, Ian, son: character, 23; RM's mortality, 27; Cannes, 29; 'krauts', 46; birth, 106; education, 119, 225; gambling, 211; visits Mirror building, 224; BPCC, 225
Maxwell, Isabel, daughter, 23, 105
Maxwell, Karin, daughter, 106
Maxwell, Kevin, son, 239, 243; character, 23; Cannes, 29; 'krauts', 46; birth, 111; independence, 117; education, 119; and RM's Russian links, 149; gambling, 211; Oxford United, 212; first visits Manor building, 224; Hollis, 225–6; relations with RM, 229; Sporting Life, 235; London Daily News, 239
Maxwell, Lt-Col., 59
Maxwell, Michael, son, 18, 85, 119–20, 152
Maxwell, Pandora, daughter-in-law, 23, 225
Maxwell, Philip, son: 40th anniversary, 18, 22; birth, 105; education, 119, 122; electioneering, 126, 166

MAXWELL, ROBERT
  Character: fears for safety, 9, 24;
    'Bouncing Czech', 10; luck, 11;
    stained-glass window, 12, 135; 'not a
    man for chums', 12; health, 13, 21–2,
    106; titles, 13; and Queen, 13, 228–9;
    lawsuits, 14; inconsistency, 14; 'only
    man who', 14; religion, 14, 40–1, 52–3,
    65; talent for languages, 16, 22, 80, 82;
    'man from Mars', 20, 25; 'jungle man',
    20; and Beaverbrook, 20; 'a Maxwell
    promise', 25; his mortality, 27;
    memory, 42, 174–5; influence of Eden,
    56, 79; 'telephone terrorist', 83, 173,
    175, 218; attitude to women, 118;
    Murdoch on RM, 141, 149–50;
    gambling, 211–12
  Names: Lodvik Hoch (Lajbi), 40, 41, 58,
    85, 106; Du Maurier, 60, 85; Jones, 64;
    Ian Maxwell, 67; Robert Maxwell, 70,
    85; military rank, 85–6, 106, 115–34
  Early life: birth, 40; education, 23, 42,
    43, 58, 59; family life, 40–3, 194
  Military career: Czech underground,
    48–50; First Czech Division, 51–6, 57,
    58; Pioneer Corps, 57–60; North
    Staffordshire Regiment, 60–7; Queen's
    Royal Regiment, 67–73, 77, 79, 80, 84;
    SHAEF, 64–7, 70; commission, 63, 66;
    MC, 68–9, 88, 113; leadership, 71;
    Sudweyne, 71–2; Berlin, 73, 77–9,
    80–4; intelligence, 80; PRISC, 81–3, 88;
    'youngest editor', 81; demobilization,
    84, 85, 86
  Marriage and family life: 40th
    anniversary, 9–18, 22–4, 27; first meets
    Betty, 19, 64–5; courtship and
    marriage, 17, 19, 24, 65–7, 70–1;
    children, 73, 85, 86, 88, 106, 111,
    119–20; naturalization, 84;
    Headington, 111, 114–15, 170;
    children's education, 118–19; death of
    Michael, 119–20, 152; driving offence,
    126
  Political career: political ambitions, 59,
    84; fails to win seat (1959), 106–14;
    wins seat (1964), 120–2, 125–7; re-
    elected (1966), 138; Catering
    Subcommittee, 147–8, 149; Committee
    of Privilege, 148–9; loses seat (1970),
    166, 167; relations with Labour Party,
    106, 110–11, 114, 119, 120–2, 166, 167,
    168, 199, 207, 208, 220–1, 224; 'High
    Tory', 106–7; Fabian Society, 109;
    maiden speech, 131–2; 'gasbag', 132;
    'not a Westminster success', 153;
    'Forward with Britain', 207
  Business career: breadth of interests,
    10, 30; Department of Trade
    judgement, 10, 16, 25, 86, 171–3;
    football, 10, 212–13, 234, 241–2; desire

  to own newspaper, 10–11, 20, 31, 122,
    123, 162, 190; *Observer*, 11, 15, 190;
    News of the World, 21, 141–7, 148, 158;
    Thatcherite, 12; Russian links, 15, 33,
    83, 97, 104, 116, 132, 149–50, 229;
    family trusts, 16, 29, 32, 33, 214–16,
    238–9; Leasco scandal, 21, 157–63,
    165, 166, 170–9, 238; 'Insight', 21, 51,
    52–3, 82, 88, 96, 97, 98, 148, 163–4,
    193; television, 24, 28–31, 32, 105, 134;
    unions, 25, 107, 189–90, 203–4, 235;
    London Daily News, 25, 27, 30, 32, 33,
    158, 235–7, 239, 240; 'Knowledge
    Market', 25, 136–41, 154, 158–9, 161;
    'Outer Darkness', 25, 92, 107, 218, 225;
    Mirror Group, 26–7, 115, 198–202, 204,
    211, 213; 'Never start a business', 31;
    Harcourt Brace Jovanovich, 30–2;
    238–9, 240; *Today*, 32, 239; Ethiopia,
    33, 37, 223, 229; Commonwealth
    Games (1986), 33, 227–9; first bank
    account, 66; *Sun*, 83, 158, 159, 161,
    162; limited liability, 86; Family
    Interests, 87, 90, 92, 93, 123, 124, 158,
    160, 169, 170, 176, 177, 225, 240; films,
    89, 134; birth of Pergamon, 90;
    Maxwell House, 92, 94, 189; 'on my
    arse', 99; Geneva conference (1955),
    103–4; 'disemployer', 107; 'Maxwell-
    grams', 112, 126, 167; work rate, 117;
    bingo, 121, 217, 218, 225; *Daily Herald*,
    123; theatre, 135; sues *Private Eye*, 135,
    207, 230–4; subscription books, 136–41,
    158–9, 161; first meets Murdoch, 141,
    142; 'Spanish Translation Rights', 154;
    Kennedy Fellowship, 169; expenses,
    174; Times Newspapers, 187; control of
    BPC, 188; *Scottish Daily News*, 191–4;
    236; *Not Private Eye*, 233–4; *Malice in
    Wonderland*, 234; reconciliation with
    Murdoch, 244; Channel Tunnel, 244
  Business ventures: *see under
    individual entries*
Maxwell Communications Corporation,
  33, 241, 243
Maxwell Communications Corporation
  Inc., 237, 238
Maxwell International Microforms
  Corporation, 154, 178
Maxwell Scientific International
  (Distribution Services) Ltd, 87, 124,
  135, 147, 172, 173, 177
Maxwell Scientific International (1964)
  Ltd, 124, 147
Maxwell Scientific International Inc.:
  established, 93; ownership, 93, 124,
  161, 162, 170; Department of Trade
  interest, 93, 124–5, 176; Simpkin
  Marshall and, 98, 99; and Pergamon
  Press Inc., 125, 161, 165; warehouse
  purchase, 153

Maxwell's Pictorial Knowledge, 137, 161
Media Week, 81
Melbourne, 144
Melbourne Herald, The, 228
Mers El Kebir, 56, 57
Meuse, River, 67, 69
Mexico, 138
Meyer, Gen. Kurt
Meynard, Elisabeth, see Maxwell,
    Elisabeth
Mezhdunarodnaya Kniga, 97
Microforms International Marketing
    Corporation, 154, 178, 214
Milan, 52
Miles, Tony, 204; editorial director of
    Mirror, 184, 197; chairman, 194, 195,
    199, 202; RM takes over, 203, 206–7,
    219; in Florida, 206
Militant Tendency, 224
Millet, Richard, 140
Milton Keynes, 166, 167
MIP-COM, 33
MIP-TV, 28, 29
Mirror, The, see Daily Mirror, The
Mirror Group Newspapers, 14, 30, 42–3,
    218; Clyde Cablevision, 13, 105, 223;
    unions, 25, 189, 190, 203–4, 235;
    flotation, 26, 196, 197–8, 199, 202, 203;
    RM acquires, 115, 198–202, 204, 211,
    213; Odhams, 136; Sun, 158; formed,
    186; journalists, 191, 194; support for
    Labour, 208; logo, 217; 'Survival Plan',
    221
Mitchell, Maj. A. W., 60
Mitchinson, Tom, 110
Mitford, Pamel   143
Mollecular De: n, 243
Molloy, Micha... RM's 40th anniversary,
    15; editor of Mirror, 195, 196–8, 235;
    background 197; and Kinnock, 199,
    200, 218; RM takes over, 202–3, 206,
    208, 219, 223; poker, 111; Keith
    Waterhouse, 220–1; Not Private Eye,
    233–4; London Daily News, 237;
    Today, 240
Montagu, Samuel, 232
Monte Carlo, 27
Montgomery, FM Bernard, 60, 63, 66, 68,
    69–70, 71, 77, 148
Montreal, 244
Moonies, 229
Moore, Mike, 204
Moorhouse, Geoffrey, 167
Moravia, 37
Morgan Grenfell, 144
Morrell, Lady Ottoline, 115
Morrisey, Patrick, 235
Morrison, Herbert, 85, 184
Moscow: British Trade Fair (1957), 104;
    Radio, 190; State University, 13, 188,
    238

Mozart, W. A.: Don Giovanni, 134
Munich Agreement (1938), 44, 45
Murdoch, Anna, 145
Murdoch, Sir Keith, 236
Murdoch, Rupert, 11, 23, 32, 33, 169;
    'Murdoch promise', 25; newspaper
    group, 26, 141, 145; Today, 32, 239;
    Sun, 32, 162, 205; RM first meets, 141,
    142; on RM, 141, 149, 211; News of
    the World, 141–2, 144–6, 158, 191;
    background, 142; on Pergamon 146;
    and Department of Trade, 168; and
    IPC, 184; on Mirror, 185; Times
    Newspapers, 187, 223, 231, 235–6;
    Collins, 189; Wapping, 223, 236;
    American citizen, 225; airline, 230;
    reconciliation with RM, 244
Mussolini, Benito, 45, 229

Nangle, Maj. Hubert 'Jock', 67, 69
National Broadcasting Corporation, 28
National Economic Development
    Council, 152
National Fund Raising Foundation, 121
National Graphical Association, 190, 236
National Savings, 59
National Society for the Prevention of
    Cruelty to Children, 191
National Union of Journalists, 200, 203
National Westminster Bank, 89, 169, 177,
    187, 201
Natkin, Mrs, sister, 49, 50, 93
Nazis, see Germany
New Caxton Encyclopaedia, 138, 139, 159
New Idea, 145
New York, 33, 93–4, 158, 161, 165, 173
New York Post, The, 244
New Yorker, The, 39
New Zealand, 136
Newell, Capt. R. G., 72
Newmarket, 59
Newnes, George, 136, 137, 201
News Corporation, 23
News International, 25, 141, 145
News of the World, The, 20, 141–2,
    142–6, 147, 158, 191, 239
Newton, John, 108
Nice, 52
North Atlantic Treaty Organization, 235
North Staffordshire Regiment, 59–67
Northcliffe, Lord, 183–4, 236
Norton Opax, 230
Norway, 53, 57
Not Private Eye, 233–4
Novello, Ivor: Perchance to Dream, 88
Nureyev, Rudolf, 134

O'Brien, Teddy, 188
Observer, The, 11, 15, 19, 190, 235
'Oceania', 96
Odhams Press Ltd, 123, 188, 202, 204,
    205, 213

OGPU, 83
Oliver, David, 241
Olney, 108, 112
Onassis, Aristotle, 144, 218
O'Neill, Bill, 240
O'Neill, Frank, 144
Open University, 120, 168
Orléans, 54
Ormrod, Bruce, 123–4, 137, 138
Orne, River, 62
Orwell, George, 241
Oxford, 109, 122
Oxford United Football Club, 10, 23, 195, 212, 216, 225, 241
Oxford University, 23, 119–20, 122, 142, 167, 225

Paarlo, 18, 67–9
Packer, Sir Frank, 145
Page, Bruce, 163, 164
Panzergrenadier Division, 61, 62, 67
Parade, 238
Paris, 17, 19, 33, 40, 70–1, 96; open city (1940), 54, 63; liberated (1944), 63; Maison Lafitte, 85, 105, 111
Paris Peace Conference (1919), 37, 38, 39
Park Royal, 188
Parkinson, Michael, 117
Pasfield, Dorothy, 237
Peat, Marwick, Mitchell & Co., 96–7
Péladeau, Pierre, 244
People, The, 26, 135, 136, 195, 206; 'Straight Talk', 233
Perchance to Dream (Novello), 88
Pergamon Holding Foundation, 215–16
Pergamon Infoline, 23, 139, 187, 243
Pergamon International Inc., 93
Pergamon Media Trust, 29, 232
Pergamon Press Inc., 16, 92, 94, 124, 125, 159, 165, 170, 172, 214
Pergamon Press Ltd: 'foundation-stone', 10; 'endless and effortless profits', 11; annual reception, 18, 24; Betty's role in, 18, 147, 167; and Leasco, 21, 157–63, 165, 166, 170, 171, 173, 175, 176, 177, 178, 179, 238; turnover, 30, 115–16, 213; and Elsevier, 32; name, 83; creation, 86, 90; Simpkin Marshall, 91–2, 94, 95–8, 98–9, 103, 106, 113, 121, 135, 146, 157; American company, 93; chairmanship, 105; move to Oxford, 109, 111, 114–15; share dealings, 123–4, 143, 159; Queen's Award for Industry (1966), 136; Newnes, 136, 137, 201; Chambers and Caxton, 136, 137, 138–9; 140, 142, 171, 201; Australasia, 142; Murdoch on, 145; warehouse purchase, 154; RM deposed, 154, 169, 172, 173–4; MIMC, 154, 178; ILSC, 158; RM regains control, 179, 186, 191, 193; RM's stock, 215; MCC, 240. *See also* British

Printing Corporation; British Printing and Communication Corporation; Department of Trade and Industry
Pergamon Reports and Surveys, 138, 161
Pergamon Subscription Books Division, 137, 139, 140
Perth, 179
Pézenas, 52
Philip, Prince, 110, 227–8, 231
Philip Hill Investment Trusts, 216
Pictorial Knowledge, 137
Pilger, John, 224
Pilson, 37
Pioneer Corps, 57–60
Pioneeren, 54, 58, 69, 113
Pitman, I. J., 91–2, 94, 113
Plunder, Operation, 71–3, 79
Podkarpatska, Rus, 38, 39, 41
Poland, 38, 39, 46, 47, 48, 50, 53, 57
Politics of Power, The (Haines), 194, 223
Poole, Henry, 16, 26–7; *Unravelling the Melmotte Skein*, 30–1
Popov, Victor, 15
Portugal, 32, 33
Prague, 37, 38, 40, 41, 47; tension, 45; Hitler in, 46, 51, 52; Russians in, 143
Press Association, 144
Press Council, 15
Pressdram, 230–4. *See also Private Eye*
Price Waterhouse, 135, 165, 176
Pringle, Gill, 224
Pringle, John, 116
Private Eye, 107, 135, 207, 230–4
Proops, Marjorie, 25
Provençale, La, 28–9, 32
Providence, Gravure, 237
Public Relations and Information Services Control, 81–2, 84, 88, 89
Purnell, 187

QANTAS, 142
Quebecor Inc., 244
Queen Elizabeth II, 192
Queen's Award for Industry, 136
Queen's Royal Regiment, 67–73, 77, 79, 80, 84

Radio Corporation of America, 23
Radio Times, 10, 20, 188
Railton, Dame Ruth, 219
Ransomes & Rapier, 232
Reading Football Club, 212, 241
Reagan, Ronald, 107
Reed International: interests, 26, 32, 186, 196; IPC, 26, 184, 185, 186; Mirror Group flotation, 27, 186, 194, 196–8, 200, 201–2, 203; sells Odhams to RM, 188; RM acquires Mirror Group, 198–205, 211, 213
Reid, Jimmy, 15
Reliance, *see* Leasco
Reuter, 23, 196, 204

Rhine, River, 66, 70, 71, 72
Ribbentrop, Joachim von, 77
Rifkind, Malcolm, 229
Rio de Janeiro, 94
Robert Maxwell Code of Conduct for Direct Sellers, 139
Robert Maxwell & Co. Ltd, 124; change of name, 91, 93; turnover, 99; *Encyclopaedia Britannica*, 137; warehouse purchase, 153; Department of Trade, 172, 173, 176
Robertson, Jillian, 144
Roer, River, 67
Romania, 38, 41
Ronson, Gerald, 191
Rosen, Sylvia, *sister*, 41, 49, 50
Rosenbluth, Lou, 52–3, 54, 55, 56, 58, 59, 79–80, 212
Rothermere, 183
Rothermere, Vere Harmsworth, Lord, 145, 237, 240
Rothschild, N. M., 143, 160, 161, 164, 175, 179
Rothschild Investment Trust, 164
Rothschilds Inc., 33
Round House, 135
Rowland, 'Tiny', 11, 15, 190, 240
Royal Air Force, 13, 24, 66, 143
Royal College of Surgeons, 33
Ruhr, the, 80
Rusbridger, Alan, 236
Russell, Dr W. Ritchie, 120
Russian Orthodox Church, 46, 47
Ruthenia, 37–50, 66, 81, 108, 238

Salazar, 45
Salzburg Festival (1954), 134
Sampson, Anthony, 19, 21
Sasakawa, Mr, 230
Sassi, Victor, 89
Scarborough, 114
Scargill, Arthur, 224
Scholtz, Arno, 81
Schwartz, Bernard, 157–63
Scottish Daily Express, The, 191
Scottish Daily News, The, 192–4, 212, 236
Scottish Daily Record, The, 26
Selby, Hugh: *Last Exit to Brooklyn*, 134
Sète, 51, 56
Shawcross, Lord, 162
She, 119
Shemara, 116
Shilling, Leonard, 138–9
Shilton, Peter, 212
Shirer, William: *Berlin Diary*, 77, 80
Shterev, Kiril, 15–16, 18
Sieff, Michael, 151
Silesia, 37
Silkin, John, 165, 172, 176, 178, 205, 216
Silkin, Sam, 172, 202, 205
Sillitoe, Fred, 193–4

Silvester, Christopher, 232
Simpkin Marshall Ltd, 157; RM acquires, 91–2, 103, 113; debt to RM, 91, 94; Wallersteiner, 95–8; liquidated, 98–9; 106, 121, 135, 146
Sinclair, Sir Clive, 13–14, 16
Sister Anne, 116
Skelton, Barbara, 143
Skoda, 37, 43, 55
Skorpios, 144
Slatina-Selo, 40–50, 66, 104
Smith, Jim, 212
Smith, John, 233
Smith, W. H., 91, 221
Smutny Jaromir, 45
Social Democratic Party, 185, 221
Society of Graphical and Allied Trades, 162, 188, 190, 200
Somerfield, Stafford, 144; *Banner Headlines*, 146
South Africa, 138, 227–8
Southern California, University of, 56
Southwood, Lord, 204
Spain, 52, 55, 58; Civil War, 51
'Spanish Translation Rights', 154, 177
Special Operations Executive, 90
Spens, Lord, 15, 17, 30. *See also* Henry Ansbacher
Sporting Life, The, 24, 26, 205, 235
Springer, Ferdinand, 87
Springer Verlag, 80, 82, 85, 87, 89
Spycatcher (Wright), 125, 204
Stable, Owen, 162, 165, 166, 171–80
Stalin, Joseph, 47
Standard, The, see Evening Standard, The
Standard Literature Company, 140
Staniszewski, Stefan, 15
Steinberg, Saul P., 157–63, 165, 166, 169, 173, 178, 238; 'Decline and Fall of IBM', 159
Stevens, Lord, 32, 216, 234
Stony Stratford, 109
Stothert & Pitt, 232
Stott, Penny, 15
Stott, Richard, 195, 206
Straka, Laszlo, 16, 158–9
Strasser, Arthur, 52, 56, 58, 59, 86
Strasser, Freddie, 52, 56, 58, 59, 86
Stratford-Lawrence, Sylvia, 109
Sudetenland, 38–50, 77
Sudweyne, 71
Sullivan, Jim, 226, 238
Sun, The, 32, 83, 123, 158, 159, 161, 162, 185, 197, 205
Sun Printers, 187
Sunday Express, The, 32, 107; 'Crossbencher', 132
Sunday Mail, The, 26
Sunday Mirror, The, 26, 135, 183, 195, 225
Sunday Pictorial, The, 183
Sunday Telegraph, The, 71, 162, 179

Sunday Times, The, 19, 149, 170, 194, 235; 'Insight', 21, 51, 52–3, 82, 88, 96, 97, 98, 148, 163–4, 193
Superwoman (Conran), 189
Supreme Headquarters Allied Expeditionary Force, 64–7, 70
Surfers Paradise Mirror, 145
Sutton Coldfield, 57, 58, 59, 60
Swadling, Samuel, 119–20
Swan Lake (Tchaikovsky), 134
Switzerland, 65, 91, 93, 124, 143, 162, 214
Sydney, 141, 142, 144, 145
Sygma, 28
'Sylvia', 59
Syria, 49, 51

Tass, 190
Tatler, The, 105
Tatra Mountains, 43
Taylor, Mike, 81
Tchaikovsky, P. I.: *Swan Lake*, 134
Telegraaf, Der, 81
television, 24, 28–31, 32, 105, 134; DBS, 28
Teng Hsiao-p'ing, 229
Terry, Capt., 63
TF-1, 28, 29, 30, 32
Thames Television, 29
Thatcher, Margaret, 216; RM's admiration, 12, 14, 107, 228; and privatization, 186; RM lectures, 212–13; *London Daily News*, 237
Thatcher, Mark, 190
Thomas, Jean, 167, 168
Thomas, Ray, 120–1
Thompson, David, 200
Thomson, Alastair, 169, 175, 178
Thomson, Lord, 145
Thornton, Clive: chairman of MGN, 194–5; MGN flotation, 196, 197–8, 200–3; 'betrayed', 200; *Standard* photograph, 205
Times, The, 110, 131, 148–9, 151, 216, 226, 231, 232
Times Newspapers, 163, 187
Tisa, River, 41, 42, 82
Today, 32, 240
Tokyo, 32
Tomalin, Nicholas, 20, 21, 153
Tombs, Sir Francis, 232
Tory, Peter, 220
Toulouse, 55
Tours, 55
Trade Union Congress, 123, 220, 222
Transylvania, 41
Trelford, Donald, 15
Trollope, Anthony: *Way We Live Now, The*, 16–17, 31
Truth, 145
Turkey, 49
Turner & Newall, 232
TV Times, 10

Ukraine, 37–40, 46, 47, 50, 64, 104
Ulysses (Joyce), 134
Union of Soviet Socialist Republics, 15, 31, 32, 37–9, 43–4, 48, 64, 229; pact with Germany, 47; annexes Ruthenia, 49–50; civil war, 51; German assault, 60, 68; invades Poland, 67; occupies Germany, 72, 77, 78, 83–4, 88; scientific research, 115; Czechoslovakia, 143
United Kingdom: Paris Peace Conference, 37, 38, 39; and Czechs, 43, 44, 45, 49; guarantee to Poland, 48; War Office, 60, 66, 84; battle for Europe, 60–73; occupation of Germany, 77–9; Home Office, 85; Foreign Office, 86, 133, 227; Ministry of Defence, 113. *See also* Department of Trade
United Nations, 111
United Newspapers, 151
United States of America: Paris Peace Conference, 37, 38, 39; battle for Europe, 60, 61, 67, 71; occupation of Germany, 77–9
United Trade Press, 243
Unravelling the Melmotte Skein (Poole), 31
USA Today, 244

Vaduz, 216
Vanden Heuvel, Count, 91
Variety, 26
Versailles, 64, 65, 67, 70; Treaty of (1919), 38
Vichy, *see* France
Victoria, Queen, 108
Victory, 236
Vienna, 37, 44
Vierst, Lt-Gen. Rudolph, 52
Viyella, 151
Vlad the Impaler, 41
Vogue, 10
Volkswagen, 84, 88

Waddington, John, 214–15
Walker, Peter, 224
Walking on the Water (Cudlipp), 184
Wall Street Journal, The, 179
Wallersteiner, Dr Kurt, 95, 96, 97–8
Wapping, 240
Warburg, S. G., 195, 200
Warner Brothers, 89
Warsaw, 67
Washington, 107, 138
Waterhouse, Keith, 220–1
Waterlows, 187, 190
Watford Chemical Company, 95, 96, 97
Watford Football Club, 213, 241–2
Watson, Maj. D. J., 67
Watson, Victor, 214–15
Way We Live Now, The (Trollope), 16–17, 31
Webb & Company, 238
Weidenfeld, George, 143

Wein, Mr Justice, 179
Wesker, Arnold, 135
West, Bill, 110
Westminster, Duke of, 191
Westminster Bank, see National
  Westminster Bank
Weygand, Gen. Maxime, 54, 55
Wharf House, 120, 167
Whitlock, Maj. J. W., 90, 95
Wilcock, Maj. A. J., 59
Wilhelm II, Kaiser, 39
Wilkins, Lt-Col., 59, 63
Williams, Charles, 187–8, 199, 234
Williams, Francis: Dangerous Estate, 196,
  197
Wilson, Bruce, 228–9
Wilson, Charles, 152
Wilson, Harold, 191, 223; RM's 40th
  anniversary, 10, 23–4; election (1964),
  125–6; Kosygin's visit, 132–3; and
  News of World, 146; 'I'm Backing
  Britain', 150; Industrial Organization
  Corporation, 187; and Joe Haines, 194,
  223; Mirror, and, 204

Wilson, Les, 217
Wilson, Woodrow, 38, 39
Windsor, Duke and Duchess of, 55
Wing, 166
Winter Supplementary Estimates, 133
Wolfson, Mark, 150
Wolverton, 120, 153
Wood, David, 131, 153
Woodcock, George, 123
Woods, Vicki, 105
World Anti-Communist League, 229
World War: First, 37, 39, 45, 49, 51, 54,
  58, 59, 123, 142, 183–4; Second, 17, 37,
  40, 48–73, 136, 142, 158, 184, 238
Wright, Peter: Spycatcher, 125, 204
Wyatt, Woodrow, 216–17, 221

York, 57
Young & Rubicam, 218
Yugoslavia, 49, 218

Zatkovic, Grigory, 39, 40
Zhukov, Marshall G. K., 77, 83, 217